Mabel Tawney-Rogers and Ernest Rogers

Family History
of
L. Mabel Tawney and Ernest F. Rogers
Their Ancestors and Descendants

Roane County, West Virginia

By Charlotte A. (Rogers) Dilno
Third Edition - May, 2010

Family History of L. Mabel Tawney-Rogers and Ernest F. Rogers

Copyright 2010

by

Charlotte A. Rogers-Dilno

_____

Printed in the United States

Dedication

This book is dedicated to my loving Mother, Mabel Rogers

In memory of my loving Father, Ernest F. Rogers

Preface to the First Edition

Many years have passed since I first began to hear the fascinating stories told by my parents about memories of their ancestors and growing up. Both my parents came from large families and it was difficult for me when I was young to understand the chronology of the people and the stories that now have become so important to me. Taking notes and then translating those notes into something that was hopefully accurate was just as difficult.

To be so fortunate to have two parents that could live into their nineties and continue to retell those stories time and again is beyond expression. I know that other members of my family feel the same way. My husband, Guy Dilno, has been my greatest source of support to bring this project to completion, with some prodding by some of my brothers and sisters.

I began the process of putting into writing a very simple Family History in 1985. It took only a few typewritten sheets of paper then for what I knew about my ancestors. My main objective in that project was to put down in writing and graph the descendants of my parents, Mabel and Ernest Rogers, and record all full names, birth dates, marriage dates and similar information for all spouses. I sent forms to my family and relatives and asked that they complete and return them to me. The response was great.

I want to express my thanks to all my family, my aunts and uncles and other relatives for providing information so that this might become a permanent reference for the generations to come. There is still much that can be done and it is my hope that the younger ones will be encouraged to do the same, especially to update new information and record any newfound information about ancestors.

Thanks to the magic of computers, this has been kept in order over the years. There have been some nervous moments to say the least but with my husband's help it always seemed to be workable. Now as I receive wedding and birth announcements, and sometimes death notices, I can keep the records up to date. Without the program, putting together this book would take many hundreds more hours and a few more years.

Now with the help of so many, I have finally put this together so that most of the lines of heritage are included under one cover.

The older photographs were borrowed from my mother and the more current photographs were on loan from my brothers and sisters, nieces and nephews and other relatives. My sincere appreciation to those who have been so cooperative and for the photographs I receive from time-to-time.

The interest has been outstanding, especially when I expressed my desire to complete this to present to my mother, Mabel Rogers, at a SURPRISE 95th BIRTHDAY CELEBRATION, at The Heritage Park Community Building, in Spencer, West Virginia, on March 24, 2001.

Part of this is an oral history of Mabel and Ernest Rogers. I requested from their children and, in some cases, their grandchildren that personal stories and letters be written as a tribute to Mother. I am fortunate to be the one to collect these. I recalled a lot of fond memories when reading those stories and enjoyed some of the humor too.

Since I began in January 2001 and set a deadline for letters and pictures so that I could complete this project for Mother's birthday, there still didn't seem to be quite enough time for everyone to submit material. Some just could not put into words what they felt in their hearts. For the future, I would encourage everyone to preserve precious letters, to write down those memories and put the notes in a special place.

As long as I am able to receive and record new information, I hope to continue this project. When I am no longer able, then my hope is that someone else will deem this important enough to continue.

First Edition, Plainwell, Michigan
Charlotte A. Dilno
March 10, 2001

Preface to the Second Edition

There were seven copies printed of the First Edition of this book. Since that time, several minor changes were necessary for the accuracy of the genealogical records. Children were added that I did not have knowledge of at the time of the first printing.

There has been a lot of interest from family and others since the first printing; and demand for additional copies. At the same time, I felt that revisions to the book were necessary as described above and one change led to another.

I have expanded the Rogers record under Robert Jahu Rodgers to include more generations. I have also included additional pages of ancestral photographs that were not included in the First Edition.

There are approximately 40 additional pages in this Second Edition and I hope that it will be that much more interesting to some or all.

May 2001

Preface to the Third Edition

There has been a lot of interest from family and others since the first and second printing, and demand for additional copies. At the same time, revisions to the book were made to more accurately reflect or update the genealogical records. Since the second edition, more children have been born and, unfortunately, some deaths have occurred. Also, I now have a more extensive and accurate record in many cases.

I eliminated some sections that were not so useful and added others. I reformatted the descendant trees and added a dedication to the military veterans in the family. Finally, the book was slightly reformatted with a new cover and in 8 x 10 for the paperback version. The hardback and coil-bound versions remain essentially 8.5 x 11. Also, the cost of the paperback version is much reduced thanks to modern "on-demand" printing capabilities.

Charlotte Dilno
Albuquerque, New Mexico
May 2010

Introduction

This book contains information about descendants of Mabel and Ernest Rogers. Mabel's ancestral lines are Tawney, Graham, Sergent, Noe, and Hughes. The Ernest Rogers ancestral lines are Rogers, McQuain, Summers, Smith, and Moore. The Genealogy Report of each line goes down only so far as the descendant is recognized. This is to avoid duplication of the later generations.

Generation numbers are shown beside the names in the reports. Where there is a report with no numbers shown, there are no known children of that person.

Several photographs were on loan for use in this book. Others I have collected and taken myself.

Table of Contents

Table of Figures

Data Methods and Comments about the Third Edition

This book was originally written and published for my mother, Lula "Mabel" Tawney-Rogers, on her 95th birthday and had a scope pertaining to her descendants. Because the information also encompassed historical information for all of the related Tawney descendants, interest in the book grew after the first two printings.

While much of the book is of more general interest, I have retained the initial pages pertaining to my mother and father, Lula Mabel Tawney and Ernest Frear Rogers. Also, many of the photographs in this book are of their descendants. I will publish a set of photographs for the entire Tawney and Rogers line at some point in the near future but this is not that book. This book is a final printing of what began as a very specific family history book.

There are a few things to know about the genealogical record. It is extremely difficult to search prior to 1800 because of the lack of written records. Most of the data prior to that period has been handed down by word of mouth and/or multiple publications of variations of that data. Much of the Johan Taney information was taken from work done by Frieda Vineyard-Tawney and Garrison Tawney, published by Clara Ross in her book *John H. Tawney*. There is more information in the *Roane County West Virginia Family History 1989* by The Roane County Family History Committee. Also, much of the early data has been taken from the *One World Tree*. With exception of census data from 1840 and beyond, I have not independently validated any of the data.

I have attempted to include the source data with each entry in the genealogy reports. These are generated by my software from data I have entered. Except as noted in those reports, most of the notes and text are mine.

Because today's online community is so diverse and the *One World Tree* is now available, there is more information available about our ancestry. Unfortunately most of it cannot be independently verified, but I keep looking.

The genealogy documented here spans 14 generations dating from about 1620. The oldest ancestors are the Preisch's who are married into the Harless line which joins the Tawney line at George William Tawney, Aaron Tawney's father. All of the Harless data is due to the One World Tree and is not independently validated.

Notes on the use and Scope of this Book

How do I use this book, how am I related to these people, and why should I care?

This book is written for the direct descendants of Mabel Tawney and Ernest Rogers and those of their brothers and sisters. Because we are interested in our roots, or genealogy, the book also provides a record of the ancestry of Mabel Tawney, Ernest Rogers, and their brothers and sisters.

A "pedigree" tree of Mabel is also valid for her brothers and sisters, and goes back through the Tawneys on her father's side and the Grahams on her mother's side. The Tawneys have been traced to the early 18th century and the Grahams to the early 19th century. The Grahams in turn married into the Sergents and Hughes. Mr. Thomas Hughes was of the first patriots and participated in the Revolutionary War and was a contemporary of the earliest Tawneys.

The United States counts its origin as the signing of the Declaration of Independence in 1776. In fact, our actual government was not in place until 1791. This means that things like basic governmental services, like county records and the like, were either nonexistent or in a state of turnover until the very late 18th century (1700's). As a consequence of this, it is very difficult to trace one's roots back before around 1800 if your ancestor was born on this continent. There are records for European immigrants if you know the region of their birth and the correct spelling of their names. Usually, however, we have an approximate spelling and region that has been passed down among the families in the form of oral history. This really is the new world!

A similar "pedigree" of Ernest Rogers shows that he is descended from the Rogers (or Rodgers) on his father's side and the McQuains and Summers on his mother's side. The McQuains can also trace themselves back to the American Revolution and the Summers (or Somers) to the early 18th century. Robert or Bobby Rodgers married into the Smiths and the Smiths to the Moores.

This book documents the early ancestors of Mabel and Ernest and you will find genealogy reports for Johan Jacob Tawney, Thomas Hughes, James P. Graham, and William Sergent, the ancestors of Mabel and her brothers and sisters. For Ernest, there is information on the John Smith who was the grandfather of Sarah Sally Smith (Ernest's Grandmother), Alexander McQuain (his Mother's paternal line), Levi Moore, and Johann Somers. If you are a descendant of Ernest or Mabel or one of their sisters and brothers, you are related to these folks.

This is not a narrative-type book of all of these people but a record of what I have been able to put together from many references. In most cases I have not traced all these people back to their origins through birth records although it has been done by others, Garrison and Frieda Tawney for the Tawneys and Mamie Tawney for the Hughes. While not perfect, it is a better record of these lines than would exist otherwise, spans some 20 generations, and is meant to be an aid to the next generation of family historians.

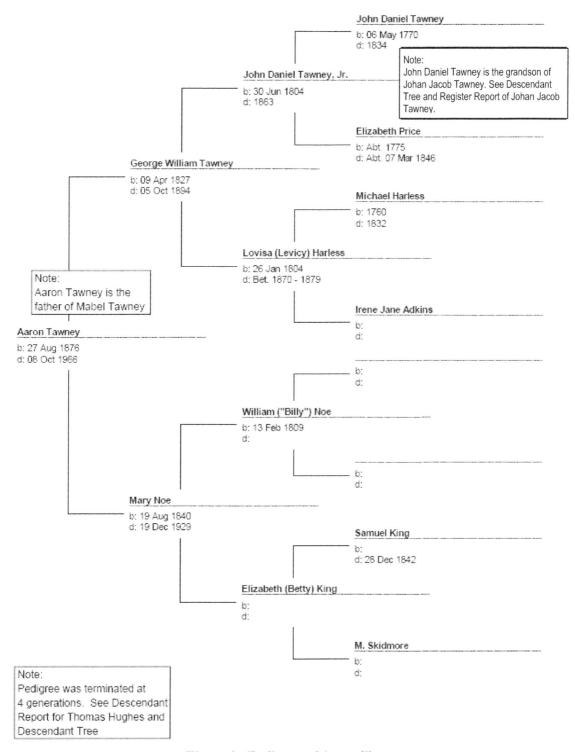

Figure 1 - Pedigree of Aaron Tawney

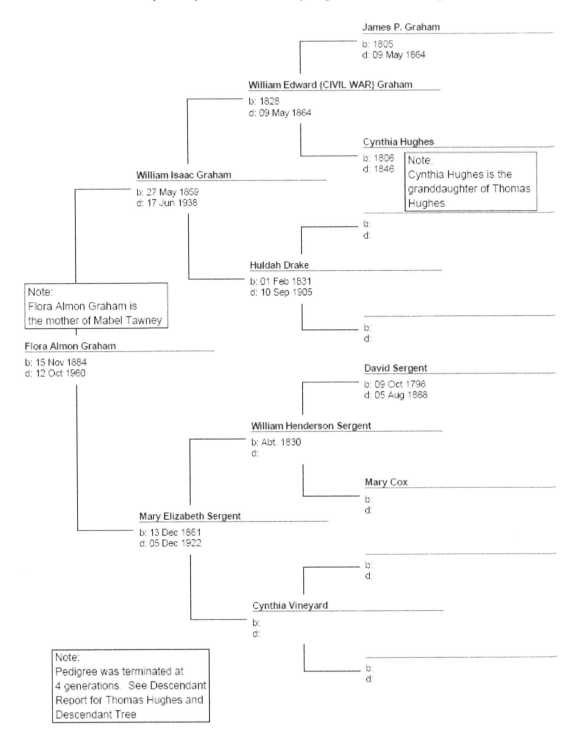

Figure 2 - Pedigree of Flora Almon Graham-Tawney

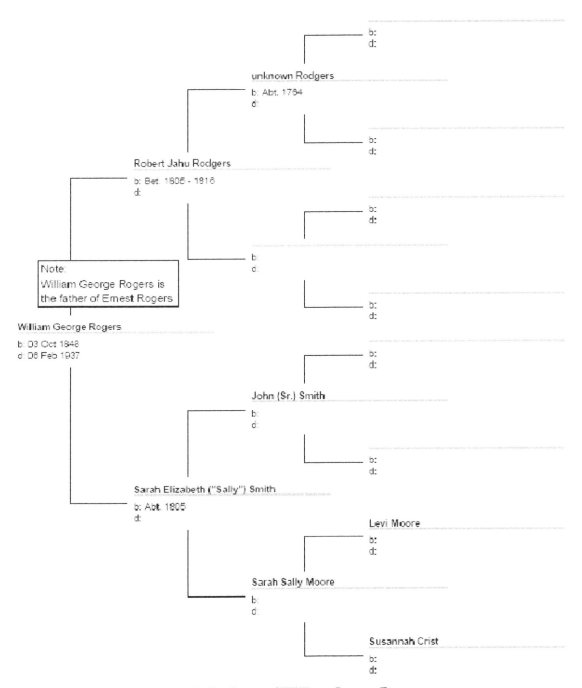

Figure 3 - Pedigree of William George Rogers

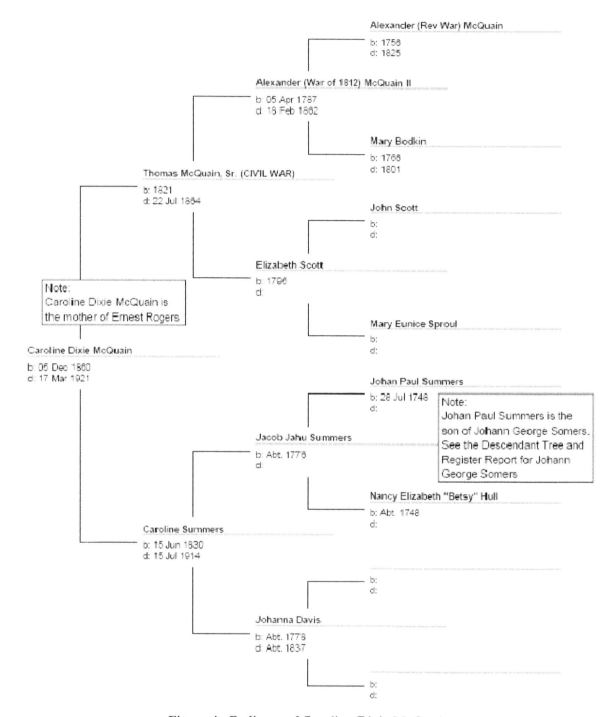

Figure 4 - Pedigree of Caroline Dixie McQuain

How to Use and Understand Genealogy Reports

Genealogy is about ancestors and descendants. A genealogy report for a person lists all of his or her descendants. The reports in the book list an entry for each child of a person. Should those children have children, they get another entry in the report. For example, the listing in the Robert Rodgers Descendant tree for Delores Rogers looks like this:

Children of ERNEST ROGERS and LULA TAWNEY are:

22.	i.	MARDELL ADELEE[5] ROGERS, b. 06 Feb 1927, Akron, Summit Co., OH.
23.	ii.	ROBERT KEITH ROGERS, b. 05 Aug 1928, Akron, Summit Co. OH; d. 23 Dec 2008, Gallipolis, OH.
24.	iii.	ALMA DELORES ROGERS, b. 23 Mar 1930, Akron, Summit Co., OH.
25.	iv.	KERMIT ADOLPH ROGERS, b. 23 Feb 1934, Newton, Roane Co., WV.
26.	v.	DORMA KATHERN ROGERS, b. 24 Mar 1936, Newton, Roane Co., WV.
27.	vi.	CARROLL AARON ROGERS, b. 10 May 1938, Newton, Roane Co., WV.
28.	vii.	CHARLOTTE ANN ROGERS, b. 16 Mar 1940, Newton, Roane Co., WV.
29.	viii.	PATRICIA RONDELL ROGERS, b. 05 Feb 1943, Newton, Roane Co., WV.
30.	ix.	BARBARA CAROLINE ROGERS, b. 07 Sep 1945, Charleston, Kanawha Co., WV; d. 05 Jun 2005, Riverside, Riverside Co., CA.

Delores is individual No. 24 of the descendants, who had children. If she did not have children, there would be no number beside her name. Since she has children, she gets another entry. Skipping down to this second entry, we get:

24. ALMA "DELORES"[5] ROGERS *(ERNEST FREAR[4], WILLIAM GEORGE[3], ROBERT JAHU[2] RODGERS, UNKNOWN[1])* was born 23 Mar 1930 in Akron, Summit Co., OH. She married (2) DELBERT DENNIS 22 Jan 1958. He was born 22 Dec 1928 in Lake Lynn, PA. More about DELBERT DENNIS and DELORES ROGERS: Marriage: 22 Jan 1958

Child of ALMA DELORES ROGERS is:

44.	i.	ANDREW JACKSON[6] ROGERS, b. 27 Mar 1952, Culver City, CA.

Child of DELORES ROGERS and DELBERT DENNIS is:

45.	ii.	SHEILA MARLENE[6] DENNIS, b. 26 Mar 1959, Union Town, PA.

Andy (44) and Sheila (45) both have children and get entries at positions 44 and 45 in the report. Skipping to Sheila we see:

45. SHEILA MARLENE[6] DENNIS *(ALMA DELORES [5] ROGERS, ERNEST FREAR[4], WILLIAM GEORGE[3], ROBERT JAHU[2] RODGERS, UNKNOWN[1])* was born 26 Mar 1959 in Union Town, PA. She married ROGER ALAN BREMER 08 Mar 1980 in Fort Wayne, IN, son of KENNETH BREMER and RUTH WOLFE. He was born 10 Sep 1960.
More about ROGER BREMER and SHEILA DENNIS:
Marriage: 08 Mar 1980, Fort Wayne, IN
Children of SHEILA DENNIS and ROGER BREMER are:

72.	i.	JAMI MARLENE[7] BREMER, b. 24 Aug 1980, Fort Wayne, IN.
	ii.	ASHLEY MARLENE BREMER, b. 29 Jul 1985, Fort Wayne, IN.

73.   iii.   LINDSEY MARLENE BREMER, b. 29 Jul 1985, Fort Wayne, IN.

Here we see the twins, Ashley and Lindsey. Lindsey has a child while Ashley, as of this writing, does not. Therefore, Lindsey gets another entry in the report and Ashley does not:

72. JAMI MARLENE[7] BREMER *(SHEILA MARLENE[6] DENNIS, ALMA DELORES[5] ROGERS, ERNEST FREAR[4], WILLIAM GEORGE[3], ROBERT JAHU[2] RODGERS, UNKNOWN[1])* was born 24 Aug 1980 in Fort Wayne, IN. She married CASEY LEE ADAMS 16 Aug 2003 in Ft. Wayne, IN. He was born 26 Nov 1978.
More about CASEY ADAMS and JAMI BREMER:
Marriage: 16 Aug 2003, Ft. Wayne, IN
Children of JAMI BREMER and CASEY ADAMS are:

   i.   SPENCER LEE[8] ADAMS, b. 01 Dec 2005, Ft. Wayne, IN.
   ii. CHLOE RENEE ADAMS, b. 17 Oct 2008, F. Wayne, IN.

73. LINDSEY MARLENE[7] BREMER *(SHEILA MARLENE[6] DENNIS, ALMA DELORES[5] ROGERS, ERNEST FREAR[4], WILLIAM GEORGE[3], ROBERT JAHU[2] RODGERS, UNKNOWN[1])* was born 29 Jul 1985 in Fort Wayne, IN.

Child of LINDSEY MARLENE BREMER is:
   i.   GRACYN RYLIN[8] SPILLERS, b. 07 Nov 2009, Ft. Wayne, IN.

This does not mean that Ashley is not important, only that there is no more genealogic information about her at the time the report was written. If she has children next year and another genealogy report is done, she would get another entry.

Notations and Letters for Mabel's 95th Birthday in 2001

ADELEE MARDELL ROGERS-JOHNSON

Dear Mother,

Happy 95th Birthday. Because of you I have had a wonderful life. Harold and I will be married fifty years this October. I have been blessed with three children, eight grandchildren and one great-granddaughter, all in good health.

My memories are many, from childhood through adulthood. You always encouraged all of us and to get as good an education as possible.

You taught us to be honest, to have the courage to stand up for what was right, and to believe in God.

You always managed for each of us to have one penny to put in the Sunday school collection plate. That taught us what you give from the heart you receive twice-fold and then more sometimes.

I remember you getting up in the mornings about 5 a.m., building a fire in the cook stove and potbelly stove and cooking us a hot breakfast. It was so cold you would have to break the ice in the water bucket in the kitchen.

I remember when you would look in the Sears Catalogue and find a dress I liked and you would make me one out of feed sack materials. I was so proud to wear the dress.

When I made mistakes, you would say, it's all right to make mistakes if you learn something from them.

When we lived on Blown Timber I remember you taking a swing up in the old rocky field and tying it up in a tree and Kermit would sit in it while we hoed corn.

Keith and I would take the horse and sled up by the rocky field and gather tomatoes. We would put some in the cold spring water that came out of the mountain and when we were finished we would sit with a salt shaker and eat as many as our stomach would hold.

Keith and I rode horses to Uler with chickens thrown over the horses and the weather was so hot they died. We had to come home without groceries. We felt so bad.

I remember when you were flying to California when I was in the hospital. Daddy brought you to the airport (in Charleston) and decided to come to California with you. He had to go out and buy clothes when he got to California. It would take a book to contain all of the wonderful memories. Thank you for your love and dedication to my family and me. I wouldn't trade you for any other mother in the world.

Love, Adelee

(Letter dated February 2000)

ALMA DELORES ROGERS-DENNIS

To Mother.

When I was little, I remember one morning you were making biscuits. I was standing by the kitchen door against the wall. When you spoke to me I just slid down the wall and sat on the floor. I had fainted.

I remember picking blackberries with you in Aunt Orva's field on her farm. I took walks with you to visit our neighbors.

It was an exciting day when I rode to the hospital in Uncle Clark's Hudson car. It was brown. You went with me. I was four years old. I was scared. I told Uncle Clark he saved my life. I believe he was my angel.

I remember quilting with you. Around noon you would say, "Why don't you go make us some donuts and we will have coffee and donuts for lunch."

I remember you always kept me clean and taught me to respect our friends and relatives, and to say "Thank you." You were a good mother to me when I was little.

I love you a bushel.

M is for the many things you did for me.

0 is for teaching me to obey and keep my house in order.

T is for telling me good advice.

H is for the hugs you gave me.

E is for the education you gave me.

R is for the little red sweater you gave me

And for all these things I thank you.

Your smallest and shortest
daughter, Delores

KERMIT A. ROGERS

To Mother on her 95th birthday,

It's hard to put into words how I feel. I just want to thank her for being there for me all the times I needed her. I only wish that every child could have a mother just like you. Mom, I won't tell the bad things, just the good things.

Mom and me went up on the hill and worked a half-day trying to build a fence to keep sheep out of the meadow. After done building the fence, we hid and watched old Susie (one of the sheep). We were so proud of the fence job we'd done. That sheep just walked out and looked at the fence and jumped right over the top of it.

I'll never be able to do enough good things to make up for the bad things

DORMA KATHERN ROGERS-DRAKE

Dear Mom,

Happy 95th birthday. If you had worked a little bit harder I would have blessed you with my appearance the day before, on your birthday. Just kidding. From what you have told me, I am lucky to be alive. I've always been a difficult child. Right?

How can I count the ways that I've been blessed to have you for a Mom? You simply amaze me with your virtues. The strength it must have taken to bear, raise, and educate all of us. The patience it must have taken just to not throw in the towel and give up as so many people do.

The love you had for me even when I was difficult. You never gave up on me even if you were tempted. The example you set for me to be a person of good integrity. You gave me strength and direction. I listened most of the time and when I didn't I was simply seeking my own independence.

I am so proud to have you for a Mom. I don't have the words to fully express my feelings for you. Just know this I love you and I've been so lucky to have you for a Mom for these past 65 years.

Again, Happy Birthday and have a wonderful day.

Love, Dorma

(Letter dated February 19, 2001)

CARROLL AARON ROGERS

Happy Birthday Mother!

What could I get for your birthday? You have been everywhere and done about everything you ever wanted, so I thought "What better way than a few memories. I've probably never really told you how much I love you. Maybe you will be able to tell from some of the things I write about.

I will always remember how happy you made me. You were always there urging me on, telling me not to give up, never to quit, you are just as good as anyone else. After a while I really did believe I could succeed. Following are some bits and pieces of those memories:

How about all those scary stories you use to tell us at bedtime? Man! We would be so scared. We stayed in bed because we were sure that if we weren't quiet or got out of bed the "Boogie Man" would get us.

There was the time when I was about 3 or 4 years old and it was Christmas time. I told you that I didn't believe in Santa Claus, that he couldn't come down the chimney because we only had a stovepipe. You told me he would probably just come in the front door. I put a washtub in front of the door and slept by the wash tub. The noise would wake me up and I would really get to see Santa Claus. I woke up the next morning in bed. You laughed and told me Santa Claus must have carried me to bed.

My first pet was "Butch" He was my pet pig, black all over, and he followed me everywhere I went, even into the house. I don't remember how you explained to me about how I was supposed to accept the fact that he was going to end up as bacon and ham on the kitchen table. I guess you did a good job of explaining because I don't remember the part about being sad or crying. I was about 3 or 4-years old.

Then there was my dog Jinx. I carried him home as a puppy under my coat from Russell Hensley's. Daddy said, "You can't keep him, he will ruin my hounds." I'll never forget how you stood up to him. You said something like "Ernest, Carroll feeds your hounds, bathes them and gets them ready for your dog shows. He deserves to have his own dog." Daddy just laughed and said that you were right, I could keep the dog." That day you were my hero! I was about 12-years old.

We rarely had our pictures taken. We had a big square Kodak. We had to hold real still. You had me convinced that the little red spot in the lens was a red bird. If we watched real close we would see the red bird.

Election Day was really a big deal. I don't know how old I was but I remember walking across the hill to the Uler Store and listening to the election returns on the radio. Grandpa Aaron Tawney had me convinced my name was Carroll Aaron Democrat. He would ask, "What's your name, young man?" I would answer proud and loud, "Carroll Aaron Democrat!" He would slap his leg and laugh Ho! Ho! Ho!

When I was a little older you sent me over to the "Linkenogger (Holler) Cherry Trees" to pick a bucket of cherries. As well as I remember I was going to get a cherry pie out of the deal. I believe Dorma and Charlotte were with me. I was up in this BIG CHERRY TREE and "the old lady" who lived on the farm came along. She said, "You get down out of that tree. Those aren't your cherries." I said, "Ma'am, we have always picked cherries from these trees and they aren't your cherries either. I'll get down when my bucket is full." I was actually pretty scared.

Then there was my dog Jinks. I carried him home as a puppy under my coat from Russell Hensley's. Daddy said, "You can't keep him. He will ruin my hounds." I'll never forget how you stood up to him. You said something like "Ernest, Carroll feeds your hounds, bathes them and gets them ready for your dog shows. He deserves to have his own dog." Daddy just laughed and said that you were right, I could keep the dog." That day you were my hero! I was about 12-years old.

Remember when I talked to you about going to college? You said, "Of course you can do it. I'll help you." Mr. Bliss Hildreth, my Vocational Agriculture (Vo-Ag) teacher also was a big positive influence on this decision. Together, we figured out how I could make enough money by raising pigs and chickens to turn into cash. Remember when my shipment of chicken feed didn't come in on time. I called down to Lee Ellis' Store to have Daddy pick up a bag of feed. He only brought a 25-pound bag of feed. This lasted my chickens only 2 or 3 days. When I asked him to bring me another bag, he couldn't believe those chickens could eat so much. He swore those chickens were going to put us in the "Poor House." I got my books out and showed him all of my expenses and how much I would make as soon as they were sold in a week or so. He still didn't believe me. You said something like, "Ernest, leave him alone, he knows what he is doing."

You helped me smoke my hams and bacons so they could be sold. As well as I remember they won Blue Ribbons at the West Virginia State FFA Ham, Bacon and Egg Show at the Daniel Boone Hotel (in Charleston). Before I graduated from West Virginia University, just before going into my senior year I still had money in the bank. Several times Daddy had asked me if I needed any spending money. I always told him, "No, I had enough." Of course I worked for seventy-five cents per hour while I was going to school. I also worked for the WV State Road and Du Pont in the summers.

You were always willing to let me try something new. I remember one time asking you why we never raised anything "really good" in the garden." You let me set out a couple of rows of strawberries. The first year I picked all the blooms off so the plants could get healthy and strong. Daddy thought I was crazy. The second year when they were ready to pick, I was away at college. Kermit said that he had never seen so many strawberries. You picked them by the bucketsful. We sure enjoyed them out of our freezer all the next winter. You loved to prove Daddy wrong and let him know it when he was enjoying them strawberries with cream and sugar.

I never thought of us as being poor. There is an old saying that "We didn't know we were poor until we went to high school." We saw how nice all the city kids dressed and the spending money they had. Then we realized us country kids were really poor. Uncle Garrison, our 8th Grade teacher and coach, took us to Spencer Grade School to play a basketball game. We had never played in a real gymnasium with a wooden floor. We had no idea we had to have gym shoes. We only had on our Brogans (work shoes). The other kids loaned us gym shoes so we could play the game. I don't remember who won.

I said that we never felt like we were poor. All the other kids in the country were pretty much the same. I can never remember going to bed hungry or not having clean clothes for school or church. I feel very blessed to have had a Mother like you. I think that every time Daddy gave you money for a new dress you spent the money on us kids.

I remember going to the store with you to get chicken feed. You would always spend a lot of time picking out the pretty patterned feed sacks. Then you made my sisters dresses from them. I could never understand why I couldn't have a pretty shirt like those dresses.

I was about 10-years old when I killed my first chicken for Sunday dinner. There was no one else there to do the job and I convinced you that I could do it. You finally agreed and I convinced Dorma to hold the chicken by the legs while I stretched the chicken's neck out across a log and prepared to chop its head off. Dorma shut her eyes and turned her head. Well, the chicken pulled her head just as I brought down the ax. I only got half the neck cut off. Dorma screamed and let the chicken go. Then you started screaming. You could never stand blood or the sight of the eyes of a dead animal, fish, frog or anything else. I finally caught the chicken and finished the job. You were always good about cooking our wild game. But I had to always dress the game and get rid of the head with those dead eyes.

When Daddy retired from Du Pont we asked if the two of you would go to California with us. We knew Daddy would only go if we convinced him we needed him to help drive. We had a great time, didn't we? We planned our trip so we could drive about 500 miles per day for five days. This worked out really well. We would wake up really early and drive a couple of hours before the kids, Marc and Shelly, woke up. Then we would drive some late in the evening. This gave us time to stop for the kid's to play at parks and other places of interest. We could hardly hold daddy down. He was always used to getting there fast and not wasting time. After about three days you convinced him to relax and enjoy the trip. You kept telling him, "Ernest, relax, you are retired now. You have nothing to do tomorrow." We pulled into Bobbie's house on the fifth day, rested, and right on schedule. Daddy said something like, "This retirement sure is nice."

Coming home we were crossing the Continental Divide and Shelly was really scared of the steep, crooked roads. She said, "Come by me, Grandma!" That was really a great trip.

Mother, I could probably write volumes about my many memories of you but all things must come to an end so I'll just have to wrap this up. It's really hard for many people, especially boys or men, to express their love for another. Despite all the hardships we have lived through as a family, I can say that I have had a really happy childhood and life. The world has truly been made better because of you.

Love,

Your son Carroll

Entry on 12-27-98. For entry on page 13 of <u>STORY OF A LIFETIME</u> - A Keepsake of Personal Memories by Charlotte Ann Dilno

WHAT DO YOU REMEMBER ABOUT YOUR OLDEST RELATIVE(S) YOU KNEW PERSONALLY?

CHARLOTTE ANN ROGERS-DILNO

My grandfather, Aaron Tawney, was the oldest relative that I remember. He was a cattleman and farmer, the father of 10 (6 sons and 4 daughters). He followed a strict schedule with meals, chores, and errands. Grandpa raised and sold cattle for a living and provided well for his family. His farm was on Route 36 (known as Dog Creek but there was no post office). The mailing address was Left Hand, West Virginia. Dog Creek is on one of the few straight stretches of road between Newton and Left Hand, WV, in Roane County. The Tawney farm on Dog Creek is about 20 miles from Spencer and 20 miles from Clay.

As I remember, Grandpa's breakfast was on the table at 6-7:00 a.m., dinner at 12 noon and supper at 5 p.m. Everyone ate together. No snacks between meals were given and nothing after the supper meal. When I was 10 years old my mother had me stay during the summer with my grandparents to help with small errands. Both my grandparents were very neat and orderly about their home and surrounding land. Nothing was ever out of place.

My Uncle Dan and wife, Hazel, lived in half of the second story of the farmhouse. At that time they had only one son, Jerry, who was about 7 years younger than I was. Later they built a home on the property just around the bend. Uncle Dan continued with all the farm work. I stayed for four summers.

When I was a freshman in high school, my mother wanted me to also stay with them during the school year for company. My grandparents were getting older and mother wanted us to be helpful to them. I stayed awhile. The evenings were very lonely and my grandparents went to bed very early. Visitors were rare, except when Grandpa had men from the cattle business for dealings. But of course, those meetings were very private and held in the parlor with closed doors. After a few months, I told mother that I just could not stay any longer.

I needed to be with my own brothers, sisters and parents, although both Grandma and Grandpa were very kind to me and undemanding. I stopped staying with them. My grandfather always listened to the 6:00 P.M. news on the radio. A rocking chair sat exactly beside the radio and that is where Grandpa sat down at exactly 6:00 o'clock every evening and expected complete silence while listening to the news. Grandma walked lightly through the house and I was expected to also walk lightly. Both my grandparents were very kind and polite. I was slightly afraid and very respectful of my grandpa, likely because Grandma instilled in me that "Pa" needed quiet while reading the paper, listening to the news or whatever it might be that he was doing.

A regular Saturday errand was when Uncle Dan drove my grandma in Grandpa's car to shop at the local general store in Left Hand (owned by Knights I believe). Grandma always took eggs with her to the store to trade for merchandise, a common practice for farm folks. The eggs were placed in a basket, which she carried on her arm. I remember that Grandma always dressed in nice clothing and wore her hat to the store. I always wished that I could go along but could not.

I remember that once Grandma took me with her at the end of the summer, near the time when I would start school. She bought me a beautiful pair of burgundy leather school shoes. I also remember that she ordered new underwear from either the J.C. Penney's or Sears catalog. I don't believe Grandpa had confidence that I was very capable.

I wanted to prove myself capable and the opportunity came one Saturday when Grandma and Uncle Dan did not return in time for Grandma to prepare dinner. I was anxious for their return to break up a boring day and watched the clock waiting for their return. I told Grandpa that it was time to start dinner and that I knew how. Grandpa said we would just wait for Ma. A half-hour passed and still they had not returned. Several times I went to Grandpa and each time I tried to tell him how I knew what to do.

Finally when they were a couple hours late, I convinced Grandpa that I could start the cornbread, then later was able to convince him that I could peel potatoes and get them started. Grandpa was very reluctant to allow me access to the kitchen to prepare food on my own. Finally Grandma arrived and when she saw that I had started supper and had it very near to putting it on the table, she was very pleased. I believe that Grandpa was also pleased. She explained her lateness, in that she had visited her brother and wife, Uncle Fred Graham and Aunt Pearl.

The farmhouse did not have indoor plumbing. My grandpa did all his bathing in a small well house right off the end of the back porch. The little building was set up with his round tin wash basin, shaving soap and a straight razor. A mirror hung on the wall. A leather razor strap for sharpening his straight razor also hung on the wall. The little well house was very orderly and neat and I can remember standing near the doorway while watching Grandpa shave. I remember visits with him while he shaved but do not remember what we talked about. I really admired my Grandpa.

When my Grandma had no more chores left for me, she would tell me to ask my Grandpa if I could be of help. There was not much I could do but I was willing to do whatever they asked of me. On wash day, Aunt Hazel did all the laundry and I would help hang the clothes on the line. On ironing day, I helped iron Grandpa's chambray work shirts and Grandma's aprons made of sackcloth.

Grandpa showed me how to use a paring knife to dig weeds from the fine grass in the yard. We both worked together on the banks around the yard. We would dig down beneath the roots to remove the entire ugly roots of the weeds. We visited and I was so proud to be helpful.

The last time I saw my Grandpa was in the summer of 1965, when I stopped on my way from California to visit my parents who still lived on Blown Timber. My Grandma was no longer living and Grandpa lived alone. I did something I have always wished I did not do. I lit a cigarette during that visit. Grandpa did not say anything at first but soon he kindly reprimanded me for smoking and told me, "Those cigarettes won't do you any good." I remember also that he complimented me on Brad as a "fine boy," and that both Kim and Brad "seemed to be well behaved." I don't remember anything about his illness, but congestive heart failure was the cause of his death.

I am glad that Mother sent me to stay with my grandparents for short periods because I had the opportunity to know them in a way that I might not otherwise remember. I learned early on what it was like to be away from my family. When I went away to work in California where my sister lived, after I graduated from high school, I soon learned the loneliness that I would experience would be with me if I were never to live close to my birthplace and my beloved family.

CHARLOTTE ANN ROGERS-DILNO

Mother,

Thinking about my early memories of you and our family in the 1940s, I remember walking with you and Daddy on the paths that curled around the Blown Timber hills to do our visiting. Sometimes it would be to visit Uncle Clark Rogers and Aunt Orva. You and Aunt Orva would save the feed sackcloth and get together occasionally with your collection to trade each other for matching fabrics, enough to sew a dress or shirt.

Daddy, with Uncle Clark, Hersey and Forrest often played fiddle, guitar, and banjo together on the weekend. The music was wonderful, since we didn't have much of a radio and there was no TV in those days. We kids would run around the yard and play games such as hide-and-seek, tag and red-rover. The same paths that were probably used by our grandparents were barren of grass and weeds. If night fell upon us and we had forgotten a lantern to light the path, we had the paths memorized. It was a little eerie though, hearing the strange and sometimes frightening sounds of the night as we passed the wooded area.

Being near you and watching you spend long hours of sewing garments was educational. To keep us occupied, you gave us small tasks. You taught us to sew a button on a plain piece of fabric, and how to create a pattern and cut out a small purse to hand sew for ourselves. Anything we knew how to do in the kitchen, you allowed us to do. The things we didn't know, you were always willing to teach us. It was funny how you could also come up with extra dirty dishes just about the time us girls thought we were finished. We kind of teased you about it. Remember?

There wasn't much time spent indoors in the warmer months, except for preparing meals for workers and the family and the daily chores. You always thought of something for us to do to help out and keep us out of trouble. That might be helping Daddy by following along behind him when he was plowing, in case he needed us, weeding carrots, or picking leaf lettuce. It might be covering the freshly planted vegetable plants to keep off a late frost with a small square of newsprint, weighted down on two sides by a hunk of dry dirt or a rock so the paper wouldn't blow away. Then by getting out to the garden early the next morning to remove the paper before the hot sun had a chance to burn the plants. It seemed that it took two hours to cover the plants and then 2 more hours to uncover them the next morning. As much as we dreaded that chore, we always seemed to find some humor in it. In actuality, it probably took less than two hours.

Humor abounded. You let us have fun in our work. Those are the best memories. Now when we get together that's where we always seem to find ourselves, recalling those times when we spent hours working together, the fun of it all at the end of the day with our family.

When I was born in 1940, the oldest child, Adelee, was living away from home and in high school. When I was 10, as I remember, there were five children at home. I don't remember having a lot of beds, but I never slept on the floor and we always had plenty of bed quilts to keep us warm. If it seemed we were getting low, you would make more. You had a quilting frame set up in the girl's bedroom upstairs for a time and that's where I did my first quilting. It was fun to learn from you. We wanted to be mischievous as I suppose all children are at times and our upstairs bedroom window was quite small. If Pat and I crunched our legs up tight to our chest we could sit facing each other and look out at the stars at night. We knew to be quiet because our parents' bedroom was just downstairs and Daddy always needed good rest because he had a job that required him to be extremely alert at all times. We must have waited until Bobbie was asleep because we three shared the room.

I know I caused a lot of extra work when I was a teenager, not for the usual reasons like other teenagers might. In the fall of 1952 when I was 12, I was with my brother, Keith, and his family on the way to a drive-in movie. We never made it to the movie. It was dark and a hound came off a bank and ran in front of the car, which caused Keith to run off the road, over a bank, and into a creek. We all suffered injuries and I was hospitalized several days with a broken arm and injured knee.

When you and Daddy brought me home from the hospital you lost a lot of sleep taking care of me. You put me in your bed and you slept on the couch, then when the pain didn't go away, you put me on the couch. Back and forth, you spent a horrible night trying to make me comfortable because I suffered severe pain. The knee was badly swollen and after about the second or third night, I was taken to a bone specialist in Charleston. He met us at the curb in front of his office at 4 a.m., and advised us that he would operate at 7 a.m. I came out with a smaller knee and a cast on my right arm. That was quite a surprise for me, but it helped diminish the pain. I lay in the hospital for two weeks and went through some therapy. It was such a lonely time and I remember that Keith came to see me. He was in pain with his back but he acted like he was just fine. He seemed very concerned for me.

A year later, I was sunbathing and my knee became sunburned, but terribly swollen. After a doctor's visit we learned that I would need some sort of cartilage surgery on my knee. Another two weeks in the hospital and a full leg cast later, you brought me home.

Yet you didn't give me away. I thought surely that parents must want to do that. None of the other children were crippled like me and they had to do chores that I would ordinarily do. Bobbie and Pat helped me while I was home recovering. It seems that I missed some of my freshmen year and when I started, I was on crutches for a long time. After the cast came off, I couldn't bend my knee very well. That improved with time. You were so kind and gentle with me. You wanted me to get well. When I went to the doctor I took up the whole back seat. When I rode on the school bus, my leg stuck out in the aisle. When I went to church, my leg stuck out in the aisle.

You were good to us. When we grew out of our clothing, you took us on a shopping trip to Charleston. It seems that I was the one who grew the fastest and had the largest feet. I always had to go with you shopping because you couldn't count on anything to fit me because I grew so fast. But, I'm sure when I left home you found that Pat and Bobbie grew fast also.

Those shopping trips were very special times. We stayed all day because we rode to Charleston with Dad and Keith, then at the end of the day they would pick us up at a designated place. It was fun going to lunch; although, I remember that we were very thrifty about it so we would have more to spend on clothing.

Thank you for all you did for us growing up and for the values you taught us. You taught us everything good that you knew about life. You encouraged us to pick our friends carefully and to choose ones that would be a good influence on us. I think you did a great job. I have tried to pass those values along to my children and grandchildren.

We've had some great fun together, hours upon hours of conversation. I'm so glad that I have a mother like you, so thankful that I've had you for so many years, so thankful that you and Daddy stuck through the hard times so that we could have great times.

I am so glad that you have a great memory and have been able to help me while I've been trying to record information about our ancestors. Thank you for the stories, some I have had a difficult time putting into writing. Forgive me for the times when I didn't have a clear understanding when we talked about our ancestors. I've done my best here and hope that you enjoy leafing through these pages and that you realize how very much you are loved by all your family and especially by me.

I didn't think about completing this project so soon but because you have a very special birthday I decided in January 2001 that there could be no better time than now to show you the results of our hard work. This book is for you. You are in my mind and my heart always, and forever I will love you.

May God be with you.

Charlotte

PATRICIA "PAT" RONDELL ROGERS-CONLEY

February 24, 2001

Pat relayed the following to me in a telephone conversation recently.

I feel blessed that I've been the one chosen to look after Mother and I've treasured every moment. There are so many memories. I've been there through almost everything. After Daddy retired, he and mother would come over and help with our garden and we would go there and help with theirs. Daddy and I did so many things together. We used to go squirrel hunting.

I just remember when we were in band and every summer Mother and Daddy saw that we got to go to band-camp. I know it must have been a lot of money to come up with then. I never could figure out how they came up with it, but they always saw that we got to go to band camp.

BARBARA CAROLYN ROGERS-BEISTLE

February 22, 2001

Happy 95th Birthday Mother,

Thank you for teaching me so many good things, like cleaning house, cooking, being polite, honesty and so many other valuable things. I have so many fond memories, especially when Daddy would go fox chasing and I would get to sleep with you. Thank you for all the wonderful holidays. The house always smelled so good, with all the aromas of spices from cooking.

I was always so proud of you and Daddy; you always looked so pretty when you went to church. I wish I could be there for your birthday, but I will be thinking of you.

Love, Bobbie

Some other notes by Barbara Rogers-Beistle.

I have fond memories when mother was a cook at Newton School. I would peek around the corner ever chance I would get just to see her.

I have wonderful memories of Mother. As we were working up the vegetables under the shade tree, Mother would tell us some great stories.

While riding in the car, I would fall asleep in Mother's arms. I remember her warm hand on my forehead, holding my head so it wouldn't fall to the side. I felt so safe. Thanks Mother.

Easter was especially wonderful. Mother bought us a new Easter outfit. My patent leather shoes were so shiny I could see myself. I felt like a princess. Thanks Mother! I love you.

SHEILA DENNIS-BREMER (Granddaughter)
Memories of Grandma's House

I will always remember watching Grandma make biscuits and always wondering what the exact recipe was. Now I know that it will be forever etched in her mind and can never be duplicated.

I would watch very carefully as she added a pinch of this and a pinch of that, and as she placed them into the oven you couldn't wait for them to come out. The smell was indescribable and they would always come out picture perfect. Where was Martha Stewart then? If there happened to be some left over, she would place them on the counter. Soon someone would walk through the door and they always knew where to look for the leftovers, whether it would be a plate of bacon or cornbread on the stove.

There was always the famous peanut butter sandwich that Grandma would suggest if you were hungry. There was always something to eat. You would never walk away hungry.

I remember how proud Grandpa was of his garden and rightfully so. I can remember standing out in the garden and Grandpa picking a fresh cucumber and peeling it right there, then pulling the salt shaker out of his pocket and we would stand right there and eat it. I can remember the huge cabbage that would fill a washtub and Grandma's fresh green beans were the best, cooked to perfection.

As a young child not growing up on a farm, I never quite understood the concept of going to the chicken house to get eggs for breakfast, let alone eat them. And milking a cow to get milk, which I tried several times as a child, but never had much success. I was always a little disappointed that I could never accomplish that task.

Who could forget the old outhouse? I have shared stories with my own girls and have gotten plenty of weird looks, especially when I explain to them that the Sears and Roebuck catalog wasn't necessarily used for reading material. I share these stories with my girls because these are things they will probably never experience.

I can remember walking down the lane at the old farm and kicking up a few rocks. When you got to the bridge you would toss them off, then maybe go down into the water and see if you could see a few craw dads that come out from underneath the rocks.

I'm sure Grandma would rather forget the day I was supposed to be upstairs taking a nap but, oh no, curious me, always intrigued by those little gas stoves. I was sitting there playing around and I caught the floor on fire. Grandma said it really scared her but I didn't really understand the seriousness of it all at that time. I was too young. I'm sorry Grandma.

I will always remember Grandpa sitting at his spot at the table and everyone bowing their heads while he said grace. What a wonderful memory!

What my family and friends will remember about Grandpa: Family was very important to him. We were all special to him in our own way and he always made you feel like you were the most important at that time.

He loved his wife, children, grandchildren and great grandchildren. He loved to fox hunt and was very proud of his dogs and his trophy's. He loved to play the banjo and when he played it was like you were at your own private concert. He believed in reading the Bible. He was just an amazing man and I am proud to say he was my Grandpa.

Grandma loves her animals I remember her dog Flip, her white cat and, of course, Sparky. The girls talk about Sparky and often ask, "Does Grandma still have a Sparky'? Funny, how we remember the pets.

Grandma loves to quilt and crotchet. She has made some of the most beautiful things. Thank you for the small pieces of lace that you crocheted for the girls. They will cherish those forever.

When you came to visit we had such a wonderful time. We enjoyed sitting around listening to you tell stories. You almost made it seem like we were right there when it happened. You have such interesting things to share.

I probably could go on and on about my memories of Grandma's house. The stories and the memories are just endless, but anyone who knows Grandma knows exactly what I am talking about.

I hope you have a great 95th birthday. Always remember how much you mean to us and how much we love you.

With Love, Hugs and Kisses

Your Granddaughter Sheila, Roger, Jami, Ashley and Lindsey

Notes for Lula Mabel Tawney

Mabel was the 2nd oldest among eleven children of Aaron Tawney 1876-1966 and Almon Graham Tawney 1884-1960.

Mabel, together with her brothers and sisters, attended the Dog Creek Grade School on Route 36, at Left Hand, WV (between Newton and Amma) on the Aaron Tawney farm. Her father donated a portion of his farm where the school could be built so that his children and other children in the community would have a place to go to school.

At the age of 15 Mabel attended Summer Normal School. Her first and only teaching experience was at Booger Hole School where she was frequently challenged by her students. Many times she has told stories about the huge pet hog that a student brought to school. On one occasion, a student brought and threatened her with a switchblade knife.

The job paid only a minimal wage and she traveled on horseback to teach. Upon the good advice of her father, she declined to return the following year.

Her oldest brother, Ernest, had a job in Akron, Ohio and her parents decided it would be OK for her to seek out employment there. Her father took her in a horse-drawn wagon to Looneyville where her Uncle Fred Graham met them and drove her to Spencer to catch a train for Akron, Ohio. At that time, it was necessary to find a boarding room to stay overnight because of the long trip. Now it's about a four-hour drive.

Many times she has told the stories of the events of her years growing up with her sisters and brothers. They are interesting and exciting and they never grow old to the ears of most, maybe all, of her children and grandchildren. She will say "I've told that story a hundred times or more." I believe she thinks we should have those stories memorized by now, but never could they be retold as she tells them. Then when she retells them and I ask her questions, I find there is still so much more to learn. Her keen memory is marveled by many, and knowing her so well, I'm almost sure that she will tell a story if she is asked. But, be careful. She can tell it as it was. You will probably find a lesson in any one of them.

Notes for Ernest Rogers

Ernest was born at home in the Blown Timber hollow near Newton, WV (Roane County) in a log cabin on the family farm. He was the youngest of eight children. He attended Blown Timber School through 6th grade.

Mabel was introduced to Ernest by her brother, Ernest Tawney, when they all lived in Akron, OH. They were married in Akron on May 17, 1926. Ernest and Mabel both worked for Goodyear in Ohio and after their third child was born, they moved back to Roane Co., WV.

They saw hard times, much the same as others during the Great Depression. Ernest took any work he could get to provide for his family, including working on the WPA. When he worked for E.I. Du Pont, Belle Plant, he started at the bottom and worked up, to earn the grade of 1st Class Pipe Fitter.

He sometimes boarded in or near Belle because of the travel distance. There were many years when he did not have an automobile. For a short time, he and the family lived at Witcher Creek, WV to be near his work. During that time, the children went to Diamond Grade School and Du Pont High School, but in 1950 their home burned.

They rented a home in Rand for the remainder of that school year, and then moved back to their farm on Blown Timber. The two oldest children were married by then. Then they were left with seven children to raise. After Ernest retired from Du Pont, he and Mabel moved from the farm to a home on a 4-acre plot they purchased at Left Hand, where Mabel still lives. He stayed active with his foxhunting sport, always planted a vegetable garden and loved traveling with Mabel to visit family and relatives nearby and in several other states.

They looked forward to visits from the children and grandchildren. Ernest and Mabel were members of the Newton Methodist Church where they regularly attended with the family. In the early 1960s, Ernest became an ordained minister and assisted with services in various churches throughout the district.

He was a foxchasing enthusiast and earned many ribbons and trophies in both bench and field trials. During his life he had excellent work ethics. He enjoyed foxchasing on weekends and made many friends in the sport. He was active in the church community and was often called upon to assist at regular church meetings and in revival services throughout the area. He encouraged his children to trust in God and to be faithful church goers. Most of all he earned the respect of his children and is remembered most for his love of family. In later years, he often expressed that his hope was that his children would always get along well with each other.

In 1985 he survived an automobile accident where he was a passenger, and suffered from a strained back. At that time, the medical expert found an abdominal aortic aneurysm and surgery was soon performed. Later he often marveled at the mystery of the accident and wondered why his life had been spared and others were lost. They soon learned that he also suffered from osteoporosis, and emphysema from smoking cigarettes.

Throughout his illness, he continued to be a friend to many and his children continued to seek him out for advice. Mabel cared for him at home until his death at the age of 91 years.

> The bracketed numbers indicate the generation number. The + sign = Husband or Wife

Descendants of L. Mabel Tawney-Rogers and Ernest Frear Rogers

1 Lula "Mabel" Tawney b: 23 Mar 1906 d: 30 May 2003 in Newton, Roane Co., WV
+Ernest Frear Rogers b: 15 Mar 1902 d: 25 Apr 1993 in Chas., Kanawha Co., WV m: 17 May 1926 in Akron, OH
.... 2 Mardell Adelee Rogers b: 06 Feb 1927
.... +Gilbert McClelland b: 23 Jun 1924 d: 20 May 1983 m: in Akron, OH, Summit Co.
.... 3 Mary Gillette "Shelley" McClelland b: 04 Jan 1945
.... +Marvin Johnson d: Jun 2005
.... 4 Katrina Leigh Johnson b: 08 Feb 1965
.... +Matt Hessler
.... 5 Kayla Ell Hessler b: 05 Aug 1989
.... *2nd Husband of Mary Gillette "Shelley" McClelland:
.... +Bill Panetti
.... 4 Mason Jeffrey Panetti b: 04 Jul 1968
.... +Nadine F. Mullen b: 27 Dec 1961
.... *2nd Husband of Mardell Adelee Rogers:
.... +Harold Edgar Johnson b: 08 Sep 1924 m: 23 Oct 1951 in Las Vegas, NV
.... 3 Dale Adolph Johnson b: 10 May 1953
.... +Sandra Ann Brown b: 10 Jul 1954 m: 18 Sep 1976 in Orange Co., CA
.... 4 Matthew Richard Johnson b: 01 Jul 1979
.... +Denisse Carolina Sanchez Soto m: 09 Dec 2006 in Los Mochis, Sinaloa, Mexico, b: 16 Dec 1986.
.... 4 Russell Kenneth Johnson b: 03 Feb 1981
.... 4 Tiffany Ann Johnson b: 10 Jul 1983
.... *2nd Wife of Dale Adolph Johnson:
.... +Deborah Jean Manuel b: 02 Jul 1950 m: 17 Mar 2002 in Las Vegas, NV
.... 4 Jason Charles Mahaffey b: 1971
.... 5 Colton David Mahaffey b: Abt. 2007
.... 4 Jaimie Elizabeth Mahaffey b: 17 Apr 1986
.... +Unknown Brewer
.... 5 Chandler E. Brewer b: Abt. 2002
.... 5 Austin A Brewer b: Abt. 2006
.... *2nd Husband of Jaimie Elizabeth Mahaffey:
.... +Unknown Bosley
.... 5 Hannah Elizabeth Bosley
.... 4 Justin Charles Mahaffey b: 01 May 1982
.... +Rosario
.... 5 Alyssia Irene Mahaffey b: Abt. 2001

The bracketed numbers indicate the generation number. The + sign = Husband or Wife

5 Jacob Charles Mahaffey b: Abt. 2002
5 Rosario Unknown b: Abt. 1994
5 Jacob Unknown b: Abt. 1998
5 Mercedes Unknown b: Abt. 1997
3 Teresa Ann Johnson b: 29 Jan 1955
+Keith Craig Jackson b: 08 May 1955 m: 10 Apr 1982 in Castro Valley, Alameda Co., CA
4 Lauren Nicole Jackson b: 21 May 1985
4 Leah Michelle Jackson b: 06 Apr 1987
4 Kyle William Jackson b: 16 Feb 1990
2 Robert Keith Rogers b: 05 Aug 1928 d: 23 Dec 2008 in Gallipolis, OH
+Nancy Larch
*2nd Wife of Robert Keith Rogers:
+Marie Parsons b: 9 Jun 1929 m: 28 Jul 1950 in Cartlettsburg, Boyd Co., KY
3 Ina Gale Rogers b: 11 Mar 1949
+James Kermit Carper b: 05 Jun 1941
4 James Darin Carper b: 27 Nov 1967
4 Brian Christopher Carper b: 23 Jun 1969
+Cindy Robinson b: 24 Feb 1970
5 Kylie Paige Carper b: 22 Jun 2003
5 Courtney Brook Carper b: 04 Feb 2005
4 Brandi Lee Carper b: 03 Feb 1975
+ James Ward
5 Morgan Nichole Carper b: 23 Mar 1994
3 Michael Keith Rogers b: 03 Oct 1950
+Deborah Leigh Legg b: 16 Aug 1955
4 Mabel Lynn Rogers b: 24 Jul 1971
5 Joshua Neil Shirey b: 17 Aug 1989
5 Loren Montana Legg b: 04 Jul 1991
5 Whitney Ray Shirey b: 09 Jun 1993
5 Christina Danielle Peck b: 09 Nov 1995
4 Chester Keith Rogers b: 26 May 1976
3 Rhonda Diane Rogers b: 10 May 1952
+Randall Keith Carper b: 21 Feb 1950 m: 27 Mar 1971 in Roane Co., WV
4 Lisa Dawn Carper b: 16 Mar 1980
+Brian Stott b: 15 Feb 1976
3 Debra Jeanne Rogers b: 08 Aug 1953
+Collen Waldeck
4 [1] Christina Lynn Conley b: 25 Jan 1970
+[2] Gary Scott Deusenberry b: 30 Dec 1969 m: Dec 1990 in Newton, WV
5 Kayla Colleen Deusenberry b: 10 Dec 1990

The bracketed numbers indicate the generation number. The + sign = Husband or Wife

..... *2nd Husband of [1] Christina Lynn Conley:
..... +[3] Mike Whitman m: Jul 2000
..... *2nd Husband of Debra Jeanne Rogers:
..... +Ivan Logsdon m: 19 Aug 1974 in Parsons, WV, Tucker Co d: 01 May 2010
..... 4 Amber Dawn Logsdon b: 21 Oct 1975
..... +Tony Huber
..... 5 Cody Lee Huber b: 10 Oct 2000
..... 5 Kindra Nicole Huber b: 02 Feb 1998
..... 4 Travis Eugene Logsdon b: 30 May 1980
..... +Heather Lynn Heaney m: 28 Jun 2003 in Vienna, WV
..... 3 Timothy Lee Rogers b: 31 Jul 1954
..... +Karen Tawney b: 23 Oct 1954
..... 4 Chadrick Lee Rogers b: 09 Feb 1977
..... 5 Jayden Rogers b: 2003
..... 4 Kelly Jo Rogers b: 19 Feb 1979
..... +David Stone
..... 5 Hayden Zane Stone b: Abt. 12 Feb 2003
..... 3 Robert Randall Rogers b: 10 Aug 1955
..... +Loraine Marie Barone
..... 4 Joseph Randall Rogers b: 23 Feb 1978
..... 2 Delores Alma Rogers b: 23 Mar 1930
..... 3 [4] Andrew Jackson Rogers b: 27 Mar 1952
..... +[5] Caroline Carte b: 23 Jun 1950. d: 03 Aug 2006 in Clay, WV
..... 4 Andrea Jacqueline Rogers b: 22 Dec 1976
..... 5 Hunter Lee Bowman b: 26 Jan 1996
..... +Robert White
..... 5 Jorja Kenzleigh White b: 13 Aug 2003
..... *2nd Wife of [4] Andrew Jackson Rogers:
..... +[6] Tammy Lynn Gray b: 27 Jun 1973 m: 05 Sep 1997 in Clifton Forge, VA
..... +Delbert Dennis b: 22 Dec 1928 m: 22 Jan 1958
..... 3 Sheila Marlene Dennis b: 26 Mar 1959
..... +Roger Alan Bremer b: 10 Sep 1960 m: 08 Mar 1980 in Fort Wayne, IN
..... 4 Jami Marlene Bremer b: 24 Aug 1980
..... +Casey Lee Adams b: 28 Nov 1978 m: 16 Aug 2003 in Ft. Wayne, IN
..... 5 Spencer Lee Adams b: 01 Dec 2005
..... 5 Chloe Renee Adams b: 17 Oct 2008
..... 4 Ashley Marlene Bremer b: 29 Jul 1985

> The bracketed numbers indicate the generation number. The + sign = Husband or Wife

.... 4 Lindsey Marlene Bremer b: 29 Jul 1985
.... 2 Kermit Adolph Rogers b: 23 Feb 1934
.... 5 Gracyn Rylin Spillers b: 07 Sep 2009
.... +Betty Lou Bird b: 29 Oct 1936 m: 12 Aug 1954
.... 3 Kathleen Ann Rogers b: 14 Jan 1955
.... +Roger Smith m: 01 Dec 1973 b: 31 Jan 1947
.... 4 Kerrie Ann Smith b: 28 Dec 1979
.... 5 Cloie Page Hart b: 04 Sep 2007
.... +James Drake m: 03 Jun 2000 in Newton, WV, Roane Co. b: 02 Mar 1939
.... *2nd Husband of Kerrie Ann Smith:
.... +Richard L. Young, Jr. m: 04 Jan 2003 in United Me. Church, Clendenin, WV
.... 5 Kaitlynn Brielle Young b: 27 Sep 2003
.... 4 Kacie Jo Smith b: 31 Oct 1985
.... 5 Mahailey Jo Smith b: 02 Dec 2005
.... +Robert Scott Holcomb b: 8 Jan 1982 m: 22 Jun 2009
.... 5 Marissa Brooke Holcomb b: 25 Jan 2010
.... *2nd Husband of Kathleen Ann Rogers:
.... +Karl Holcomb
.... 3 Cheryl Lynn Rogers b: 10 Mar 1956
.... +Paul Holcomb b: 16 Jun 1949 m: 22 Sep 1973
.... 4 Jennifer Dawn Holcomb b: 22 Oct 1974
.... +Mark Tanner b: 05 Apr 1973 m: 22 Apr 2000 in Monroe, NC
.... 4 Leah Michele Holcomb b: 07 Nov 1976
.... +Jeremy Quinn b: 30 Jun 1974
.... 5 Garrett Monteville Quinn b: 10 Mar 2001
.... 5 Jackson Henry Quinn b: 09 Jun 2006
.... 3 Dawn Arlene Rogers b: 15 May 1960
.... +Charles Richard Wilkinson b: 26 Nov 1949 m: in Arnoldsburg, WV, Calhoun Co.
.... 4 Luke Aaron Wilkinson b: 27 Jul 1979
.... 5 Kylin Levi Wilkinson b: 29 Jan 1999
.... 4 Carrissa Dawn Wilkinson b: 08 Oct 1980
.... +James Foster
.... 4 Jessy Kathlynn Wilkinson b: 20 Oct 1984
.... 4 Rebecca Kay Wilkinson b: 08 May 1986
.... +Adam Duane Stock b: 03 Feb 1982
.... 5 Braxton Graham Stock b: 30 Jun 2006
.... 5 Owen Bradford Stock b: 24 Oct 2008
.... 4 Julie Marie Wilkinson b: 11 Oct 1988

> The bracketed numbers indicate the generation number. The + sign = Husband or Wife

2 Dorma Kathern Rogers b: 24 Mar 1936
.... +James Henry Bird b: 12 Jun 1933 d: May 1986 m: Sep 1955
.... 3 Jimmy Lee Bird b: 12 Jul 1956
.... 3 Nena Marie Bird b: 11 Mar 1958
.... +Ricky Gene Coppock b: 11 Sep 1957 d: 10 May 2000 m: 19 Jun 1976 in Huntington, IN
.... 4 Scott Lee Coppock b: 15 Jul 1978
.... +Lillian E Frosyni Douramacos b: 15 Oct 1978 m: 08 Jun 2002 in Alexandria, IN
.... 5 David James Coppock b: 11 Jun 2008
.... 4 Kathryn Irene Coppock b: 29 Sep 1982
.... +Chase Garrett Hill m: 28 Dec 2002 in First Baptist Church, Alexandria, IN
.... 3 Lisa Carol Bird b: 30 Jun 1960
.... +Steve Tackett b: 17 Oct 1956 m: 03 Aug 1979
.... 4 Bobby Wayne Tackett b: 19 Aug 1980
.... 4 James Lee Tackett Jr. b: 19 Aug 1980
.... +Kristine Louise White b: 29 Oct 1983
.... 5 Haley Kristine Tackett b: 14 Jul 2004
.... 5 James Lee Tackett II b: 02 Nov 2001
.... 5 Christian David Tackett b: 04 Feb 2008
.... 4 Steven Daniel Tackett b: 20 May 1987
.... 3 Ernest Scott Bird b: 16 Aug 1962
.... +April Shoemaker m: 14 Nov 2008
.... 4 Kylie May Bird b: 30 Dec 1992
.... 4 McKenna Shoemaker b: 25 Aug 2000
.... 4 Joseph Scott Bird b: 05 May 2005
.... *2nd Husband of Dorma Kathern Rogers:
.... +James Drake m: 22 Jul 1997 in Gatlinburg, Tennessee
2 Carroll Aaron Rogers b: 10 May 1938
.... +Maria Felicia Greco b: 25 May 1941 m: 19 Nov 1960 in Morgantown, WV
.... 3 Marc Robert Rogers b: 05 May 1962
.... +Melanie Baker b: 01 May 1964 m: 19 Dec 1998 in Wesley Methodist Church, High St., Morgantow
.... 4 Matthew Perry Rogers b: 02 Feb 2001
.... 4 Mikala Polina Rogers b: 01 Sep 2003
.... 3 Michele Lynn Rogers b: 06 Apr 1964
.... +Michael Tarrantini m: 19 Nov 1960
.... *2nd Husband of Michele Lynn Rogers:
.... +Gregoy Wes McDonald b: 22 Oct 1963 m: 20 Sep 1992 in Morgantown, WV, Monongalia Co.
.... 4 Heather Noel McDonald b: 15 Dec 1993
.... 4 Wesley Aaron McDonald b: 10 May 1997

The bracketed numbers indicate the generation number. The + sign = Husband or Wife

..... 3 Nathan Eric Rogers b: 10 Jul 1970
..... +Vickie Sue DeCarlo b: 26 Jun 1970 m: 22 Jun 1996 in Morgantown, WV, Monogalia Co.
.... 4 Isiah Jackson Rogers b: 24 Oct 2001
.... 4 Franklin Jeremiah Rogers b: 26 Jun 2003
.... 4 Winston Nehemiah Rogers b: 26 Jun 2003
.... 4 Hudson Elijah Rogers b: 13 Oct 2008
..... 2 Charlotte Ann Rogers b: 16 Mar 1940
..... +David Alexander Richmond b: 02 Jun 1937 d: 03 Aug 2008 m: 22 Aug 1959 in Inglewood, LA Co., CA
.... 3 Brad Alexander Richmond b: 17 Sep 1960
..... +Dawn Marie Gauthier b: 17 Jul 1961 m: 30 Nov 1979 in Otsego, Allegan Co., MI
.... 4 Brooke Alexandria Richmond b: 27 Jun 1983
.... 4 Brenton Alexander Richmond b: 11 Jan 1987
.... 4 Brittany Anastasia Richmond b: 24 Feb 1990
..... *2nd Wife of Brad Alexander Richmond:
..... +Vickie Lynne Nickelson b: 09 Jan 1962 m: 22 Aug 2008 in Rockford, MI
.... 4 Martin Andrew Monzo b: 19 Mar 1991
.... 4 Rachel Monzo b: 25 Jun 1993
.... 3 Kimberly Anne Richmond b: 11 Nov 1963
..... +Michael Charles Hickey b: 26 May 1961 m: 09 Apr 1982 in Yucca Valley, CA
.... 4 Matthew Michael Hickey b: 15 Nov 1984
..... +Rochelle Lynn Dovin b: 11 Mar, 1985 m: Aug 2005 in Plainwell, Allegan Co., MI
.... 5 Ryleigh Elizabeth Hickey b: 06 Feb 2006
.... 5 Jackson Matthew Hickey b: 31 May 2009
.... 4 Kristin Ann Hickey b: 30 Oct 1988
..... +Jeffery Lorsung m: 10 Feb 2009 in Radcliff, Kentucky
..... *2nd Husband of Charlotte Ann Rogers:
..... +Donald John Ostrom b: 20 Mar 1939 m: 30 Oct 1972 in Las Vegas, Clark Co., NV
.... 3 Lance John Ostrom b: 29 Feb 1972
..... +Laurel Lee LaCour b: 14 Apr 1975 m: 09 Sep 2001 in Saline, MI
.... 4 Jacob Davis Ostrom b: 18 Jun 2008
.... 4 Claire Ann Ostrom b: 21 Apr 2010
.... 4 Maya Jean Ostrom b: 21 Apr 2010
..... *3rd Husband of Charlotte Ann Rogers:
..... +Guy LeRoy Dilno b: 22 Aug 1946 m: 14 Dec 1980 in Plainwell, Allegan Co., MI
..... 2 Patricia Rondell Rogers b: 05 Feb 1943
..... +Homer Lee Conley b: 14 Mar 1940 m: 11 Aug 1962 in Clover Ridge, Roane Co., WV
.... 3 Gregory Lee Conley b: 24 Jul 1963
..... +Priscilla Cathern Naylor b: 11 Nov 1965 m: 24 Feb 1993 in Newton, Roane Co., WV.
.... 3 Michael Garrett Conley b: 22 Jan 1966
..... +Shanna Claudine Pugh m: Jul 1988 in March AFB, Riverside Co., CA

The bracketed numbers indicate the generation number. The + sign = Husband or Wife

.... *2nd Wife of Michael Garrett Conley:

.... +Jennifer Rebecca French b: 14 Aug 1969 m: 30 Jun 1996

.... *3rd Wife of Michael Garrett Conley:

.... +Shirley Ann Bird b: 02 Jun 1952 m: 19 May 2009 in Newton, Roane Co., WV

...... 3 Stephen Wayne Conley b: 28 Sep 1967

.... +Vera Ellen Highlander

.... 4 Gabriel Wayne Conley b: 30 Dec 2001

.... 4 Joshua Highlander Conley b: 25 Apr 2006

.... + Child of Stephen Wayne Conley and Melissa Bailey

............4 Ashley Nicole Bailey b: 12 Feb 1993. Melissa Bailey

.... 5 Braydonn James Bailey b: 05 Jul 2009

...... 3 Stacy Rondell Conley b: 21 Sep 1972

.... +Aaron Michael Romano b: 07 Sep 1971 m: 30 May 1992 in Newton, WV, Roane Co.

.... 4 Bryan Gregory Romano b: 03 May 1994

.... 4 Justin Matthew Romano b: 17 Oct 1995

.... 4 Sara Elizabeth Romano b: 07 Sep 1998

...... 3 [1] Christina Lynn Conley b: 25 Jan 1970

.... +[2] Gary Scott Deusenberry b: 30 Dec 1969 m: 30 Dec 1988 in Newton, WV

.... *2nd Husband of [1] Christina Lynn Conley:

.... +[3] Mike Whittman m: 22 Jul 2000

.... 2 Barbara Caroline Rogers b: 07 Sep 1945 d: 05 Jun 2005 in Riverside, Riverside Co., CA

.... +Roger Beistle b: 25 Jul 1941 m: in Las Vegas, NV

...... 3 Gregory Allen Beistle b: 19 Jan 1966

...... 3 Therese Marie Beistle b: 19 Jun 1968

.... +Kevin Pederson

.... 4 Britney Taylor Pederson b: 28 Jan 1994

.... 4 Christian Kevin Pederson b: 25 Apr 1995

.... 2 [4] Andrew Jackson Rogers b: 27 Mar 1952

.... +[5] Caroline Carte d: 03 Aug 2006 in Clay, WV

.... *2nd Wife of [4] Andrew Jackson Rogers:

.... +[6] Tammy Lynn Gray b: 27 Jun 1973 m: 05 Sep 1997 in Clifton Forge, VA

31

Notes about the Genealogy Report for Johan Jacob Tawney

I have included all of the generations under John Jacob Tawney because his line is the most often quoted among the descendants of Aaron and Almon Tawney. By including all generations, each descendant can see where she or he fits into the line.

In the case of Almon's ancestors, I terminated the reports at Almon so you might consider referring to either the John Jacob Tawney or Thomas Hughes report to see the remainder of the generations. This results in the least amount of redundancy.

Genealogy Report of Johan Jacob Tawney

Generation No. 1

1. JOHAN JACOB[1] TAWNEY was born Abt. 1720 in Germany, and died 1790 in Berks Co., PA. He married CHARLOTTE UNKNOWN.

Notes for Johan Jacob Tawney:

The following was compiled by my Uncle Garrison Tawney and provided in writing to Aunt Anna (Tawney) Desposito who gave it to me for the book.

According to these notes, Johan Jacob (Johan Adam Tanny) was born of the Palatines heritage near the Bavarian border, Southwestern portion of Hesse, in West Germany. They arrived in Philadelphia, PA on September 3, 1739, on the ship Royal Judith, Commander Edward Painter from Rotterdam last from Deal with 315 passengers. After taking the oath of allegiance, Jacob made his way inland, and settled in Bethel Township, now Berks County. He died there about 1790.

He was living near the present site of Rehersburg when his second child was born February 28, 1747. The baby was named John George. He was baptized by the Lutheran Minister John Casper Stover. Twenty-one years later Reverend Stover officiated at the marriage of George Thany and Elizabeth Truckmuller, both of Bethel.

The young couple eventually migrated to Virginia, where George served in the Augusta County Militia, from 1781 to 1783 during the Revolutionary War. He died at his South Fork home on Reed Wythe Creek in Wythe County, July 4, 1817. He and Elizabeth had seven children, one of whom was John Daniel Tawney, born May 6, 1770 in Berks County, PA. Daniel served in Captain John Morris Rangers in Kanawha County which was in Virginia at the time but is West Virginia now. They fought against the Indians, in 1792 and 1793. Later he was Lieutenant in Wythe County.

In 1796 Daniel married Elizabeth Price, daughter of David and Katherine Price, Early New River settlers. Daniel acquired a good deal of land, mostly on Sinking Creek, Giles County. Daniel died in 1834 and leaving his wife and three known children: Sally Hendricks, Mary Elizabeth and Daniel Jr. (1804-1863). He was the first of our line to live in what is now Roane County. Daniel Tawney Jr. came from Russell County, Virginia where he and his family for about six years and in 1853 bought 254 acres on Potalico River, then in Kanawha County. He sold the land in 1856 to William Price, whereupon he returned to Virginia.

His oldest son George W. Tawney (1827-1894) promptly bought 605 acres of land on Big Sandy Creek branch of Elk River. He assumed charge of his family consisting of his mother Lovisa, daughter of Michael and Irene Adkins, also his brothers Christopher P., William H. and John H; also his sisters Sara Jane, Elizabeth and Amanda. Another brother David J. had married and was living nearby.

During the Civil War the five brothers and Alexander Tawney (relationship unknown) served in the 126th Regiment Militia, Clay County Scouts, enlisting from Roane County.

In 1863 John Tawney, less than 16 years old, but over six-feet-tall transferred to the regular Union Army for the remainder of the war.

George W. Tawney, born April 9, 1827 and died October 6, 1894, had married Mary Noe on Valentine's Day 1857. She was the daughter of William and Elizabeth King-Noe, who had come from Pike County, Kentucky, before 1840 to settle on Dog Creek Branch of Big Sandy Creek. After some years, George sold some of his land to his brothers Christopher and William and bought some land from his father-in-law. George and Mary were parents of 11 children. George and Mary's ninth child Aaron was born 1876 and died 1966. He was a farmer, Methodist religion, and school trustee like his father.

He and his wife Flora Almon Graham-Tawney had eleven children. Almon was the oldest child and was the daughter of William Isaac Graham and Mary Ellen Sergent, born December 13, 1861. William Graham was born May 27, 1859 and died at Left Hand, Roane County June 17, 1938. He was the son of William Edward Graham (1828) in Nicholas County. He died at Cloyds Mountain during the Civil War, Virginia May 9. 1864.

Their children were: William Ernest, married Mable Varney; Lula Mable Tawney-Rogers married Ernest Rogers; Ruby Mamie Tawney-Haines married Irving Haines; Clement Tawney married Opal Nester; Florence Tawney-Dalton married Jack Dalton; George Garrison Tawney married Frieda Vineyard; Champ "Clark" Tawney married Beatrice Summers; Harry Marshall , died as child (10-24-1917 to May 18, 1920); Jarrett Tawney married Frances Roberts; Elizabeth Anna Tawney married Michael Edward Desposito; Daniel Aaron Tawney married Hazel Short.

My notes:
Johan Jacob Tawney was born in Germany and arrived in Philadelphia from Rotterdam, Holland, aboard the ship "Loyal Judith" in Sept. 1739. He settled in Bethel Township in Berks Co., PA. He died there in 1790. The last name of his wife, Charlotte, is not known.

Child of JOHAN TAWNEY and CHARLOTTE UNKNOWN is:
2.   i.   JOHN GEORGE[2] TAWNEY.

Generation No. 2

2. JOHN GEORGE[2] TAWNEY *(JOHAN JACOB[1])* He met (1) MARGARETHA ELISABETH TRUCKEMULLER 30 May 1768 in Bethel.   He married (2) ELIZABETH GODBEY 19 Dec 1806 in Montgomery Co, VA.

Notes for JOHN GEORGE TAWNEY: John George Tawney served in the Augusta Co. VA Militia from 1781 to 1783 during the American Revolution.

More about JOHN TAWNEY and MARGARETHA TRUCKEMULLER:
Single: 30 May 1768, Bethel

Children of JOHN TAWNEY and MARGARETHA TRUCKEMULLER are:
3.   i.   JOHN DANIEL[3] TAWNEY, b. 06 May 1770, Berks Co., PA; d. 1834, Giles Co., VA.
           ii.   CHRISTIAN TAWNEY,   b. 11 Sep 1771.
4.   iii.   JANE TAWNEY, b. 1772; d. Abt. 1859.
           iv.   ELIZABETH TAWNEY, b. Abt. 1773; m. JOHN WILLIAMS.
            v.   JOHN GEORGE TAWNEY, JR, b. Abt. 1775; d. Abt. 1799; m. CATEY STALEY, 01 Feb 1797.

More about JOHN TAWNEY and CATEY STALEY:
Marriage: 01 Feb 1797

5. vi.   JOHN TAWNEY, b. Abt. 1776; d. Abt. 1856.
    vii. BARBARA TAWNEY, b. Abt. 1777; m. JACOB OLINGER, Abt. 1795.

    More about JACOB OLINGER and BARBARA TAWNEY:
    Marriage: Abt. 1795

    viii. CATHERINE TAWNEY, b. Abt. 1779; m. JOHN LEFTWICH; b. 16 Nov 1797.

Generation No. 3

3. JOHN DANIEL[3] TAWNEY *(JOHN GEORGE[2], JOHAN JACOB[1])* was born 06 May 1770 in Berks Co., PA, and died 1834 in Giles Co., VA.   He married ELIZABETH PRICE 06 Dec 1796 in Montgomery Co., VA, daughter of DAVID PRICE and KATHERINE UNKNOWN.   She was born Abt. 1775, and died Abt. 07 Mar 1846.

Notes for JOHN DANIEL TAWNEY:
John Daniel Tawney served in Capt. John Morris's Company of Kanawha Rangers against the Indians in 1792 and 1793.

Children of JOHN TAWNEY and ELIZABETH PRICE are:
6. i.   JOHN DANIEL[4] TAWNEY, JR. , b. 30 Jun 1804, Montgomery Co., VA; d. 1863, Russell Co., VA.
    ii.   SARAH "SALLY" TAWNEY, b. Abt. 1798; m. ABRAHAM HEDRICK, 27 Sep 1814.
    iii. MARY ELIZABETH TAWNEY, b. Abt. 1800; m. ROBERT M. HUTCHISON.

4. JANE[3] TAWNEY *(JOHN GEORGE[2], JOHAN JACOB[1])* was born 1772, and died Abt. 1859.   She married JOHN BARGER.

Children of JANE TAWNEY and JOHN BARGER are:
    i.   GEORGE WASHINGTON[4] BARGER.
    ii.   WILLIAM I. BARGER.
    iii. JAMES JR. BARGER.
    iv.   JOHN JR. BARGER.
    v.   POLLY BARGER.
    vi.   PHILLIP BARGER.
    vii. DANIEL BARGER.
    viii. NANCY BARGER.
    ix.   HARRIET BARGER.
    x.   ABRAM H. BARGER.

5. JOHN[3] TAWNEY *(JOHN GEORGE[2], JOHAN JACOB[1])* was born Abt. 1776, and died Abt. 1856. He married MARY ANN PRICE 07 May 1799.

Children of JOHN TAWNEY and MARY PRICE are:

	i.	LETTICE[4] TAWNEY, d. 18 Mar 1876.
	ii.	JOHN TAWNEY.
7.	iii.	MARY "POLLY" TAWNEY.
	iv.	AGNES TAWNEY, m. THOMAS EAGLESON.
	v.	KATHERINE TAWNEY, b. Abt. 1813.
	vi.	WILLIAM TAWNEY, m. ELIZABETH HUNTER, 24 Mar 1843.
	vii.	DAVID JAMES TAWNEY, b. 1823; m. CYNTHIA/SYNTHA LAWRENCE.
	viii.	GEORGE TAWNEY, b. 1825.
	ix.	JACOB TAWNEY, b. 1838.

Generation No. 4

6. JOHN DANIEL[4] TAWNEY, JR. *(JOHN DANIEL[3], JOHN GEORGE[2], JOHAN JACOB[1])* was born 30 Jun 1804 in Montgomery Co., VA, and died 1863 in Russell Co., VA[1]. He married LOVISA (LEVICY) HARLESS 30 Jun 1827 in Elana, WV, Roane Co., daughter of MICHAEL HARLESS and IRENE ADKINS. She was born 26 Jan 1804 in Montgomery Co., VA, and died between 1870 - 1879 in Roane Co., WV.

Children of JOHN TAWNEY and LOVISA HARLESS are:

8.	i.	GEORGE WILLIAM[5] TAWNEY, b. 09 Apr 1827, Giles Co., VA; d. 05 Oct 1894, Newton, WV, Roane Co.
9.	ii.	CHRISTOPHER P. TAWNEY, b. Abt. 1829.
10.	iii.	DAVID J. TAWNEY, b. 1832.
11.	iv.	SARAH JANE TAWNEY, b. 1833.
12.	v.	ELIZABETH TAWNEY, b. 19 Nov 1834.
13.	vi.	WILLIAM H. TAWNEY, b. 01 Aug 1836.
	vii.	AMANDA TAWNEY, b. Abt. 1842.
14.	viii.	JOHN HAMILTON TAWNEY, b. 22 Mar 1848, Giles Co., VA; d. 01 Oct 1916, Roane Co., WV.
	ix.	ALEXANDER TAWNEY, b. Abt. 1844.

7. MARY "POLLY"[4] TAWNEY *(JOHN[3], JOHN GEORGE[2], JOHAN JACOB[1])* She married HIRAM ATKINS 26 Apr 1831. He was born 1808, and died 24 May 1888.

Children of MARY "POLLY" TAWNEY and HIRAM ATKINS are:

i.	JOHN[5] ATKINS.
ii.	ROBERT ATKINS, d. 1863, Gettysburg, PA.
iii.	MOSES ATKINS, d. 1864, Cloyds Mountain.
iv.	CLARISSA "CLARY" ATKINS, b. Abt. 1835; m. HARRISON P. ECHOLS; b. Abt. 1830.
v.	MARY JANE ATKINS, b. Abt. 1836; m. WILLIAM H. BELLER, 04 Dec 1856; b. Abt. 1834.
vi.	LEWIS ATKINS, b. 22 Jun 1845; d. Abt. 1883; m. CLEOPATRIC TINSLEY.
vii.	ALBERT J. ATKINS, b. 1847; m. NANNIE E. BELLER, 07 Jan 1872.
viii.	GEORGE H. ATKINS, b. 1854; d. 1935.

Generation No. 5

8. GEORGE WILLIAM[5] TAWNEY *(JOHN DANIEL[4], JOHN DANIEL[3], JOHN GEORGE[2], JOHAN JACOB[1])* was born 09 Apr 1827 in Giles Co., VA, and died 05 Oct 1894 in Newton, WV, Roane Co.   He married MARY NOE 14 Feb 1857, daughter of WILLIAM NOE and ELIZABETH KING.   She was born 19 Aug 1840 in Kanawha Co., VA (now WV), and died 19 Dec 1929 in Newton, Roane Co., WV.

Notes for GEORGE WILLIAM TAWNEY:
He lived next door to the Newton Post Office.   Data from the 1870 Census indicates that neither he nor Mary could read or write.   His son Aaron Tawney was very strong on education and was responsible for the construction of the Dog Creek School on his farm.

Notes for MARY NOE:
On her tombstone "He who dies believing dies safely through thy love."

Children of GEORGE TAWNEY and MARY NOE are:

	i.	MIRANDA[6] TAWNEY, b. Abt. 1859, Elana, Roane Co., WV; d. 24 Jul 1863, Unknown.

More about MIRANDA TAWNEY:
Burial: 24 Jul 1863, Unknown

15.	ii.	DANIEL W. "LINK" TAWNEY, b. 27 Mar 1861, Newton, WV; d. 1948.
16.	iii.	SARA ELIZABETH "BETT" TAWNEY, b. 25 Feb 1863.
17.	iv.	DAVID JACKSON TAWNEY, b. 06 May 1865; d. 09 Sep 1951.
	v.	HIRAM J. "HIGH" TAWNEY, b. 16 Aug 1867; d. 15 Apr 1912.
	vi.	LOUVISA TAWNEY, b. 06 Oct 1869; d. 02 Sep 1877, Newton, WV, Roane Co.
	vii.	GEORGE WILLIAMTAWNEY, b. 14 Apr 1872; d. 05 Oct 1894.
	viii.	SAMUEL RICHARD TAWNEY, b. 07 Jun 1874; m. ELLEN HELMICK, 23 May 1897, Roane Co., WV.
18.	ix.	AARON TAWNEY, b. 27 Aug 1876, Roane Co., WV; d. 08 Oct 1966, Left Hand, Roane Co., WV.
	x.	JAMES M. TAWNEY, b. 21 Dec 1879; d. Nov 1901.
	xi.	FLORENCE TAWNEY, m. WILL SERGENT; d. St. Louis, MO.
	xii.	CHRISTOPHER TAWNEY, b. Unknown; d. Unknown.
	xiii.	WILLIAM H. TAWNEY, b. Unknown; d. Unknown.

9. CHRISTOPHER P.[5] TAWNEY *(JOHN DANIEL[4], JOHN DANIEL[3], JOHN GEORGE[2], JOHAN JACOB[1])* was born Abt. 1829.   He married LUCRETIA UNKNOWN.

Children of CHRISTOPHER TAWNEY and LUCRETIA UNKNOWN are:

	i.	MARTHA A.[6] TAWNEY, b. Abt. 1856.
	ii.	WILLIAM TAWNEY, b. Abt. 1859.
	iii.	REBECCA J. ` TAWNEY, b. Abt. Jan 1863; m. GEORGE SCOTT, 19 Sep 1888.
	iv.	MARY F. TAWNEY, b. Abt. 1864.
	v.	ARMETHA A. TAWNEY, b. Abt. 1865.
	vi.	ARMITTA E. TAWNEY, b. Abt. 15 Aug 1866; m. ANTHONY BUCHANNON.

10. DAVID J.[5] TAWNEY *(JOHN DANIEL[4], JOHN DANIEL[3], JOHN GEORGE[2], JOHAN JACOB[1])* was born 1832.   He married ELIZABETH E. YOUNG 14 Jul 1854.

Children of DAVID TAWNEY and ELIZABETH YOUNG are:
      i.   WILLIAM P.[6] TAWNEY, b. Abt. 1856.
     ii.   LEWIS C. TAWNEY, b. 07 Oct 1858.
    iii.   ARMENTHA M. TAWNEY, b. 24 Sep 1859.
    iv.   MARY A. TAWNEY, b. 22 Apr 1861.
     v.   PHILLIP G. TAWNEY, b. 14 Jul 1866.
    vi.   EDWIN A. TAWNEY, b. Abt. 1868.
   vii.   MABEL TAWNEY, b. Bet. 1869 - 1870.
  viii.   EMMA TAWNEY, b. Abt. 1872.
    ix.   JOHN D. TAWNEY, b. Abt. 1875.
     x.   MATTIE L. TAWNEY, b. Abt. 1877.
    xi.   ERNEST R. TAWNEY, b. Abt. 1880.

11. SARAH JANE[5] TAWNEY *(JOHN DANIEL[4], JOHN DANIEL[3], JOHN GEORGE[2], JOHAN JACOB[1])* was born 1833.

Children of SARAH JANE TAWNEY are:
      i.   WILLIAM M.[6] TAWNEY, b. 27 Oct 1850.
     ii.   FLOYD M. TAWNEY, b. 30 Jul 1861.
    iii.   JAMES M. TAWNEY, b. Abt. 1863.
    iv.   ALBERT/HERBERT TAWNEY, b. 15 Sep 1865; d. Abt. 1865.

12. ELIZABETH[5] TAWNEY *(JOHN DANIEL[4], JOHN DANIEL[3], JOHN GEORGE[2], JOHAN JACOB[1])* was born 19 Nov 1834.   She married ISAAC M. ROSS 07 Mar 1858.

Children of ELIZABETH TAWNEY and ISAAC ROSS are:
      i.   ARMETHA L.[6] ROSS, b. 10 Dec 1859.
     ii.   MARY J. ROSS, b. 10 Oct 1861.
    iii.   JOHN A. ROSS, b. 19 Nov 1864; m. MARY F. SMITH, 03 Feb 1893.
    iv.   W.C./WILLIAM ROSS, b. 14 Nov 1878; d. Unknown.

13. WILLIAM H.[5] TAWNEY *(JOHN DANIEL[4], JOHN DANIEL[3], JOHN GEORGE[2], JOHAN JACOB[1])* was born 01 Aug 1836.   He married LOUISA GRIFFITH 20 Nov 1863.

Children of WILLIAM TAWNEY and LOUISA GRIFFITH are:
      i.   HUGH H.[6] TAWNEY, b. 09 Dec 1864; m. (1) JULIA A. DRAKE, 25 Apr 1904; m. (2) NANCY A. BARNES, 02 Aug 1920.
     ii.   LOVICA M. TAWNEY, b. 17 Nov 1867.
    iii.   INFANT TAWNEY.

14. JOHN HAMILTON[5] TAWNEY *(JOHN DANIEL[4], JOHN DANIEL[3], JOHN GEORGE[2], JOHAN JACOB[1])* was born 22 Mar 1848 in Giles Co., VA, and died 01 Oct 1916 in Roane Co., WV. He married (1) ELIZABETH JANE KEEN 20 Apr 1867 in Roane Co., WV census, daughter of NANCY (KING) KEEN. She was born 22 Feb 1851 in Kanawha Co. (now WV), and died 01 Jun 1901 in Roane Co., WV. He married (2) COLUMBIA (DOUGLAS) ROE 27 Nov 1901. She was born 20 Apr 1853, and died 29 Jan 1918.

Notes for COLUMBIA (DOUGLAS) ROE:
She was the widow of Grandville Roe

Children of JOHN TAWNEY and ELIZABETH KEEN are:
19.	i.	DORA ELLEN[6] TAWNEY, b. 19 Jun 1868; d. 06 Jun 1928.
20.	ii.	JAMES WELLINGTON TAWNEY, b. 22 Dec 1868; d. 11 Sep 1958.
21.	iii.	NANCY EMMA TAWNEY, b. 02 May 1871, Newton, WV, Roane Co.; d. 26 May 1896.
22.	iv.	DANIEL CAREY TAWNEY, b. 23 Aug 1872; d. 24 Apr 1953.
23.	v.	LUCY ALAPHAIR TAWNEY, b. 28 Feb 1874, Roane Co., WV; d. 05 Nov 1955.
24.	vi.	MAE BELLE TAWNEY, b. 03 Dec 1875, Roane Co., WV; d. 26 Dec 1902.
25.	vii.	MARY ELIZABETH TAWNEY , b. 19 Oct 1877; d. 25 Oct 1962.
	viii.	ROBERT L. TAWNEY, b. 28 Sep 1879; d. Unknown.
26.	ix.	ROSA FORREST TAWNEY, b. 10 Jun 1881; d. 22 Mar 1917.
27.	x.	JOHN SPENCER TAWNEY, b. 04 May 1883; d. 02 Jun 1958.
28.	xi.	CLARA ESTER TAWNEY, b. 04 Sep 1885, Roane Co., WV; d. Unknown.
29.	xii.	ROXIE FAY TAWNEY, b. 02 Mar 1888, Roane Co., WV; d. Unknown.
	xiii.	STILLBORN TAWNEY, b. 19 Jun 1890; d. Stillborn.
	xiv.	STILLBORN TAWNEY, b. 15 Aug 1891; d. 15 Aug 1891.
	xv.	WILLIAM TAWNEY, b. 06 Jun 1893; d. Infant.

Generation No. 6

15. DANIEL W. "LINK"[6] TAWNEY *(GEORGE WILLIAM[5], JOHN DANIEL[4], JOHN DANIEL[3], JOHN GEORGE[2], JOHAN JACOB[1])* was born 27 Mar 1861 in Newton, WV, and died 1948. He married MARY MOLLY HALEY. She was born 1869, and died 1963.

Children of DANIEL TAWNEY and MARY HALEY are:
	i.	JOHN[7] TAWNEY, m. LOCIE GREATHOUSE.
	ii.	JENNINGS TAWNEY, m. DONA HUNT.
	iii.	GEORGE TAWNEY, m. RUBY BOGGS.
	iv.	WILSON TAWNEY, m. MARY MARKS.
	v.	RHUAMI FLORENCE TAWNEY, m. HOMER WHITE.
	vi.	EMMA TAWNEY, m. FLOYD DRAKE.
30.	vii.	MAGGIE TAWNEY, d. 05 Mar 1999.
	viii.	STELLA TAWNEY, m. JOHN NIDA.

16. SARA ELIZABETH "BETT"[6] TAWNEY *(GEORGE WILLIAM[5], JOHN DANIEL[4], JOHN DANIEL[3], JOHN GEORGE[2], JOHAN JACOB[1])* was born 25 Feb 1863. She married PETE RADABAUGH.

Children of SARA TAWNEY and PETE RADABAUGH are:

31.   i.   KISTA CHRISTENIA[7] RADABAUGH, b. 01 Sep 1890, Spencer, WV; d. 20 Dec 1971, Salem, Arkansas.
       ii. OMAR RADABAUGH.
       iii. HOWARD RADABAUGH.
       iv. MARY RADABAUGH.

17.   DAVID JACKSON[6] TAWNEY *(GEORGE WILLIAM[5], JOHN DANIEL[4], JOHN DANIEL[3], JOHN GEORGE[2], JOHAN JACOB[1])* was born 06 May 1865, and died 09 Sep 1951.   He married CYNTHIA MAY CARPER.

Children of DAVID JACKSON TAWNEY and CYNTHIA CARPER are:
       i.   ADD S.[7] TAWNEY, b. 1892; d. Jan 1936.
       ii.   CLARA TAWNEY.
       iii. CLARK TAWNEY.
       iv.   CORA TAWNEY.
       v.   FLORENCE TAWNEY.
       vi.   GROVER TAWNEY, b. 1890; d. 1959.
       vii. GYPSY TAWNEY.
       viii. HESTER TAWNEY.
       ix.   JAMES HENRY TAWNEY.
       x.   MARY TAWNEY.
32.   xi.   PRESTON J. TAWNEY, b. 02 Feb 1900; d. 12 Sep 1985.
       xii. W. CLAY TAWNEY.

18.   AARON[6] TAWNEY *(GEORGE WILLIAM[5], JOHN DANIEL[4], JOHN DANIEL[3], JOHN GEORGE[2], JOHAN JACOB[1])* was born 27 Aug 1876 in Roane Co., WV, and died 08 Oct 1966 in Left Hand, Roane Co., WV.   He married FLORA ALMON GRAHAM 22 Aug 1903 in Left Hand, Roane Co., WV, daughter of WILLIAM GRAHAM and MARY SERGENT.   She was born 15 Nov 1884 in Left Hand, Roane Co., WV, and died 12 Oct 1960 in Parkersburg, Wood Co., WV.

Notes for AARON TAWNEY:
Aaron was a member of the Methodist Church, Newton, WV.   He was a farmer.

More about AARON TAWNEY:
Burial: Tawney Family Cemetery, Newton, WV
Cause of Death: Congestive Heart Failure

Marriage Notes for AARON TAWNEY and FLORA GRAHAM:
Married by Rev. Albright

Children of AARON TAWNEY and FLORA GRAHAM are:
33.   i.   WILLIAM "ERNEST"[7] TAWNEY, b. 01 Sep 1904, Left Hand, Roane Co., WV; d. 24 Mar 1966, Charleston, Kanawha Co., WV.
34.   ii.   LULA "MABEL" TAWNEY, b. 23 Mar 1906, Left Hand, Roane Co., WV; d. 30 May 2003, Newton, Roane Co., WV.
       iii. RUBY "MAMIE" TAWNEY, b. 24 Sep 1907, Left Hand, Roane Co., WV; m. IRVING CHARLES HAINES, 05 Oct 1953, Akron, Ohio; b. 1905; d. 1982.
35.   iv.   CLEMENT LUTHER TAWNEY, b. 19 Jul 1909, Left Hand, Roane Co., WV; d. 22 Oct 2009, Charleston, WV, Kanawha Co.

| | v. | FLORENCE MARY TAWNEY, b. 29 Jan 1911, Left Hand, Roane Co., WV; d. 06 Feb 2009, Charleston, WV, Kanawha Co.; m. JACK DALTON, 04 Jun 1945, Newcomerstown, Ohio; d. 02 Apr 1981, Parkersburg, WV. |

36.   vi.   GEORGE "GARRISON" TAWNEY, b. 11 Nov 1913, Left Hand, Roane Co., WV; d. 14 Sep 2004, Looneyville, Roane Co., WV.

37.   vii.   CHAMP "CLARK" TAWNEY (KNOWN AS CLARK) , b. 28 Nov 1915, Left Hand, Roane Co., WV; d. 27 Aug 2007.

viii.   HARRY MARSHALL TAWNEY, b. 24 Oct 1917, Left Hand, Roane Co., WV; d. 18 May 1920, Left Hand, Roane Co., WV.

38.   ix.   JARRETT ("BUZZ") TAWNEY, b. 02 Apr 1919, Left Hand,   Roane Co., WV.

39.   x.   ANNA ELIZABETH TAWNEY, b. 11 Sep 1921, Left Hand,   Roane Co., WV.

40.   xi.   DANIEL AARON TAWNEY, b. 04 Jun 1923, Left Hand,   Roane Co., WV.

19.   DORA ELLEN[6] TAWNEY *(JOHN HAMILTON[5], JOHN DANIEL[4], JOHN DANIEL[3], JOHN GEORGE[2], JOHAN JACOB[1])* was born 19 Jun 1868, and died 06 Jun 1928.   She married ROBERT FILMORE WILSON 18 Dec 1883, son of WALTER WILSON and JULIA COX.   He was born 10 Apr 1863.

Children of DORA TAWNEY and ROBERT WILSON are:

i.   CLIDA[7] WILSON, b. 1885; d. 1961; m. SAMUEL WITTE.

ii.   CLARK WILSON, m. (1) DORA KING; m. (2) LYNNE ENGLE.

iii.   EVERETT WILSON, b. 06 May 1889; d. 03 Jun 1952; m. MAHALIA ENGLE.

iv.   JULIA WILSON, b. 12 Jun 1891; d. Unknown; m. CHARLES NESTER.

v.   HUNTER WILSON, b. 27 Oct 1893; d. Unknown; m. FANNIE SMITH; d. Unknown.

vi.   CLARA WILSON, b. 13 Feb 1896; d. Unknown; m. STANLEY F. ROSS; d. Unknown.

vii.   BUENA WILSON, b. 05 Feb 1898; d. Unknown; m. ROBBERT KELLIS OGDEN.

viii.   ROBERT WILSON, b. 23 Aug 1901; d. Unknown; m. MAYZEL PARSONS.

ix.   FANNIE WILSON, b. 09 Nov 1903; d. Unknown; m. TIMOTHY MORRISON.

x.   HARRY WILSON, b. 15 Jan 1906; d. Unknown; m. ELLA SMITH.

xi.   GOFF WILSON, b. 17 Apr 1907; d. 09 Apr 1971; m. (1) NANCY AUDRA TAWNEY, 12 Sep 1931; m. (2) NANCY AUDRA TAWNEY, 12 Sep 1931; b. 1905; d. 1988.

xii.   CORA WILSON, b. 04 Nov 1908; m. (1) PORTER SIERS; m. (2) PATRICK HENRY FOX.

xiii.   JOHN W. WILSON.

xiv.   THELMA WILSON.

20. JAMES WELLINGTON[6] TAWNEY *(JOHN HAMILTON[5], JOHN DANIEL[4], JOHN DANIEL[3], JOHN GEORGE[2], JOHAN JACOB[1])* was born 22 Dec 1868, and died 11 Sep 1958. He married NANCY ANNABELLE ROSS, daughter of GEORGE ROSS and NANCY ROSS.

Children of JAMES TAWNEY and NANCY ROSS are:

	i.	VESTA G.[7] TAWNEY, m. (1) ANTHONY MATHENEY; m. (2) WHIT TUCKER; m. (3) HARRISON DALE HALL.
	ii.	FREDDIE D. TAWNEY, m. ZOE WHITE.
	iii.	ARLIE M. TAWNEY, m. WALTER B. SMITH.
	iv.	LOCIE D. TAWNEY, m. ERNEST WHITE.
	v.	INA TAWNEY, m. LOWELL SWAIN.
41.	vi.	W. CECIL TAWNEY.
42.	vii.	GEORGE W. TAWNEY, b. 02 Oct 1905, Elana, WV; d. 07 Nov 1996.
	viii.	JAMES DELMAR TAWNEY, m. MARTHA HUNT.
	ix.	BERNICE G. TAWNEY, m. CONKLIN BELKNAP.
	x.	ELBERT L. TAWNEY, m. MARILYN STARCHER.

21. NANCY EMMA[6] TAWNEY *(JOHN HAMILTON[5], JOHN DANIEL[4], JOHN DANIEL[3], JOHN GEORGE[2], JOHAN JACOB[1])* was born 02 May 1871 in Newton, WV, Roane Co., and died 26 May 1896. She married ULYSSES SIMPSON ROSS 24 Oct 1891 in Roane Co., WV census, son of DAVIDSON ROSS and NANCY DRAKE. He was born 27 Feb 1867 in Newton, WV, Roane Co., and died 19 Mar 1930.

More about NANCY EMMA TAWNEY:
Burial: Ogden Cemetery near Uler, WV

Children of NANCY TAWNEY and ULYSSES ROSS are:

43.	i.	DIXIE ARTIE[7] ROSS, b. 26 Jul 1892; d. 28 Nov 1983.
44.	ii.	REX PHILIP ROSS, b. 04 Jul 1894; d. 19 Aug 1976.
45.	iii.	MAX HAMILTON ROSS, b. 05 Apr 1896; d. 20 May 1967.
	iv.	HOMER DANIEL ROSS, b. 08 Feb 1886, Roane Co. Census, WV; d. 15 Jun 1971.

22. DANIEL CAREY[6] TAWNEY *(JOHN HAMILTON[5], JOHN DANIEL[4], JOHN DANIEL[3], JOHN GEORGE[2], JOHAN JACOB[1])* was born 23 Aug 1872, and died 24 Apr 1953. He married LULA S. DRAKE, daughter of SUTTON DRAKE and JANE DEEL. She was born 23 Aug 1872.

Children of DANIEL TAWNEY   and LULA DRAKE are:

	i.	EVA[7] ETHEL TAWNEY, m. AARON J. NOE.
	ii.	IRIS ETHEL TAWNEY, m. JOSEPH H. ELLISON.
	iii.	NORA HESTER TAWNEY, b. Abt. 1900; d. Unknown; m. LESTER RAY SAMMS; d. Unknown.
	iv.	CARL HAMILTON TAWNEY, b. Abt. 1912; m. VIRGINIA L. ROSE.
	v.	CLARA FAY TAWNEY, b. Abt. 1914; m. RAYMOND SMITH.
	vi.	DONALD CLYDE TAWNEY, b. Abt. 1911; m. (1) ZELDA DAVISSON; m. (2) VIRGINIA MCGANN.
	vii.	EUPHA IONA TAWNEY, b. 23 Oct 1908.
	viii.	RUSSELL D. TAWNEY, m. VIRGINIA SMITH.
	ix.	CARRIE NEVA TAWNEY, b. Abt. 1915; m. HOLLY DAVIS MACE.

23. LUCY ALAPHAIR[6] TAWNEY *(JOHN HAMILTON[5], JOHN DANIEL[4], JOHN DANIEL[3], JOHN GEORGE[2], JOHAN JACOB[1])* was born 28 Feb 1874 in Roane Co., WV, and died 05 Nov 1955. She married SPURGEON CHARLES ROSS, son of DAVIDSON ROSS and NANCY DRAKE.

Children of LUCY ALAPHAIR TAWNEY and SPURGEON ROSS are:
  i.   HARLEY E.[7] ROSS, m. MABEL KING.
  ii. WILLIS C. ROSS, m. (1) REBECCA IGO; m. (2) ODESSA W. BURDETTE.
  iii. DON L. ROSS, m. LILLIE SMITH.
  iv. DALLAS C. ROSS, m. MAUDE HAROLD.
  v.   LYNN ROSS, m. GRACE WHITE.

24. MAE BELLE[6] TAWNEY *(JOHN HAMILTON[5], JOHN DANIEL[4], JOHN DANIEL[3], JOHN GEORGE[2], JOHAN JACOB[1])* was born 03 Dec 1875 in Roane Co., WV, and died 26 Dec 1902. She married CHARLES W. DRAKE, son of SUTTON DRAKE and JANE DEEL.

Children of MAE BELLE TAWNEY and CHARLES DRAKE are:
  i.   LESTER H.[7] DRAKE, m. JESSIE HAROLD.
  ii. OTMER S. DRAKE, m. MATOKA UNKNOWN.
  iii. DARRELL W. DRAKE, m. MYRTLE RAMSEY.
  iv. CARLOS DRAKE.
  v.   OLLIE DRAKE.
  vi. OLIVE DRAKE.

25. MARY[6] ELIZABETH *(JOHN HAMILTON[5] TAWNEY, JOHNDANIEL[4], JOHN DANIEL[3], JOHN GEORGE[2], JOHAN JACOB[1])* was born 19 Oct 1877, and died 25 Oct 1962. She married OKEY E. WHITE, son of JAMES WHITE and LUCINDA GILLENWATER.

Children of MARY ELIZABETH and OKEY WHITE are:
  i.   DIXIE A.[7] WHITE, m. (1) CHARLES KANSKE; m. (2) CARL W. SIMMONS.
  ii. BRUCE H. WHITE, m. (1) SHIRLEY ENGLE; m. (2) FANNY BROWNING.
  iii. OLIVE C. WHITE, m. (1) JOHN SPERLING; m. (2) HENNING PEARSON.
  iv. JOHN W. WHITE, m. RUBY ERICKSON.

26. ROSA FORREST[6] TAWNEY *(JOHN HAMILTON[5], JOHN DANIEL[4], JOHN DANIEL[3], JOHN GEORGE[2], JOHAN JACOB[1])* was born 10 Jun 1881, and died 22 Mar 1917.

Children of ROSA FORREST TAWNEY are:
  i.   CLAUDE MARK[7] ROSS, d. Unknown; m. MATTIE LUCILLE NEXTER.
  ii. DORIS RUTH ROSS, m. WILLIAM CLYDE SMITH.
  iii. JOHN TAWNEY, m. STELLA G. ASHLEY.
  iv. RUBY CLAIRE ROSS, m. RABE LEE SHAW.
  v.   IMOGENE ROSS, m. WILLIAM BIRCHARD.

27. JOHN SPENCER[6] TAWNEY *(JOHN HAMILTON[5], JOHN DANIEL[4], JOHN DANIEL[3], JOHN GEORGE[2], JOHAN JACOB[1])* was born 04 May 1883, and died 02 Jun 1958. He married LEONA ROSS, daughter of GEORGE ROSS and NANCY BELCHER. She was born 15 Jan 1879, and died 15 Apr 1956.

Children of JOHN TAWNEY and LEONA ROSS are:

   i. OMAR WILLARD[7] TAWNEY, b. 1902; d. 1979; m. ROXIE SYLVIA FALLS.
   ii. BETTY GLADYS TAWNEY, b. 1903; d. 1982.
   iii. NANCY AUDRA TAWNEY, b. 1905; d. 1988; m. (1) JOHN HAROLD; m. (2) GOFF WILSON, 12 Sep 1931; b. 17 Apr 1907; d. 09 Apr 1971.
    More about GOFF WILSON and NANCY TAWNEY:
    Marriage: 12 Sep 1931
46. iv. LEONA HELEN TAWNEY, b. 28 Jun 1923, Elana, Roane Co, WV; d. 12 Apr 2001.

28. CLARA ESTER[6] TAWNEY *(JOHN HAMILTON[5], JOHN DANIEL[4], JOHN DANIEL[3], JOHN GEORGE[2], JOHAN JACOB[1])* was born 04 Sep 1885 in Roane Co., WV, and died Unknown. She married WILLIAM HOMER ENGLE, son of JOSEPH ENGLE and JULIA HOFF.

Children of CLARA TAWNEY and WILLIAM ENGLE are:

   i. GLADYS[7] ENGLE, m. GREELY JARVIS.
   ii. AURA ENGLE, m. (1) HARRY W. LAWRENCE; m. (2) CHARLES C. AYER.
   iii. ORVA ENGLE, m. OLE MALM.
   iv. JULIA E. ENGLE.
   v. THURLEY ENGLE.
   vi. JOHN J. "JOE" ENGLE, m. DORIS E. SOUTHWORTH.

29. ROXIE FAY[6] TAWNEY *(JOHN HAMILTON[5], JOHN DANIEL[4], JOHN DANIEL[3], JOHN GEORGE[2], JOHAN JACOB[1])* was born 02 Mar 1888 in Roane Co., WV, and died Unknown. She married (1) RUSSELL FARRER. She married (2) PETER T. SUTPHIN. She married (3) JOHN W. MILSTER. She married (4) JOHN F. GOEBEL.

Child of ROXIE TAWNEY and PETER SUTPHIN is:

   i. HAZEL M.[7] SUTPHIN, m. JAKE KING.

Generation No. 7

30. MAGGIE[7] TAWNEY *(DANIEL W. "LINK"[6], GEORGE WILLIAM[5], JOHN DANIEL[4], JOHN DANIEL[3], JOHN GEORGE[2], JOHAN JACOB[1])* died 05 Mar 1999. She married ALBERT L. SMITH, son of JOHN SMITH and BERTHA. He died in Newton, WV, Roane Co.

Children of MAGGIE TAWNEY and ALBERT SMITH are:

   i. CAROLYN SUE[8] SMITH.
   ii. MARY LOU SMITH.
   iii. JO ANN SMITH, m. BILL GOODWIN.
   iv. ROBERT L. SMITH, d. 13 Feb 2001.
   v. JOHN B. SMITH.

31. KISTA CHRISTENIA[7] RADABAUGH *(SARA ELIZABETH "BETT"[6] TAWNEY, GEORGE WILLIAM[5], JOHN DANIEL[4], JOHN DANIEL[3], JOHN GEORGE[2], JOHAN JACOB[1])* was born 01 Sep 1890 in Spencer, WV, and died 20 Dec 1971 in Salem, Arkansas. She married I. W. ARMSTEAD 08 Dec 1915 in Clendenin, WV.

Children of KISTA RADABAUGH and I. ARMSTEAD are:
- i. GEORGE[8] ARMSTEAD.
- ii. HAROLD ARMSTEAD.
- iii. RICHARD ARMSTEAD.
- iv. FREDA ARMSTEAD.
- v. FAYE ARMSTEAD.
- vi. UNKNOWN ARMSTEAD.

32. PRESTON J.[7] TAWNEY *(DAVID JACKSON[6], GEORGE WILLIAM[5], JOHN DANIEL[4], JOHN DANIEL[3], JOHN GEORGE[2], JOHAN JACOB[1])* was born 02 Feb 1900, and died 12 Sep 1985. He married RETTA ROGERS, daughter of JOHN ROGERS and JOANNA MCQUAIN.

Children of PRESTON TAWNEY and RETTA ROGERS are:
- i. JACK L.[8] TAWNEY, b. Newton, Roane Co., WV; d. 10 Jan 2007.
- ii. JUANITA FLORENCE TAWNEY, b. Abt. 1926, Newton, Roane Co., West Virginia.
- iii. FRANKLIN D. TAWNEY.
- iv. WANDA LEE TAWNEY, m. UNKNOWN SIMMONS.

33. WILLIAM "ERNEST"[7] TAWNEY *(AARON[6], GEORGE WILLIAM[5], JOHN DANIEL[4], JOHN DANIEL[3], JOHN GEORGE[2], JOHAN JACOB[1])* was born 01 Sep 1904 in Left Hand, Roane Co., WV, and died 24 Mar 1966 in Charleston, Kanawha Co., WV. He married MABEL VARNIE 23 Aug 1934. She died 1997 in Kanawha Co, WV.

Child of WILLIAM TAWNEY and MABEL VARNIE is:
- 47. i. GENE[8] TAWNEY.

34. LULA "MABEL"[7] TAWNEY *(AARON[6], GEORGE WILLIAM[5], JOHN DANIEL[4], JOHN DANIEL[3], JOHN GEORGE[2], JOHAN JACOB[1])* was born 23 Mar 1906 in Left Hand, Roane Co., WV, and died 30 May 2003 in Newton, Roane Co., WV. She met ERNEST FREAR ROGERS 17 May 1926 in Akron, OH, son of WILLIAM ROGERS and CAROLINE MCQUAIN. He was born 15 Mar 1902 in Newton, Roane Co., WV, and died 25 Apr 1993 in Charleston, Kanawha Co., WV.

Notes for LULA "MABEL" TAWNEY – See Page 23
More about LULA "MABEL" TAWNEY: Burial: 04 Jun 2003, Tawney Family Cemetery
Medical Information: Gull bladder operation. Later years had respiratory problems (including asthma). Put on nebulizer in 2000 to treat chronic obstructive pulmonary disease (COPD); Pneumonia a few times over the years; and congestive heart disease.

Notes for ERNEST FREAR ROGERS: - See Page 24
More about ERNEST FREAR ROGERS:
Burial: Tawney Family Cemetery
Cause of Death: arteriosclerosis
Medical Information: Emphysema in later years (due to smoking to the age of about 62). Hernia surgery. Prostrate trouble. Ernest suffered from emphyscma and osteoporosis.

Children of LULA TAWNEY and ERNEST ROGERS are:

48.   i.   MARDELL ADELEE[8] ROGERS, b. 06 Feb 1927, Akron, Summit Co., OH.
49.   ii.   ROBERT KEITH ROGERS, b. 05 Aug 1928, Akron, Summit Co. OH; d. 23 Dec 2008, Gallipolis, OH.
50.   iii. ALMA DELORES ROGERS, b. 23 Mar 1930, Akron, Summit Co., OH.
51.   iv. KERMIT ADOLPH ROGERS, b. 23 Feb 1934, Newton, Roane Co., WV.
52.   v.   DORMA KATHERN ROGERS, b. 24 Mar 1936, Newton, Roane Co., WV.
53.   vi. CARROLL AARON ROGERS, b. 10 May 1938, Newton, Roane Co., WV.
54.   vii. CHARLOTTE ANN ROGERS, b. 16 Mar 1940, Newton, Roane Co., WV.
55.   viii. PATRICIA RONDELL ROGERS, b. 05 Feb 1943, Newton, Roane Co., WV.
56.   ix. BARBARA CAROLINE ROGERS, b. 07 Sep 1945, Charleston, Kanawha Co., WV; d. 05 Jun 2005, Riverside, Riverside Co., CA.

35. CLEMENT LUTHER[7] TAWNEY *(AARON[6], GEORGE WILLIAM[5], JOHN DANIEL[4], JOHN DANIEL[3], JOHN GEORGE[2], JOHAN JACOB[1])* was born 19 Jul 1909 in Left Hand, Roane Co., WV, and died 22 Oct 2009 in Charleston, WV, Kanawha Co.   He married AVA OPAL NESTER 10 Jul 1930 in Gandeeville, WV, daughter of HARLEY NESTER and LIZZY TROUT.   She was born 15 May 1911 in Left Hand, WV, Roane Co., and died 2002.

Notes for AVA OPAL NESTER:
Form   completed by Lamoine Tawney-King, September 3, 1996

Children of CLEMENT TAWNEY and AVA NESTER are:
57.   i.   EWUELL JEROME[8] TAWNEY, b. 24 Sep 1930, Left Hand, WV, Roane Co.
58.   ii.   KENNETH JENOAL TAWNEY, b. 13 Aug 1932, Left Hand, WV, Roane Co.
59.   iii. JACK LANDIS TAWNEY, b. 05 Jul 1934, Left Hand, WV, Roane Co.
60.   iv. BARBARA LAMOINE TAWNEY, b. 19 May 1936, Left Hand, WV, Roane Co.
         v.   CLEMENT JOE TAWNEY, b. 20 Feb 1939, Left Hand, WV, Roane Co.; d. 22 Feb 1939.

36. GEORGE "GARRISON"[7] TAWNEY *(AARON[6], GEORGE WILLIAM[5], JOHN DANIEL[4], JOHN DANIEL[3], JOHN GEORGE[2], JOHAN JACOB[1])* was born 11 Nov 1913 in Left Hand, Roane Co., WV, and died 14 Sep 2004 in Looneyville, Roane Co., WV.   He married FRIEDA E. VINEYARD 24 Jun 1939 in Green Co., KY, daughter of FREDERICK VINEYARD and NANCY BOGGS.   She was born 07 Dec 1916 in Looneyville, Roane Co., WV, and died 12 Aug 1999.

Notes for GEORGE "GARRISON" TAWNEY:
Graduate of Spencer High School, Spencer, WV 1935. Graduate of Marshall College 1940. Member of Alpha Kappa Pi.   Schoolteacher and principal in Roane County for 36 years before retiring from Left Hand Elementary School in 1976. His greatest love was cattle farming. His hobby was gas well leasing. In his younger years, he enjoyed foxchasing; deer and turkey hunting. He is buried in the Vineyard Family Cemetery, Looneyville, WV.

Children of GEORGE TAWNEY and FRIEDA VINEYARD are:
61.   i.   LELA ANNE[8] TAWNEY, b. 07 Jan 1943, Spencer, Roane Co., WV.
62.   ii.   JANICE EVELYN TAWNEY, b. 18 Oct 1945, Spencer, Roane Co., WV.

37. CHAMP "CLARK" TAWNEY (KNOWN AS[7] CLARK) *(AARON[6] TAWNEY, GEORGE WILLIAM[5], JOHN DANIEL[4], JOHN DANIEL[3], JOHN GEORGE[2], JOHAN JACOB[1])* was born 28 Nov 1915 in Left Hand, Roane Co., WV, and died 27 Aug 2007. He married BEATRICE ALMEDA SUMMERS 28 Jun 1944. She was born 28 Jun 1917 in Wallback, WV Clay County.

Notes for CHAMP "CLARK" TAWNEY (KNOWN AS CLARK) :
He served in the US Army from October 1941 until June 11, 1943.

Child of CHAMP CLARK and BEATRICE SUMMERS is:
63.   i.   BERNICE JEAN[8] TAWNEY, b. 13 May 1945, Spencer, WV Roane Co.

38. JARRETT ("BUZZ")[7] TAWNEY *(AARON[6], GEORGE WILLIAM[5], JOHN DANIEL[4], JOHN DANIEL[3], JOHN GEORGE[2], JOHAN JACOB[1])* was born 02 Apr 1919 in Left Hand, Roane Co., WV. He married FRANCIS ROBERTS 13 Sep 1940, daughter of JAMES ROBERTS and MARTHA BAILEY.

Children of JARRETT TAWNEY and FRANCIS ROBERTS are:
64.   i.   NANCY ELLEN[8] TAWNEY, b. 04 Oct 1955.
        ii.   FREDERICK JARRETT TAWNEY, b. 23 Apr 1960; m. JANEEN SKELLY, 27 May 1989.

Notes about Buzz Tawney:
Uncle Buzz served in WWII from 1943-1946. He was with the 634th Engineers, Light Equipment Co., 9th Army, 13th Corps. He was in Germany during the Battle of the Bulge. He told me that the terrain was extremely rough. It was very cold and snowy and the soldiers didn't even have boots, only low top shoes. He ran a road grader and said they would take turns riding close to the engine on the grader to get warm. When the war was over he was stationed in California where his sister Anna was stationed. They are pictured together in Figure 141. His major was Biology in college. He graduated from Marshall University, the same as his brother Garrison Tawney and he taught Biology at Spencer High where he was a coach for many years.

39. ANNA ELIZABETH[7] TAWNEY *(AARON[6], GEORGE WILLIAM[5], JOHN DANIEL[4], JOHN DANIEL[3], JOHN GEORGE[2], JOHAN JACOB[1])* was born 11 Sep 1921 in Left Hand, Roane Co., WV. She married MICHAEL EDWARD DESPOSITO 11 Aug 1945 in Bakersfield, CA, son of JOSEPH DESPOSITO and ILENE FLYNN. He was born 05 Mar 1921.

Notes for ANNA ELIZABETH TAWNEY:
1943. Anna Elizabeth Tawney of Newton, WV, Roane Co., passed entrance tests to become the first female, not only from Roane County, WV, but was also in the first group of women to serve in the U.S. Marines. There were not yet any accommodation for women in the Marines for training, and Hunter College in New York was taken over by the government to house the first boot camp for women. "Ann" was later stationed in the Mohave Desert, California. She served from 1943 to 1945. Her husband Michael Edward Desposito served in the U.S. Marines from 1942 to 1945. They lived on Long Island, NY after their service. They now live in Rio Rancho, NM. Aunt Ann and Uncle Mike are wonderful friends to us. Ann volunteered for the Veteran's Hospital for several years. They belong to the New York Club in Rio Rancho, NM. Uncle Mike is a retired policeman (from NY) and volunteers some of his time to helping other people who are not so able, driving them to appointments.

Children of ANNA TAWNEY and MICHAEL DESPOSITO are:
65.   I.   MICHAEL (JR) EDWARD[8] DESPOSITO, b. 18 Feb 1947, Manhattan, NY.
66.   ii.   DANIEL JOHN DESPOSITO, b. 03 Nov 1950, Queens Co., Flushing, NY.

67.   iii.   JOSEPH MARTIN DESPOSITO, b. 14 Oct 1957, Queens Co., NY; d. Jan 1998, Phoenix, AZ., from complications of melanoma.
68.   iv.   PATRICIA ANN DESPOSITO, b. 30 Jul 1962, Queens Co., NY.

40. DANIEL AARON[7] TAWNEY *(AARON[6], GEORGE WILLIAM[5], JOHN DANIEL[4], JOHN DANIEL[3], JOHN GEORGE[2], JOHAN JACOB[1])* was born 04 Jun 1923 in Left Hand, Roane Co., WV. He married HAZEL MAXINE SHORT 19 Jun 1943, daughter of TRACY SHORT and BEATRICE HIVELY.   She was born 22 Apr 1923 in 2008.

More about DANIEL AARON TAWNEY:
Burial: Tawney Family Cemetery

Children of DANIEL TAWNEY and HAZEL SHORT are:
69.   i.   JERRY WAYNE[8] TAWNEY, b. 17 Jan 1944, WV; d. 15 Jun 2001, Charleston, WV, Kanawha Co.
70.   ii.   KAREN ALMON TAWNEY, b. 22 Oct 1960, Charleston, WV, Kanawha Co.; d. 25 Sep 1997, Charleston, WV, Kanawha Co.
71.   iii.   SANDRA SUE TAWNEY, b. 20 Aug 1952, WV.

41. W. CECIL[7] TAWNEY *(JAMES WELLINGTON[6], JOHN HAMILTON[5], JOHN DANIEL[4], JOHN DANIEL[3], JOHN GEORGE[2], JOHAN JACOB[1])*   He married GENEVA SMITH.

Children of W. TAWNEY and GENEVA SMITH are:
       i.   SANDRA[8] TAWNEY.
       ii.   CHARLES TAWNEY.

42. GEORGE W.[7] TAWNEY *(JAMES WELLINGTON[6], JOHN HAMILTON[5], JOHN DANIEL[4], JOHN DANIEL[3], JOHN GEORGE[2], JOHAN JACOB[1])* was born 02 Oct 1905 in Elana, WV, and died 07 Nov 1996.   He married LULA ERMAL MCCLAIN, daughter of RANDOLPH MIDDLETON and STELLA SNODGRASS.   She was born 06 Jul 1911 in Calhoun Co.

Children of GEORGE TAWNEY and LULA MCCLAIN are:
       i.   REGINA FAY[8] TAWNEY.
       ii.   VIVIAN JOYCE TAWNEY.
       iii.   FREDA MAE TAWNEY.
72.   iv.   WANDA LEE TAWNEY.

43. DIXIE ARTIE[7] ROSS *(NANCY EMMA[6] TAWNEY, JOHN[5], JOHN DANIEL[4], JOHN DANIEL[3], JOHN GEORGE[2], JOHAN JACOB[1])* was born 26 Jul 1892, and died 28 Nov 1983.   She married CHARLES H. HAROLD 08 Oct 1911.

Children of DIXIE ROSS and CHARLES HAROLD are:
       i.   GOLDIE E.[8] HAROLD, b. 27 Feb 1913; m. (1) FREDDIE D. ALLEN; b. 10 Jun 1933; m. (2) JAMES G. DRAKE.
       ii.   RALPH R. HAROLD, b. 06 Dec 1915; m. EVELYN M. GREATHOUSE.
73.   iii.   REX K. HAROLD, b. 17 Jul 1917.

44. REX PHILIP[7] ROSS *(NANCY EMMA[6] TAWNEY, JOHN[5], JOHN DANIEL[4], JOHN DANIEL[3], JOHN GEORGE[2], JOHAN JACOB[1])* was born 04 Jul 1894, and died 19 Aug 1976. He married MINNIE D. STEVENS 09 Jun 1923.

Child of REX ROSS and MINNIE STEVENS is:

    i.   PAUL H.[8] ROSS, b. 01 Apr 1925; m. (1) LAURA M. CROSS, 22 Jan 1949; m. (2) MARY L. (CAREY) CRABTREE, 19 Feb 1994.

45. MAX HAMILTON[7] ROSS *(NANCY EMMA[6] TAWNEY, JOHN[5], JOHN DANIEL[4], JOHN DANIEL[3], JOHN GEORGE[2], JOHAN JACOB[1])* was born 05 Apr 1896, and died 20 May 1967. He married MARY W. MURRAY 01 Nov 1919.

Children of MAX ROSS and MARY MURRAY are:

    i.   EMMA E.[8] ROSS, b. 01 Sep 1920; m. ROSCOE R. FLINT, 23 Jan 1937.

    ii.   MAX H. ROSS, b. 20 Aug 1923; m. CAROL J. TITUS, 19 Mar 1945.

    iii.   RICHARD C. ROSS, b. 12 Apr 1926; m. DONNA J. MACK, 10 Jun 1949.

46. LEONA HELEN[7] TAWNEY *(JOHN SPENCER[6], JOHN HAMILTON[5], JOHN DANIEL[4], JOHN DANIEL[3], JOHN GEORGE[2], JOHAN JACOB[1])* was born 28 Jun 1923 in Elana, Roane Co, WV, and died 12 Apr 2001. She married JOHN HENRY MCCLAIN 02 Jan 1940.

Children of LEONA TAWNEY and JOHN MCCLAIN are:

    i.   ALAN R.[8] MCCLAIN.

    ii.   JOHN L. MCCLAIN.

    iii.   EDWARD B. MCCLAIN.

    iv.   CAROLL MCCLAIN.

    v.   DIANNE MCCLAIN.

    vi.   KATHY MCCLAIN.

    vii.   GLEN MCCLAIN.

    viii.   FERRELL MCCLAIN.

    ix.   DAVID MCCLAIN.

Generation No. 8

47. GENE[8] TAWNEY *(WILLIAM "ERNEST"[7], AARON[6], GEORGE WILLIAM[5], JOHN DANIEL[4], JOHN DANIEL[3], JOHN GEORGE[2], JOHAN JACOB[1])*

Children of GENE TAWNEY are:
74.   i.   TERRI[9] TAWNEY, b. 11 Nov 1962.
75.   ii.   CATHY TAWNEY, b. 06 Jul 1960.

48. MARDELL ADELEE[8] ROGERS *(LULA "MABEL"[7] TAWNEY, AARON[6], GEORGE WILLIAM[5], JOHN DANIEL[4], JOHN DANIEL[3], JOHN GEORGE[2], JOHAN JACOB[1])* was born 06 Feb 1927 in Akron, Summit Co., OH.   She met (1) GILBERT MCCLELLAND in Akron, OH, Summit Co., son of STANLEY MCCLELLAND and MARY DAVIS.   He was born 23 Jun 1924, and died 20 May 1983.   She married (2) HAROLD EDGAR JOHNSON 23 Oct 1951 in Las Vegas, NV, son of ADOLPH JOHNSON and ERNA BROOE.   He was born 08 Sep 1924.

Child of MARDELL ROGERS and GILBERT MCCLELLAND is:
76.   i.   MARY GILLETTE "SHELLEY"[9] MCCLELLAND, b. 04 Jan 1945, Akron, OH.

Children of MARDELL ROGERS and HAROLD JOHNSON are:
77.   ii.   DALE ADOLPH[9] JOHNSON, b. 10 May 1953, Santa Monica, Los Angeles Co., CA.
78.   iii. TERESA ANN JOHNSON, b. 29 Jan 1955, Torrance, Los Angeles Co., CA.

49. ROBERT KEITH[8] ROGERS *(LULA "MABEL"[7] TAWNEY, AARON[6], GEORGE WILLIAM[5], JOHN DANIEL[4], JOHN DANIEL[3], JOHN GEORGE[2], JOHAN JACOB[1])* was born 05 Aug 1928 in Akron, Summit Co. OH, and died 23 Dec 2008 in Gallipolis, OH[2].   He married (1) MARIE PARSONS 28 Jul 1950 in Cartlettsburg, Boyd Co., KY, daughter of WILLIAM PARSONS and ICIE BISHOP.   She was born 9 Jun 1929.   He married (2) NANCY LARCH, daughter of WESLEY ADAMS LARCH.

Notes for ROBERT KEITH ROGERS:

Keith remembers being in the woods with Ernest and, at the age of 75, Ernest was swinging on a grapevine. Keith, like his Dad, was also a foxchasing enthusiast. They hunted together from the time Keith was young, until Ernest was no longer able to go on the hills. At the age of 85, however, Ernest was still able to go on the hills. After that, Keith visited and they talked about the hunt and their fox hounds.   They both worked at Du Pont and rode together for many years.

Children of ROBERT ROGERS and MARIE PARSONS are:
79.   i.   INA GALE[9] ROGERS, b. 11 Mar 1949, Charleston, Kanawha Co., WV.
80.   ii.   MICHAEL KEITH ROGERS, b. 03 Oct 1950, Charleston, Kanawha Co., WV.
81.   iii. RHONDA DIANE ROGERS, b. 10 May 1952, Charleston, Kanawha Co., WV.
82.   iv.   DEBRA JEANNE ROGERS, b. 08 Aug 1953, Charleston, Kanawha Co., WV.
83.   v.   TIMOTHY LEE ROGERS, b. 31 Jul 1954, Charleston, Kanawha Co., WV.
84.   vi.   ROBERT RANDALL ROGERS, b. 10 Aug 1955, Charleston, Kanawha Co., WV.

50. ALMA DELORES[8] ROGERS *(LULA "MABEL"[7] TAWNEY, AARON[6], GEORGE WILLIAM[5], JOHN DANIEL[4], JOHN DANIEL[3], JOHN GEORGE[2], JOHAN JACOB[1])* was born 23 Mar 1930 in Akron, Summit Co., OH. She married (2) DELBERT DENNIS 22 Jan 1958. He was born 22 Dec 1928 in Lake Lynn, PA.

Child of ALMA DELORES ROGERS is:
85.   i.   ANDREW JACKSON[9] ROGERS, b. 27 Mar 1952, Culver City, CA.

Child of ALMA DELORES ROGERS and DELBERT DENNIS is:
86.   ii.   SHEILA MARLENE[9] DENNIS, b. 26 Mar 1959, Union Town, PA.

51. KERMIT ADOLPH[8] ROGERS *(LULA "MABEL"[7] TAWNEY, AARON[6], GEORGE WILLIAM[5], JOHN DANIEL[4], JOHN DANIEL[3], JOHN GEORGE[2], JOHAN JACOB[1])* was born 23 Feb 1934 in Newton, Roane Co., WV. He married BETTY LOU BIRD 12 Aug 1954, daughter of ALFRED BIRD and ORA TRUMAN. She was born 29 Oct 1936 in Clay Co., WV.

Notes for KERMIT ADOLPH ROGERS:
Form completed by Betty Rogers Sept. 30, 1996.

Children of KERMIT ROGERS and BETTY BIRD are:
87.   i.   KATHLEEN ANN[9] ROGERS, b. 14 Jan 1955, Charleston, WV, Kanawha Co.
88.   ii.   CHERYL LYNN ROGERS, b. 10 Mar 1956, Charleston, WV, Kanawha Co.
89.   iii. DAWN ARLENE ROGERS, b. 15 May 1960, Charleston, WV, Kanawha Co.

52. DORMA KATHERN[8] ROGERS *(LULA "MABEL"[7] TAWNEY, AARON[6], GEORGE WILLIAM[5], JOHN DANIEL[4], JOHN DANIEL[3], JOHN GEORGE[2], JOHAN JACOB[1])* was born 24 Mar 1936 in Newton, Roane Co., WV. She married (1) JAMES HENRY BIRD Sep 1955, son of ALFRED BIRD. He was born 12 Jun 1933 and died May 1986. She married (2) JAMES DRAKE 22 Jul 1997 in Gatlinburg, Tennessee. He was born 02 Mar 1939.

Children of DORMA ROGERS and JAMES BIRD are:
           i.   JIMMY LEE[9] BIRD, b. 12 Jul 1956.
90.   ii.   NENA MARIE BIRD, b. 11 Mar 1958, Charleston, WV, Kanawha Co.
91.   iii. LISA CAROL BIRD, b. 30 Jun 1960.
92.   iv.   ERNEST SCOTT BIRD, b. 16 Aug 1962, Huntington, IN.

53. CARROLL AARON[8] ROGERS *(LULA "MABEL"[7] TAWNEY, AARON[6], GEORGE WILLIAM[5], JOHN DANIEL[4], JOHN DANIEL[3], JOHN GEORGE[2], JOHAN JACOB[1])* was born 10 May 1938 in Newton, Roane Co., WV. He married MARIA FELICIA GRECO 19 Nov 1960 in Morgantown, WV, daughter of FRANK GRECO and LOUISE NAPOLILLO. She was born 25 May 1941.

Children of CARROLL ROGERS and MARIA GRECO are:
93.   i.   MARC ROBERT[9] ROGERS, b. 05 May 1962, Morgantown, WV, Monongalia Co.
94.   ii.   MICHELE LYNN ROGERS, b. 06 Apr 1964, Springfield, OH, Clark Co.
95.   iii. NATHAN ERIC ROGERS, b. 10 Jul 1970, Morgantown, WV, Monongalia Co.

54. CHARLOTTE ANN[8] ROGERS *(LULA MABEL[7] TAWNEY, AARON[6], GEORGE WILLIAM[5], JOHN DANIEL[4], JOHN DANIEL[3], JOHN GEORGE[2], JOHAN JACOB[1])* was born 16 Mar 1940 in Newton, Roane Co., WV.   She married (1) DAVID ALEXANDER RICHMOND 22 Aug 1959 in Inglewood, LA Co., CA, son of JAMES RICHMOND and LOIS FLEMING AKA. LOIS HEMING . He was born 02 Jun 1937 in Boston, Suffolk Co., Mass, and died 03 Aug 2008.   She married (2) DONALD JOHN OSTROM 30 Oct 1972 in Las Vegas, Clark Co., NV, son of RALPH OSTROM and ESTELLE DUDLEY.   He was born 20 Mar 1939 in Oconomowoc, Waukesha Co., WI.   She married (3) GUY LEROY DILNO 14 Dec 1980 in Plainwell, Allegan Co., MI, son of MILFORD DILNO and WILDA PHILLIPS.   He was born 22 Aug 1946 in Kalamazoo, MI, Kalamazoo Co.

More about CHARLOTTE ANN ROGERS:
Divorced: 16 Nov 1969, Santa Ana, Orange Co., CA
Medical Information: Osteoarthritis (left knee, surgery 1952); diagnosed in 1976.   Osteoarthritis in left and right hips, lower spine; polyneuropathy (cause unknown).

More about DAVID ALEXANDER RICHMOND:
Divorced: 16 Nov 1969, Santa Ana, Orange Co., CA
Medical Information: Polio at 9 years of age.

More about DAVID RICHMOND and CHARLOTTE ROGERS:
Divorce: 16 Nov 1969, Santa Ana, Orange Co., California
Marriage: 22 Aug 1959, Inglewood, LA Co., CA

More about DONALD OSTROM and CHARLOTTE ROGERS:
Divorce: 02 Nov 1979, Allegan, MI (Allegan Co.)
Marriage: 30 Oct 1972, Las Vegas, Clark Co., NV

More about GUY DILNO and CHARLOTTE ROGERS:
Marriage: 14 Dec 1980, Plainwell, Allegan Co., MI

Children of CHARLOTTE ROGERS and DAVID RICHMOND are:
96.   i.   BRAD ALEXANDER[9] RICHMOND, b. 17 Sep 1960, Inglewood, Los Angeles Co., CA.
97.   ii.   KIMBERLY ANNE RICHMOND, b. 11 Nov 1963, Riverside, Riverside Co., CA.

Child of CHARLOTTE ROGERS and DONALD OSTROM is:
98.   iii. LANCE JOHN[9] OSTROM, b. 29 Feb 1972, Phoenix, Maricopa Co., AZ.

55. PATRICIA RONDELL[8] ROGERS *(LULA "MABEL"[7] TAWNEY, AARON[6], GEORGE WILLIAM[5], JOHN DANIEL[4], JOHN DANIEL[3], JOHN GEORGE[2], JOHAN JACOB[1])* was born 05 Feb 1943 in Newton, Roane Co., WV. She married HOMER LEE CONLEY 11 Aug 1962 in Clover Ridge, Roane Co., WV, son of HOWARD CONLEY and LOCIE MILLER. He was born 14 Mar 1940 in Uler, Roane Co., WV.

More about HOMER CONLEY and PATRICIA ROGERS:
Marriage: 11 Aug 1962, Clover Ridge, Roane Co., WV

Children of PATRICIA ROGERS and HOMER CONLEY are:

      i.   GREGORY LEE[9] CONLEY, b. 24 Jul 1963; m. PRISCILLA CATHERN NAYLOR, 24 Feb 1993, Newton, Roane Co., WV; b. 11 Nov 1965.

           More about GREGORY LEE CONLEY: Date born 2: 24 Jul 1963, Fort Knox, KY

     ii.   MICHAEL GARRETT CONLEY, b. 22 Jan 1966; m. (1) SHANNA CLAUDINE PUGH, Jul 1988, March AFB, Riverside Co., CA; m. (2) JENNIFER REBECCA FRENCH, 30 Jun 1996; b. 14 Aug 1969, Grand Forks, ND; m. (3) SHIRLEY ANN BIRD, 19 May 2009, Newton, Roane Co., WV; b. 02 Jun 1952.

           More about MICHAEL CONLEY and SHANNA PUGH: Marriage: Jul 1988, March AFB, Riverside Co., CA

           Marriage Notes for MICHAEL CONLEY and JENNIFER FRENCH: Divorced.

99.   iii.   STEPHEN WAYNE CONLEY, b. 28 Sep 1967.
100.   iv.   STACY RONDELL CONLEY, b. 21 Sep 1972, Charleston, Kanawha Co., WV.

56. BARBARA CAROLINE[8] ROGERS *(LULA "MABEL"[7] TAWNEY, AARON[6], GEORGE WILLIAM[5], JOHN DANIEL[4], JOHN DANIEL[3], JOHN GEORGE[2], JOHAN JACOB[1])* was born 07 Sep 1945 in Charleston, Kanawha Co., WV, and died 05 Jun 2005 in Riverside, Riverside Co., CA. She married ROGER BEISTLE in Las Vegas, NV. He was born 25 Jul 1941 in Riverside Co., CA.

Notes for BARBARA CAROLINE ROGERS:
Bobbie was her nickname most of her life.   When she graduated from Spencer High School, Spencer, WV, she went to California where she worked as a waitress.   She met her husband Roger Beistle and they dated for a year or more before they eloped and got married in Las Vegas, NV.   They lived in Riverside and had two children.   Bobbie battled lung cancer approximately 2 years or more before it took her life.

Children of BARBARA ROGERS and ROGER BEISTLE are:
      i.   GREGORY ALLEN[9] BEISTLE, b. 19 Jan 1966, Riverside, CA, Riverside Co.
101.   ii   THERESE MARIE BEISTLE, b. 19 Jun 1968, Riverside, CA, Riverside Co.

57. EWUELL JEROME[8] TAWNEY *(CLEMENT LUTHER[7], AARON[6], GEORGE WILLIAM[5], JOHN DANIEL[4], JOHN DANIEL[3], JOHN GEORGE[2], JOHAN JACOB[1])* was born 24 Sep 1930 in Left Hand, WV, Roane Co. He married BETTY JEAN SHEPPARD 14 Sep 1952 in Linden, WV, Roane Co., daughter of JENNINGS SHEPPARD and DOLA YOUNG. She was born 18 Apr 1933.

Children of EWUELL TAWNEY and BETTY SHEPPARD are:
102.   i.   DEBRA JEAN[9] TAWNEY, b. 17 Aug 1953.
         ii.   JANET LYNN TAWNEY, b. 13 Jul 1954; d. 14 Jul 1954.
103.   iii. JEFFREY JEROME TAWNEY, b. 21 Dec 1956.

58. KENNETH JENOAL[8] TAWNEY *(CLEMENT LUTHER[7], AARON[6], GEORGE WILLIAM[5], JOHN DANIEL[4], JOHN DANIEL[3], JOHN GEORGE[2], JOHAN JACOB[1])* was born 13 Aug 1932 in Left Hand, WV, Roane Co. He married (1) RETHA JEAN HOSTUTLER. She died 04 Mar 1992. He married (2) PAULINE MARIE MARTIN 29 Jan 1976 in Nazareth, PA, daughter of UNKNOWN MARTIN. She was born 09 May 1945 in Liberty NY, Sullivan Co.

Children of KENNETH TAWNEY and RETHA HOSTUTLER are:
         i.   GUYLA JEAN[9] TAWNEY, b. 28 Jan 1957, Spencer, WV, Roane Co.; m. PAUL ALAN BLACK, 06 Aug 1977, Clendenin, WV.
104.   ii.   DREMA LYNN TAWNEY, b. 28 Jul 1959, Charleston, WV, Kanawha Co.
105.   iii. KENNETH JAY TAWNEY, b. 07 Nov 1961, Charleston, WV, Kanawha Co.

Children of KENNETH TAWNEY and PAULINE MARTIN are:
         iv.   BONITA LOUISE[9] TAWNEY, b. 08 Mar 1961, Clifton Springs, NY; Adopted child; m. JAMES RUTH, Parkersburg, WV.
         v.   SANDRA ANN TAWNEY, b. 03 Apr 1962, Geneva, NY; Stepchild; m. GLENN MATHESS, Parkersburg, WV.
         vi.   SUZANNE MARIE TAWNEY, b. 12 Feb 1964, Clifton Springs, NY; Adopted child; m. RANDY ENOCH, Parkersburg, WV.
         vii. TAMMY LYNN TAWNEY, b. 24 Dec 1965, Canandaigua, NY; Adopted child; m. MATTHEW MILLER, Parkersburg, WV.

59. JACK LANDIS[8] TAWNEY *(CLEMENT LUTHER[7], AARON[6], GEORGE WILLIAM[5], JOHN DANIEL[4], JOHN DANIEL[3], JOHN GEORGE[2], JOHAN JACOB[1])* was born 05 Jul 1934 in Left Hand, WV, Roane Co. He married FRANCES ELOISE BULLARD in Minnora, WV, daughter of BURL BULLARD and HAZEL ELLISON.

Notes for FRANCES ELOISE BULLARD: Information about Frances (Bullard) Tawney and her ancestors: Form completed by Frances Bullard-Tawney dated 1 Sep 1996.

Children of JACK TAWNEY and FRANCES BULLARD are:
         i.   DAVID ALLEN[9] TAWNEY, b. 29 Dec 1961, Charleston, WV, Kanawha Co.; m. LOIS GRIFFIN, 15 Oct 1988, Charleston, WV, Kanawha Co.

               Notes for DAVID ALLEN TAWNEY: Works for law firm of Calif and Handleman, Reynoldsburg, Ohio

         ii.   JACK LANDIS TAWNEY II, b. 09 Aug 1965, Charleston, WV, Kanawha Co.; m. KATHALEEN MCCANNS, 17 Oct 1992, Raleigh, NC.

60. BARBARA LAMOINE[8] TAWNEY *(CLEMENT LUTHER[7], AARON[6], GEORGE WILLIAM[5], JOHN DANIEL[4], JOHN DANIEL[3], JOHN GEORGE[2], JOHAN JACOB[1])* was born 19 May 1936 in Left Hand, WV, Roane Co. She married WILLIAM R. "BUD" KING 18 Sep 1953 in Huntington, WV, son of WILLIAM KING and NETTIE NIDA. He was born 17 May 1935.

Notes for BARBARA LAMOINE TAWNEY:
Form completed by Lamoine Tawney-King, Sep 4, 1996.
Children of BARBARA TAWNEY and WILLIAM KING are:
106.   i.   SHERRY LOUISE[9] KING, b. 23 May 1954, Charleston, WV, Kanawha Co.; d. 03 Jun 1998.
        ii.   WILLIAM RICHARD KING, b. 22 Apr 1960, Charleston, WV, Kanawha Co.

61. LELA ANNE[8] TAWNEY *(GEORGE "GARRISON"[7], AARON[6], GEORGE WILLIAM[5], JOHN DANIEL[4], JOHN DANIEL[3], JOHN GEORGE[2], JOHAN JACOB[1])* was born 07 Jan 1943 in Spencer, Roane Co., WV. She married "DICK" VERNON ELLIS GOFF 30 May 1964 in Looneyville, WV, Roane Co., son of LAWRENCE GOFF and VELMA GILLISPIE. He was born 17 Mar 1942 in Fraziers Bottom, WV, Putnam Co.

Children of LELA TAWNEY and "DICK" are:
        i.   MATTHEW GARRISON[9] GOFF, b. 06 Nov 1969, Charleston, WV, Kanawha Co. He married PENELOPE LYNN GRITT 17 Sep 1994 in Scott Depot, WV, Putnam Co. She was born 20 Nov 1960.

107.   ii.   NATHAN LAWRENCE GOFF, b. 10 Nov 1972, Charleston, WV, Kanawha Co.
108.   iii.   ADAM CARTER GOFF, b. 01 Oct 1977, South Charleston, WV, Kanawha Co.

62. JANICE EVELYN[8] TAWNEY *(GEORGE "GARRISON"[7], AARON[6], GEORGE WILLIAM[5], JOHN DANIEL[4], JOHN DANIEL[3], JOHN GEORGE[2], JOHAN JACOB[1])* was born 18 Oct 1945 in Spencer, Roane Co., WV. She married CLIFFORD PAYNE COOPER 30 Nov 1968 in Salisbury, MD, Wicomico Co., son of LEVIN COOPER and ELLEN PAYNE. He was born 04 Jun 1945.

Child of JANICE TAWNEY and CLIFFORD COOPER is:
109.   i.   AARON ROY[9] COOPER, b. 06 Dec 1975, Salisbury, MD, Wicomico Co.

63. BERNICE JEAN[8] TAWNEY *(CHAMP "CLARK" TAWNEY (KNOWN AS[7] CLARK), AARON[6] TAWNEY, GEORGE WILLIAM[5], JOHN DANIEL[4], JOHN DANIEL[3], JOHN GEORGE[2], JOHAN JACOB[1])* was born 13 May 1945 in Spencer, WV Roane Co. She married MARK HAPPNEY. He was born 22 May 1940.

Children of BERNICE JEAN TAWNEY and MARK HAPPNEY are:
110.   i.   KIMBERLY SUE[9] HAPPNEY, b. 12 Nov 1963, Bellflower, CA.
111.   ii.   TAMMY ANNE HAPPNEY, b. 20 Jan 1967, Ripley WV Jackson Co.

Family History of L. Mabel Tawney-Rogers and Ernest F. Rogers

64. NANCY ELLEN[8] TAWNEY *(JARRETT ("BUZZ")[7], AARON[6], GEORGE WILLIAM[5], JOHN DANIEL[4], JOHN DANIEL[3], JOHN GEORGE[2], JOHAN JACOB[1])* was born 04 Oct 1955. She married DANIEL M. SETTLE Feb 1987.

Child of NANCY TAWNEY and DANIEL SETTLE is:
      i. KACI ELLYN[9] SETTLE, b. 02 Jun 1989.
      ii. SUSAN DANIELLE SETTLE, b. 24 Jan 1992

65. MICHAEL EDWARD[8] DESPOSITO, JR. *(ANNA ELIZABETH[7] TAWNEY, AARON[6], GEORGE WILLIAM[5], JOHN DANIEL[4], JOHN DANIEL[3], JOHN GEORGE[2], JOHAN JACOB[1])* was born 18 Feb 1947 in Manhattan, NY. He married LINDA SPENSIERI 11 Jan 1969 in Huntington, Nassau Co., NY. She was born 01 Aug 1948 in Queens, NY.

Children of MICHAEL DESPOSITO and LINDA SPENSIERI are:
112.   i. MICHAEL SCOTT[9] DESPOSITO, b. 24 Feb 1970, Queens, NY.
113.   ii. MARC CHRISTOPHER DESPOSITO, b. 15 Dec 1974, Syosset, NY.
114.   iii. LORI LYNN DESPOSITO, b. 19 Oct 1971, Huntington, Nassau Co., NY.

66. DANIEL JOHN[8] DESPOSITO *(ANNA ELIZABETH[7] TAWNEY, AARON[6], GEORGE WILLIAM[5], JOHN DANIEL[4], JOHN DANIEL[3], JOHN GEORGE[2], JOHAN JACOB[1])* was born 03 Nov 1950 in Queens Co., Flushing, NY. He married JANICE ANDERSON 08 Mar 1974 in Rio Rancho, NM. She was born 29 Aug 1953.

Children of DANIEL DESPOSITO and JANICE ANDERSON are:
115.   i. BRIAN[9] DESPOSITO, b. 20 Jun 1975.
116.   ii. COURTNEY DESPOSITO, b. 01 Feb 1977, Pete AFB.

67. JOSEPH MARTIN[8] DESPOSITO *(ANNA ELIZABETH[7] TAWNEY, AARON[6], GEORGE WILLIAM[5], JOHN DANIEL[4], JOHN DANIEL[3], JOHN GEORGE[2], JOHAN JACOB[1])* was born 14 Oct 1957 in Queens Co., NY, and died Jan 1998 in Phoenix, AZ. He married LORI VIGIL, daughter of STEVEN VIGIL and BERTHA TAFOYA. She was born 02 Dec 1961.

Notes for JOSEPH MARTIN DESPOSITO:
Joe lived in Phoenix, AZ with his wife Lorie and children. He died there from complications of melanoma.

Children of JOSEPH DESPOSITO and LORI VIGIL are:
      i. DANIEL KEITH[9] DESPOSITO, b. 24 Feb 1987.
      ii. KATHY ANN DESPOSITO, b. 07 Jun 1988.

68. PATRICIA ANN[8] DESPOSITO *(ANNA ELIZABETH[7] TAWNEY, AARON[6], GEORGE WILLIAM[5], JOHN DANIEL[4], JOHN DANIEL[3], JOHN GEORGE[2], JOHAN JACOB[1])* was born 30 Jul 1962 in Queens Co., NY. She married (1) MARK JOHN DONAHUE 05 Sep 1987. Divorced. She married (2) STEVEN WAYNE DURANCEAU 02 Dec 1991.

Child of PATRICIA ANN DESPOSITO and MARK DONAHUE is:
117.   i. KRISTINA ELIZABETH[9] DURANCEAU, b. 05 Oct 1989.

56

Children of PATRICIA DESPOSITO and STEVEN DURANCEAU are:
    ii.   MATTHEW[9] LOREN DURANCEAU, b. 12 Sep 1996.
   iii.   ASHLEY NICOLE DURANCEAU, b. 14 Sep 1992.

69. JERRY WAYNE[8] TAWNEY *(DANIEL AARON[7], AARON[6], GEORGE WILLIAM[5], JOHN DANIEL[4], JOHN DANIEL[3], JOHN GEORGE[2], JOHAN JACOB[1])* was born 17 Jan 1944 in WV, and died 15 Jun 2001 in Charleston, WV, Kanawha Co. He married (1) BRENDA NICHOLS; divorced. He married (2) LINDA BUTCHER.

Children of JERRY WAYNE TAWNEY and LINDA BUTCHER are:
     i.   JERRY W.[9] TAWNEY II, d. 2004.
118.   ii.   PAMELA SUE TAWNEY.
   iii.   JAMES MATTHEW TAWNEY.

70. KAREN ALMON[8] TAWNEY *(DANIEL AARON[7], AARON[6], GEORGE WILLIAM[5], JOHN DANIEL[4], JOHN DANIEL[3], JOHN GEORGE[2], JOHAN JACOB[1])* was born 22 Oct 1960 in Charleston, WV, Kanawha Co., and died 25 Sep 1997 in Charleston, WV, Kanawha Co. She married GARY WAYNE TAWNEY 20 Oct 1978. He was born 17 Mar 1960.

Children of KAREN TAWNEY and GARY TAWNEY are:
     i.   AMIE ERIN[9] TAWNEY, b. 21 Jun 1986, Jackson Co. Hospital, Ripley, WV.
    ii.   COLE GARRETT TAWNEY, b. 07 May 1991, Jackson Co. Hospital, Ripley, WV.
119.   iii.   BRANDY NICOLE TAWNEY, b. 15 Sep 1981, Jackson Co. Hospital, Ripley, WV.

71. SANDRA SUE[8] TAWNEY *(DANIEL AARON[7], AARON[6], GEORGE WILLIAM[5], JOHN DANIEL[4], JOHN DANIEL[3], JOHN GEORGE[2], JOHAN JACOB[1])* was born 20 Aug 1952 in WV. She married SHIRLEY WYATT (JR.) GRAY in WV, son of SHIRLEY GRAY and HAZEL WEST. He was born 12 May 1954 in Sutton, WV.

Children of SANDRA TAWNEY and SHIRLEY GRAY are:
120.   i.   STACIE LEA[9] TAWNEY, b. 22 Jun 1971, Jackson Co. Hospital, Ripley, WV.
    ii.   TAMMY LYNN GRAY, b. 27 Jun 1973, Jackson Co. Hospital, Ripley, WV.

Notes for ANDREW JACKSON ROGERS :
        Andy was adopted in 1966 by his grandparents, Mabel and Ernest Rogers.

72. WANDA LEE[8] TAWNEY *(GEORGE W.[7], JAMES WELLINGTON[6], JOHN HAMILTON[5], JOHN DANIEL[4], JOHN DANIEL[3], JOHN GEORGE[2], JOHAN JACOB[1]).* She married STEPHEN BLAKE SMITH.

Child of WANDA TAWNEY and STEPHEN SMITH is:
     i.   CARY STEPHEN[9] SMITH, b. 01 Aug 1973.

73. REX K.[8] HAROLD *(DIXIE ARTIE[7] ROSS, NANCY EMMA[6] TAWNEY, JOHN[5], JOHN DANIEL[4], JOHN DANIEL[3], JOHN GEORGE[2], JOHAN JACOB[1])* was born 17 Jul 1917. He married HELEN G. ALLEN 15 Oct 1938.

Child of REX HAROLD and HELEN ALLEN is:
      i.   PAUL H.[9] HAROLD, b. 01 Apr 1925.

Generation No. 9

74. TERRI[9] TAWNEY *(GENE[8], WILLIAM "ERNEST"[7], AARON[6], GEORGE WILLIAM[5], JOHN DANIEL[4], JOHN DANIEL[3], JOHN GEORGE[2], JOHAN JACOB[1])* was born 11 Nov 1962. She married MIKE FISHER. He was born 24 Sep 1961.

Children of TERRI TAWNEY and MIKE FISHER are:
      i.   SAM[10] FISHER, b. 13 Jul 1990.
     ii.   SARA FISHER, b. 16 Mar 1993.

75. CATHY[9] TAWNEY *(GENE[8], WILLIAM "ERNEST"[7], AARON[6], GEORGE WILLIAM[5], JOHN DANIEL[4], JOHN DANIEL[3], JOHN GEORGE[2], JOHAN JACOB[1])* was born 06 Jul 1960. She married NAME UNKNOWN.

Children of CATHY TAWNEY and NAME UNKNOWN are:
      i.   SHAWN[10] SUPPA, b. 21 Dec 1983.
     ii.   JENNA SUPPA, b. 10 Nov 1985.
    iii.   ANGELA SUPPA, b. 31 May 1987.
    iv.   MADISON SUPPA, b. 21 Dec 1996.

76. MARY GILLETTE "SHELLEY"[9] MCCLELLAND *(MARDELL ADELEE[8] ROGERS, LULA "MABEL"[7] TAWNEY, AARON[6], GEORGE WILLIAM[5], JOHN DANIEL[4], JOHN DANIEL[3], JOHN GEORGE[2], JOHAN JACOB[1])* was born 04 Jan 1945 in Akron, OH. She married (1) MARVIN JOHNSON. He died Jun 2005. She married (2) BILL PANETTI.

Child of MARY MCCLELLAND and MARVIN JOHNSON is:
121.   i.   KATRINA LEIGH[10] JOHNSON, b. 08 Feb 1965.

Child of MARY MCCLELLAND and BILL PANETTI is:
     ii.   MASON JEFFREY[10] PANETTI, b. 04 Jul 1968; m. NADINE F. MULLEN; b. 27 Dec 1961, Perth, Western Australia.

77. DALE ADOLPH[9] JOHNSON *(MARDELL ADELEE[8] ROGERS, LULA "MABEL"[7] TAWNEY, AARON[6], GEORGE WILLIAM[5], JOHN DANIEL[4], JOHN DANIEL[3], JOHN GEORGE[2], JOHAN JACOB[1])* was born 10 May 1953 in Santa Monica, Los Angeles Co., CA. He married (1) SANDRA ANN BROWN 18 Sep 1976 in Orange Co., CA. She was born 10 Jul 1954. He married (2) DEBORAH JEAN MANUEL 17 Mar 2002 in Las Vegas, NV, daughter of UNKNOWN MANUEL and UNKNOWN WATSON. She was born 02 Jul 1950 in Tallahassee, Florida.

Notes for SANDRA ANN BROWN:
Divorced.

Children of DALE JOHNSON and SANDRA BROWN are:
  i. MATTHEW RICHARD[10] JOHNSON, b. 01 Jul 1979; m. DENISSE CAROLINA SANCHEZ SOTO 09 Dec 2006, in Los Mochis, Sinaloa, Mexico. She was born 16 Dec 1986.
  ii. RUSSELL KENNETH JOHNSON, b. 03 Feb 1981.
  iii. TIFFANY ANN JOHNSON, b. 10 Jul 1983.

78. TERESA ANN[9] JOHNSON *(MARDELL ADELEE[8] ROGERS, LULA "MABEL"[7] TAWNEY, AARON[6], GEORGE WILLIAM[5], JOHN DANIEL[4], JOHN DANIEL[3], JOHN GEORGE[2], JOHAN JACOB[1])* was born 29 Jan 1955 in Torrance, Los Angeles Co., CA. She married KEITH CRAIG JACKSON 10 Apr 1982 in Castro Valley, Alameda Co., CA, son of WILLIAM JACKSON and MARY READING. He was born 08 May 1955.

Children of TERESA JOHNSON and KEITH JACKSON are:
  i. LAUREN NICOLE[10] JACKSON, b. 21 May 1985, Petaluma, Sonoma Co., CA.
  ii. LEAH MICHELLE JACKSON, b. 06 Apr 1987, Petaluma, Sonoma Co., CA.
  iii. KYLE WILLIAM JACKSON, b. 16 Feb 1990, Petaluma, Sonoma Co., CA.

79. INA GALE[9] ROGERS *(ROBERT KEITH[8], LULA "MABEL"[7] TAWNEY, AARON[6], GEORGE WILLIAM[5], JOHN DANIEL[4], JOHN DANIEL[3], JOHN GEORGE[2], JOHAN JACOB[1])* was born 11 Mar 1949 in Charleston, Kanawha Co., WV. She married JAMES KERMIT CARPER, son of GUY CARPER and RUBY GRAHAM. He was born 05 Jun 1941.

Children of INA ROGERS and JAMES CARPER are:
       i. JAMES DARIN[10] CARPER, b. 27 Nov 1967.
122.   ii. BRIAN CHRISTOPHER CARPER, b. 23 Jun 1969.
123.   iii. BRANDI LEE CARPER, b. 03 Feb 1975.

80. MICHAEL KEITH[9] ROGERS *(ROBERT KEITH[8], LULA "MABEL"[7] TAWNEY, AARON[6], GEORGE WILLIAM[5], JOHN DANIEL[4], JOHN DANIEL[3], JOHN GEORGE[2], JOHAN JACOB[1])* was born 03 Oct 1950 in Charleston, Kanawha Co., WV. He married DEBORAH LEIGH LEGG; divorced. She was born 16 Aug 1955.

Children of MICHAEL ROGERS and DEBORAH LEGG are:
124.   i. MABEL LYNN[10] ROGERS, b. 24 Jul 1971.
       ii. CHESTER KEITH ROGERS, b. 26 May 1976.

81. RHONDA DIANE[9] ROGERS *(ROBERT KEITH[8], LULA "MABEL"[7] TAWNEY, AARON[6], GEORGE WILLIAM[5], JOHN DANIEL[4], JOHN DANIEL[3], JOHN GEORGE[2], JOHAN JACOB[1])* was born 10 May 1952 in Charleston, Kanawha Co., WV. She married RANDALL KEITH CARPER 27 Mar 1971 in Roane Co., WV, son of BRADFORD CARPER and MABEL WESTFALL. He was born 21 Feb 1950.

Child of RHONDA ROGERS and RANDALL CARPER is:
  i. LISA DAWN[10] CARPER, b. 16 Mar 1980, Cuyahoga Falls, OH; m. BRIAN STOTT; b. 15 Feb 1976, Cuyahoga Falls, OH.

82. DEBRA JEANNE[9] ROGERS *(ROBERT KEITH[8], LULA "MABEL"[7] TAWNEY, AARON[6], GEORGE WILLIAM[5], JOHN DANIEL[4], JOHN DANIEL[3], JOHN GEORGE[2], JOHAN JACOB[1])* was born 08 Aug 1953 in Charleston, Kanawha Co., WV. She married (1) COLLEN WALDECK. She married (2) IVAN LOGSDON 19 Aug 1974 in Parsons, WV, Tucker Cop; he died 1 May 2010.

Child of DEBRA ROGERS and COLLEN WALDECK is:
125.   i.   CHRISTINA LYNN[10] CONLEY, b. 25 Jan 1970, Parkersburg, WV, Wood Co.

Children of DEBRA ROGERS and IVAN LOGSDON are:
126.   ii. AMBER DAWN[10] LOGSDON, b. 21 Oct 1975, Parkersburg, WV, Wood Co.
        iii. TRAVIS EUGENE LOGSDON, b. 30 May 1980, Parkersburg, WV, Wood Co.; m. HEATHER LYNN HEANEY, 28 Jun 2003, Vienna, WV.

83. TIMOTHY LEE[9] ROGERS *(ROBERT KEITH[8], LULA "MABEL"[7] TAWNEY, AARON[6], GEORGE WILLIAM[5], JOHN DANIEL[4], JOHN DANIEL[3], JOHN GEORGE[2], JOHAN JACOB[1])* was born 31 Jul 1954 in Charleston, Kanawha Co., WV. He married KAREN TAWNEY; divorced. She was born 23 Oct 1954.

Children of TIMOTHY ROGERS and KAREN TAWNEY are:
127.   i.   CHADRICK LEE[10] ROGERS, b. 09 Feb 1977.
128.   ii. KELLY JO ROGERS, b. 19 Feb 1979.

84. ROBERT RANDALL[9] ROGERS *(ROBERT KEITH[8], LULA "MABEL"[7] TAWNEY, AARON[6], GEORGE WILLIAM[5], JOHN DANIEL[4], JOHN DANIEL[3], JOHN GEORGE[2], JOHAN JACOB[1])* was born 10 Aug 1955 in Charleston, Kanawha Co., WV. He married LORAINE MARIE BARONE, daughter of VITO BARONE and ANGELA UNKNOWN.

Child of ROBERT ROGERS and LORAINE BARONE is:
        i.   JOSEPH RANDALL[10] ROGERS, b. 23 Feb 1978, Akron, OH, Summit Co.

85. ANDREW JACKSON[9] ROGERS *(ALMA DELORES[8], LULA "MABEL"[7] TAWNEY, AARON[6], GEORGE WILLIAM[5], JOHN DANIEL[4], JOHN DANIEL[3], JOHN GEORGE[2], JOHAN JACOB[1])* was born 27 Mar 1952 in Culver City, CA. He married (1) CAROLINE CARTE. She was born 23 Jun 1950 and died 03 Aug 2006 in Clay, WV. He married (2) TAMMY LYNN GRAY 05 Sep 1997 in Clifton Forge, VA, daughter of SHIRLEY GRAY and SANDRA TAWNEY. She was born 27 Jun 1973 in Jackson Co. Hospital, Ripley, WV.

Notes for ANDREW JACKSON ROGERS - See Page 57

Child of ANDREW ROGERS and CAROLINE CARTE is:
129.   i.   ANDREA JACQUELINE[10] ROGERS, b. 22 Dec 1976.

86. SHEILA MARLENE[9] DENNIS *(ALMA DELORES[8] ROGERS, LULA "MABEL"[7] TAWNEY, AARON[6], GEORGE WILLIAM[5], JOHN DANIEL[4], JOHN DANIEL[3], JOHN GEORGE[2], JOHAN JACOB[1])* was born 26 Mar 1959 in Union Town, PA. She married ROGER ALAN BREMER 08 Mar 1980 in Fort Wayne, IN, son of KENNETH BREMER and RUTH WOLFE. He was born 10 Sep 1960.

Children of SHEILA DENNIS and ROGER BREMER are:
130. i. JAMI MARLENE[10] BREMER, b. 24 Aug 1980, Fort Wayne, IN.
      ii. ASHLEY MARLENE BREMER, b. 29 Jul 1985, Fort Wayne, IN.
131. iii. LINDSEY MARLENE BREMER, b. 29 Jul 1985, Fort Wayne, IN.

87. KATHLEEN ANN[9] ROGERS *(KERMIT ADOLPH[8], LULA "MABEL"[7] TAWNEY, AARON[6], GEORGE WILLIAM[5], JOHN DANIEL[4], JOHN DANIEL[3], JOHN GEORGE[2], JOHAN JACOB[1])* was born 14 Jan 1955 in Charleston, WV, Kanawha Co. She married (1) ROGER SMITH 01 Dec 1973; divorced. He was born 31 Jan 1947. She married (2) KARL HOLCOMB; divorced.

Children of KATHLEEN ROGERS and ROGER SMITH are:
132. i. KERRIE ANN[10] SMITH, b. 28 Dec 1979.
133. ii. KACIE JO SMITH, b. 31 Oct 1985.

88. CHERYL LYNN[9] ROGERS *(KERMIT ADOLPH[8], LULA "MABEL"[7] TAWNEY, AARON[6], GEORGE WILLIAM[5], JOHN DANIEL[4], JOHN DANIEL[3], JOHN GEORGE[2], JOHAN JACOB[1])* was born 10 Mar 1956 in Charleston, WV, Kanawha Co. She met PAUL HOLCOMB 22 Sep 1973; divorced. He was born 16 Jun 1949 in Indore, Clay Co., WV.

Children of CHERYL ROGERS and PAUL HOLCOMB are:
      i. JENNIFER DAWN[10] HOLCOMB, b. 22 Oct 1974, Charleston, Kanawha Co., West Virginia; m. MARK TANNER, 22 Apr 2000, Monroe, NC; b. 05 Apr 1973, Charleston, Kanawha Co., West Virginia.

134. ii. LEAH MICHELE HOLCOMB, b. 07 Nov 1976, Charleston, Kanawha Co., West Virginia.

89. DAWN ARLENE[9] ROGERS *(KERMIT ADOLPH[8], LULA "MABEL"[7] TAWNEY, AARON[6], GEORGE WILLIAM[5], JOHN DANIEL[4], JOHN DANIEL[3], JOHN GEORGE[2], JOHAN JACOB[1])* was born 15 May 1960 in Charleston, WV, Kanawha Co. She married CHARLES RICHARD WILKINSON in Arnoldsburg, WV, Calhoun Co. He was born 26 Nov 1949.

Children of DAWN ROGERS and CHARLES WILKINSON are:
135. i. LUKE AARON[10] WILKINSON, b. 27 Jul 1979.
      ii. CARRISSA DAWN WILKINSON, b. 08 Oct 1980; m. JAMES FOSTER.
      iii. JESSY KATHLYNN WILKINSON, b. 20 Oct 1984.
136. iv. REBECCA KAY WILKINSON, b. 08 May 1986.
      v. JULIE MARIE WILKINSON, b. 11 Oct 1988.

90. NENA MARIE[9] BIRD *(DORMA KATHERN[8] ROGERS, LULA "MABEL"[7] TAWNEY, AARON[6], GEORGE WILLIAM[5], JOHN DANIEL[4], JOHN DANIEL[3], JOHN GEORGE[2], JOHAN JACOB[1])* was born 11 Mar 1958 in Charleston, WV, Kanawha Co. She married RICKY GENE COPPOCK 19 Jun 1976 in Huntington, IN, son of HARRY COPPOCK and EVELYN CAMPBELL. He was born 11 Sep 1957, and died 10 May 2000.

Children of NENA BIRD and RICKY COPPOCK are:
137.   i.   SCOTT LEE[10] COPPOCK, b. 15 Jul 1978, Bluffton, Indiana, Wells Co.
          ii.   KATHRYN IRENE COPPOCK, b. 29 Sep 1982, Hartford City, IN, Blackford Co.; m. CHASE GARRETT HILL on 28 Dec 2002, First Baptist Church, Alexandria, IN. He was born 04 Aug 1983.

             Notes for KATHRYN IRENE COPPOCK:
             Nena said Kathryn Irene was named after grandmothers.

91. LISA CAROL[9] BIRD *(DORMA KATHERN[8] ROGERS, LULA "MABEL"[7] TAWNEY, AARON[6], GEORGE WILLIAM[5], JOHN DANIEL[4], JOHN DANIEL[3], JOHN GEORGE[2], JOHAN JACOB[1])* was born 30 Jun 1960. She married STEVE TACKETT on 03 Aug 1979. He was born 17 Oct 1956.

Children of LISA BIRD and STEVE TACKETT are:
          i.   BOBBY WAYNE[10] TACKETT, b. 19 Aug 1980.
138.   ii.   JAMES LEE TACKETT JR., b. 19 Aug 1980.
          iii.   STEVEN DANIEL TACKETT, b. 20 May 1987.

92. ERNEST SCOTT[9] BIRD *(DORMA KATHERN[8] ROGERS, LULA "MABEL"[7] TAWNEY, AARON[6], GEORGE WILLIAM[5], JOHN DANIEL[4], JOHN DANIEL[3], JOHN GEORGE[2], JOHAN JACOB[1])* was born 16 Aug 1962 in Huntington, IN. He married APRIL SHOEMAKER 14 Nov 2008.

Children of ERNEST BIRD and APRIL SHOEMAKER are:
          i.   KYLIE MAY[10] BIRD, b. 30 Dec 1992.
          ii.   MCKENNA SHOEMAKER, b. 25 Aug 2000.
          iii.   JOSEPH SCOTT BIRD, b. 05 May 2005.

93. MARC ROBERT[9] ROGERS *(CARROLL AARON[8], LULA "MABEL"[7] TAWNEY, AARON[6], GEORGE WILLIAM[5], JOHN DANIEL[4], JOHN DANIEL[3], JOHN GEORGE[2], JOHAN JACOB[1])* was born 05 May 1962 in Morgantown, WV, Monongalia Co. He married MELANIE BAKER 19 Dec 1998 in Wesley Methodist Church, High St., Morgantown, WV. She was born 01 May 1964 in Honolulu, Hawaii.

Children of MARC ROGERS and MELANIE BAKER are:
          i.   MATTHEW PERRY[10] ROGERS, b. 02 Feb 2001.
          ii.   POLINA ROGERS, b. 01 Sep 2003.

94. MICHELE LYNN[9] ROGERS *(CARROLL AARON[8], LULA "MABEL"[7] TAWNEY, AARON[6], GEORGE WILLIAM[5], JOHN DANIEL[4], JOHN DANIEL[3], JOHN GEORGE[2], JOHAN JACOB[1])* was born 06 Apr 1964 in Springfield, OH, Clark Co. She married (1) MICHAEL TARRANTINI; divorced. She married (2) GREGORY WES MCDONALD 20 Sep 1992 in Morgantown, WV, Monongalia Co. He was born 22 Oct 1963.

Children of MICHELE ROGERS and GREGORY MCDONALD are:
    i.   HEATHER NOEL[10] MCDONALD, b. 15 Dec 1993, Morgantown, WV, Monongalia Co.
    ii. WESLEY AARON MCDONALD, b. 10 May 1997, Morgantown, WV, Monongalia Co.

95. NATHAN ERIC[9] ROGERS *(CARROLL AARON[8], LULA "MABEL"[7] TAWNEY, AARON[6], GEORGE WILLIAM[5], JOHN DANIEL[4], JOHN DANIEL[3], JOHN GEORGE[2], JOHAN JACOB[1])* was born 10 Jul 1970 in Morgantown, WV, Monongalia Co. He married VICKIE SUE DECARLO 22 Jun 1996 in Morgantown, WV, Monongalia Co., daughter of DONALD DECARLO and SANDRA ASHLEY. She was born 26 Jun 1970 in Warren, OH, Trumbell Co.

Children of NATHAN ROGERS and VICKIE DECARLO are:
    i.   ISIAH JACKSON[10] ROGERS, b. 24 Oct 2001.
    ii. FRANKLIN JEREMIAH ROGERS, b. 26 Jun 2003.
    iii. WINSTON NEHEMIAH ROGERS, b. 26 Jun 2003.
    iv. HUDSON ELIJAH ROGERS, b. 13 Oct 2008.

96. BRAD ALEXANDER[9] RICHMOND *(CHARLOTTE ANN[8] ROGERS, LULA "MABEL"[7] TAWNEY, AARON[6], GEORGE WILLIAM[5], JOHN DANIEL[4], JOHN DANIEL[3], JOHN GEORGE[2], JOHAN JACOB[1])* was born 17 Sep 1960 in Inglewood, Los Angeles Co., CA. He married (1) DAWN MARIE GAUTHIER 30 Nov 1979 in Otsego, Allegan Co., MI, daughter of GEORGE GAUTHIER and BEATRICE BARBER; divorced. She was born 17 Jul 1961 in Plainwell, Allegan Co., MI. He married (2) VICKIE LYNNE NICKELSON 22 Aug 2008 in Rockford, MI. She was born 09 Jan 1962 in Henipin County, Minneapolis, MN.

Notes for BRAD ALEXANDER RICHMOND:
Born at Daniel Freeman Hospital in Inglewood (Los Angeles County), California, at 9:50 P.M., 8 lbs., 2 oz; delivered by Dr. Glicklick of Westchester Medical Group in Inglewood, California. Graduated from Plainwell High School 1979; graduated from National Institute of Technology in Grand Rapids, Michigan in 1986. He completed an Associates Degree in Quality Science at Grand Rapids Junior College in 1998. He completed a Bachelors Degree from the University of Phoenix in 2010.

Children of BRAD RICHMOND and DAWN GAUTHIER are:
    i.   BROOKE ALEXANDRIA[10] RICHMOND, b. 27 Jun 1983, Plainwell, Allegan Co., MI.
    ii. BRENTON ALEXANDER RICHMOND, b. 11 Jan 1987, Plainwell, Allegan Co., MI.
    iii. BRITTANY ANASTASIA RICHMOND, b. 24 Feb 1990, Plainwell, Allegan Co., MI.

Children of BRAD RICHMOND and VICKIE NICKELSON are:
    iv. MARTIN ANDREW[10] MONZO, b. 19 Mar 1991, Ingham County, Lansing, MI.
    v. RACHEL LYNNE MONZO, b. 25 Jun 1993, Kent County, Grand Rapids, MI.

97. KIMBERLY ANNE[9] RICHMOND *(CHARLOTTE ANN[8] ROGERS, LULA "MABEL"[7] TAWNEY, AARON[6], GEORGE WILLIAM[5], JOHN DANIEL[4], JOHN DANIEL[3], JOHN GEORGE[2], JOHAN JACOB[1])* was born 11 Nov 1963 in Riverside, Riverside Co., CA. She married MICHAEL CHARLES HICKEY 09 Apr 1982 in Yucca Valley, CA, son of PATRICIA WEBSTER. He was born 26 May 1961 in Pittsburgh, PA.

Notes for KIMBERLY ANNE RICHMOND:
Kim weighed 7 lbs., 7 oz., at birth and was 19 1/2 inches long. Kim was delivered by Dr. Trotter at Riverside Hospital in Riverside, California.

Kim served in the U.S. Army. Discharged in Germany. Served in the National Guard in Washington, Louisiana, Mississippi and Texas. She was on the first Old Miss Women's Rifle Team as Captain, with an athletic scholarship where she completed her Bachelors Degree in Elementary Education. Taught English to 7th and 8th grade students. In 2009 is teaching 3rd Grade, then 4th Grade in Kentucky.
Medical Information: Scoliosis. Chickenpox at age 21, melanoma.

Notes for MICHAEL CHARLES HICKEY:
Career: U.S. Army, Rank E9 at Ft. Polk, Louisiana. Promoted to Sgt. Major in Summer of 2003, stationed in Germany 2004. Two tours of duty in the Iraqi theater February 2004. Retired after 30 years of service. Awarded the Bronze Star.

Children of KIMBERLY RICHMOND and MICHAEL HICKEY are:
139.　　i.　MATTHEW MICHAEL[10] HICKEY, b. 15 Nov 1984, Nuremberg, Germany.
　　　　ii.　KRISTIN ANN HICKEY, b. 30 Oct 1988, Spanaway, Washington; m. JEFFERY LORSUNG; divorced.

98. LANCE JOHN[9] OSTROM *(CHARLOTTE ANN[8] ROGERS, LULA "MABEL"[7] TAWNEY, AARON[6], GEORGE WILLIAM[5], JOHN DANIEL[4], JOHN DANIEL[3], JOHN GEORGE[2], JOHAN JACOB[1])* was born 29 Feb 1972 in Phoenix, Maricopa Co., AZ. He married LAUREL LEE LACOUR 09 Sep 2001 in Saline, MI, daughter of CHARLES LACOUR and JEAN. She was born 14 Apr 1975.

Notes for LANCE JOHN OSTROM:
Lance graduated in 1990 from Plainwell High School, Plainwell, Allegan Co., MI. Served in the U.S. Army from 1990 to 1993 out of Ft. Benning, GA. Based in Germany and spent time in Kuwait during Desert Storm. After being discharged he used his benefits for college. He went to Kalamazoo Valley Community College, Kalamazoo, MI and transferred to the University of Michigan, Ann Arbor, MI where he earned a Bachelor of Science Degree in Biology. He was a Research Associate for the University of Michigan Hospital and served with the National Guard, rank E6 Staff Sergeant, since 1993 out of Grand Rapids, MI. He was activated to Cuba in August 2004 and was discharged in 2006. Obtained Master's Degree in Biology from Harvard University, Boston, MA. 2009.

Children of LANCE OSTROM and LAUREL LACOUR is:
　　　　i.　JACOB DAVIS[10] OSTROM, b. 18 Jun 2008, Concord, MA.
　　　　ii.　MAYA JEAN OSTROM, b. 21 Apr 2010, Concore, MA.
　　　　iii.　CLAIRE ANN OSTROM, b. 21 Apr 2010, Concord, MA.

Notes for JACOB DAVIS OSTROM:

Jacob David Ostrom was born at 12:32 p.m., Wednesday, June 18, 2008.   He was born at Emerson Hospital in Concord, MA.   His weight at birth 7 lbs. 13 1/2 oz., 21 1/2 inches long. At birth he had lots of dark brown hair and brown eyes.

Notes for CLAIRE ANN OSTROM and MAYA JEAN OSTROM:

Claire Ann Ostrom and Maya Jean Ostrom were born on 21 Apr 2010, at Emerson Hospital in Concord, MA., weighing in at 8 lbs. 3 oz. and 8 lbs. 4 oz, at 4:04 and 4:12 p.m., 21" and 21 ½" respectively.

99.   STEPHEN WAYNE[9] CONLEY *(PATRICIA RONDELL[8] ROGERS, LULA "MABEL"[7] TAWNEY, AARON[6], GEORGE WILLIAM[5], JOHN DANIEL[4], JOHN DANIEL[3], JOHN GEORGE[2], JOHAN JACOB[1])* was born 28 Sep 1967.   He married (1) VERA ELLEN HIGHLANDER

Children of STEPHEN CONLEY and VERA HIGHLANDER are:
      i.   GABRIEL WAYNE[10] CONLEY, b. 30 Dec 2001, West Virginia.

          Notes for GABRIEL WAYNE CONLEY: Born at Thomas Memorial Hospital.

      ii. JOSHUA HIGHLANDER CONLEY, b. 25 Apr 2006, West Virginia.

          Notes for JOSHUA HIGHLANDER CONLEY: Born at Thomas Memorial Hospital.

Child of STEPHEN CONLEY and MELISSA BAILEY is:
140.   iii. ASHLEY NICOLE[10] BAILEY, b. 12 Feb 1993, So. Charleston, Kanawha Co., WV.

100.   STACY RONDELL[9] CONLEY *(PATRICIA RONDELL[8] ROGERS, LULA "MABEL"[7] TAWNEY, AARON[6], GEORGE WILLIAM[5], JOHN DANIEL[4], JOHN DANIEL[3], JOHN GEORGE[2], JOHAN JACOB[1])* was born 21 Sep 1972 in Charleston, Kanawha Co., WV.   She married AARON MICHAEL ROMANO 30 May 1992 in Newton, WV, Roane Co., son of JOHN ROMANO and RUTH SHEPPER.   He was born 07 Sep 1971.

Notes for STACY RONDELL CONLEY:
Stacy Conley completed C.Dilno's form Sept. 4, 1996.
Entered by C. Dilno 12-2-96Born Charleston Memorial Hospital.

Children of STACY CONLEY and AARON ROMANO are:
      i.   BRYAN GREGORY[10] ROMANO, b. 03 May 1994, Spencer, WV, Roane Co.

          Notes for BRYAN GREGORY ROMANO: Born Roane General Hospital

      ii. JUSTIN MATTHEW ROMANO, b. 17 Oct 1995, Great Falls, Montana.

          Notes for JUSTIN MATTHEW ROMANO: Born Columbus Hospital.

      iii. SARA ELIZABETH ROMANO, b. 07 Sep 1998, Florida.

          Notes for SARA ELIZABETH ROMANO: Born at University of Florida.

101. THERESE MARIE[9] BEISTLE *(BARBARA CAROLINE[8] ROGERS, LULA "MABEL"[7] TAWNEY, AARON[6], GEORGE WILLIAM[5], JOHN DANIEL[4], JOHN DANIEL[3], JOHN GEORGE[2], JOHAN JACOB[1])* was born 19 Jun 1968 in Riverside, CA, Riverside Co. She married KEVIN PEDERSON.

Children of THERESE BEISTLE and KEVIN PEDERSON are:
    i.   BRITNEY TAYLOR[10] PEDERSON, b. 28 Jan 1994, Riverside, CA, Riverside Co.
    ii. CHRISTIAN KEVIN PEDERSON, b. 25 Apr 1995, Riverside, CA, Riverside Co.

102. DEBRA JEAN[9] TAWNEY *(EWUELL JEROME[8], CLEMENT LUTHER[7], AARON[6], GEORGE WILLIAM[5], JOHN DANIEL[4], JOHN DANIEL[3], JOHN GEORGE[2], JOHAN JACOB[1])* was born 17 Aug 1953. She married FRED E. BRADLEY 22 Aug 1965. He was born 22 May 1954.

Children of DEBRA TAWNEY and FRED BRADLEY are:
    i.   ANGELA DENISE[10] BRADLEY, b. 10 Sep 1981.
    ii. JENNIFER LYNN BRADLEY, b. 16 Oct 1983.

103. JEFFREY JEROME[9] TAWNEY *(EWUELL JEROME[8], CLEMENT LUTHER[7], AARON[6], GEORGE WILLIAM[5], JOHN DANIEL[4], JOHN DANIEL[3], JOHN GEORGE[2], JOHAN JACOB[1])* was born 21 Dec 1956. He married CAROL D. BARKER 09 Apr 1982. She was born 23 Oct 1957.

Child of JEFFREY TAWNEY and CAROL BARKER is:
    i.   ADAM CHRISTOPHER[10] TAWNEY, b. 20 Jan 1993.

104. DREMA LYNN[9] TAWNEY *(KENNETH JENOAL[8], CLEMENT LUTHER[7], AARON[6], GEORGE WILLIAM[5], JOHN DANIEL[4], JOHN DANIEL[3], JOHN GEORGE[2], JOHAN JACOB[1])* was born 28 Jul 1959 in Charleston, WV, Kanawha Co. She married (1) STEVEN JOSEPH VELTRI. She married (2) JAMES WILLIAM DENNEWITZ 14 Feb 1985 in Charleston, WV, son of WALLACE DENNEWITZ and DOROTHY MCMILLON.

Notes for DREMA LYNN TAWNEY:
Drema L. Dennewitz furnished all information on Sept. 1, 1996.
.
Children of DREMA TAWNEY and STEVEN VELTRI are:
    i.   CHRISTOPHER JOSEPH[10] VELTRI, b. 24 Dec 1979, Kanawha Co., Charleston, WV.
    ii. STEPHANIE MARIE VELTRI, b. 23 Jul 1982, Kanawha Co., Charleston, WV.

105. KENNETH JAY[9] TAWNEY *(KENNETH JENOAL[8], CLEMENT LUTHER[7], AARON[6], GEORGE WILLIAM[5], JOHN DANIEL[4], JOHN DANIEL[3], JOHN GEORGE[2], JOHAN JACOB[1])* was born 07 Nov 1961 in Charleston, WV, Kanawha Co. He married (2) WENDY ANDERSON.

Notes for KENNETH JAY TAWNEY:
Form completed by oldest sister, Guyla Black, of Joseph Logan Tawney, September 1, 1996

Child of KENNETH JAY TAWNEY is:
    i.   KENNETH JOSEPH[10] TAWNEY, b. 24 Feb 1992, Charleston, WV, Kanawha Co.

       Notes for KENNETH JOSEPH TAWNEY: Mother's name is: Wendy Anderson

106. SHERRY LOUISE[9] KING *(BARBARA LAMOINE[8] TAWNEY, CLEMENT LUTHER[7], AARON[6], GEORGE WILLIAM[5], JOHN DANIEL[4], JOHN DANIEL[3], JOHN GEORGE[2], JOHAN JACOB[1])* was born 23 May 1954 in Charleston, WV, Kanawha Co., and died 03 Jun 1998. She married (1) CLYDE MCQUAIN. He was born 05 Sep 1952. She married (2) DELBERT BROWNING 06 Jun 1970 in Left Hand (Roane Co.), WV.
Children of SHERRY KING and CLYDE MCQUAIN are:
141.   i.   TRAVIS SCOTT[10] MCQUAIN, b. 15 May 1971.
142.   ii.   CRYSTAL LYNN MCQUAIN, b. 30 Aug 1974.

107. NATHAN LAWRENCE[9] GOFF *(LELA ANNE[8] TAWNEY, GEORGE "GARRISON"[7], AARON[6], GEORGE WILLIAM[5], JOHN DANIEL[4], JOHN DANIEL[3], JOHN GEORGE[2], JOHAN JACOB[1])* was born 10 Nov 1972 in Charleston, WV, Kanawha Co. He married AMY MARIE SHEETS 05 Jun 2004. She was born 27 Dec 1973.

Child of NATHAN GOFF and AMY SHEETS is:
         i.   ADELEE[10] ELIZABETH GOFF, b. 01 Apr 2008, California.

108. ADAM CARTER[9] GOFF *(LELA ANNE[8] TAWNEY, GEORGE "GARRISON"[7], AARON[6], GEORGE WILLIAM[5], JOHN DANIEL[4], JOHN DANIEL[3], JOHN GEORGE[2], JOHAN JACOB[1])* was born 01 Oct 1977 in South Charleston, WV, Kanawha Co. He married CAREN TAHAN 12 Jul 2003 in Woodbridge, VA, Prince William Co. She was born 25 Sep 1978 in Beirut, Lebanon.

Child of ADAM GOFF and CAREN TAHAN is:
         i.   ANNABELLE LILY[10] GOFF, b. 09 Oct 2007, Charlottesville, VA, Abermarle Co.
         ii.   LUKE HARRISON GOFF, b. 04 Apr 2010, Charlottesville, VA, Abermarle Co.

109. AARON ROY[9] COOPER *(JANICE EVELYN[8] TAWNEY, GEORGE "GARRISON"[7], AARON[6], GEORGE WILLIAM[5], JOHN DANIEL[4], JOHN DANIEL[3], JOHN GEORGE[2], JOHAN JACOB[1])* was born 06 Dec 1975 in Salisbury, MD, Wicomico Co. He married BETSEY FAITH FOSTER 15 Jul 2000, daughter of ROBERT FOSTER and PATTY UPDIKE. She was born 02 Jun 1976 in Charlottesville, VA, Charlottesville City.

Children of AARON COOPER and BETSEY FOSTER are:
         i.   THOMAS CLAY[10] COOPER, b. 27 Apr 2006, Annapolis, MD, Anne Arundel Co.
         ii.   PEYTON LEE COOPER, b. 18 Apr 2008, Salisbury, MD, Wicomico Co.

110. KIMBERLY SUE[9] HAPPNEY *(BERNICE JEAN[8] TAWNEY, CHAMP "CLARK" TAWNEY (KNOWN AS[7] CLARK), AARON[6] TAWNEY, GEORGE WILLIAM[5], JOHN DANIEL[4], JOHN DANIEL[3], JOHN GEORGE[2], JOHAN JACOB[1])* was born 12 Nov 1963 in Bellflower, CA. She married DEAN MURRAY. He was born 11 Sep 1962.

Children of KIMBERLY HAPPNEY and DEAN MURRAY are:
         i.   CORY THOMAS[10] MURRAY, b. 07 Apr 1990, Parkersburg WV, Wood Co.
         ii.   LUKE DAVID MURRAY, b. 30 Apr 1992, Parkersburg WV, Wood Co.

111. TAMMY ANNE[9] HAPPNEY *(BERNICE JEAN[8] TAWNEY, CHAMP "CLARK" TAWNEY (KNOWN AS[7] CLARK), AARON[6] TAWNEY, GEORGE WILLIAM[5], JOHN DANIEL[4], JOHN DANIEL[3], JOHN GEORGE[2], JOHAN JACOB[1])* was born 20 Jan 1967 in Ripley WV Jackson Co.   She married GREG OXLEY.   He was born 19 Aug 1961.

Children of TAMMY HAPPNEY and GREG OXLEY are:
> i.   KAYLA ANNE[10] OXLEY, b. 08 Nov 1991.
> ii.   NICHOLAS GREGORY OXLEY, b. 30 Dec 1994.

112. MICHAEL SCOTT[9] DESPOSITO *(MICHAEL (JR) EDWARD[8], ANNA ELIZABETH[7] TAWNEY, AARON[6], GEORGE WILLIAM[5], JOHN DANIEL[4], JOHN DANIEL[3], JOHN GEORGE[2], JOHAN JACOB[1])* was born 24 Feb 1970 in Queens, NY.   He married (1) JANEEN LACAUSI 01 Aug 1992.   He married (2) KATIE COOPER 10 Jul 1999.   She was born 04 Oct 1975.

Child of MICHAEL DESPOSITO and JANEEN LACAUSI is:
> i.   SERINA[10] DESPOSITO, b. 03 Dec 1993.

113. MARC CHRISTOPHER[9] DESPOSITO *(MICHAEL (JR) EDWARD[8], ANNA ELIZABETH[7] TAWNEY, AARON[6], GEORGE WILLIAM[5], JOHN DANIEL[4], JOHN DANIEL[3], JOHN GEORGE[2], JOHAN JACOB[1])* was born 15 Dec 1974 in Syosset, NY.   He married JEANENNE JOY DOUGLAS 01 Dec 2001.   She was born 15 Jun 1976.

Children of MARC DESPOSITO and JEANENNE DOUGLAS are:
> i.   BRIANNA MEGAN[10] DESPOSITO, b. 07 Nov 2003.
> ii.   OLIVIA LOGAN DESPOSITO, b. 01 May 2008.

114. LORI LYNN[9] DESPOSITO *(MICHAEL (JR) EDWARD[8], ANNA ELIZABETH[7] TAWNEY, AARON[6], GEORGE WILLIAM[5], JOHN DANIEL[4], JOHN DANIEL[3], JOHN GEORGE[2], JOHAN JACOB[1])* was born 19 Oct 1971 in Huntington, Nassau Co., NY.   She married RAYMOND CRANE   02 Mar 1992.   He was born 15 Nov 1969.

Children of LORI DESPOSITO and RAYMOND CRANE are:
> i.   AMANDA[10] CRANE, b. 14 Dec 1991.
> ii.   VICTORIA ROSE CRANE, b. 07 Oct 1996.
> iii.   RAYMOND MICHAEL CRANE, (Jr.); b. 19 Jul 2000.
> iv.   CHRISTOPHER CRANE, b. 22 May 2003.

115. BRIAN[9] DESPOSITO *(DANIEL JOHN[8], ANNA ELIZABETH[7] TAWNEY, AARON[6], GEORGE WILLIAM[5], JOHN DANIEL[4], JOHN DANIEL[3], JOHN GEORGE[2], JOHAN JACOB[1])* was born 20 Jun 1975.   He married LESLIE MCCARTHY.

Notes for LESLIE MCCARTHY:
Has two daughters from previous marriage.

Child of BRIAN DESPOSITO and LESLIE MCCARTHY is:
> i.   JOSEPH KEITH[10] DESPOSITO.

116. COURTNEY[9] DESPOSITO *(DANIEL JOHN[8], ANNA ELIZABETH[7] TAWNEY, AARON[6], GEORGE WILLIAM[5], JOHN DANIEL[4], JOHN DANIEL[3], JOHN GEORGE[2], JOHAN JACOB[1])* was born 01 Feb 1977 in Pete AFB.   She married BRANDON REEVES.

Children of COURTNEY DESPOSITO and BRANDON REEVES are:
  i. CALEB[10] REEVES.
  ii. MOLLY MARGARET REEVES, b. 10 Jan 2007.

117. KRISTINA ELIZABETH[9] DURANCEAU *(PATRICIA ANN[8] DESPOSITO, ANNA ELIZABETH[7] TAWNEY, AARON[6], GEORGE WILLIAM[5], JOHN DANIEL[4], JOHN DANIEL[3], JOHN GEORGE[2], JOHAN JACOB[1])* was born 05 Oct 1989.

Child of KRISTINA ELIZABETH DURANCEAU AND GEORGE GURULE is:
  i. MICHAEL ANTHONY GURULE[10], b. 23 May 2008.

118. PAMELA SUE[9] TAWNEY *(JERRY WAYNE[8], DANIEL AARON[7], AARON[6], GEORGE WILLIAM[5], JOHN DANIEL[4], JOHN DANIEL[3], JOHN GEORGE[2], JOHAN JACOB[1])*   She married RICHARD PROSS.

Child of PAMELA TAWNEY and RICHARD PROSS is:
  i. JOSHUA MATTHEW[10] PROSS.

119. BRANDY NICOLE[9] TAWNEY *(KAREN ALMON[8], DANIEL AARON[7], AARON[6], GEORGE WILLIAM[5], JOHN DANIEL[4], JOHN DANIEL[3], JOHN GEORGE[2], JOHAN JACOB[1])* was born 15 Sep 1981 in Jackson Co. Hospital, Ripley, WV.   She married STEPHEN LEWIS PORTILLO 21 Nov 2005, son of LOUIS PORTILLO and JANET VINEYARD.   He was born 11 Jun 1978.

Child of BRANDY TAWNEY and STEPHEN PORTILLO is:
  i. JOBE ALEXANDER[10] PORTILLO, b. 03 Feb 2006.

120. STACIE LEA[9] TAWNEY *(SANDRA SUE[8], DANIEL AARON[7], AARON[6], GEORGE WILLIAM[5], JOHN DANIEL[4], JOHN DANIEL[3], JOHN GEORGE[2], JOHAN JACOB[1])[3]* was born 22 Jun 1971 in Jackson Co. Hospital, Ripley, WV.   She married MICHAEL ALLEN PETERSON 15 Jun 1996 in Newton, WV, Roane Co.

Notes for STACIE LEA TAWNEY
Furnished by Brandy Portillo

Stacie got out of the military around 1995-1996 after Desert Storm. She and Mike first married while they were stationed in Japan (95-96). They had Alexander Daniel on October 17, 1998 when they moved back to Washington State. Stacie has stayed home with Alex as they moved around while Mike was earning degrees and training. After Washington State they moved to Colorado (which is where Mike was raised) for a couple years. Then they went to Germany for 3-4 years. There she started her BA in Sociology. They moved back to Monterey CA spring of 05' for Mike to attend DLI/ post-graduate school there. After that they moved to Beavercreek, OH its outside Dayton. Mike is stationed there at Wright-Patterson Air Force base.

Currently, he travels a lot with his job as he is a Special Agent. In 2008 he spent 6 months of the year in China working at the US Embassy. Stacie and Alex went to visit him there for about 8 weeks last summer.

Stacie & Alex left about a week before the Olympics started. Stacie is working on her Masters Degree in Library Science. I love it that she's so close after all these years. When I went to visit her in Germany one day we just mapped our way into the French countryside and drove around. I never felt so free. Anyway, fond memories. This is part of a note received from Brandy Portillo, Stacie's niece.   Love, the Portillos

Marriage Notes for STACIE TAWNEY and MICHAEL PETERSON:
They were married in Japan before the marriage ceremony at Newton, WV. All the family attended the ceremony at Newton Baptist Church, Roane Co., WV.

Stacie served in the 82nd Airborne of the U.S. Army during Desert Storm, stationed in Saudi Arabia. She served a total of seven years.

Michael, her husband, served in the U.S. Army. In 1999, they are stationed in the State of Washington.

Child of STACIE TAWNEY and MICHAEL PETERSON is:
      i.   ALEXANDER DANIEL[10] PETERSON, b. 17 Oct 1998.

Generation No. 10

121.   KATRINA LEIGH[10] JOHNSON *(MARY GILLETTE "SHELLEY"[9] MCCLELLAND, MARDELL ADELEE[8] ROGERS, LULA "MABEL"[7] TAWNEY, AARON[6], GEORGE WILLIAM[5], JOHN DANIEL[4], JOHN DANIEL[3], JOHN GEORGE[2], JOHAN JACOB[1])* was born 08 Feb 1965.   She married MATT HESSLER.

Child of KATRINA JOHNSON and MATT HESSLER is:
      i.   KAYLA ELL[11] HESSLER, b. 05 Aug 1989.

122.   BRIAN CHRISTOPHER[10] CARPER *(INA GALE[9] ROGERS, ROBERT KEITH[8], LULA "MABEL"[7] TAWNEY, AARON[6], GEORGE WILLIAM[5], JOHN DANIEL[4], JOHN DANIEL[3], JOHN GEORGE[2], JOHAN JACOB[1])* was born 23 Jun 1969.

Child of BRIAN CHRISTOPHER CARPER is:
      i.   KYLIE PAIGE[8] CARPER, b. 22 Jun 2003.
      ii. COURTNEY BROOK CARPER, b. 04 Feb, 2005

123.   BRANDI LEE[10] CARPER *(INA GALE[9] ROGERS, ROBERT KEITH[8], LULA "MABEL"[7] TAWNEY, AARON[6], GEORGE WILLIAM[5], JOHN DANIEL[4], JOHN DANIEL[3], JOHN GEORGE[2], JOHAN JACOB[1])* was born 03 Feb 1975.   She is married to James Ward.

Child of BRANDI LEE CARPER is:
      i.   MORGAN NICHOLE[11] CARPER, b. 23 Mar 1994.

124.   MABEL LYNN[10] ROGERS *(MICHAEL KEITH[9], ROBERT KEITH[8], LULA "MABEL"[7] TAWNEY, AARON[6], GEORGE WILLIAM[5], JOHN DANIEL[4], JOHN DANIEL[3], JOHN GEORGE[2], JOHAN JACOB[1])* was born 24 Jul 1971.

Children of MABEL LYNN ROGERS are:
>   i.   JOSHUA NEIL[11] SHIREY, b. 17 Aug 1989.
>   ii.   LOREN MONTANA LEGG, b. 04 Jul 1991.

>   iii.   WHITNEY RAY SHIREY, b. 09 Jun 1993.
>   iv.   CHRISTINA DANIELLE PECK, b. 09 Nov 1995.

125.   CHRISTINA LYNN[10] CONLEY *(DEBRA JEANNE[9] ROGERS, ROBERT KEITH[8], LULA "MABEL"[7] TAWNEY, AARON[6], GEORGE WILLIAM[5], JOHN DANIEL[4], JOHN DANIEL[3], JOHN GEORGE[2], JOHAN JACOB[1])* was born 25 Jan 1970 in Parkersburg, WV, Wood Co.   She married (1) GARY SCOTT DEUSENBERRY 30 Dec 1988 in Newton, WV.   He was born 30 Dec 1969. Divorced 1996.   She married (2) MIKE WHITTMAN 22 Jul 2000. He was born 25 Nov 1969.

Child of CHRISTINA CONLEY and GARY DEUSENBERRY is:
>   i.   KAYLA COLLEEN[11] DEUSENBERRY, b. 10 Dec 1990.

126.   AMBER DAWN[10] LOGSDON *(DEBRA JEANNE[9] ROGERS, ROBERT KEITH[8], LULA "MABEL"[7] TAWNEY, AARON[6], GEORGE WILLIAM[5], JOHN DANIEL[4], JOHN DANIEL[3], JOHN GEORGE[2], JOHAN JACOB[1])* was born 21 Oct 1975 in Parkersburg, WV, Wood Co.   She married TONY HUBER.

Children of AMBER LOGSDON and TONY HUBER are:
>   i.   CODY LEE[11] HUBER, b. 10 Oct 2000.
>   ii.   KINDRA NICOLE HUBER, b. 02 Feb 1998.

127.   CHADRICK LEE[10] ROGERS *(TIMOTHY LEE[9], ROBERT KEITH[8], LULA "MABEL"[7] TAWNEY, AARON[6], GEORGE WILLIAM[5], JOHN DANIEL[4], JOHN DANIEL[3], JOHN GEORGE[2], JOHAN JACOB[1])* was born 09 Feb 1977.

Child of CHADRICK LEE ROGERS is:
>   i.   JAYDEN[11] ROGERS, b. 2003.

128.   KELLY JO[10] ROGERS *(TIMOTHY LEE[9], ROBERT KEITH[8], LULA "MABEL"[7] TAWNEY, AARON[6], GEORGE WILLIAM[5], JOHN DANIEL[4], JOHN DANIEL[3], JOHN GEORGE[2], JOHAN JACOB[1])* was born 19 Feb 1979.   She married DAVID STONE ; divorced.

Child of KELLY ROGERS and DAVID STONE is:
>   i.   HAYDEN ZANE[11] STONE, b. Abt. 12 Feb 2003.

129. ANDREA JACQUELINE[10] ROGERS *(ANDREW JACKSON[9], ALMA DELORES[8], LULA "MABEL"[7] TAWNEY, AARON[6], GEORGE WILLIAM[5], JOHN DANIEL[4], JOHN DANIEL[3], JOHN GEORGE[2], JOHAN JACOB[1])* was born 22 Dec 1976.   She married (2) ROBERT WHITE.

Child of ANDREA JACQUELINE ROGERS is:
      i.   HUNTER LEE[11] BOWMAN, b. 26 Jan 1996.

          Notes for HUNTER LEE BOWMAN:
          Hunter's   biological father is Larry Bowman of Virginia.   Larry is also enlisted with the U.S.M.C.   as of 3-1-99.

Child of ANDREA ROGERS and ROBERT WHITE is:
      ii.   JORJA KENZLEIGH[11] WHITE, b. 13 Aug 2003.
          At birth: 7 pounds, 19 inches long.

130. JAMI MARLENE[10] BREMER *(SHEILA MARLENE[9] DENNIS, ALMA DELORES[8] ROGERS, LULA "MABEL"[7] TAWNEY, AARON[6], GEORGE WILLIAM[5], JOHN DANIEL[4], JOHN DANIEL[3], JOHN GEORGE[2], JOHAN JACOB[1])* was born 24 Aug 1980 in Fort Wayne, IN.   She married CASEY LEE ADAMS 16 Aug 2003 in Ft. Wayne, IN.   He was born 28 Nov 1978.

Children of JAMI BREMER and CASEY ADAMS are:
      i.   SPENCER LEE[11] ADAMS, b. 01 Dec 2005, Ft. Wayne, IN.
      ii.   CHLOE RENEE ADAMS, b. 17 Oct 2008, F. Wayne, IN.

131. LINDSEY MARLENE[10] BREMER *(SHEILA MARLENE[9] DENNIS, ALMA DELORES[8] ROGERS, LULA "MABEL"[7] TAWNEY, AARON[6], GEORGE WILLIAM[5], JOHN DANIEL[4], JOHN DANIEL[3], JOHN GEORGE[2], JOHAN JACOB[1])* was born 29 Jul 1985 in Fort Wayne, IN.

Child of LINDSEY MARLENE BREMER is:
      i.   GRACYN RYLIN[11] SPILLERS, b. 07 Nov 2009, Ft. Wayne, IN., DuPont Hospital.

132. KERRIE ANN[10] SMITH *(KATHLEEN ANN[9] ROGERS, KERMIT ADOLPH[8], LULA "MABEL"[7] TAWNEY, AARON[6], GEORGE WILLIAM[5], JOHN DANIEL[4], JOHN DANIEL[3], JOHN GEORGE[2], JOHAN JACOB[1])* was born 28 Dec 1979.   She married (2) JAMES DRAKE 03 Jun 2000 in Newton, WV,   Roane Co.   She married (3) RICHARD L. YOUNG, JR. 04 Jan 2003 in United Church, Clendenin, WV.

Child of KERRIE ANN SMITH is:
      i.   CLOIE PAGE[11] HART, b. 04 Sep 2007.

Child of KERRIE SMITH and RICHARD YOUNG. is:
      ii.   KAITLYNN BRIELLE[11] YOUNG, b. 27 Sep 2003.

133. KACIE JO[10] SMITH *(KATHLEEN ANN[9] ROGERS, KERMIT ADOLPH[8], LULA "MABEL"[7] TAWNEY, AARON[6], GEORGE WILLIAM[5], JOHN DANIEL[4], JOHN DANIEL[3], JOHN GEORGE[2], JOHAN JACOB[1])* was born 31 Oct 1985.   She married (2) ROBERT SCOTT HOLCOMB 22 Jun 2009. He was born 08 Jan 1982.

Child of KACIE JO SMITH is:
>   i.   MAHAILEY JO[11] SMITH, b. 02 Dec 2005.

Child of KACIE JO SMITH AND SCOTT HOLCOMB is:
>   ii.   MARISSA BROOKE HOLCOMB b. 25 Jan 2010.

134. LEAH MICHELE[10] HOLCOMB *(CHERYL LYNN[9] ROGERS, KERMIT ADOLPH[8], LULA "MABEL"[7] TAWNEY, AARON[6], GEORGE WILLIAM[5], JOHN DANIEL[4], JOHN DANIEL[3], JOHN GEORGE[2], JOHAN JACOB[1])* was born 07 Nov 1976 in Charleston, Kanawha Co., West Virginia.   She married JEREMY QUINN.   He was born 30 Jun 1974 in Charleston, Kanawha Co., West Virginia.

Children of LEAH HOLCOMB and JEREMY QUINN are:
>   i.   GARRETT MONTEVILLE[11] QUINN, b. 10 Mar 2001.
>   ii.   JACKSON HENRY QUINN, b. 09 Jun 2006, Mecklenburg County, SC.

135. LUKE AARON[10] WILKINSON *(DAWN ARLENE[9] ROGERS, KERMIT ADOLPH[8], LULA "MABEL"[7] TAWNEY, AARON[6], GEORGE WILLIAM[5], JOHN DANIEL[4], JOHN DANIEL[3], JOHN GEORGE[2], JOHAN JACOB[1])* was born 27 Jul 1979.

Child of LUKE AARON WILKINSON is:
>   i.   KYLIN LEVI[11] WILKINSON, b. 29 Jan 1999, Kirksville, MO.

136. REBECCA KAY[10] WILKINSON *(DAWN ARLENE[9] ROGERS, KERMIT ADOLPH[8], LULA "MABEL"[7] TAWNEY, AARON[6], GEORGE WILLIAM[5], JOHN DANIEL[4], JOHN DANIEL[3], JOHN GEORGE[2], JOHAN JACOB[1])* was born 08 May 1986.   She married ADAM DUANE STOCK.   He was born 03 Feb 1982 in Alexandria, LA.

Children of REBECCA WILKINSON and ADAM STOCK are:
>   i.   BRAXTON GRAHAM[11] STOCK, b. 30 Jun 2006, Missouri.
>   ii.   OWEN BRADFORD STOCK, b. 24 Oct 2008.

137. SCOTT LEE[10] COPPOCK *(NENA MARIE[9] BIRD, DORMA KATHERN[8] ROGERS, LULA "MABEL"[7] TAWNEY, AARON[6], GEORGE WILLIAM[5], JOHN DANIEL[4], JOHN DANIEL[3], JOHN GEORGE[2], JOHAN JACOB[1])* was born 15 Jul 1978 in Bluffton, Indiana, Wells Co.   He married LILLIAN E. "FROSYNI" DOURAMACOS 08 Jun 2002 in Alexandria, IN.   She was born 15 Oct 1978 in Anderson, IN, Madison Co.

Notes for SCOTT LEE COPPOCK: Scott's mother said he was named after three uncles.

Notes for LILLIAN E. "FROSYNI" DOURAMACOS: Married at First Christina Church, 215 West Berry, Alexandria, IN

Child of SCOTT COPPOCK and FROSYNI DOURAMACOS is:
>   i.   DAVID JAMES[11] COPPOCK, b. 11 Jun 2008, Carmel, Indiana.

138. JAMES LEE TACKETT[10] JR. *(LISA CAROL[9] BIRD, DORMA KATHERN[8] ROGERS, LULA "MABEL"[7] TAWNEY, AARON[6], GEORGE WILLIAM[5], JOHN DANIEL[4], JOHN DANIEL[3], JOHN GEORGE[2], JOHAN JACOB[1])* was born 19 Aug 1980. He married KRISTINE LOUISE WHITE. She was born 29 Oct 1983.

Children of JAMES JR. and KRISTINE WHITE are:
- i. HALEY KRISTINE[11] TACKETT, b. 14 Jul 2004.
- ii. JAMES LEE TACKETT II, b. 02 Nov 2001.
- iii. CHRISTIAN DAVID TACKETT, b. 04 Feb 2008.

139. MATTHEW MICHAEL[10] HICKEY *(KIMBERLY ANNE[9] RICHMOND, CHARLOTTE ANN[8] ROGERS, LULA "MABEL"[7] TAWNEY, AARON[6], GEORGE WILLIAM[5], JOHN DANIEL[4], JOHN DANIEL[3], JOHN GEORGE[2], JOHAN JACOB[1])* was born 15 Nov 1984 in Nuremberg, Germany. He married ROCHELLE LYNN DOVIN in Plainwell, Allegan Co., MI, daughter of DAMIAN DOVIN and KARINA DOVIN. Rochelle was born 11 Mar, 1985.

Children of MATTHEW HICKEY and ROCHELLE DOVIN are:
- i. RYLEIGH ELIZABETH[11] HICKEY, b. 06 Feb 2006, Kalamazoo, Kalamazoo Co., MI.
- ii. JACKSON MATTHEW HICKEY, b. 31 May 2009, Kalamazoo, Kalamazoo Co., MI.

140. ASHLEY NICOLE[10] BAILEY *(STEPHEN WAYNE[9] CONLEY, PATRICIA RONDELL[8] ROGERS, LULA "MABEL"[7] TAWNEY, AARON[6], GEORGE WILLIAM[5], JOHN DANIEL[4], JOHN DANIEL[3], JOHN GEORGE[2], JOHAN JACOB[1])* was born 12 Feb 1993 in So. Charleston, Kanawha Co., WV, Thomas Memorial Hospital.

Child of ASHLEY NICOLE BAILEY is:
- i. BRAYDONN JAMES[11] BAILEY, b. 05 Jul 2009, Ohio.

141. TRAVIS SCOTT[10] MCQUAIN *(SHERRY LOUISE[9] KING, BARBARA LAMOINE[8] TAWNEY, CLEMENT LUTHER[7], AARON[6], GEORGE WILLIAM[5], JOHN DANIEL[4], JOHN DANIEL[3], JOHN GEORGE[2], JOHAN JACOB[1])* was born 15 May 1971. He married (1) RHONDA MUSIC. She was born 02 Apr 1972. He married (2) HEATHER ROGERS. She was born 13 Jan 1971.

Children of TRAVIS MCQUAIN and RHONDA MUSIC are:
- i. CHELSEY NICOLE[11] MCQUAIN, b. 30 Jan 1993.
- ii. ZACHARY CALEB MCQUAIN, b. 30 Apr 1994.

Child of TRAVIS MCQUAIN and HEATHER ROGERS is:
- iii. MEADOW ROSE[11] MCQUAIN, b. 20 Feb 2007.

142. CRYSTAL LYNN[10] MCQUAIN *(SHERRY LOUISE[9] KING, BARBARA LAMOINE[8] TAWNEY, CLEMENT LUTHER[7], AARON[6], GEORGE WILLIAM[5], JOHN DANIEL[4], JOHN DANIEL[3], JOHN GEORGE[2], JOHAN JACOB[1])* was born 30 Aug 1974. She married (1) ROY YOUNG. He was born 05 Aug 1973. She married (2) GREG JAMES.

Child of CRYSTAL MCQUAIN and ROY YOUNG is:
      i.   CASSIDY AVA[11] YOUNG, b. 07 Dec 1999.

Child of CRYSTAL MCQUAIN and GREG JAMES is:
     ii.   COTY ALLEN[11] JAMES, b. 19 Jul 1993.

Endnotes

1.   Garrison Tawney found latest record...He was living in 1860 in Giles Co., VA census.
3.   Brandy Tawney Portillo E-Mail.

Genealogy Report of Thomas Hughes

Notes about Genealogy Report for Thomas Hughes

I have included the generations under Thomas Hughes because this is the most common line used for entry into the Daughters of the American Revolution. I have included down to the 4th generation under Thomas Hughes and the remaider after the 4th are included elsewhere in the book.

Generation No. 1

1. THOMAS[1] HUGHES was born Abt. 1740 in Virginia, and died 27 Jun 1794 in Hughes Fort, Augusta Co. VA (now Hugheston), Kanawha Co., VA. He married NELLIE FOSTER[1].

Notes for THOMAS HUGHES:
Thomas Hughes, Private. He served as private in Capt. Smith's Augusta Militia.
Reference: John H. Gwathancy's Historical Record of Virginia in Revolutionary War. Page 400.

More about THOMAS HUGHES:
Baptism: NAT 37631
Christened: Augusta Co, Virginia (now WV); resided during the Revolutionary War.

Children of THOMAS HUGHES and NELLIE FOSTER are:
	i.	ROBERT[2] HUGHES, b. 1760.
2.	ii.	EDWARD HUGHES, b. 1762, VA; d. 1839, Kanawha Co., VA (now WV).
	iii.	NANCY HUGHES, b. Bet. 1774 - 1776; m. JOHN CAMPBELL.
	iv.	THOMAS JR. HUGHES, b. 1778; m. NANCY KINCAID.

Generation No. 2

2. EDWARD[2] HUGHES *(THOMAS[1])* was born 1762 in VA, and died 1839 in Kanawha Co., VA (now WV). He married NANCY FOSTER 01 Oct 1793 in Greenbrier Co., VA. She was born in Greenbrier Co., VA, and died in Nicholas Co., VA.

Child of EDWARD HUGHES and NANCY FOSTER is:
| 3. | i. | CYNTHIA[3] HUGHES, b. 1806, Kanawha Co., VA (now WV); d. 1846, Kanawha Co, VA (now WV), at Cloyds Mt., Va. |

Generation No. 3

3. CYNTHIA[3] HUGHES *(EDWARD[2] HUGHES, THOMAS[1] HUGHES)* was born 1806 in Kanawha Co., VA (now WV), and died 1846 in Kanawha Co, VA (now WV), at Cloyds Mt., Va. She married JAMES P. GRAHAM 10 Mar 1827 in Kanawha County, VA. He was born 1805 in Ohio, and died 09 May 1864 in Kanawha Co., VA (now WV).

Child of CYNTHIA HUGHES and JAMES GRAHAM is:
| 4. | i. | WILLIAM EDWARD (CIVIL WAR)[4] GRAHAM, b. 1828, Nicholas Co., VA; d. 09 May 1864, Cloyds Mountain, Pulaski Co., VA. |

Generation No. 4

4. WILLIAM EDWARD (CIVIL WAR)[4] GRAHAM *(CYNTHIA[3] HUGHES, EDWARD HUGHES[2], THOMAS[1])* was born 1828 in Nicholas Co., VA, and died 09 May 1864 in Cloyds Mountain, Pulaski Co., VA. He married HULDAH DRAKE 05 Oct 1848 in Kanawha County, VA. She was born 01 Feb 1831 in Pike Co., KY, and died 10 Sep 1905 in Elana, Roane Co., WV.

Children of WILLIAM EDWARD GRAHAM and HULDAH DRAKE are:

5.   i.   WILLIAM ISAAC[5] GRAHAM, b. 27 May 1859, Meigs Co., OH; d. 17 Jun 1938, Left Hand, Roane Co., WV.
      ii.   M. R. GRAHAM[1].
     iii. JOHN M. GRAHAM, b. Jul 1850.
     iv. COLUMBUS GRAHAM, b. Abt 1853, Newton, WV. d. 29 Jan 1930
      v. SARAH ALCINDA GRAHAM, b. 11 Sep 1852, Pennsylvania.
     vi. EDWARD S. GRAHAM, b. 1862. d. Apr 1932
    vii. MARTHA GRAHAM.

Generation No. 5

5. WILLIAM ISAAC[5] GRAHAM *(WILLIAM EDWARD (CIVIL WAR)[4], CYNTHIA[3] HUGHES, EDWARD[2], THOMAS[1])* was born 27 May 1859 in Meigs Co., OH, and died 17 Jun 1938 in Left Hand, Roane Co., WV. He married MARY ELIZABETH SERGENT 22 Dec 1883 in Left Hand, Roane Co., WV, daughter of WILLIAM SERGENT and CYNTHIA VINEYARD. She was born 13 Dec 1861 in Left Hand, Roane Co., WV, and died 05 Dec 1922 in Left Hand, Roane Co., WV. Marriage by: D. W. Ross (recorded in poetry book of Graham's).

Children of WILLIAM ISAAC GRAHAM and MARY SERGENT are:

      i.   FLORA ALMON[6] GRAHAM, b. 15 Nov 1884, Left Hand, Roane Co., WV; d. 12 Oct 1960, Parkersburg, Wood Co., WV; m. AARON TAWNEY, 22 Aug 1903, Left Hand, Roane Co., WV; b. 27 Aug 1876, Roane Co., WV; d. 08 Oct 1966, Left Hand, Roane Co., WV. Cause of death: Cancer

           Notes for AARON TAWNEY – See page 40

           More about AARON TAWNEY:
           Burial: Tawney Family Cemetery, Newton, WV
           Cause of Death: Congestive Heart Failure

           Marriage Notes for FLORA GRAHAM and AARON TAWNEY:
           Married by Rev. Albright.

      ii.   WOODY GAY GRAHAM, b. 27 Jan 1887; d. 01 Sep 1964; married Lula Orpha Moore, 18 Mar 1911. She was born 1893 and died 1976.

     iii. CHARLEY GOFF GRAHAM, b. 11 Aug 1889; d. Unknown.

           Notes for CHARLEY GOFF GRAHAM:
           Served in World War I.

iv. FREDERIC LUTHER GRAHAM, b. 01 Jan 1893, Left Hand, Roane Co., WV; d. Sep 1985, Left Hand, Roane Co., WV; m. PEARLE FLORENCE GROVES, 31 Dec 1922; b. 03 Nov 1899; d. 05 Mar 1990, Spencer, WV.

Notes for FREDERIC LUTHER GRAHAM:
Served during World War I.

Fred married Pearl, and they lived in Fred's birthplace where they raised their family. Fred was 6-feet 6-inches tall, a kind and gentle man with a good sense of humor.   Both his mother and only daughter Marie were 6-feet tall.   It seems that the height in my own family was inherited from the Grahams.   William Isaac Graham is my great-grandfather. He was the son of William Edward Graham (known as "Eddie").   Eddie served in the Civil War.   He was my great-great-grandfather (or 2nd great-grandfather).

v. GRACIE ANN GRAHAM, b. 01 May 1896; d. 22 Oct 1937.
vi. ROMEO HENDERSON GRAHAM, b. 08 Aug 1893; d. Oct 1979.

Genealogy Report of James P. Graham

Generation No. 1

1. JAMES P.[1] GRAHAM was born 1805 in Ohio, and died in Kanawha Co., VA (now WV). He married CYNTHIA HUGHES 10 Mar 1827 in Kanawha County, VA, daughter of EDWARD HUGHES and NANCY FOSTER. She was born 1806 in Kanawha Co., VA (now WV), and died 1846 in Kanawha Co, VA (now WV), at Cloyds Mt., Va.

Child of JAMES GRAHAM and CYNTHIA HUGHES is:
2.   i.   WILLIAM EDWARD (CIVIL WAR)[2] GRAHAM, b. 1828, Nicholas Co., VA; d. 09 May 1864, Cloyds Mountain, Pulaski Co., VA.

Generation No. 2

2. WILLIAM EDWARD (CIVIL WAR)[2] GRAHAM *(JAMES P.[1])* was born 1828 in Nicholas Co., VA, and died 09 May 1864 in Cloyds Mountain, Pulaski Co., VA. He married HULDAH DRAKE 05 Oct 1848 in Kanawha County, VA. She was born 01 Feb 1831 in Pike Co., KY, and died 10 Sep 1905 in Elana, Roane Co., WV.

Children of WILLIAM GRAHAM and HULDAH DRAKE are:
3.   i.   WILLIAM ISAAC[3] GRAHAM, b. 27 May 1859, Meigs Co., OH; d. 17 Jun 1938, Left Hand, Roane Co., WV.
        ii.   M. R. GRAHAM[1].
      iii.   JOHN M. GRAHAM, b. Jul 1850.
      iv.   COLUMBUS GRAHAM, b. Abt 1853, Newton, WV. d. 29 Jan 1930
       v.   SARAH ALCINDA GRAHAM, b. 11 Sep 1852, Pennsylvania.
      vi.   EDWARD S. GRAHAM, b. 1862. d. Apr 1932
     vii.   MARTHA GRAHAM.

Generation No. 3

3. WILLIAM ISAAC[3] GRAHAM *(WILLIAM EDWARD (CIVIL WAR)[2], JAMES P.[1])* was born 27 May 1859 in Meigs Co., OH, and died 17 Jun 1938 in Left Hand, Roane Co., WV. He married MARY ELIZABETH SERGENT 22 Dec 1883 in Left Hand, Roane Co., WV, daughter of WILLIAM SERGENT and CYNTHIA VINEYARD. She was born 13 Dec 1861 in Left Hand, Roane Co., WV, and died 05 Dec 1922 in Left Hand, Roane Co., WV.

Children of WILLIAM GRAHAM and MARY SERGENT are:
4.   i.   FLORA ALMON[4] GRAHAM, b. 15 Nov 1884, Left Hand, Roane Co., WV; d. 12 Oct 1960, Parkersburg, Wood Co., WV.
5.   ii.   WOODY GAY GRAHAM, b. 27 Jan 1887; d. 01 Sep 1964.
      iii.   CHARLEY GOFF GRAHAM, b. 11 Aug 1889; d. Unknown.
6.   iv.   FREDERIC LUTHER GRAHAM, b. 01 Jan 1893, Left Hand, Roane Co., WV; d. Sep 1985, Left Hand, Roane Co., WV.
7.   v.   GRACIE ANN GRAHAM, b. 01 May 1896; d. 22 Oct 1937.
      vi.   ROMEO HENDERSON GRAHAM, b. 08 Aug 1893; d. Oct 1879 (SS Index)

Generation No. 4

4. FLORA ALMON[4] GRAHAM *(WILLIAM ISAAC[3], WILLIAM EDWARD (CIVIL WAR)[2], JAMES P.[1])* was born 15 Nov 1884 in Left Hand, Roane Co., WV, and died 12 Oct 1960 in Parkersburg, Wood Co., WV.   She married AARON TAWNEY 22 Aug 1903 in Left Hand, Roane Co., WV, son of GEORGE TAWNEY and MARY NOE.   He was born 27 Aug 1876 in Roane Co., WV, and died 08 Oct 1966 in Left Hand, Roane Co., WV.

Children of FLORA GRAHAM and AARON TAWNEY are:

- i.   WILLIAM "ERNEST"[5] TAWNEY, b. 01 Sep 1904, Left Hand, Roane Co., WV; d. 24 Mar 1966, Charleston, Kanawha Co., WV; m. MABEL VARNIE, 23 Aug 1934; d. 1997, Kanawha Co, WV.
- ii.   LULA "MABEL" TAWNEY, b. 23 Mar 1906, Left Hand, Roane Co., WV; d. 30 May 2003, Newton, Roane Co., WV; m. ERNEST FREAR ROGERS, 17 May 1926, Akron, OH; b. 15 Mar 1902, Newton, Roane Co., WV; d. 25 Apr 1993, Chas., Kanawha Co., WV.
- iii.   **RUBY "MAMIE" TAWNEY**, b. 24 Sep 1907, Left Hand, Roane Co., WV; m. IRVING CHARLES HAINES, 05 Oct 1953, Akron, Ohio; b. 1905; d. 1982.
- iv.   **CLEMENT LUTHER TAWNEY**, b. 19 Jul 1909, Left Hand, Roane Co., WV; d. 22 Oct 2009, Charleston, WV, Kanawha Co.; m. AVA OPAL NESTER, 10 Jul 1930, Gandeeville, WV; b. 15 May 1911, Left Hand, WV, Roane Co.; d. 2002.
- v.   FLORENCE MARY TAWNEY, b. 29 Jan 1911, Left Hand, Roane Co., WV; d. 06 Feb 2009, Charleston, WV, Kanawha Co.; m. JACK DALTON, 04 Jun 1945, Newcomerstown, Ohio; d. 02 Apr 1981, Parkersburg, WV.
- vi.   GEORGE "GARRISON" TAWNEY, b. 11 Nov 1913, Left Hand, Roane Co., WV; d. 14 Sep 2004, Looneyville, Roane Co., WV; m. FRIEDA E. VINEYARD, 24 Jun 1939, Green Co., KY; b. 07 Dec 1916, Looneyville, Roane Co., WV; d. 12 Aug 1999.
- vii.   CHAMP "CLARK" TAWNEY (KNOWN AS CLARK), b. 28 Nov 1915, Left Hand, Roane Co., WV; d. 27 Aug 2007; m. BEATRICE ALMEDA SUMMERS, 28 Jun 1944; b. 28 Jun 1917, Wallback, WV Clay County.
- viii.   HARRY MARSHALL TAWNEY, b. 24 Oct 1917, Left Hand, Roane Co., WV; d. 18 May 1920, Left Hand, Roane Co., WV.
- ix.   JARRETT ("BUZZ") TAWNEY, b. 02 Apr 1919, Left Hand, Roane Co., WV; m. FRANCIS ROBERTS, 13 Sep 1940.
- x.   ANNA ELIZABETH TAWNEY, b. 11 Sep 1921, Left Hand,   Roane Co., WV; m. MICHAEL EDWARD DESPOSITO, 11 Aug 1945, Bakersfield, CA; b. 05 Mar 1921.
- xi.   DANIEL AARON TAWNEY, b. 04 Jun 1923, Left Hand,   Roane Co., WV; m. HAZEL MAXINE SHORT, 19 Jun 1943; b. 22 Apr 1923, 2008.

5. WOODY GAY[4] GRAHAM *(WILLIAM ISAAC[3], WILLIAM EDWARD (CIVIL WAR)[2], JAMES P.[1])* was born 21 Jan 1887 in Left Hand, Roane Co., WV, and died 1976 in Left Hand, Roane Co., WV.   He married Lula Orpha Moore, 18 Mar 1911. She was born 1893 and died 1976.

Children of WOODY GAY GRAHAM and LULA ORPHA MOORE are:

- i.   GEORGE[5] GRAHAM, b. 15 Aug 1911.
- ii.   ALFRED R. GRAHAM, b. 10 Nov 1912.
- iii.   REX GRAHAM, b. 29 Oct 1913 and died 04 Jan 1914.
- iv.   ALICE RUTH GRAHAM, b. 08 Aug 1915.
- v.   RALPH GRAHAM, b. 06 Apr 1970.
- vi.   DARRELL H. GRAHAM,   b. 1920 and died 21 May 1986.

    vii.   DORIS (HARDING) GRAHAM, b. 11 Oct 1921.
   viii.   MARY ELIZABETH GRAHAM, b. 04 Feb 1924.
    ix.   WOODY GAY GRAHAM, b. 10 May 1925.
     x.   GLEN EUGENE GRAHAM, b. 08 May 1929.
    xi.   RUBY ELLEN GRAHAM, b. 1919.

6. FREDERIC LUTHER[4] GRAHAM *(WILLIAM ISAAC[3], WILLIAM EDWARD (CIVIL WAR)[2], JAMES P.[1])* was born 01 Jan 1893 in Left Hand, Roane Co., WV, and died Sep 1985 in Left Hand, Roane Co., WV.   He married PEARLE FLORENCE GROVES 31 Dec 1922, daughter of ELLIS GROVES and EMZY GANDEE.   She was born 03 Nov 1899, and died 05 Mar 1990 in Spencer, WV.

Children of FREDERIC GRAHAM and PEARLE GROVES are:
     i.   NELL MARIE[5] GRAHAM, b. 14 Aug 1924; died 24 Jul 2002
    ii.   LUTHER EDWARD GRAHAM, b. 10 Dec 1927.
   iii.   WILLIAM BARNEY GRAHAM, b. 27 Sep 1929; died 01 Jan 2008.
   iv.   DELBERT RICHARD GRAHAM, b. 12 Apr 1935.

7. GRACIE ANN[4] GRAHAM *(WILLIAM ISAAC[3], WILLIAM EDWARD (CIVIL WAR)[2], JAMES P.[1])* was born 04 May 1896; died 22 Oct 1937. She married BILL RAMSEY.

Children of GRACIE ANN GRAHAM are:
     i.   LAVAUGHN[5] RAMSEY
    ii.   GRANVILLE RAMSEY

Genealogy Report of William Sergent

Generation No. 1

1. WILLIAM[1] SERGENT was born Bet. 1700 - 1710, and died 1768 in Orange Co., NC. He married SARAH LEE 1715.

Child of WILLIAM SERGENT and SARAH LEE is:
2.   i.   STEPHEN[2] SERGENT,   b. 1740; d. 1815, Orange Co., NC.

Generation No. 2

2. STEPHEN[2] SERGENT *(WILLIAM[1])* was born 1740, and died 1815 in Orange Co., NC. He married MARGARET GOLD.

Child of STEPHEN SERGENT and MARGARET GOLD is:
3.   i.   EPHRAIM[3] SERGENT, b. 1761; d. 1844.

Generation No. 3

3. EPHRAIM[3] SERGENT *(STEPHEN[2], WILLIAM[1])* was born 1761, and died 1844. He married ELIZABETH HODGE 1792.

Child of EPHRAIM SERGENT and ELIZABETH HODGE is:
4.   i.   DAVID[4] SERGENT, b. 09 Oct 1798, VA; d. 05 Aug 1868.

Generation No. 4

4. DAVID[4] SERGENT *(EPHRAIM[3], STEPHEN[2], WILLIAM[1])* was born 09 Oct 1798 in VA, and died 05 Aug 1868. He married (1) REBECCA LOCKHART 1820.   He married (2) MARY COX 1860. She was born in PA.

Children of DAVID SERGENT and REBECCA LOCKHART are:
          i.   HENDERSON[5] SERGENT.
          ii.   JAMES MADISON SERGENT.
5.   iii. HENRY DAVID SERGENT, b. 20 Sep 1836; d. 17 Dec 1924.
          iv.   LEAH SINNETT SERGENT.
          v.   ELIZABETH KELLY SERGENT.
          vi.   SARAH COMBS SERGENT.

Child of DAVID SERGENT and MARY COX is:

6.   vii. WILLIAM HENDERSON[5] SERGENT, b. Abt. 1830.

Generation No. 5

5. HENRY DAVID[5] SERGENT *(DAVID[4], EPHRAIM[3], STEPHEN[2], WILLIAM[1])* was born 20 Sep 1836, and died 17 Dec 1924. He married FINETTA DRAKE 04 Nov 1858.

Children of HENRY SERGENT and FINETTA DRAKE are:
7.   i.   WILLIAM MADISON[6] SERGENT, b. 05 Feb 1879; d. 08 Jun 1972.
        ii.   FANNIE SERGENT.
       iii.   ROXIE SERGENT.
        iv.   SARAH SERGENT.
         v.   EMMA DAUGHERTY.
        vi.   MARY SMITH.

6. WILLIAM HENDERSON[5] SERGENT *(DAVID[4], EPHRAIM[3], STEPHEN[2], WILLIAM[1])* was born Abt. 1830. He married (1) CYNTHIA VINEYARD 1849 in Roane Co., WV. He married (2) MARY RUNNION 20 Nov 1896 in Roane Co., WV. He married (3) RUAMIE TAWNEY 21 Sep 1902.

Children of WILLIAM SERGENT and CYNTHIA VINEYARD are:
         i.   RACHEL A.[6] SERGENT, b. Abt. 1850, Kanawha Co., VA (now WV); m. CALLAHAN CALVIN CARPER, 02 Apr 1869, Roane Co., WV.
        ii.   DAVID SERGENT, b. Abt. 1851.
       iii.   PRESLEY SERGENT, b. Abt. 1852; m. P. D. LOONEY, 11 Nov 1878, Roane Co., WV, at residence of Pastor Albright..
        iv.   PETER SERGENT, b. Abt. 1854; m. MARGARET CROMWELL, 16 May 1892, Roane Co., WV; b. 1854.
         v.   EPHRAIM SERGENT, b. 1855, Jackson Co., WV; m. CAROLINE COOK, 08 Oct 1878, Roane Co., WV.
        vi.   CHARITY SERGENT, b. Abt. 1857.
8.   vii.   MARY ELIZABETH SERGENT, b. 13 Dec 1861, Left Hand, Roane Co., WV; d. 05 Dec 1922, Left Hand, Roane Co., WV.
       viii.   MALISSA SERGENT, b. Abt. 1866; m. C. C. COOK, 10 Feb 1883, Roane Co., WV.
        ix.   ANNIE SERGENT, b. Abt. 1869.

Generation No. 6

7. WILLIAM MADISON[6] SERGENT *(HENRY DAVID[5], DAVID[4], EPHRAIM[3], STEPHEN[2], WILLIAM[1])* was born 05 Feb 1879, and died 08 Jun 1972. He married MAUDE VINEYARD.

Children of WILLIAM MADISON SERGENTand MAUDE VINEYARD are:
9.   i.   HENRY CARL[7] SERGENT, b. 20 Aug 1903; d. 30 Jun 1972.
        ii.   WILLIAM DARYL SERGENT.
       iii.   RUBY DAUGHERTY.

8. MARY ELIZABETH[6] SERGENT *(WILLIAM HENDERSON[5], DAVID[4], EPHRAIM[3], STEPHEN[2], WILLIAM[1])* was born 13 Dec 1861 in Left Hand, Roane Co., WV, and died 05 Dec 1922 in Left Hand, Roane Co., WV. She married WILLIAM ISAAC GRAHAM 22 Dec 1883 in Left Hand, Roane Co., WV, son of WILLIAM GRAHAM and HULDAH DRAKE. He was born 27 May 1859 in Meigs Co., OH, and died 17 Jun 1938 in Left Hand, Roane Co., WV.

Notes for Mary Sergent: She died from a burst appendix while being transported by wagon to the doctor.

Children of MARY SERGENT and WILLIAM GRAHAM are:

10. i.   FLORA ALMON[7] GRAHAM, b. 15 Nov 1884, Left Hand, Roane Co., WV; d. 12 Oct 1960, Parkersburg, Wood Co., WV.
11. ii.   WOODY GAY GRAHAM, b. 27 Jan 1887; d. 01 Sep 1964.
     iii. CHARLEY GOFF GRAHAM, b. 11 Aug 1889; d. Unknown.
12. iv.   FREDERIC LUTHER GRAHAM, b. 01 Jan 1893, Left Hand, Roane Co., WV; d. Sep 1985, Left Hand, Roane Co., WV.
13. v.   GRACIE ANN GRAHAM, b. 01 May 1896; d. 22 Oct 1937.
     vi.   ROMEO HENDERSON GRAHAM, b. 08 Aug 1893; d. Oct 1879 (SS Index)

Generation No. 7

9. HENRY CARL[7] SERGENT (*WILLIAM MADISON[6], HENRY DAVID[5], DAVID[4], EPHRAIM[3], STEPHEN[2], WILLIAM[1]*) was born 20 Aug 1903, and died 30 Jun 1972. He married RUBY MILDRED DYE 10 Feb 1923.

Children of HENRY CARL SERGENT and RUBY DYE are:
     i.   RALPH EDWARD[8] SERGENT.
     ii.   ROBERT LAWRENCE SERGENT, b. 30 Oct 1930; m. GEORGIA PAULINE REED, 1953.

10. FLORA ALMON[7] GRAHAM (*MARY ELIZABETH[6] SERGENT, WILLIAM HENDERSON[5], DAVID[4], EPHRAIM[3], STEPHEN[2], WILLIAM[1]*) was born 15 Nov 1884 in Left Hand, Roane Co., WV, and died 12 Oct 1960 in Parkersburg, Wood Co., WV. She married AARON TAWNEY 22 Aug 1903 in Left Hand, Roane Co., WV, son of GEORGE TAWNEY and MARY NOE. He was born 27 Aug 1876 in Roane Co., WV, and died 08 Oct 1966 in Left Hand, Roane Co., WV.

Children of FLORA GRAHAM and AARON TAWNEY are:
     i.   WILLIAM "ERNEST"[8] TAWNEY, b. 01 Sep 1904, Left Hand, Roane Co., WV; d. 24 Mar 1966, Charleston, Kanawha Co., WV; m. MABEL VARNIE, 23 Aug 1934; d. 1997, Kanawha Co, WV.
     ii.   LULA "MABEL" TAWNEY, b. 23 Mar 1906, Left Hand, Roane Co., WV; d. 30 May 2003, Newton, Roane Co., WV; m. ERNEST FREAR ROGERS, 17 May 1926, Akron, OH; b. 15 Mar 1902, Newton, Roane Co., WV; d. 25 Apr 1993, Chas., Kanawha Co., WV.
     iii. RUBY "MAMIE" TAWNEY, b. 24 Sep 1907, Left Hand, Roane Co., WV; m. IRVING CHARLES HAINES, 05 Oct 1953, Akron, Ohio; b. 1905; d. 1982.
     iv.   CLEMENT LUTHER TAWNEY, b. 19 Jul 1909, Left Hand, Roane Co., WV; d. 22 Oct 2009, Charleston, WV, Kanawha Co.; m. AVA OPAL NESTER, 10 Jul 1930, Gandeeville, WV; b. 15 May 1911, Left Hand, WV, Roane Co.; d. 2002.
     v.   FLORENCE MARY TAWNEY, b. 29 Jan 1911, Left Hand, Roane Co., WV; d. 06 Feb 2009, Charleston, WV, Kanawha Co.; m. JACK DALTON, 04 Jun 1945, Newcomerstown, Ohio; d. 02 Apr 1981, Parkersburg, Wv.
     vi.   GEORGE "GARRISON" TAWNEY, b. 11 Nov 1913, Left Hand, Roane Co., WV; d. 14 Sep 2004, Looneyville, Roane Co., WV; m. FRIEDA E. VINEYARD, 24 Jun 1939, Green Co., KY; b. 07 Dec 1916, Looneyville, Roane Co., WV; d. 12 Aug 1999.

   vii. CHAMP "CLARK" TAWNEY, b. 28 Nov 1915, Left Hand, Roane Co., WV; d. 27 Aug 2007; m. BEATRICE ALMEDA SUMMERS, 28 Jun 1944; b. 28 Jun 1917, Wallback, WV Clay County.

   viii. HARRY MARSHALL TAWNEY, b. 24 Oct 1917, Left Hand, Roane Co., WV; d. 18 May 1920, Left Hand, Roane Co., WV.

   ix. JARRETT "BUZZ" TAWNEY, b. 02 Apr 1919, Left Hand, Roane Co., WV; m. FRANCIS ROBERTS, 13 Sep 1940.

   x. ANNA ELIZABETH TAWNEY, b. 11 Sep 1921, Left Hand, Roane Co., WV; m. MICHAEL EDWARD DESPOSITO, 11 Aug 1945, Bakersfield, CA; b. 05 Mar 1921.

   xi. DANIEL AARON TAWNEY, b. 04 Jun 1923, Left Hand, Roane Co., WV; m. HAZEL MAXINE SHORT, 19 Jun 1943; b. 22 Apr 1923, 2008.

11. WOODY GAY[7] GRAHAM *(WILLIAM ISAAC[3], WILLIAM EDWARD (CIVIL WAR)[2], JAMES P.[1])* was born 21 Jan 1887 in Left Hand, Roane Co., WV, and died 1976 in Left Hand, Roane Co., WV. He married Lula Orpha Moore, 18 Mar 1911. She was born 1893 and died 1976.

Children of WOODY GAY GRAHAM and LULA ORPHA MOORE are:
   i. GEORGE[8] GRAHAM, b. 15 Aug 1911.
   ii. ALFRED R. GRAHAM, b. 10 Nov 1912.
   iii. REX GRAHAM, b. 29 Oct 1913 and died 04 Jan 1914.
   iv. ALICE RUTH GRAHAM, b. 08 Aug 1915.
   v. RALPH GRAHAM, b. 06 Apr 1970.
   vi. DARRELL H. GRAHAM, b. 1920 and died 21 May 1986.
   vii. DORIS (HARDING) GRAHAM, b. 11 Oct 1921.
   viii. MARY ELIZABETH GRAHAM, b. 04 Feb 1924.
   ix. WOODY GAY GRAHAM, b. 10 May 1925.
   x. GLEN EUGENE GRAHAM, b. 08 May 1929.
   xi. RUBY ELLEN GRAHAM, b. 1919.

12. FREDERIC LUTHER[7] GRAHAM *(MARY ELIZABETH[6] SERGENT, WILLIAM HENDERSON[5], DAVID[4], EPHRAIM[3], STEPHEN[2], WILLIAM[1])* was born 01 Jan 1893 in Left Hand, Roane Co., WV, and died Sep 1985 in Left Hand, Roane Co., WV. He married PEARLE FLORENCE GROVES 31 Dec 1922, daughter of ELLIS GROVES and EMZY GANDEE. She was born 03 Nov 1899, and died 05 Mar 1990 in Spencer, WV.

Children of FREDERIC GRAHAM and PEARLE GROVES are:
   i. NELL MARIE[8] GRAHAM, b. 14 Aug 1924; died 24 Jul 2002
   ii. LUTHER EDWARD GRAHAM, b. 10 Dec 1927.
   iii. WILLIAM BARNEY GRAHAM, b. 27 Sep 1929; died 01 Jan 2008.
   iv. DELBERT RICHARD GRAHAM, b. 12 Apr 1935.

13. GRACIE ANN[7] GRAHAM *(WILLIAM ISAAC[3], WILLIAM EDWARD (CIVIL WAR)[2], JAMES P.[1])* was born 04 May 1896; died 22 Oct 1937. Husband's name not known.

Children of GRACIE ANN GRAHAM are:
   i. LAVAUGHN[8] RAMSEY
   ii. GRANVILLE RAMSEY

Genealogy Report of William ("Billy") Noe

Generation No. 1

1. WILLIAM "BILLY"[1] NOE was born 13 Feb 1809 in Patrick Co., VA. He married ELIZABETH (BETTY) KING, daughter of SAMUEL KING and M. SKIDMORE. She was born in Pike Co., KY.

Children of WILLIAM NOE and ELIZABETH KING are:
2.   i.   MARY[2] NOE, b. 19 Aug 1840, Kanawha Co., VA (now WV); d. 19 Dec 1929, Newton, Roane Co., WV.
3.   ii. SALLY NOE.
        iii. HIRAM NOE, b. 31 Jan 1838; d. 13 Sep 1920.

Generation No. 2

2. MARY[2] NOE *(WILLIAM "BILLY"[1])* was born 19 Aug 1840 in Kanawha Co., VA (now WV), and died 19 Dec 1929 in Newton, Roane Co., WV. She married GEORGE WILLIAM TAWNEY 14 Feb 1857, son of JOHN TAWNEY and LOVISA HARLESS. He was born 09 Apr 1827 in Giles Co., VA, and died 05 Oct 1894 in Newton, WV, Roane Co.

Children of MARY NOE and GEORGE TAWNEY are:
        i.   MIRANDA[3] TAWNEY, b. Abt. 1859, Elana, Roane Co., WV; d. 24 Jul 1863, Unknown.
4.   ii.   DANIEL W. "LINK" TAWNEY, b. 27 Mar 1861, Newton, WV; d. 1948.
5.   iii. SARA ELIZABETH "BETT" TAWNEY, b. 25 Feb 1863.
6.   iv.   DAVID JACKSON TAWNEY, b. 06 May 1865; d. 09 Sep 1951.
        v.   HIRAM J. "HIGH" TAWNEY, b. 16 Aug 1867; d. 15 Apr 1912.
        vi.   LOUVISA TAWNEY, b. 06 Oct 1869; d. 02 Sep 1877, Newton, WV, Roane Co.
        vii. GEORGE WILLIAM TAWNEY, b. 14 Apr 1872; d. 05 Oct 1894.
        viii. SAMUEL RICHARD TAWNEY, b. 07 Jun 1874; m. ELLEN HELMICK, 23 May 1897, Roane Co., WV.
7.   ix.   AARON TAWNEY, b. 27 Aug 1876, Roane Co., WV; d. 08 Oct 1966, Left Hand, Roane Co., WV.
        x.   JAMES M. TAWNEY, b. 21 Dec 1879; d. Nov 1901.
        xi.   FLORENCE TAWNEY, m. WILL SERGENT; d. St. Louis, MO.
        xii. CHRISTOPHER TAWNEY, b. Unknown; d. Unknown.
        xiii. WILLIAM H. TAWNEY, b. Unknown; d. Unknown.

3. SALLY[2] NOE *(WILLIAM ("BILLY")[1])* She married BILLY KNIGHT.

Child of SALLY NOE and William (Billy) KNIGHT is:
        i.   SMITH[3] KNIGHT, m. NORMA KEE.

Generation No. 3

4. DANIEL W. "LINK"³ TAWNEY *(MARY² NOE, WILLIAM "BILLY"¹)* was born 27 Mar 1861 in Newton, WV, and died 1948.   He married MARY MOLLY HALEY.   She was born 1869, and died 1963.

Children of DANIEL TAWNEYand MARY HALEY are:
-   i.   JOHN⁴, TAWNEY m. LOCIE GREATHOUSE.
-   ii.   JENNINGS TAWNEY, m. DONA HUNT.
-   iii. GEORGE TAWNEY, m. RUBY BOGGS.
-   iv.   WILSON TAWNEY, m. MARY MARKS.
-   v.   RHUAMI FLORENCE TAWNEY, m. HOMER WHITE.
-   vi.   EMMA TAWNEY, m. FLOYD DRAKE.
-   vii. MAGGIE TAWNEY, d. 05 Mar 1999; m. ALBERT L. SMITH; d. Newton, WV, Roane Co.
-   viii. STELLA TAWNEY, m. JOHN NIDA.

5. SARA ELIZABETH "BETT"³ TAWNEY *(MARY² NOE, WILLIAM ("BILLY")¹)* was born 25 Feb 1863.   She married PETE RADABAUGH.

Children of SARA TAWNEY and PETE RADABAUGH are:
-   i.   KISTA CHRISTENIA⁴ RADABAUGH, b. 01 Sep 1890, Spencer, WV; d. 20 Dec 1971, Salem, Arkansas; m. I. W. ARMSTEAD, 08 Dec 1915, Clendenin, WV.
-   ii.   OMAR RADABAUGH.
-   iii. HOWARD RADABAUGH.
-   iv.   MARY RADABAUGH.

6. DAVID JACKSON³ TAWNEY *(MARY² NOE, WILLIAM ("BILLY")¹)* was born 06 May 1865, and died 09 Sep 1951.   He married CYNTHIA MAY CARPER.

Children of DAVID TAWNEY and CYNTHIA CARPER are:
-   i.   ADD S.⁴ TAWNEY, b. 1892; d. Jan 1936.
-   ii.   CLARA TAWNEY
-   iii.   CLARK TAWNEY.
-   iv.   CORA TAWNEY.
-   v.   FLORENCE TAWNEY
-   vi.   GROVER TAWNEY, b. 1890; d. 1959.
-   vii.   GYPSY TAWNEY.
-   viii. HESTER TAWNEY.
-   ix.   JAMES HENRY TAWNEY.
-   x.   MARY TAWNEY
-   xi.   PRESTON J. TAWNEY, b. 02 Feb 1900; d. 12 Sep 1985; m. RETTA ROGERS.
-   xii.   W. CLAY TAWNEY.

7. AARON[3] TAWNEY *(MARY[2] NOE, WILLIAM[1])* was born 27 Aug 1876 in Roane Co., WV, and died 08 Oct 1966 in Left Hand, Roane Co., WV. He married FLORA ALMON GRAHAM 22 Aug 1903 in Left Hand, Roane Co., WV, daughter of WILLIAM GRAHAM and MARY SERGENT. She was born 15 Nov 1884 in Left Hand, Roane Co., WV, and died 12 Oct 1960 in Parkersburg, Wood Co., WV.

Children of AARON TAWNEY and FLORA GRAHAM are:

  i.   WILLIAM "ERNEST"[4] TAWNEY, b. 01 Sep 1904, Left Hand, Roane Co., WV; d. 24 Mar 1966, Charleston, Kanawha Co., WV; m. MABEL VARNIE, 23 Aug 1934; d. 1997, Kanawha Co, WV.

  ii. LULA "MABEL" TAWNEY, b. 23 Mar 1906, Left Hand, Roane Co., WV; d. 30 May 2003, Newton, Roane Co., WV; m. ERNEST FREAR ROGERS, 17 May 1926, Akron, OH; b. 15 Mar 1902, Newton, Roane Co., WV; d. 25 Apr 1993, Chas., Kanawha Co., WV.

  iii. RUBY "MAMIE" TAWNEY, b. 24 Sep 1907, Left Hand, Roane Co., WV; m. IRVING CHARLES HAINES, 05 Oct 1953, Akron, Ohio; b. 1905; d. 1982.

  iv. CLEMENT LUTHER TAWNEY, b. 19 Jul 1909, Left Hand, Roane Co., WV; d. 22 Oct 2009, Charleston, WV, Kanawha Co.; m. AVA OPAL NESTER, 10 Jul 1930, Gandeeville, WV; b. 15 May 1911, Left Hand, WV, Roane Co.; d. 2002.

  v.   FLORENCE MARY TAWNEY, b. 29 Jan 1911, Left Hand, Roane Co., WV; d. 06 Feb 2009, Charleston, WV, Kanawha Co.; m. JACK DALTON, 04 Jun 1945, Newcomerstown, Ohio; d. 02 Apr 1981, Parkersburg, Wv.

  vi. GEORGE "GARRISON" TAWNEY, b. 11 Nov 1913, Left Hand, Roane Co., WV; d. 14 Sep 2004, Looneyville, Roane Co., WV; m. FRIEDA E. VINEYARD, 24 Jun 1939, Green Co., KY; b. 07 Dec 1916, Looneyville, Roane Co., WV; d. 12 Aug 1999.

  vii. CHAMP "CLARK" TAWNEY (KNOWN AS CLARK), b. 28 Nov 1915, Left Hand, Roane Co., WV; d. 27 Aug 2007; m. BEATRICE ALMEDA SUMMERS, 28 Jun 1944; b. 28 Jun 1917, Wallback, WV Clay County.

  viii. HARRY MARSHALL TAWNEY, b. 24 Oct 1917, Left Hand, Roane Co., WV; d. 18 May 1920, Left Hand, Roane Co., WV.

  ix. JARRETT "BUZZ" TAWNEY, b. 02 Apr 1919, Left Hand, Roane Co., WV; m. FRANCIS ROBERTS, 13 Sep 1940.

  x.   ANNA ELIZABETH TAWNEY, b. 11 Sep 1921, Left Hand, Roane Co., WV; m. MICHAEL EDWARD DESPOSITO, 11 Aug 1945, Bakersfield, CA; b. 05 Mar 1921.

  xi. DANIEL AARON TAWNEY, b. 04 Jun 1923, Left Hand, Roane Co., WV; m. HAZEL MAXINE SHORT, 19 Jun 1943; b. 22 Apr 1923, 2008.

Genealogy Report of Levi Moore

Generation No. 1

1. LEVI[1] MOORE was born in Wales.   He married SUSANNAH CRIST.

Child of LEVI MOORE and SUSANNAH CRIST is:
2.   i.   SARAH SALLY[2] MOORE, b. Edray, Pocahontas Co., VA.

Generation No. 2

2. SARAH SALLY[2] MOORE *(LEVI[1])* was born in Edray, Pocahontas Co., VA.   She married JOHN (SR.) SMITH 01 Jan 1794 in Bath Co., VA.   He was born in Ireland.

Notes for JOHN (SR.) SMITH:
He came through Pennsylvania when he emigrated from Ireland.

Children of SARAH MOORE and JOHN SMITH are:
              i.   ANDREW[3] SMITH.
3.   ii.   JOHN JR. SMITH, b. 19 Mar 1815; d. 22 Aug 1862.
            iii.   ELIZABETH (1) SMITH.
             iv.   ANN SMITH.
              v.   REBECCA SMITH.
4.   vi.   SARAH ELIZABETH "SALLY" SMITH, b. Abt. 1805, Stony Creek, Pocahontas Co., VA;
                   d. Nicholas Co., WV.
            vii.   MARTHA SMITH.

Generation No. 3

3. JOHN JR.[3] SMITH *(SARAH SALLY[2] MOORE, LEVI[1])* was born 19 Mar 1815, and died 22 Aug 1862.   He married FRANCES ("FANNIE") COCHRAN 12 Nov 1835, daughter of JOHN COCHRAN and ELIZABETH JAMES.   She was born 15 Jul 1814, and died 20 Apr 1895.

Notes for JOHN JR. SMITH:
John and Frances Smith came to Roane Co. in 1843 and settled on Blown Timber Run, east of Newton. John Smith, Jr. served with his two sons, William Y and Newton, in the Union Army. Newton went to Kansas in 1869 and homesteaded a tract of land near Chanute, Kansas.

Children of JOHN SMITHand FRANCES COCHRAN are:
              i.   WILLIAM YOUNG[4] SMITH, b. 15 Dec 1840, Pocahontas Co., VA; d. 31 Jul 1925; m. (1)
                   MELISSA JARRETT; d. 1868; m. (2) JULIA ANN (COX) WILSON, 01 Sep 1870, Roane
                   Co., WV; b. 16 Mar 1839, Lewis Co., VA; d. 05 Mar 1929, Uler, WV, Roane Co.

              Notes for WILLIAM YOUNG SMITH:
              William Y. Smith served 3 years in the Union Army, Quarter Master, re-enlisted in Co. B. 4th
              West Virginia Reg. Cavalry. He attained the rank of Sergeant in the Cavalry. He served ten
              years as school trustee; one term in the WV Legislature from Roane Co.

  ii. MARGARET SMITH, b. 1838; d. 1868.
  iii. MARY SMITH, b. 1844; d. 1922.
  iv. LECTA SMITH, b. 02 Feb 1848, Kanawha Co., WV; d. 12 Mar 1937, Roane Co., WV; m. WILLIAM CAREY KEEN, 08 Dec 1877, Roane Co., WV; b. 30 Aug 1854, Kanawha Co., WV; d. 25 Jun 1938.
  v. LYDIA SMITH, b. 1853; d. 1927.
  vi. ELIZABETH SMITH, b. 1856; d. 1929.
  vii. NEWTON SMITH, b. 1842; d. 1925.
  viii. MARTHA SMITH, b. 1847; d. 1889.
  ix. JOSEPH NELSON SMITH, b. 1854; d. 1944.
  x. FRANKLIN SMITH, b. 1858; d. 1861.
  xi. JAMES JOHN JR SMITH, b. 25 Oct 1836, Pocahontas Co., VA (now WV); d. 1915; m. EMMA ROGERS, 06 Dec 1860, Clay Co., WV; b. 29 Apr 1846; d. 22 Apr 1890, Roane Co., WV.
  xii. DAVID D. SMITH.

4. SARAH ELIZABETH "SALLY"³ SMITH *(SARAH SALLY² MOORE, LEVI¹)* was born Abt. 1805 in Stony Creek, Pocahontas Co., VA, and died in Nicholas Co., WV. She married ROBERT JAHU RODGERS 14 May 1835 in Pocahontas Co., VA (now WV), son of UNKNOWN RODGERS. He was born Bet. 1805 - 1816 in Nicholas Co., Virginia, and died in Newton, WV, Roane Co.

Notes for ROBERT JAHU RODGERS:
Ernest Rogers always told us that his Grandfather Robert Rodgers was a Confederate Scout. William George Rogers (son of Robert Rodgers) recalled to Ernest that he remembered troops arriving and Robert leaving with them on a horse and would tell them something such as "I'll be back" or "I'll see you." Ernest always told that Robert's full name was Robert Jahu Rodgers and he was called by "Bobby," the name on his headstone in the family cemetery.

Both the 1850 Census in Nicholas Co., VA   (now WV) has him listed as just Robert Rodgers and his wife listed as just Sarah Rogers.

Kermit Rogers told that William Rogers came to the Blown Timber area with his parents and they moved into the Clay Smith hollow off the Blown Timber Road, Newton, WV. William Rogers was 12 at the time, 1861. They came to this area with other relatives (the Smiths).

Marriage Notes for SARAH SMITH and ROBERT RODGERS:
Married by Rev. E. A. Nicholson, page 84, Roane Co. Marriage Index. William George Rogers told his son, Ernest, that he came to the Roane Co. area when he was twelve years old. His parents settled in the Clay Hollow off the Blown Timber Road. William George bought the Rogers farm and a deed is recorded in the Roane County Records, Spencer, WV.

Children of SARAH SMITH and ROBERT RODGERS are:
  i.   JOHN HERSEY[4] ROGERS, b. Abt. 1838, VA.

       Notes for JOHN HERSEY ROGERS:
       He died when ambushed serving in the Civil War in Webster County.

  ii. ELIZABETH ROGERS, b. Abt. 1836.

       Notes for ELIZABETH ROGERS:
       Elizabeth is buried on the Russell Hensley property on Blown Timber, near Newton, at the
       top of a hill. William George Rogers told Mabel Rogers that Elizabeth was buried by a pine
       tree to mark the spot. I believe that Kermit Rogers remembers this story about where she
       was buried and our Mother Mabel talked about it several times to her children. There are
       now markers there.

  iii. SARAH ROGERS, b. Abt. 1837.
  iv. JULIE A. ROGERS, b. Abt. 1846.
  v.   WILLIAM GEORGE ROGERS, b. 03 Oct 1848, Webster Co., Virginia; d. 06 Feb 1937,
       Newton, Roane Co., WV; m. CAROLINE DIXIE MCQUAIN, 09 Oct 1884, Roane Co.,
       WV; b. 05 Dec 1860, Clay Co., WV; d. 17 Mar 1921, Newton, WV, Roane Co.

       Notes for WILLIAM GEORGE ROGERS:
       William George Rogers told his son Ernest that he came to the Roane Co. area when he was
       twelve years old. His parents settled in the Clay hollow off Blown Timber Road. William
       George Rogers bought the Rogers farm and a deed is recorded in the Roane Co. Records.

       Marriage Notes for WILLIAM ROGERS and CAROLINE MCQUAIN:
       Marriage License of Wm. G. Rogers and Caroline McQuain.   Married in bride's residence,
       by E. A. Nicholson, minister of the N.P. (or M.P.) Church).   Bride was 23 and born in Clay
       Co., WV.   Groom born in Webster Co., VA. (Roane Co. Records, Marriage Index, page 84).

  vi. JAMES H. ROGERS, b. Abt. 1852, Kanawha Co., VA; m. ANNIE SCHOOLCRAFT, 04
       Oct 1896.

       Notes for JAMES H. ROGERS:
       It is noted Ernest Rogers said that James Rogers moved to Oklahoma and they never heard
       from him again. It is thought that he died of pneumonia after going West. It is said that he
       had two sons.

Genealogy Report of John (Sr.) Smith

Generation No. 1

1. JOHN (SR.)[1] SMITH was born in Ireland. He married SARAH SALLY MOORE 01 Jan 1794 in Bath Co., VA, daughter of LEVI MOORE and SUSANNAH CRIST. She was born in Edray, Pocahontas Co., VA.

Children of JOHN SMITH and SARAH MOORE are:

        i.   ANDREW[2] SMITH.
2.   ii.   JOHN JR. SMITH, b. 19 Mar 1815; d. 22 Aug 1862.
      iii.   ELIZABETH (1) SMITH.
      iv.   ANN SMITH.
       v.   REBECCA SMITH.
3.   vi.   SARAH ELIZABETH "SALLY" SMITH, b. Abt. 1805, Stony Creek, Pocahontas Co., VA; d. Nicholas Co., WV.
      vii.   MARTHA SMITH.

Generation No. 2

2. JOHN JR.[2] SMITH *(JOHN (SR.)[1])* was born 19 Mar 1815, and died 22 Aug 1862. He married FRANCES ("FANNIE") COCHRAN 12 Nov 1835, daughter of JOHN COCHRAN and ELIZABETH JAMES. She was born 15 Jul 1814, and died 20 Apr 1895.

Children of JOHN SMITH and FRANCES COCHRAN are:
4.   i.   WILLIAM YOUNG[3] SMITH, b. 15 Dec 1840, Pocahontas Co., VA; d. 31 Jul 1925.
      ii.   MARGARET SMITH, b. 1838; d. 1868.
     iii.   MARY SMITH, b. 1844; d. 1922.
5.   iv.   LECTA SMITH, b. 02 Feb 1848, Kanawha Co., WV; d. 12 Mar 1937, Roane Co., WV.
      v.   LYDIA SMITH, b. 1853; d. 1927.
     vi.   ELIZABETH SMITH, b. 1856; d. 1929.
    vii.   NEWTON SMITH, b. 1842; d. 1925.
   viii.   MARTHA SMITH, b. 1847; d. 1889.
     ix.   JOSEPH NELSON SMITH, b. 1854; d. 1944.
      x.   FRANKLIN SMITH, b. 1858; d. 1861.
6.   xi.   JAMES JOHN JR SMITH, b. 25 Oct 1836, Pocahontas Co., VA (now WV); d. 1915.
     xii.   DAVID D. SMITH.

3. SARAH ELIZABETH "SALLY"[2] SMITH *(JOHN (SR.)[1])* was born Abt. 1805 in Stony Creek, Pocahontas Co., VA, and died in Nicholas Co., WV. She married ROBERT JAHU RODGERS 14 May 1835 in Pocahontas Co., VA (now WV), son of UNKNOWN RODGERS. He was born Bet. 1805 - 1816 in Nicholas Co., Virginia, and died in Newton, WV, Roane Co.

Children of SARAH SMITH and ROBERT RODGERS are:
       i.   JOHN HERSEY[3] ROGERS, b. Abt. 1838, VA.
      ii.   ELIZABETH ROGERS, b. Abt. 1836.
     iii.   SARAH ROGERS, b. Abt. 1837.
     iv.   JULIE A. ROGERS, b. Abt. 1846.

7. v. WILLIAM GEORGE ROGERS, b. 03 Oct 1848, Webster Co., Virginia; d. 06 Feb 1937, Newton, Roane Co., West Virginia.
   vi. JAMES H. ROGERS, b. Abt. 1852, Kanawha Co., VA; m. ANNIE SCHOOLCRAFT, 04 Oct 1896.

Generation No. 3

4. WILLIAM YOUNG³ SMITH *(JOHN JR.², JOHN (SR.)¹)* was born 15 Dec 1840 in Pocahontas Co., VA, and died 31 Jul 1925.   He married (1) MELISSA JARRETT .   She died 1868.   He married (2) JULIA ANN (COX) WILSON 01 Sep 1870 in Roane Co., WV, daughter of ISAAC COX and MARY KNISELY. She was born 16 Mar 1839 in Lewis Co., VA, and died 05 Mar 1929 in Uler, WV, Roane Co.

Children of WILLIAM SMITH and MELISSA JARRETT are:
   i. ALICE D.⁴ SMITH, b. 1866; m. MCCLELLAN HART.
   ii. BUENA A. SMITH, b. 1868; d. 1868.

Children of WILLIAM SMITH and JULIA WILSON are:
8. iii. JOHN (OF BLOWN TIMBER)⁴ SMITH, b. 1871.
9. iv. CARRIE SMITH.
10. v. THOMAS FREDERICK SMITH, b. 07 Dec 1881, Roane Co.; d. 22 Apr 1950, Uler, WV.
   vi. FLOYD SMITH.

5. LECTA³ SMITH *(JOHN JR.², JOHN (SR.)¹)* was born 02 Feb 1848 in Kanawha Co., WV, and died 12 Mar 1937 in Roane Co., WV.   She married WILLIAM CAREY KEEN 08 Dec 1877 in Roane Co., WV. He was born 30 Aug 1854 in Kanawha Co., WV, and died 25 Jun 1938.

Child of LECTA SMITH and WILLIAM KEEN is:
11. i. WESLEY FRANKLIN⁴ KEEN, b. 23 Jan 1881, Roane Co., WV; d. 16 Jul 1957, Washington Co., OH.

6. JAMES JOHN JR³ SMITH *(JOHN JR.², JOHN (SR.)¹)* was born 25 Oct 1836 in Pocahontas Co., VA (now WV), and died 1915.   He met EMMA ROGERS 06 Dec 1860 in Clay Co., WV, daughter of LEVI ROGERS and NAOMA SKIDMORE.   She was born 29 Apr 1846, and died 22 Apr 1890 in Roane Co., WV.

Children of JAMES SMITH and EMMA ROGERS are:
12. i. GEORGE BROOKS⁴ SMITH, b. 1862.
   ii. NEWTON JASPER SMITH.
   iii. HANNAH VIRGINIA SMITH, b. 1866.
   iv. FREDERICK SMITH, b. 1868.
   v. JULIA SMITH, b. 1869.
   vi. ANNA SUSAN SMITH, b. 1871.
   vii. JAMES CARY SMITH, b. 1873; d. 1875.
   viii. CHARLES L. SMITH, b. 1876.
   ix. FLORA GALE SMITH, b. 1878.
   x. IDA SMITH, b. 1879; d. 1879.
   xi. JAMES CLAY SMITH, b. 1880.
13. xii. WILLIAM HUNTER SMITH, b. 14 Jul 1882; d. 01 Apr 1951.

xiii.   JACOB BLAINE SMITH.
xiv.   IRA D. SMITH.
xv.   EMMA SMITH.

7.   WILLIAM GEORGE[3] ROGERS *(SARAH ELIZABETH "SALLY"[2] SMITH, JOHN (SR.)[1])* was born 03 Oct 1848 in Webster Co., Virginia, and died 06 Feb 1937 in Newton, Roane Co., West Virginia. He married CAROLINE DIXIE MCQUAIN 09 Oct 1884 in Roane Co., WV, daughter of THOMAS MCQUAIN and CAROLINE SUMMERS.   She was born 05 Dec 1860 in Clay Co., WV, and died 17 Mar 1921 in Newton, WV, Roane Co.

Children of WILLIAM ROGERS and CAROLINE MCQUAIN are:
14.   i.   CORA BELLE[4] ROGERS, b. 10 Jan 1882, Virginia; d. Unknown.
15.   ii.   ALICE BLANCHE ROGERS, b. 23 Aug 1885, Roane Co.,   WV; d. 1964.
16.   iii.   NEWTON PAUL ROGERS, b. 02 Nov 1886, Roane Co., WV; d. 19 Jan 1919.
17.   iv.   SARA ELIZABETH ROGERS, b. 19 Feb 1892, Roane Co.,   WV; d. 25 Jan 1962.
18.   v.   LUCY JONE ROGERS, b. 19 Sep 1894, Roane Co.,   WV; d. 19 Sep 1981, Springdale, (Fayette Co.) WV.
            vi.   WILLIAM CHARLES ROGERS, b. 22 Aug 1896, Roane Co., WV; d. 04 Sep 1933, Roane Co., WV.
19.   vii.   JAHU CLARK ROGERS, b. 12 Aug 1899, Newton, WV, Roane Co.; d. Abt. Oct 1961, Newton, WV, Roane Co.
20.   viii.   ERNEST FREAR ROGERS, b. 15 Mar 1902, Newton, Roane Co., WV; d. 25 Apr 1993, Charleston, Kanawha Co., WV.

Generation No. 4

8.   JOHN (of BLOWN TIMBER)[4] SMITH *(WILLIAM YOUNG[3], JOHN JR.[2], JOHN (SR.)[1])* was born in 1871.   He married BERTHA.

Children of JOHN SMITH and BERTHA are:
21.   i.   ALBERT L.[5] SMITH, d. Newton, WV, Roane Co.
           ii.   JIM SMITH, m. GENEVA ROGERS.
          iii.   LUCY SMITH.
           iv.   LAURA SMITH.
            v.   LONA SMITH.
           vi.   ROSA SMITH.
          vii.   GLADYS SMITH.
         viii.   MARGARETTE SMITH.
22.   ix.   GLEN SMITH.

9.   CARRIE[4] SMITH *(WILLIAM YOUNG[3], JOHN JR.[2], JOHN (SR.)[1])*

Child of CARRIE SMITH is:
            i.   LIONEL[5] SMITH.

10.   THOMAS FREDERICK[4] SMITH   *(WILLIAM YOUNG[3], JOHN JR.[2], JOHN (SR.)[1])* was born 07 Dec 1881 in Roane Co., and died 22 Apr 1950 in Uler, WV.   He married DEBORAH JARVIS, daughter of JOSIAH JARVIS and ELIZA ARNOLD.   She was born 25 Apr 1878 in Calhoun Co., WV, and died 08

Mar 1952 in Akron, OH, Summit Co.

Child of THOMAS SMITH and DEBORAH JARVIS is:

23. i. KENNETH[5] SMITH, b. 28 Jun 1911, Uler, WV; d. 28 Oct 1974, Uler, WV.

11. WESLEY FRANKLIN[4] KEEN *(LECTA[3] SMITH, JOHN JR.[2], JOHN (SR.)[1])* was born 23 Jan 1881 in Roane Co., WV, and died 16 Jul 1957 in Washington Co., OH.   He married LILLIAN ELLIS.   She was born 14 Jul 1880 in Roane Co., WV, and died 09 Feb 1968 in Portage Co., OH.

Child of WESLEY KEEN and LILLIAN ELLIS is:

24. i. LOISE[5] KEEN, b. 09 Dec 1907, Newton, Roane Co.,   WV.

12. GEORGE BROOKS[4] SMITH *(JAMES JOHN JR[3], JOHN JR.[2], JOHN (SR.)[1])* was born 1862.

Children of GEORGE BROOKS SMITH are:

    i. GENEVA[5] SMITH.
    ii. MILDRED SMITH.
    iii. BROOKS SMITH.
    iv. RAYMOND SMITH.

13. WILLIAM HUNTER[4] SMITH *(JAMES JOHN JR[3], JOHN JR.[2], JOHN (SR.)[1])* was born 14 Jul 1882, and died 01 Apr 1951.   He married (1) ROXIE GAY SIEBERT, daughter of JOHN SIEBERT and SUSAN EAKLE.   She was born 1897, and died 1920.   He married (2) MATTIE JANE HALL 14 May 1924, daughter of CALVIN HALL and MATILDA MCCOY.   She was born 1889, and died 1985.

Children of WILLIAM SMITH and ROXIE SIEBERT are:

    i. ROSE MARY[5] SMITH.
25. ii. HUNTER PAUL SMITH, b. 14 Aug 1920, Elana, WV.

Child of WILLIAM SMITH and MATTIE HALL is:

26. iii. JOHN CALVIN[5] SMITH, b. 04 Sep 1930.

14. CORA BELLE[4] ROGERS *(WILLIAM GEORGE[3], SARAH ELIZABETH "SALLY"[2] SMITH, JOHN (SR.)[1])* was born 10 Jan 1882 in Virginia, and died Unknown.   She married WILLIAM ROBERT SMITH.   He was born Abt. 1882, and died Unknown.

Children of CORA ROGERS and WILLIAM SMITH are:

    i. JASON CARL[5] SMITH, d. Apr 1993; m. IRENE.
    ii. KERMIT SMITH, d. Unknown.
27. iii. ELIZABETH SMITH, d. Unknown.
28. iv. VIRGINIA BELLE SMITH, b. 24 Jul 1916, Fayette Co., WV.

15. ALICE BLANCHE[4] ROGERS *(WILLIAM GEORGE[3], SARAH ELIZABETH "SALLY"[2] SMITH, JO (SR.)[1])* was born 23 Aug 1885 in Roane Co.,   WV, and died 1964.   She married ROBERT SAMUEL HENSLEY; divorced.

Children of ALICE ROGERS and ROBERT HENSLEY are:

29.	i.	CLIFFORD[5] HENSLEY, d. Unknown.
30.	ii.	RAYMOND HENSLEY, b. 27 Jun 1923.
31.	iii.	OLIVER HENSLEY, b. 03 Oct 1926.
	iv.	PIERCE HENSLEY, b. 03 Aug 1929.
32.	v.	HENSLEY, b. Abt. 1907.
	vi.	DIXIE FAY HENSLEY-DOUGLAS, m. ERWIN DOUGLAS.
33.	vii.	OPAL HENSLEY-DOUGLAS.
	viii.	CHLOISE HENSLEY.
	ix.	GLADYS HENSLEY, b. Abt. 03 Oct.
	x.	VIRGINIA HENSLEY-WILLIAMS, m. UNKNOWN WILLIAMS.
	xi.	WILLARD HENSLEY.

16. NEWTON PAUL[4] ROGERS *(WILLIAM GEORGE[3], SARAH ELIZABETH "SALLY"[2] SMITH, JOHN (SR.)[1])* was born 02 Nov 1886 in Roane Co., WV, and died 19 Jan 1919.   He married HESTER BOGGS 21 Nov 1913 in Roane Co., WV.   She was born 1892, death date unknown.

Children of NEWTON ROGERS and HESTER BOGGS are:
34.	i.	SNOWDEN[5] ROGERS, death date unknown.
	ii.	LESLIE ROGERS, death date unknown.
	iii.	IMOGENE ROGERS, m. UNKNOWN GESBRECHT.

17. SARA ELIZABETH[4] ROGERS *(WILLIAM GEORGE[3], SARAH ELIZABETH "SALLY"[2] SMITH, JO (SR.)[1])* was born 19 Feb 1892 in Roane Co.,   WV, and died 25 Jan 1962.   She married EDWARD HUGHES.   Death date unknown.

Child of SARA ROGERS and EDWARD HUGHES is:
35.	i.	ROLAND KESTER[5] ROGERS, b. Abt. 1911; death date unknown.

18. LUCY JONE[4] ROGERS *(WILLIAM GEORGE[3], SARAH ELIZABETH "SALLY"[2] SMITH, JOHN (SR.)[1])* was born 19 Sep 1894 in Roane Co.,   WV, and died 19 Sep 1981 in Springdale, WV, Fayette Co.   She married WILLIAM LOWRY.   He was born 22 Oct 1892, and died 26 Feb 1968 in Springdale, WV, Fayette Co.

Children of LUCY ROGERS and WILLIAM LOWRY are:
	i.	IMOGENE[5] LOWRY.
	ii.	ADELEE LOWRY.
	iii.	JOAN LOWRY.
	iv.	ROGER LOWRY.

19. JAHU CLARK[4] ROGERS *(WILLIAM GEORGE[3], SARAH ELIZABETH "SALLY"[2] JOHN SMITH, JOHN (SR.)[1])* was born 12 Aug 1899 in Newton, WV, Roane Co., and died Abt. Oct 1961 in Newton, WV, Roane Co. He married ORVA HICKS. She was born 17 Feb 1903, and died 27 Apr 1992 in Spencer, WV, Roane Co.

Children of JAHU ROGERS and ORVA HICKS are:

36.	i.	HENRY HERSEY[5] ROGERS, b. 24 Apr 1924, Newton, WV; d. Sep 1993, Spencer, WV, Roane Co.
37.	ii.	WILLIAM GAIL ROGERS, b. Abt. 1926, Newton, WV, Roane Co.
	iii.	JAMES FORREST ROGERS, b. 22 Jan 1930, Newton, WV, Roane Co.; d. 06 Dec 1993, Spencer, WV, Roane Co.; m. NORA MARCEL MULLIN, 10 Apr 1962.
38.	iv.	LAWANDA ROGERS, b. 03 Aug 1932, Newton, WV, Roane Co.

20. ERNEST FREAR[4] ROGERS *(WILLIAM GEORGE[3], SARAH ELIZABETH "SALLY"[2] SMITH, JOHN (SR.)[1])* was born 15 Mar 1902 in Newton, Roane Co., WV, and died 25 Apr 1993 in Chas., Kanawha Co., WV. He met LULA "MABEL" TAWNEY 17 May 1926 in Akron, OH, daughter of AARON TAWNEY and FLORA GRAHAM. She was born 23 Mar 1906 in Left Hand, Roane Co., WV, and died 30 May 2003 in Newton, Roane Co., WV.

Children of ERNEST ROGERS and LULA TAWNEY are:

39.	i.	MARDELL "ADELEE"[5] ROGERS, b. 06 Feb 1927, Akron, Summit Co., OH.
40.	ii.	ROBERT "KEITH" ROGERS, b. 05 Aug 1928, Akron, Summit Co. OH; d. 23 Dec 2008, Gallipolis, OH.
41.	iii.	ALMA "DELORES" ROGERS, b. 23 Mar 1930, Akron, Summit Co., OH.
42.	iv.	KERMIT ADOLPH ROGERS, b. 23 Feb 1934, Newton, Roane Co., WV.
43.	v.	DORMA KATHERN ROGERS, b. 24 Mar 1936, Newton, Roane Co., WV.
44.	vi.	CARROLL AARON ROGERS, b. 10 May 1938, Newton, Roane Co., WV.
45.	vii.	CHARLOTTE ANN ROGERS, b. 16 Mar 1940, Newton, Roane Co., WV.
46.	viii.	PATRICIA RONDELL ROGERS, b. 05 Feb 1943, Newton, Roane Co., WV.
47.	ix.	BARBARA CAROLINE "Bobbie" ROGERS, b. 07 Sep 1945, Charleston, Kanawha Co., WV; d. 05 Jun 2005, Riverside, Riverside Co., CA.

Generation No. 5

21. ALBERT L.[5] SMITH *(JOHN (OF BLOWN TIMBER)[4], WILLIAM YOUNG[3], JOHN JR.[2], JOHN (SR.)[1])* died in Newton, WV, Roane Co. He married MAGGIE TAWNEY, daughter of DANIEL TAWNEY and MARY HALEY. She died 05 Mar 1999.

Children of ALBERT SMITH and MAGGIE TAWNEY are:

i.	CAROLYN SUE[6] SMITH.
ii.	MARY LOU SMITH.
iii.	JO ANN SMITH, m. BILL GOODWIN.
iv.	ROBERT L. SMITH, d. 13 Feb 2001.
v.	JOHN B. SMITH.

22. GLEN[5] SMITH *(JOHN (OF BLOWN TIMBER)[4], WILLIAM YOUNG[3], JOHN JR.[2], JOHN (SR.)[1])* He married GLADYS NESTER.

Children of GLEN SMITH and GLADYS NESTER are:
   i. COY[6] SMITH, b. Abt. 1935; d. 08 Jul 1994.
   ii. WILLIAM SMITH, b. Abt. 1937; death date unknown.
   iii. GLEN SMITH, b. Abt. 1943.
   iv. LORETTA SMITH, b. Abt. 1940; death date unknown.
   v. THERESA SMITH.
   vi. DIANE SMITH.
   vii. DEBRA SMITH.
   viii. DAVID SMITH.
   ix. GARY SMITH.
   x. BARBARA JEAN SMITH.
   xi. REBECCA SMITH.

23. KENNETH[5] SMITH *(THOMAS FREDERICK[4], WILLIAM YOUNG[3], JOHN JR.[2], JOHN (SR.)[1])* was born 28 Jun 1911 in Uler, WV, and died 28 Oct 1974 in Uler, WV. He married ELVA ETHEL DRAKE, daughter of CHARLES DRAKE and LUCY KEEN. She was born 18 Jan 1915 in Newton, WV, Roane Co., and died 07 Feb 1972 in Uler, WV.

Children of KENNETH SMITH and ELVA DRAKE are:
   i. MERLE LOUISE[6] SMITH, b. 08 Jul 1946, Uler, WV, Roane Co.; m. EARLIE GENE KING, 01 Feb 1964, Linden, WV; b. 31 May 1943, Left Hand, WV.
   ii. ELOISE SMITH.
   iii. WANDA SMITH.
   iv. TOM SMITH.

24. LOISE[5] KEEN *(WESLEY FRANKLIN[4], LECTA[3] SMITH, JOHN JR.[2], JOHN (SR.)[1])* was born 09 Dec 1907 in Newton, Roane Co., WV. She married EZRA SPENCER 23 Nov 1927 in Parkersburg, Wood Co., WV. He was born 10 Oct 1896 in Calhoun Co., WV, and died 23 Oct 1953 in Washington Co., OH.

Child of LOISE KEEN and EZRA SPENCER is:
   i. CLIFFORD DUANE[6] SPENCER, b. 16 Jan 1934, Smithfield, Roane Co., WV; m. ADITH ALEEN COPEN, 24 Dec 1955, Vienna, Wood Co., WV; b. 15 Sep 1936, Wirt Co., WV.

25. HUNTER PAUL[5] SMITH *(WILLIAM HUNTER[4], JAMES JOHN JR[3], JOHN JR.[2], JOHN (SR.)[1])* was born 14 Aug 1920 in Elana, WV. He married VIRGINIA DAUGHTERY 01 Jan 1942, daughter of ROME DAUGHTERY and PEARL CALDWELL. She was born 19 May 1923 in Bomont, Clay Co, WV.

Children of HUNTER SMITH and VIRGINIA DAUGHTERY are:
   i. VIRGINIA GAY[6] SMITH, b. 1944; m. EDWARD HAMRIC, 07 Jul 1967.
   ii. HUNTER PAUL SMITH, b. 1952.
   iii. SCOTT ANDREW SMITH, b. 1957.
   iv. ERIC CHARLES SMITH, b. 1959.

26. JOHN CALVIN[5] SMITH *(WILLIAM HUNTER[4], JAMES JOHN JR[3], JOHN JR.[2], JOHN (SR.)[1])* was born 04 Sep 1930. He married MARY LOU CLENDENEN 16 May 1964, daughter of ROBERT CLENDENEN and ONA BRANCH. She was born 26 Dec 1935.

Children of JOHN SMITH and MARY CLENDENEN are:
    i.   DAVID HALL[6] SMITH, b. 29 Sep 1965.
    ii. ELLEN SUZANNE SMITH, b. 11 Dec 1967.

27. ELIZABETH[5] SMITH *(CORA BELLE[4] ROGERS, WILLIAM GEORGE[3], SARAH ELIZABETH "SALLY"[2] SMITH, JOHN, SR.[1])*; death date unknown.

Child of ELIZABETH SMITH is:
    i.   LINDA CAMPBELL[6] SMITH.

28. VIRGINIA BELLE[5] SMITH *(CORA BELLE[4] ROGERS, WILLIAM GEORGE[3], SARAH ELIZABETH "SALLY"[2] SMITH, JOHN (SR.)[1])* was born 24 Jul 1916 in Fayette Co., WV. She married BASIL ESTES COOK 17 Aug 1934 in Logan Co., WV, son of JAMES COOK and JOSEPHINE BALLARD. He was born in Logan Co., WV, and died 23 Dec 2004.

Children of VIRGINIA SMITH and BASIL COOK are:
    i.   WILLIAM ROBERT[6] COOK, b. 14 Aug 1935, Logan Co., WV; m. PATTI L. STANLEY, 31 Jul 1956, Raleigh, NC.
    ii. BETTY JEAN COOK, b. 02 Oct 1937; m. EARL LANCTOT. Betty is deceased.

29. CLIFFORD[5] HENSLEY *(ALICE BLANCHE[4] ROGERS, WILLIAM GEORGE[3], SARAH ELIZABETH "SALLY"[2] SMITH, JOHN, SR.[1])*; death date unknown. He married ANN UNKNOWN.

Child of CLIFFORD HENSLEY and ANN UNKNOWN is:
    i.   DANNY[6] HENSLEY.

30. RAYMOND[5] HENSLEY *(ALICE BLANCHE[4] ROGERS, WILLIAM GEORGE[3], SARAH ELIZABETH "SALLY"[2] SMITH, JOHN (SR.)[1])* was born 27 Jun 1923. He married RUTH MAE UNKNOWN.

Children of RAYMOND HENSLEY and RUTH UNKNOWN are:
    i.   JUDY MAE[6] HENSLEY, Adopted child; m. DENNIS LEROY ACHESON.
    ii. JOANNE MARIE HENSLEY, m. TERRY CONLEY.

31. OLIVER[5] HENSLEY *(ALICE BLANCHE[4] ROGERS, WILLIAM GEORGE[3], SARAH ELIZABETH "SALLY"[2] SMITH, JOHN SR[1])* was born 03 Oct 1926. He married LELA MAE UNKNOWN.

Child of OLIVER HENSLEY and LELA UNKNOWN is:
    i.   SUSAN[6] HENSLEY.

32. HENSLEY[5] *(ALICE BLANCHE[4] ROGERS, WILLIAM GEORGE[3], SARAH ELIZABETH "SALLY"[2] SMITH, JOHN (SR.)[1])* was born Abt. 1907.   She married EARL RAFFERTY.

Children of (First name not known) HENSLEY and EARL RAFFERTY are:
 i.   DALE[6] RAFFERTY.
 ii. GEORGE RAFFERTY.
 iii. ALMA RAFFERTY-MCFADDEN, m. UNKNOWN MCFADDEN.
 iv. ALICE RAFFERTY-BUSH, m. UNKNOWN BUSH.
 v.   MARY RAFFERTY-LAKE, m. UNKNOWN LAKE.

33. OPAL[5] HENSLEY-DOUGLAS *(ALICE BLANCHE[4] ROGERS, WILLIAM GEORGE[3], SARAH ELIZABET "SALLY"[2] SMITH, JO SR)[1])*   She married VERNON DOUGLAS.

Child of OPAL HENSLEY-DOUGLAS and VERNON DOUGLAS is:
 i.   HERBIE[6] DOUGLAS.

34. SNOWDEN[5] ROGERS *(NEWTON PAUL[4], WILLIAM GEORGE[3], SARAH ELIZABETH "SALLY"[2] SMITH, JO SR[1])*. He married HATTIE UNKNOWN.   He is deceased.

Children of SNOWDEN ROGERS and HATTIE UNKNOWN are:
 i.   WADE[6] ROGERS, birthdate unknown.
 ii. JAMES ROGERS, b. Abt. 1943.

35. ROLAND KESTER[5] ROGERS *(SARA ELIZABETH[4], WILLIAM GEORGE[3], SARAH ELIZABETH "SALLY"[2] SMITH, JOHN (SR.)[1])* was born Abt. 1911. He is deceased.

Children of ROLAND KESTER ROGERS are:
 i.   MARY BETH[6] ROGERS.
 ii. LINDA ROGERS.
 iii. KAREN ROGERS.

36. HENRY HERSEY[5] ROGERS *(JAHU CLARK[4], WILLIAM GEORGE[3], SARAH ELIZABETH "SALLY"[2] SMITH, JOHN (SR.)[1])* was born 24 Apr 1924 in Newton, WV, and died Sep 1993 in Spencer, WV, Roane Co.   He married MARY BELLE JUSTICE.

Children of HENRY ROGERS and MARY JUSTICE are:
 i.   MARILYN ANN[6] ROGERS, b. 22 May 1957.
 ii. INFANT ROGERS, b. 14 May 1959; d. Abt. 14 May 1959.

37. WILLIAM GAIL[5] ROGERS *(JAHU CLARK[4], WILLIAM GEORGE[3], SARAH ELIZABETH "SALLY"[2] SMITH, JOHN (SR.)[1])* was born Abt. 1926 in Newton, WV, Roane Co.

Children of WILLIAM GAIL ROGERS are:
 i.   THOMAS[6] ROGERS, b. 25 Jan 1946; d. Unknown.
 ii. LARRY ROGERS, b. 31 Jan 1946; d. Unknown.

38. LAWANDA[5] ROGERS *(JAHU CLARK[4], WILLIAM GEORGE[3], SARAH ELIZABETH "SALLY"[2] SMITH, JOHN (SR.)[1])* was born 03 Aug 1932 in Newton, WV, Roane Co. She married PAUL HICKLE. He was born Abt. 1932, and died in Maryland.

Children of LAWANDA ROGERS and PAUL HICKLE are:
- i. BRYAN[6] HICKLE.
- ii. BOY HICKLE.

39. MARDELL ADELEE[5] ROGERS *(ERNEST FREAR[4], WILLIAM GEORGE[3], SARAH ELIZABETH "SALLY"[2] SMITH, JOHN (SR.)[1])* was born 06 Feb 1927 in Akron, Summit Co., OH. She met (1) GILBERT MCCLELLAND in Akron, OH, Summit Co., son of STANLEY MCCLELLAND and MARY DAVIS. He was born 23 Jun 1924, and died 20 May 1983. She married (2) HAROLD EDGAR JOHNSON 23 Oct 1951 in Las Vegas, NV, son of ADOLPH JOHNSON and ERNA BROOE. He was born 08 Sep 1924.

Child of MARDELL ROGERS and GILBERT MCCLELLAND is:
- i. MARY GILLETTE "SHELLEY"[6] MCCLELLAND, b. 04 Jan 1945, Akron, OH; m. (1) MARVIN JOHNSON; d. Jun 2005; m. (2) BILL PANETTI; Divorced.

Children of MARDELL ROGERS and HAROLD JOHNSON are:
- ii. DALE ADOLPH[6] JOHNSON, b. 10 May 1953, Santa Monica, Los Angeles Co., CA; m. (1) SANDRA ANN BROWN, 18 Sep 1976, Orange Co., CA; b. 10 Jul 1954; m. (2) DEBORAH JEAN MANUEL, 17 Mar 2002, Las Vegas, NV; b. 02 Jul 1950, Tallahassee, Florida.
- iii. TERESA ANN JOHNSON, b. 29 Jan 1955, Torrance, Los Angeles Co., CA; m. KEITH CRAIG JACKSON, 10 Apr 1982, Castro Valley, Alameda Co., CA; b. 08 May 1955.

40. ROBERT KEITH[5] ROGERS *(ERNEST FREAR[4], WILLIAM GEORGE[3], SARAH ELIZABETH "SALLY"[2] SMITH, JOHN (SR.)[1])* was born 05 Aug 1928 in Akron, Summit Co. OH, and died 23 Dec 2008 in Gallipolis, OH[1]. He married (1) MARIE PARSONS 28 Jul 1950 in Cartlettsburg, Boyd Co., KY, daughter of WILLIAM PARSONS and ICIE BISHOP. She was born 9 Jun 1929. He married (2) NANCY LARCH, daughter of WESLEY ADAMS LARCH.

Children of ROBERT ROGERS and MARIE PARSONS are:
- i. INA GALE[6] ROGERS, b. 11 Mar 1949, Charleston, Kanawha Co., WV; m. JAMES KERMIT CARPER; b. 05 Jun 1941.
- ii. MICHAEL KEITH ROGERS, b. 03 Oct 1950, Charleston, Kanawha Co., WV; m. DEBORAH LEIGH LEGG; b. 16 Aug 1955.
- iii. RHONDA DIANE ROGERS, b. 10 May 1952, Charleston, Kanawha Co., WV; m. RANDALL KEITH CARPER, 27 Mar 1971, Roane Co., WV; b. 21 Feb 1950.
- iv. DEBRA JEANNE ROGERS, b. 08 Aug 1953, Charleston, Kanawha Co., WV; m. (1) COLLEN WALDECK; m. (2) IVAN LOGSDON, 19 Aug 1974, Parsons, WV, Tucker Co.
- v. TIMOTHY LEE ROGERS, b. 31 Jul 1954, Charleston, Kanawha Co., WV; m. KAREN TAWNEY; b. 23 Oct 1954.
- vi. ROBERT RANDALL ROGERS, b. 10 Aug 1955, Charleston, Kanawha Co., WV; m. LORAINE MARIE BARONE.

41. ALMA "DELORES" [5] ROGERS *(ERNEST FREAR[4], WILLIAM GEORGE[3], SARAH ELIZABETH "SALLY"[2] SMITH, JOHN (SR.)[1])* was born 23 Mar 1930 in Akron, Summit Co., OH. She married (2) DELBERT DENNIS 22 Jan 1958. He was born 22 Dec 1928 in Lake Lynn, PA.

Child of DELORES ROGERS is:

    i.   ANDREW JACKSON[6] ROGERS, b. 27 Mar 1952, Culver City, CA; m. (1) CAROLINE CARTE; b. 23 Jun 1950, d. 03 Aug 2006, Clay, WV; m. (2) TAMMY LYNN GRAY, 05 Sep 1997, Clifton Forge, VA; b. 27 Jun 1973, Jackson Co. Hospital, Ripley, WV.

Child of DELORES ROGERS and DELBERT DENNIS is:

    ii. SHEILA MARLENE[6] DENNIS, b. 26 Mar 1959, Union Town, PA; m. ROGER ALAN BREMER, 08 Mar 1980, Fort Wayne, IN; b. 10 Sep 1960.

42. KERMIT ADOLPH[5] ROGERS *(ERNEST FREAR[4], WILLIAM GEORGE[3], SARAH ELIZABETH "SALLY"[2] SMITH, JOHN (SR.)[1])* was born 23 Feb 1934 in Newton, Roane Co., WV. He married BETTY LOU BIRD 12 Aug 1954, daughter of ALFRED BIRD and ORA TRUMAN. She was born 29 Oct 1936 in Clay Co., WV.

Children of KERMIT ROGERS and BETTY BIRD are:

    i.   KATHLEEN ANN[6] ROGERS, b. 14 Jan 1955, Charleston, WV, Kanawha Co.; m. (1) KARL HOLCOMB; m. (2) ROGER SMITH, 01 Dec 1973, b 31Jan 1947.

    ii. CHERYL LYNN ROGERS, b. 10 Mar 1956, Charleston, WV, Kanawha Co.; m. PAUL HOLCOMB, 22 Sep 1973; b. 16 Jun 1949, Indore, Clay Co., WV.

    iii. DAWN ARLENE ROGERS, b. 15 May 1960, Charleston, WV, Kanawha Co.; m. CHARLES RICHARD WILKINSON, Arnoldsburg, WV, Calhoun Co.; b. 26 Nov 1949.

43. DORMA KATHERN[5] ROGERS *(ERNEST FREAR[4], WILLIAM GEORGE[3], SARAH ELIZABETH "SALLY"[2] SMITH, JOHN (SR.)[1])* was born 24 Mar 1936 in Newton, Roane Co., WV. She married (1) JAMES HENRY BIRD Sep 1955, son of ALFRED BIRD and UNKNOWN SPOUSE. He was born 12 Jun 1933, and died May 1986. She married (2) JAMES DRAKE 22 Jul 1997 in Gatlinburg, Tennessee. He was born 02 Mar 1939.

Children of DORMA ROGERS and JAMES BIRD are:

    i.   JIMMY LEE[6] BIRD, b. 12 Jul 1956.

    ii. NENA MARIE BIRD, b. 11 Mar 1958, Charleston, WV, Kanawha Co.; m. RICKY GENE COPPOCK, 19 Jun 1976, Huntington, IN; b. 11 Sep 1957; d. 10 May 2000.

    iii. LISA CAROL BIRD, b. 30 Jun 1960; m. STEVE TACKETT, 03 Aug 1979; b. 17 Oct 1956.

    iv. ERNEST SCOTT BIRD, b. 16 Aug 1962, Huntington, IN; m. APRIL SHOEMAKER, 14 Nov 2008.

44. CARROLL AARON[5] ROGERS *(ERNEST FREAR[4], WILLIAM GEORGE[3], SARAH ELIZABETH "SALLY"[2] SMITH, JOHN (SR.)[1])* was born 10 May 1938 in Newton, Roane Co., WV. He married MARIA FELICIA GRECO 19 Nov 1960 in Morgantown, WV, daughter of FRANK GRECO and LOUISE NAPOLILLO. She was born 25 May 1941.

Children of CARROLL ROGERS and MARIA GRECO are:

    i.   MARC ROBERT[6] ROGERS, b. 05 May 1962, Morgantown, WV, Monongalia Co.; m. MELANIE BAKER, 19 Dec 1998, Wesley Methodist Church, High St., Morgantown, WV;

b. 01 May 1964, Honolulu, Hawaii.

    ii.   MICHELE LYNN ROGERS, b. 06 Apr 1964, Springfield, OH, Clark Co.; m. (1) MICHAEL TARRANTINI; m. (2) GREGORY WES MCDONALD, 20 Sep 1992, Morgantown, WV, Monongalia Co.; b. 22 Oct 1963.

    iii.   NATHAN ERIC ROGERS, b. 10 Jul 1970, Morgantown, WV, Monongalia Co.; m. VICKIE SUE DECARLO, 22 Jun 1996, Morgantown, WV, Monongalia Co.; b. 26 Jun 1970, Warren, OH, Trumbell Co.

45. CHARLOTTE ANN[5] ROGERS *(ERNEST FREAR[4], WILLIAM GEORGE[3], SARAH ELIZABETH "SALLY"[2] SMITH, JOHN (SR.)[1])* was born 16 Mar 1940 in Newton, Roane Co., WV. She married (1) DAVID ALEXANDER RICHMOND 22 Aug 1959 in Inglewood, LA Co., CA, son of JAMES RICHMOND and LOIS HEMING. He was born 02 Jun 1937 in Boston, Suffolk Co., Mass and died 03 Aug 2008. She married (2) DONALD JOHN OSTROM 30 Oct 1972 in Las Vegas, Clark Co., NV, son of RALPH OSTROM and ESTELLE DUDLEY. He was born 20 Mar 1939 in Oconomowoc, Waukesha Co., WI. She married (3) GUY LEROY DILNO 14 Dec 1980 in Plainwell, Allegan Co., MI, son of MILFORD DILNO and WILDA PHILLIPS. He was born 22 Aug 1946 in Kalamazoo, MI, Kalamazoo Co.

Children of CHARLOTTE ROGERS and DAVID RICHMOND are:

    i.   BRAD ALEXANDER[6] RICHMOND, b. 17 Sep 1960, Inglewood, Los Angeles Co., CA; m. (1) DAWN MARIE GAUTHIER, 30 Nov 1979, Otsego, Allegan Co., MI; b. 17 Jul 1961, Plainwell, Allegan Co., MI; m. (2) VICKIE LYNNE NICKELSON, 22 Aug 2008, Rockford, MI; b. 09 Jan 1962, Henipin County, Minneapolis, MN.

    ii.   KIMBERLY ANNE RICHMOND, b. 11 Nov 1963, Riverside, Riverside Co., CA; m. MICHAEL CHARLES HICKEY, 09 Apr 1982, Yucca Valley, CA; b. 26 May 1961, Pittsburgh, PA.

Child of CHARLOTTE ROGERS and DONALD OSTROM is:

    iii.   LANCE JOHN[6] OSTROM, b. 29 Feb 1972, Phoenix, Maricopa Co., AZ; m. LAUREL LEE LACOUR, 09 Sep 2001, Saline, MI; b. 14 Apr 1975.

46. PATRICIA RONDELL[5] ROGERS *(ERNEST FREAR[4], WILLIAM GEORGE[3], SARAH ELIZABETH "SALLY"[2] SMITH, JOHN (SR.)[1])* was born 05 Feb 1943 in Newton, Roane Co., WV. She married HOMER LEE CONLEY 11 Aug 1962 in Clover Ridge, Roane Co., WV, son of HOWARD CONLEY and LOCIE MILLER. He was born 14 Mar 1940 in Uler, Roane Co., WV.

Children of PATRICIA ROGERS and HOMER CONLEY are:

    i.   GREGORY LEE[6] CONLEY, b. 24 Jul 1963; m. PRISCILLA CATHERN NAYLOR, 24 Feb 1993, Newton, Roane Co., WV; b. 11 Nov 1965.

    ii.   MICHAEL GARRETT CONLEY, b. 22 Jan 1966; m. (1) SHANNA CLAUDINE PUGH, Jul 1988, March AFB, Riverside Co., CA; m. (2) JENNIFER REBECCA FRENCH, 30 Jun 1996; b. 14 Aug 1969, Grand Forks, ND; m. (3) SHIRLEY ANN BIRD, 19 May 2009, Newton, Roane Co., WV; b. 02 Jun 1952.

    iii.   STEPHEN WAYNE CONLEY, b. 28 Sep 1967; m. VERA ELLEN HIGHLANDER.

    iv.   STACY RONDELL CONLEY, b. 21 Sep 1972, Charleston, Kanawha Co., WV; m. AARON MICHAEL ROMANO, 30 May 1992, Newton, WV, Roane Co.; b. 07 Sep 1971.

47. BARBARA CAROLINE[5] ROGERS *(ERNEST FREAR[4], WILLIAM GEORGE[3], SARAH ELIZABETH "SALLY"[2] SMITH, JOHN (SR.)[1])* was born 07 Sep 1945 in Charleston, Kanawha Co., WV, and died 05 Jun 2005 in Riverside, Riverside Co., CA.   She married ROGER BEISTLE in Las Vegas, NV. He was born 25 Jul 1941 in Riverside Co., CA.

Children of BARBARA ROGERS and ROGER BEISTLE are:
  i.   GREGORY ALLEN[6] BEISTLE, b. 19 Jan 1966, Riverside, CA, Riverside Co.
  ii. THERESE MARIE BEISTLE, b. 19 Jun 1968, Riverside, CA, Riverside Co.; m. KEVIN PEDERSON.

Genealogy Report of Johann George Somers

Generation No. 1

1. JOHANN GEORGE[1] SOMERS was born Abt. 1713 in Germany, and died Bef. 26 Apr 1787 in Shenandoah Co, VA. He married MARIA MARGARETHA METZ.

More about JOHANN GEORGE SOMERS:
Burial: Bef. 26 Apr 1787, Tom's Brook, Shenandoah Co, VA

Child of JOHANN SOMERS and MARIA METZ is:
2.   i.   JOHAN PAUL[2] SUMMERS, b. 28 Jul 1748, Douglas Township, Montgomery Co, PA.

Generation No. 2

2. JOHAN PAUL[2] SUMMERS *(JOHANN GEORGE[1] SOMERS)* was born 28 Jul 1748 in Douglas Township, Montgomery Co, PA. He married NANCY ELIZABETH "BETSY" HULL, daughter of PETER HULL. She was born Abt. 1748.

More about JOHAN PAUL SUMMERS:
Burial: Enon, Nicholas Co, VA

Child of JOHAN SUMMERS and NANCY HULL is:
3.   i.   JACOB JAHU[3] SUMMERS, b. Abt. 1776.

Generation No. 3

3. JACOB JAHU[3] SUMMERS *(JOHAN PAUL[2], JOHANN GEORGE[1] SOMERS)* was born Abt. 1776. He married (1) JOHANNA DAVIS. She was born Abt. 1778, and died Abt. 1837. He married (2) MARIAN COZUALD.

Children of JACOB SUMMERS and JOHANNA DAVIS are:
4.   i.   CAROLINE[4] SUMMERS, b. 15 Jun 1830, Nicholas Co., VA; d. 15 Jul 1914, Newton, Roane Co., WV.
        ii.   WILLIAM HARRISON SUMMERS.
      iii.   PAUL SUMMERS (TWIN TO JAHU).
      iv.   MARGARET "PAGA" SUMMERS, m. UNKNOWN PIERSON.
       v.   HENRIETTA SUMMERS, m. UNKNOWN NICHOLAS.
      vi.   JOHANNA SUMMERS, m. UNKNOWN NICHOLAS.
     vii.   SUSAN SUMMERS, m. UNKNOWN SHANNON.
    viii.   DELIA SUMMERS, m. UNKNOWN BAILES.
      ix.   PAULINE SUMMERS, m. UNKNOWN NICHOLAS.
       x.   SALLY SUMMERS, m. UNKNOWN SCHOONOVER.
      xi.   JAHU (TWIN TO PAUL) SUMMERS.

Children of JACOB SUMMERS and MARIAN COZUALD are:
- xii.   ANDREW JACKSON[4] SUMMERS.
- xiii.   DAVID CROCKETT SUMMERS, Wallback, WV, Clay Co.
- xiv.   THOMAS BENTON SUMMERS.
- xv.   GEORGE CLARKE SUMMERS.
- xvi.   LOIS SUMMERS, m. UNKNOWN BOGGS.
- xvii.   ALMIRA SUMMERS, m. CRUICKSHANK UNKNOWN.
- xviii.   AMERICA SUMMERS, m. UNKNOWN CRUICKSHANK.

Generation No. 4

4. CAROLINE[4] SUMMERS *(JACOB JAHU[3], JOHAN PAUL[2], JOHANN GEORGE[1] SOMERS)* was born 15 Jun 1830 in Nicholas Co., VA, and died 15 Jul 1914 in Newton, Roane Co., WV. She married (1) THOMAS MCQUAIN, SR. (CIVIL WAR) in VA, son of ALEXANDER MCQUAIN and ELIZABETH SCOTT. He was born 1821 in Gilmer Co., VA, at McQuain Farm, Big Cove Creek, and died 22 Jul 1864 in Ft. Delaware, NJ. She married (2) ALFRED M. ROGERS 22 Jun 1868, son of JOHN ROGERS and MALINDA WILSON. He was born 21 Jan 1823 in Roane Co, WV, and died 07 Aug 1879 in Roane Co, WV.

Notes for CAROLINE SUMMERS:
She is listed in Nicholas Co., in 1850 census. In later years, she lived at Rogers Fork, WV, with her sons Luke and Paul "Pat."

More about CAROLINE SUMMERS:
Cause of Death: Old age.

Notes for , SR. (CIVIL WAR):
He was in the Civil War, was captured and taken prisoner at Ft. Delaware, NJ. While in prison camp he came down with typhoid fever and died.   He is buried in Ft. Pinns National Cemetery, Salem, NJ. He was captured and died in Ft. Delaware, NJ. While Thomas McQuain was in New Jersey, he wrote McQuain relatives to go and get Caroline, that she was having a hard time.   They brought her to Gilmer Co., then to Roane to care for her. (Information from Garnette Yates).

In the summer of 2002, Charlotte Dilno, Guy Dilno and Mabel Tawney-Rogers visited John McQuain in Clendenin, WV. He had a copy of a letter written by Thomas McQuain was transcribed and displayed on a clothesline at a family reunion as follows:

Dated: the 12th of March 1864, Prison No. 3, Map 11, Camp Chase, Ohio.

Addressed to: Mrs. Caroline McQuain. Signed by Thomas McQuain

My Dear Wife,

It is with the greatest pleasure that I address you on the present occasion and am truly rejoiced to hear that you and the children are all in good health & safe landed in Gilmer Co. which is where you have always wanted to go ever since we were married.   I hope that you are satisfied with the exchange.   I think you can do better there than you could in Roane Co.   I am sorry that I can't be with you to assist along the rough road over which you have to pass. I am also aware that you have had a hard time to get along but you have been equal to the task and got along beyond my expectations.   I would therefore say to you to be in good heart and always remember that you alone lives in my affection as the only one on this earth that is of Woman Kind that has a place in my heart and you are always upper most in my thoughts.   And I always think of you as a true and devoted wife in whom I am willing to trust my most Secret Rights and I truly hope that we will soon meet again.   I shall avail myself of the first chance that offers itself to obtain my liberty so that I can get home.   Give my love to the children, tell them that I would be glad to see them to see how much they have grown.   I expect that I will go on exchange in a few days. If I am not sent off I will write you again.   You need not write to me until you hear from me again.

I will write to you as often as I can.   Do the best you can. If I am released from prison I will come home and try to assist you all I can.   I would like to know what is your chance to get provisions this summer.   Charles wrote that times was very hard in Gilmer.   I hope that you can get along well.   I have had my health very well since I have been a prisoner.   I am well treated considering I am a Rebel.   Give my respects to all of my brothers, their wives and children.

I remain your devoted husband.   Hoping that when this cruel war is over that we will meet again.

More about THOMAS MCQUAIN, SR. (CIVIL WAR):
Burial: Ft. Pinns Cemetery, Salem, NJ (source Garnette Yates)
Cause of Death: Typhoid fever.

Children of CAROLINE SUMMERS and THOMAS MCQUAIN are:
-   i.   CHARLIE⁵ MCQUAIN.

        Notes for CHARLIE MCQUAIN:
        He was a blacksmith and lived at Silver Maple, WV, Roane Co., WV.

-   ii. DUNCAN MCQUAIN.
-   iii. ELIE MCQUAIN.

        Notes for ELIE MCQUAIN:
        He disappeared when he was a young man, as told by Mabel Rogers.

5.   iv.   JOANNA MCQUAIN, b. 17 Aug 1847, Whitewater, Nicholas Co., VA; d. 22 Feb 1922, Roane Co., WV.
-       v.   ALEXANDER HAMILTON MCQUAIN, b. 1849.
6.   vi.   JOHN S. MCQUAIN, b. 1851, Nicholas Co., VA.
7.   vii. WILLIAM PITT MCQUAIN, b. 1854, VA.
8.   viii. THOMAS MARSHALL MCQUAIN, b. 24 Oct 1855, Nicholas Co., VA; d. 1928, Kanawha Co., WV.
-       ix.   ELIZABETH SCOTT MCQUAIN, b. 1859; m. MARSHALL GRENBERRY "GREEN" DRAKE, 19 Nov 1874.
9.   x.   CAROLINE DIXIE MCQUAIN, b. 05 Dec 1860, Clay Co., WV; d. 17 Mar 1921, Newton, WV, Roane Co.

Children of CAROLINE SUMMERS and ALFRED ROGERS are:
-   xi.   PAUL S.⁵ ROGERS, b. 08 Mar 1869; m. HANNAH A. HANSHAW, 12 Nov 1891.
-   xii. SILAS B. ROGERS, b. 09 Mar 1869; d. Feb 1876.
-   xiii. LUKE ROGERS, b. 25 Sep 1871.

        Notes for LUKE ROGERS:
        Luke was a Blacksmith at Silver Maple, WV, Roane Co. His mother, Caroline Summers-McQuain-Rogers, in later years, lived with he and his brother Paul at Silver Maple.

Generation No. 5

5. JOANNA⁵ MCQUAIN *(CAROLINE⁴ SUMMERS, JACOB JAHU³, JOHAN PAUL², JOHANN GEORGE¹ SOMERS)* was born 17 Aug 1847 in Whitewater, Nicholas Co., VA, and died 22 Feb 1922 in Roane Co., WV. She married JOHN WALLBACK ROGERS 06 Aug 1867 in Clay Co., WV, son of ELIJAH ROGERS and ELLEN SKIDMORE. He was born 29 May 1841, and died 25 Jul 1925 in Roane Co., WV.

Children of JOANNA MCQUAIN and JOHN ROGERS are:
-   i.   LON EARL⁶ ROGERS, b. 04 Oct 1868; d. 14 Nov 1954; m. (1) ELLIZABETH COOPMAN; m. (2) MINNIE YARRA.
-   ii. TYRE BENNETT ROGERS, b. 07 May 1870; d. 16 Mar 1933; m. (1) SARA SEARS; b. 5/12/1928; m. (2) EFFIE SMITH, 01 Mar 1896.

     iii.   FREDERICK ALFRED ROGERS, b. 23 Jan 1873; d. 22 Oct 1957; m. FLORA E. ROLLYSON, 06 Apr 1905.

     iv.   MAHALA CAROLINE ROGERS, b. 16 Feb 1876; d. 28 Jul 1939.

     v.   JAMES JOHN ROGERS, b. 05 Apr 1882; d. 19 Feb 1932; m. (1) NETTIE PHILLIPS; m. (2) EVELEEN BROWN, 11 Sep 1904.

     vi.   LILLIE ELLEN ROGERS, b. 12 Mar 1885; d. 21 May 1971; m. SILAS M. MOORE, 03 Feb 1903.

     vii.   WILLIAM PITT ROGERS, b. 29 Apr 1888; d. 01 Dec 1975; m. (1) FLORA COOK, 01 Jun 1919; m. (2) RUTH BOGGS-SNYDER, 09 Oct 1966.

10.   viii.   RETTA ROGERS.

11.   ix.   ESTER ELIZABETH ROGERS, b. 22 Jun 1880, Roane Co, WV; d. 09 Aug 1956, Clay Co, WV.

     x.   CLEMIN ROGERS.

6. JOHN S.[5] MCQUAIN *(CAROLINE[4] SUMMERS, JACOB JAHU[3], JOHAN PAUL[2], JOHANN GEORGE[1] SOMERS)* was born 1851 in Nicholas Co., VA.   He married NANCY GRIFFITH.

Notes for JOHN S. MCQUAIN:
Mabel Rogers gave me a photograph of the John S. McQuain and Nancy Griffith McQuain family. She said the other people in the photograph were their children. John S. McQuain is the father of Lewis McQuain, not in the photograph. John S. McQuain was referred to as "Uncle Jafe." The photograph is in the Rogers scrapbook. (This information obtained in 2000).

Children of JOHN MCQUAIN and NANCY GRIFFITH are:
     i.   LEWIS[6] MCQUAIN.
     ii.   ROBERT "BUB" MCQUAIN.
     iii.   THOMAS MCQUAIN.
     iv.   MARIAM "PUSS" MCQUAIN.
     v.   "BIRD" MCQUAIN.
     vi.   LULA MCQUAIN.
12.   vii.   GROVER CLEVELAND MCQUAIN.
     viii.   LAURA MCQUAIN.

7. WILLIAM PITT[5] MCQUAIN *(CAROLINE[4] SUMMERS, JACOB JAHU[3], JOHAN PAUL[2], JOHANN GEORGE[1] SOMERS)* was born 1854 in VA.

Child of WILLIAM PITT MCQUAIN is:
     i.   LOUIS[6] MCQUAIN.

8. THOMAS MARSHALL[5] MCQUAIN *(CAROLINE[4] SUMMERS, JACOB JAHU[3], JOHAN PAUL[2], JOHANN GEORGE[1] SOMERS)* was born 24 Oct 1855 in Nicholas Co., VA, and died 1928 in Kanawha Co., WV.   He married MAHALA ROSE ANN DRAKE 21 Mar 1878 in Roane Co., WV, daughter of CHARLES DRAKE and SARAH BISHOP.   She was born 11 May 1855.

Notes for MAHALA ROSE ANN DRAKE:
Mahala Drake is related to the Grahams.

Children of THOMAS MCQUAIN and MAHALA DRAKE are:

13.   i.   LEWIS WETZEL[6] MCQUAIN, b. 01 Feb 1879, Roane Co. Census, WV; d. 10 Oct 1957, Cotton, WV, Roane Co.

          ii.   CHARLES MCQUAIN, b. Mar 1886; d. Nov 1950; m. LOLA BOWYER.

Notes for CHARLES MCQUAIN:
Called Sugar Bowl McQuain, because he was hit on his head by a waitress.

9.   CAROLINE DIXIE[5] MCQUAIN *(CAROLINE[4] SUMMERS, JACOB JAHU[3], JOHAN PAUL[2], JOHANN GEORGE[1] SOMERS)* was born 05 Dec 1860 in Clay Co., WV, and died 17 Mar 1921 in Newton, WV, Roane Co. She married WILLIAM GEORGE ROGERS 09 Oct 1884 in Roane Co., WV, son of ROBERT RODGERS and SARAH SMITH. He was born 03 Oct 1848 in Webster Co., Virginia, and died 06 Feb 1937 in Newton, Roane Co., West Virginia.

Notes for WILLIAM GEORGE ROGERS – See page 91

Children of CAROLINE MCQUAIN and WILLIAM ROGERS are:

14.   i.   CORA BELLE[6] ROGERS, b. 10 Jan 1882, Virginia; d. Unknown.
15.   ii.   ALICE BLANCHE ROGERS, b. 23 Aug 1885, Roane Co., WV; d. 1964.
16.   iii. NEWTON PAUL ROGERS, b. 02 Nov 1886, Roane Co., WV; d. 19 Jan 1919.
17.   iv. SARA ELIZABETH ROGERS, b. 19 Feb 1892, Roane Co., WV; d. 25 Jan 1962.
18.   v.   LUCY JONE ROGERS, b. 19 Sep 1894, Roane Co., WV; d. 19 Sep 1981, Springdale, WV, Fayette Co.

          vi. WILLIAM CHARLES ROGERS, b. 22 Aug 1896, Roane Co., WV; d. 04 Sep 1933, Roane Co., WV.

Notes for WILLIAM CHARLES ROGERS: Roane Co. WV Death Index, page 143.

More about WILLIAM CHARLES ROGERS: Cause of Death: He was shot at Blown Timber.

19.   vii. JAHU CLARK ROGERS, b. 12 Aug 1899, Newton, WV, Roane Co.; d. Abt. Oct 1961, Newton, WV, Roane Co.
20.   viii. ERNEST FREAR ROGERS, b. 15 Mar 1902, Newton, Roane Co., WV; d. 25 Apr 1993, Chas., Kanawha Co., WV.

Generation No. 6

10.   RETTA[6] ROGERS *(JOANNA[5] MCQUAIN, CAROLINE[4] SUMMERS, JACOB JAHU SUMMERS[3], JOHAN PAUL[2], JOHANN GEORGE[1] SOMERS)* She married PRESTON J. TAWNEY, son of DAVID TAWNEYfor and CYNTHIA CARPER. He was born 02 Feb 1900, and died 12 Sep 1985.

Children of RETTA ROGERS and PRESTON TAWNEY are:
          i.   JACK L.[7] TAWNEY.
          ii.   JUANITA FLORENCE TAWNEY, b. Abt. 1926, Newton, Roane Co., West Virginia.
          iii. FRANKLIN D. TAWNEY.
          iv. WANDA LEE TAWNEY, m. UNKNOWN SIMMONS.

11. ESTER ELIZABETH[6] ROGERS *(JOANNA[5] MCQUAIN, CAROLINE[4] SUMMERS, JACOB JAHU[3], JOHAN PAUL[2], JOHANN GEORGE[1] SOMERS)* was born 22 Jun 1880 in Roane Co, WV, and died 09 Aug 1956 in Clay Co, WV. She married EARLY BRAGG 18 May 1899 in Clay Co, WV, son of MORGAN BRAGG and SARAH FRAME. He was born 08 Dec 1871 in Clay Co, WV, and died 17 Sep 1949 in Clay Co, WV.

Children of ESTER ROGERS and EARLY BRAGG are:
 i. ORVILLE[7] BRAGG, b. 08 Mar 1900, Clay Co, WV; d. Unknown.
 ii. PEARL BRAGG, b. 13 Dec 1902, Clay Co, WV; d. Unknown; m. FRANK WHITE, 29 Apr 1924; d. Unknown.
 iii. JODA "JOANNA" BRAGG, b. 14 Jun 1905, Clay Co, WV; d. Unknown; m. LANTE SEARS, 12 Apr 1927; d. Unknown.
 iv. WARDEN EMMETT BRAGG, b. 17 Aug 1907, Clay Co, WV; m. BESSIE JONES, 24 Dec 1930.
 v. JOHN MORGAN BRAGG, b. 19 Feb 1910, Clay Co, WV; d. 18 Dec 1944, WV.
 vi. ELSIE HATTIE BRAGG, b. 19 Jan 1912, Clay Co, WV; m. DAYTON WILMOTH, 06 Oct 1933.
 vii. THOMAS WOODEROW BRAGG, b. 02 Aug 1914, Clay Co, WV; m. JUANITA WILMOTH, 07 Nov 1940.
 viii. WILLIAM IRA BRAGG, b. 31 Mar 1917, Clay Co, WV; m. HALCIE MATHENY, 31 Jul 1949.
 ix. ALICE MARION BRAGG, b. 15 Dec 1919, Clay Co, WV; m. JAMES HEFLIN, 05 Dec 1938.
 x. DOROTHY ANNABELLE BRAGG, b. 28 Sep 1923, Clay Co, WV; m. CHARLES CARROLL, 14 Jun 1946.
 xi. CLIFTON STERRETT BRAGG, b. 15 Dec 1925, Clay Co, WV.

12. GROVER CLEVELAND[6] MCQUAIN *(JOHN S.[5], CAROLINE[4] SUMMERS, JACOB JAHU SUMMERS[3], JOHAN PAUL[2], JOHANN GEORGE[1] SOMERS)*

Children of GROVER CLEVELAND MCQUAIN are:
 i. GEORGE[7] MCQUAIN.
 ii. FRANK MCQUAIN.
 iii. UNKNOWN MCQUAIN.
 iv. UNKNOWN MCQUAIN.
 v. UNKNOWN MCQUAIN.
 vi. UNKNOWN MCQUAIN.

13. LEWIS WETZEL[6] MCQUAIN *(THOMAS MARSHALL[5], CAROLINE[4] SUMMERS, JACOB JAHU SUMMERS[3], JOHAN PAUL[2], JOHANN GEORGE[1] SOMERS)* was born 01 Feb 1879 in Roane Co. Census, WV, and died 10 Oct 1957 in Cotton, WV, Roane Co. He married (1) LILLY ALICE FIELDS. She was born 1884, and died May 1925. He married (2) DOROTHY MCKOWN 1899.

Notes for LEWIS WETZEL MCQUAIN:
Dedicated bridge on I-79. Lewis McQuain, He used to live on old road to Charleston, at the foot of hill. Close to Clendenin exit about 4 miles. Burial: Grannies Creek Cemetery, Roane Co, WV

Notes for LILLY ALICE FIELDS:
She died giving birth to twin sons, one of which died. The youngest living son is George who has lived at

Big Piney, Wyoming about 30 years, according to information given by John McQuain during a phone conversation between Charlotte Dilno and John on Dec 6, 1997.

More about LILLY ALICE FIELDS: Cause of Death from Childbirth.

Children of LEWIS MCQUAIN and LILLY FIELDS are:
     i.   JOHN ALBERT[7] MCQUAIN, b. 12 Jul 1921; m. RUTH ANN UNKNOWN.

           Notes for JOHN ALBERT MCQUAIN:
           There were ten sons in the family that were in the military service at the same time during WWII. One brother, Earl, could not go because he was injured, was an engineer on the railroad.

           John lives near where Big Sandy runs into the Elk River. Go down 119 to dead end, go over bridge that crosses Big Sandy and turn left, then take another left on Cobb Street. He lives right across from the swimming pool.

     ii.   MABEL GRACE MCQUAIN, b. 01 Feb 1905; d. Unknown; m. CLARENCE HENSLEY.
    iii.   GEORGE LEWIS MCQUAIN, b. 1925.
    iv.   EARL MCQUAIN, b. 1927.
     v.   EVELYN MCQUAIN, b. 1913.
    vi.   UNKNOWN MCQUAIN.
   vii.   UNKNOWN MCQUAIN.
  viii.   UNKNOWN MCQUAIN.
    ix.   UNKNOWN MCQUAIN.
     x.   UNKNOWN MCQUAIN.
    xi.   UNKNOWN MCQUAIN.
   xii.   UNKNOWN MCQUAIN.

Children of LEWIS MCQUAIN and DOROTHY MCKOWN are:
   xiii.   UNKNOWN[7] MCQUAIN.
   xiv.   UNKNOWN MCQUAIN.
    xv.   UNKNOWN MCQUAIN.
   xvi.   UNKNOWN MCQUAIN.

14. CORA BELLE[6] ROGERS (*CAROLINE DIXIE[5] MCQUAIN, CAROLINE[4] SUMMERS, JACOB JAHU[3], JOHAN PAUL[2], JOHANN GEORGE[1] SOMERS*) was born 10 Jan 1882 in Virginia, and died Unknown. She married WILLIAM ROBERT SMITH. He was born Abt. 1882, and death date is unknown.

Notes for WILLIAM ROBERT SMITH:
William Robert Smith had a store and Ernest Rogers worked for him.

Children of CORA ROGERS and WILLIAM SMITH are:
     i.   JASON CARL[7] SMITH, d. Apr 1993; m. IRENE.
    ii.   KERMIT SMITH, d. Unknown.
   iii.   ELIZABETH (Betty) SMITH, d. Unknown.
   iv.   VIRGINIA BELLE SMITH, b. 24 Jul 1916, Fayette Co., WV; m. BASIL ESTES COOK, 17 Aug 1934, Logan Co., WV; b. Logan Co., WV; d. 23 Dec 2004.

15. ALICE BLANCHE[6] ROGERS *(CAROLINE DIXIE[5] MCQUAIN, CAROLINE[4] SUMMERS, JACOB JAHU[3], JOHAN PAUL[2], JOHANN GEORGE[1] SOMERS)* was born 23 Aug 1885 in Roane Co., WV, and died 1964.   She married ROBERT SAMUEL HENSLEY.

Children of ALICE ROGERS and ROBERT HENSLEY are:
    i.   CLIFFORD[7] HENSLEY, d. Unknown; m. ANN UNKNOWN.
    ii.   RAYMOND HENSLEY, b. 27 Jun 1923; m. RUTH MAE UNKNOWN.
    iii.   OLIVER HENSLEY, b. 03 Oct 1926; m. LELA MAE UNKNOWN.
    iv.   PIERCE HENSLEY, b. 03 Aug 1929.
    v.   HENSLEY, b. Abt. 1907; m. EARL RAFFERTY.
    vi.   DIXIE FAY HENSLEY-DOUGLAS, m. ERWIN DOUGLAS.
    vii.   OPAL HENSLEY-DOUGLAS, m. VERNON DOUGLAS.
    viii.   CHLOISE HENSLEY.
    ix.   GLADYS HENSLEY, b. Abt. 03 Oct.
    x.   VIRGINIA HENSLEY-WILLIAMS, m. UNKNOWN WILLIAMS.
    xi.   WILLARD HENSLEY.

16. NEWTON PAUL[6] ROGERS *(CAROLINE DIXIE[5] MCQUAIN, CAROLINE[4] SUMMERS, JACOB JAHU[3], JOHAN PAUL[2], JOHANN GEORGE[1] SOMERS)* was born 02 Nov 1886 in Roane Co., WV, and died 19 Jan 1919.   He married HESTER BOGGS 21 Nov 1913 in Roane Co., WV.   She was born 1892; death date unknown.

Children of NEWTON ROGERS and HESTER BOGGS are:
    i.   SNOWDEN[7] ROGERS, death date unknown; m. HATTIE UNKNOWN.
    ii.   LESLIE ROGERS, d. Unknown.
    iii.   IMOGENE ROGERS, m. UNKNOWN GESBRECHT.

17. SARA ELIZABETH[6] ROGERS *(CAROLINE DIXIE[5] MCQUAIN, CAROLINE[4] SUMMERS, JACOB JAHU[3], JOHAN PAUL[2], JOHANN GEORGE[1] SOMERS)* was born 19 Feb 1892 in Roane Co., WV, and died 25 Jan 1962.   She married EDWARD HUGHES.   He died Unknown.

Child of SARA ROGERS and EDWARD HUGHES is:
    i.   ROLAND KESTER[7] ROGERS, b. Abt. 1911; d. Unknown.

18. LUCY JONE[6] ROGERS *(CAROLINE DIXIE[5] MCQUAIN, CAROLINE[4] SUMMERS, JACOB JAHU[3], JOHAN PAUL[2], JOHANN GEORGE[1] SOMERS)* was born 19 Sep 1894 in Roane Co.,   WV, and died 19 Sep 1981 in Springdale, WV, Fayette Co.   She married WILLIAM LOWRY.   He was born 22 Oct 1892, and died 26 Feb 1968 in Springdale, WV, Fayette Co.

Children of LUCY ROGERS and WILLIAM LOWRY are:
    i.   IMOGENE[7] LOWRY.
    ii.   ADELEE LOWRY.
    iii.   JOAN LOWRY.
    iv.   ROGER LOWRY.

19. JAHU CLARK[6] ROGERS *(CAROLINE DIXIE[5] MCQUAIN, CAROLINE[4] SUMMERS, JACOB JAHU[3], JOHAN PAUL[2], JOHANN GEORGE[1] SOMERS)* was born 12 Aug 1899 in Newton, WV, Roane Co., and died Abt. Oct 1961 in Newton, WV, Roane Co. He married ORVA HICKS. She was born 17 Feb 1903, and died 27 Apr 1992 in Spencer, WV, Roane Co.

Children of JAHU ROGERS and ORVA HICKS are:

    i.   HENRY HERSEY[7] ROGERS, b. 24 Apr 1924, Newton, WV; d. Sep 1993, Spencer, WV, Roane Co.; m. MARY BELLE JUSTICE.

    ii.   WILLIAM GAIL ROGERS, b. Abt. 1926, Newton, WV, Roane Co.

    iii.   JAMES FORREST ROGERS, b. 22 Jan 1930, Newton, WV, Roane Co.; d. 06 Dec 1993, Spencer, WV, Roane Co.; m. NORA MARCEL MULLIN, 10 Apr 1962.

    iv.   LAWANDA ROGERS, b. 03 Aug 1932, Newton, WV, Roane Co.; m. PAUL HICKLE; b. Abt. 1932.

20. ERNEST FREAR[6] ROGERS *(CAROLINE DIXIE[5] MCQUAIN, CAROLINE[4] SUMMERS, JACOB JAHU[3], JOHAN PAUL[2], JOHANN GEORGE[1] SOMERS)* was born 15 Mar 1902 in Newton, Roane Co., WV, and died 25 Apr 1993 in Charleston, Kanawha Co., WV. He met LULA "MABEL" TAWNEY 17 May 1926 in Akron, OH, daughter of AARON TAWNEY and FLORA GRAHAM. She was born 23 Mar 1906 in Left Hand, Roane Co., WV, and died 30 May 2003 in Newton, Roane Co., WV. Burial: 04 Jun 2003, Tawney Family Cemetery on Route 36.

Notes for ERNEST FREAR ROGERS – See page 24:

More about ERNEST FREAR ROGERS:
Burial: Tawney Family Cemetery
Cause of Death: arteriosclerosis
Medical Information: Emphysema in later years (He was a smoker to the age of about 62). Hernia surgery. Prostrate surgery. Ernest suffered from emphysema and osteoporosis.

Notes for LULA "MABEL" TAWNEY – See page 23

More about MABEL TAWNEY:
Burial: 04 Jun 2003, Tawney Family Cemetery
Medical Information: Gull bladder surgery. Later years had respiratory problems (including asthma). Used a nebulizer in 2000 and later oxygen. She had pneumonia a few times over the years. Congestive heart disease.

Children of ERNEST ROGERS and MABEL TAWNEY are:

    i.   MARDELL ADELEE[7] ROGERS, b. 06 Feb 1927, Akron, Summit Co., OH; m. (1) GILBERT MCCLELLAND, Akron, OH, Summit Co.; b. 23 Jun 1924; d. 20 May 1983; m. (2) HAROLD EDGAR JOHNSON, 23 Oct 1951, Las Vegas, NV; b. 08 Sep 1924.

    ii.   ROBERT KEITH ROGERS, b. 05 Aug 1928, Akron, Summit Co. OH; d. 23 Dec 2008, Gallipolis, OH; m. (1) MARIE PARSONS, 28 Jul 1950, Cartlettsburg, Boyd Co., KY; b. 9 Jun 1929; m. (2) NANCY LARCH.

        Notes for ROBERT KEITH ROGERS – See page 50

    iii.   ALMA "DELORES" ROGERS, b. 23 Mar 1930, Akron, Summit Co., OH; m. (2) DELBERT DENNIS, 22 Jan 1958; b. 22 Dec 1928, Lake Lynn, PA.

iv.   KERMIT ADOLPH ROGERS, b. 23 Feb 1934, Newton, Roane Co., WV; m. BETTY LOU BIRD, 12 Aug 1954; b. 29 Oct 1936, Clay Co., WV.

Notes for KERMIT ADOLPH ROGERS:
Form completed by Betty Rogers Sept. 30, 1996.

v.   DORMA KATHERN ROGERS, b. 24 Mar 1936, Newton, Roane Co., WV; m. (1) JAMES HENRY BIRD, Sep 1955; b. 12 Jun 1933; d. May 1986; m. (2) JAMES DRAKE, 22 Jul 1997, Gatlinburg, Tennessee; b: 02 Mar 1939.

vi.   CARROLL AARON ROGERS, b. 10 May 1938, Newton, Roane Co., WV; m. MARIA FELICIA GRECO, 19 Nov 1960, Morgantown, WV; b. 25 May 1941.

vii. CHARLOTTE ANN ROGERS, b. 16 Mar 1940, Newton, Roane Co., WV; m. (1) DAVID ALEXANDER RICHMOND, 22 Aug 1959, Inglewood, LA Co., CA; b. 02 Jun 1937, Boston, Suffolk Co., Mass; d. 03 Aug 2008; m. (2) DONALD JOHN OSTROM, 30 Oct 1972, Las Vegas, Clark Co., NV; b. 20 Mar 1939, Oconomowoc, Waukesha Co., WI; m. (3) GUY LEROY DILNO, 14 Dec 1980, Plainwell, Allegan Co., MI; b. 22 Aug 1946, Kalamazoo, MI, Kalamazoo Co.

More about CHARLOTTE ANN ROGERS:
Divorced: 16 Nov 1969, Santa Ana, Orange Co., CA

More about DAVID ALEXANDER RICHMOND:
Divorced: 16 Nov 1969, Santa Ana, Orange Co., CA
Medical Information: Polio at 9 years of age.

More about DAVID RICHMOND and CHARLOTTE ROGERS:
Divorce: 16 Nov 1969, Santa Ana, Orange Co., California
Marriage: 22 Aug 1959, Inglewood, LA Co., CA

More about DONALD OSTROM and CHARLOTTE ROGERS:
Divorce: 02 Nov 1979, Allegan, MI (Allegan Co.)
Marriage: 30 Oct 1972, Las Vegas, Clark Co., NV

More about GUY DILNO and CHARLOTTE ROGERS:
Marriage: 14 Dec 1980, Plainwell, Allegan Co., MI

viii. PATRICIA "Pat" RONDELL ROGERS, b. 05 Feb 1943, Newton, Roane Co., WV; m. HOMER LEE CONLEY, 11 Aug 1962, Clover Ridge, Roane Co., WV; b. 14 Mar 1940, Uler, Roane Co., WV.

ix.   BARBARA CAROLINE ROGERS, b. 07 Sep 1945, Charleston, Kanawha Co., WV; d. 05 Jun 2005, Riverside, Riverside Co., CA; m. ROGER BEISTLE, Las Vegas, NV; b. 25 Jul 1941, Riverside Co., CA.

Notes for BARBARA CAROLINE ROGERS – See page 53

Genealogy Report of Alexander (Rev War) McQuain

Generation No. 1

1. ALEXANDER (REV WAR)[1] MCQUAIN was born 1756 in Scotland, and died 1825 in Pendleton Co., VA, at McQuain Farm, Black Thorn Creek, Bodkin Ridge. He married MARY BODKIN Abt. 1785 in Pendleton Co, VA. She was born 1766 in Augusta, VA, and died 1801 in Pendleton Co., VA, at McQuain Farm, Bodkin Ridge, Black Thorn Creek.

Notes for ALEXANDER (REV WAR) MCQUAIN:
He served the Colonies in the American Revolution in Captain Peter Hull's company of the 2nd Battalion of the Augusta Militia. He was at Yorktown, VA for Cornwallis' surrender and received 2 guns, a mess pot, and a small amount of cash as his share of the loot from the British Army.

In 1997, Garnette Yates of Norfolk, VA, told me that there is a 3-legged kettle that belongs to a McQuain of Florida and at the time was on display at the museum in Glenville, WV.

In a letter from Garnette in 1997, she wrote about the McQuains and the many reunions held throughout West Virginia; in Gilmer Co., Pendleton Co., one near Lewisburg and the largest in Webster Co., Ohio. She told that there are McQuain farms at Little and Big Cove Creeks and that there is a one lane road with a few wide places to pass oncoming cars. She wrote, " Perry McQuain still lives on 50 acres of the Alexander, Jr. McQuain place. At one time the two brothers, Hugh and Alex, Jr., owned 700 acres and they moved there about 1821. There is a cemetery on each of the farms and most of those McQuains are buried there. The old house that Perry lives in has been there a long time." She also wrote, "I never get to talk to Perry at the reunions, always someone else talking to him."

Children of ALEXANDER MCQUAIN and MARY BODKIN are:

	i.	ELIZABETH[2] MCQUAIN.
	ii.	ESTHER MCQUAIN.
	iii.	ISABELLA MCQUAIN.
	iv.	JANE MCQUAIN.
	v.	NANCY MCQUAIN.
	vi.	THOMAS MCQUAIN.
	vii.	WILLIAM MCQUAIN.
	viii.	DUNCAN MCQUAIN, b. 1783; d. 1862.
	ix.	HUGH MCQUAIN, b. 1784; d. 1855.
2.	x.	ALEXANDER (WAR OF 1812) MCQUAIN II, b. 05 Apr 1787, Pendleton Co., VA, at McQuain Farm, Black Thorn Creek; d. 18 Feb 1862, Gilmer Co., VA, at McQuain Farm, Big Cove Creek.
	xi.	JOHN MCQUAIN, b. 1799; d. 1878.

Generation No. 2

2. ALEXANDER (WAR OF 1812)[2] MCQUAIN II *(ALEXANDER (REV WAR)[1])* was born 05 Apr 1787 in Pendleton Co., VA, at McQuain Farm, Black Thorn Creek, and died 18 Feb 1862 in Gilmer Co., VA, at McQuain Farm, Big Cove Creek. He married ELIZABETH SCOTT 12 Apr 1815 in Randolph Co, VA, daughter of JOHN SCOTT and MARY SPROUL. She was born 1796 in Pennsylvania, and died in Gilmer Co., WV, at McQuain Farm, near Troy.

Notes for ALEXANDER (WAR OF 1812) MCQUAIN II:
This information provided by Garnette Yates in correspondence to Charlotte Dilno, April 1997.

Notes for ELIZABETH SCOTT:
Info from Garnette Yates shows parents of Elizabeth Scott to be Alexander Scott and Rebecca Crawford.

Children of ALEXANDER MCQUAIN and ELIZABETH SCOTT are:

	i.	CASSIDY[3] MCQUAIN, m. DENNIS BURK.
	ii.	JANE MCQUAIN, m. JOHN CROLLEY.
3.	iii.	HUGH MCQUAIN, b. 1817, Lewis Co., VA (WV); d. 1892.
4.	iv.	GEORGE HILL MCQUAIN, b. 1818; d. 1899, Gilmer Co., VA (WV).
5.	v.	THOMAS MCQUAIN, SR. (CIVIL WAR), b. 1821, Gilmer Co., VA, at McQuain Farm, Big Cove Creek; d. 22 Jul 1864, Ft. Delaware, NJ.
6.	vi.	CHARLES JACOB MCQUAIN, b. 1828, Lewis Co., VA (WV); d. 1872, Gilmer Co., VA (WV).
	vii.	REBECCA MCQUAIN, b. 1831; m. WALTER WEST.
	viii.	NANCY MCQUAIN, b. 1833; m. ALEXANDER CAIN.
	ix.	WILLIAM MCQUAIN, b. 1834.

Generation No. 3

3. HUGH[3] MCQUAIN *(ALEXANDER (WAR OF 1812)[2], ALEXANDER (REV WAR)[1])* was born 1817 in Lewis Co., VA (WV), and died 1892. He married (1) EUNICE MARTNEY SCOTT, daughter of THOMAS SCOTT and MARY SKIDMORE. She was born 1821 in Randolph Co., VA, and died 1881 in Gilmer Co., VA (WV). He married (2) LOUISA PARKER.

Children of HUGH MCQUAIN and EUNICE SCOTT are:

	i.	GEORGE WILLIAM[4] MCQUAIN, b. 1850; d. 1871; m. MARIAH SLEETH.
7.	ii.	THOMAS CHARLES MCQUAIN, b. 1852, Gilmer Co., VA (WV); d. 1940.
	iii.	OLIVER CROMWELL MCQUAIN, b. 1854; d. 1921; m. LONA BALL.
	iv.	NANCY ELIZABETH MCQUAIN, b. 1857; d. 1920.
	v.	ALEXANDER MARSHALL MCQUAIN, b. 1857; d. 1939; m. ALLIE ELEANOR MEANS; b. 1857; d. 1939.
	vi.	MARIE COLUMBIA MCQUAIN, b. 1859; d. 1938; m. RENO PARKER.
	vii.	ADAM SCOTT MCQUAIN, b. 1860; d. 1898.
	viii.	JOHN ELLET HAYS MCQUAIN, b. 1862; d. 1934; m. MARY MARGARET DOLAN.
	ix.	MARY DIANA "MOLLY" MCQUAIN, b. 1865; d. 1949.

4. GEORGE HILL[3] MCQUAIN *(ALEXANDER (WAR OF 1812)[2], ALEXANDER (REV WAR)[1])* was born 1818, and died 1899 in Gilmer Co., VA (WV). He married MARIA LOUISE SLEETH 10 Jun 1841 in Lewis Co., VA (WV), daughter of ALEXANDER SLEETH and KATHERN WOLFE. She was born 18 May 1818 in Harrison Co., VA.

More about MARIA LOUISE SLEETH:
Burial: Gilmer Co. WV, Cove Creek, near Troy, WV

Children of GEORGE MCQUAIN and MARIA SLEETH are:
    i.   CATHERINE K.[4] MCQUAIN, b. 1846; m. WILLIAM COOKMAN, 10 Jan 1865, Gilmer Co., VA.
    ii.   ALEXANDER SCOTT MCQUAIN, b. 1848.
    iii.   CATHERINE E. MCQUAIN, b. 1845.
    iv.   ROSETTA JANE MCQUAIN.
    v.   MARY A. MCQUAIN. (Sarah and Mary were twins)
    vi.   SARAH C. MCQUAIN. (Sarah and Mary were twins)
    vii.   GEORGE NEWTON MCQUAIN, b. 22 Jun 1859; m. IDA EAKLE, 30 Oct 1879, Gilmer Co., VA (WV); b. 1879.

5. THOMAS[3] MCQUAIN, SR. (CIVIL WAR) *(ALEXANDER (WAR OF 1812)[2], ALEXANDER (REV WAR)[1])* was born 1821 in Gilmer Co., VA, at the McQuain Farm, Big Cove Creek, and died 22 Jul 1864 in Ft. Delaware, NJ. He married CAROLINE SUMMERS in VA, daughter of JACOB SUMMERS and JOHANNA DAVIS. She was born 15 Jun 1830 in Nicholas Co., VA, and died 15 Jul 1914 in Newton, Roane Co., WV.

Notes for THOMAS MCQUAIN, SR. (CIVIL WAR) – See page 106

More about THOMAS MCQUAIN, SR. (CIVIL WAR) :
Burial: Ft. Pinns Cemetery, Salem, NJ (source Garnette Yates)
Cause of Death: Typhoid fever.

Notes for CAROLINE SUMMERS – See page 106

More about CAROLINE SUMMERS: Cause of Death: Old age.

Children of THOMAS MCQUAIN and CAROLINE SUMMERS are:
    i.   CHARLIE[4] MCQUAIN.

    Notes for CHARLIE MCQUAIN: He was a blacksmith and lived at Silver Maple, WV, Roane Co., WV.

    ii.   DUNCAN MCQUAIN.
    iii.   ELIE MCQUAIN.

    Notes for ELIE MCQUAIN: He disappeared when he was a young man, as told by Mabel Rogers.

8.   iv.   JOANNA MCQUAIN, b. 17 Aug 1847, Whitewater, Nicholas Co., VA; d. 22 Feb 1922, Roane Co., WV.

	v.	ALEXANDER HAMILTON MCQUAIN, b. 1849.
9.	vi.	JOHN S. MCQUAIN, b. 1851, Nicholas Co., VA.
10.	vii.	WILLIAM PITT MCQUAIN, b. 1854, VA.
11.	viii.	THOMAS MARSHALL MCQUAIN, b. 24 Oct 1855, Nicholas Co., VA; d. 1928, Kanawha Co., WV.
	ix.	ELIZABETH SCOTT MCQUAIN, b. 1859; m. MARSHALL GRENBERRY "GREEN" DRAKE, 19 Nov 1874.
12.	x.	CAROLINE DIXIE MCQUAIN, b. 05 Dec 1860, Clay Co., WV; d. 17 Mar 1921, Newton, WV, Roane Co.

6. CHARLES JACOB[3] MCQUAIN *(ALEXANDER (WAR OF 1812)[2], ALEXANDER (REV WAR)[1])* was born 1828 in Lewis Co., VA (WV), and died 1872 in Gilmer Co., VA (WV). He married MARY DIANA VAN HORN, daughter of THOMAS VAN HORN and ELEANOR BROWN. She was born 05 Oct 1822 in Harrison Co., VA.

Children of CHARLES MCQUAIN and MARY VAN HORN are:
-   i.   MARY JANE[4] MCQUAIN, b. 1847; d. 1823; m. THOMAS SCOTT.
-   ii. ELLEN LUVERNIA MCQUAIN, b. 1854; d. 1931; m. RICHARD SCOTT.

Generation No. 4

7. THOMAS CHARLES[4] MCQUAIN *(HUGH[3], ALEXANDER (WAR OF 1812)[2], ALEXANDER (REV WAR)[1])* was born 1852 in Gilmer Co., VA (WV), and died 1940. He married JESSIE LEWIS 16 Oct 1895, daughter of OLIVER PERRY and ELIZABETH LEWIS. She was born 1870, and died 1961.

Children of THOMAS MCQUAIN and JESSIE LEWIS are:
13.	i.	THOMAS BRYAN[5] MCQUAIN, b. 09 Apr 1897; d. 11 Nov 1988.
	ii.	GEORGE WILLIAM MCQUAIN, b. 09 Aug 1898; d. 01 Jun 1977; m. LUCILLE LORETA TERESA LOCKE, 27 Oct 1934.
	iii.	EUNICE ELIZABETH MCQUAIN, b. 19 Feb 1900; d. 1979; m. CORNELIUS I.D. WISE, 17 Mar 1937; b. 19 Feb 1900; d. 17 Aug 1979.
	iv.	CLEMMIE LOIS MCQUAIN, b. 13 Feb 1902; d. 06 Dec 1974.
	v.	EDNA COLUMBIA MCQUAIN, b. 21 Jul 1903; d. 18 Feb 1945.

More about EDNA COLUMBIA MCQUAIN:
Christened: Died in World War II

	vi.	HELEN LEAH MCQUAIN, b. 25 Nov 1905; d. Unknown; m. AUBREY BERWIN CURTIS, 03 Jul 1930.
	vii.	MYRA PAULINE MCQUAIN, b. 05 Apr 1909; d. 22 Dec 1986.
	viii.	PERRY HUGH MCQUAIN, b. 14 Nov 1911.

8. JOANNA[4] MCQUAIN *(THOMAS[3], ALEXANDER (WAR OF 1812)[2], ALEXANDER (REV WAR)[1])* was born 17 Aug 1847 in Whitewater, Nicholas Co., VA, and died 22 Feb 1922 in Roane Co., WV. She married JOHN WALLBACK ROGERS 06 Aug 1867 in Clay Co., WV, son of ELIJAH ROGERS and ELLEN SKIDMORE. He was born 29 May 1841, and died 25 Jul 1925 in Roane Co., WV.

Children of JOANNA MCQUAIN and JOHN ROGERS are:

	i.	LON EARL[5] ROGERS, b. 04 Oct 1868; d. 14 Nov 1954; m. (1) ELIZABETH COOPMAN; m. (2) MINNIE YARRA.
	ii.	TYRE BENNETT ROGERS, b. 07 May 1870; d. 16 Mar 1933; m. (1) SARA SEARS; b. 5/12/1928; m. (2) EFFIE SMITH, 01 Mar 1896.
	iii.	FREDERICK ALFRED ROGERS, b. 23 Jan 1873; d. 22 Oct 1957; m. FLORA E. ROLLYSON, 06 Apr 1905.
	iv.	MAHALA CAROLINE ROGERS, b. 16 Feb 1876; d. 28 Jul 1939.
	v.	JAMES JOHN ROGERS, b. 05 Apr 1882; d. 19 Feb 1932; m. (1) NETTIE PHILLIPS; m. (2) EVELEEN BROWN, 11 Sep 1904.
	vi.	LILLIE ELLEN ROGERS, b. 12 Mar 1885; d. 21 May 1971; m. SILAS M. MOORE, 03 Feb 1903.
	vii.	WILLIAM PITT ROGERS, b. 29 Apr 1888; d. 01 Dec 1975; m. (1) FLORA COOK, 01 Jun 1919; m. (2) RUTH BOGGS-SNYDER, 09 Oct 1966.
14.	viii.	RETTA ROGERS.
15.	ix.	ESTER ELIZABETH ROGERS, b. 22 Jun 1880, Roane Co, WV; d. 09 Aug 1956, Clay Co, WV.
	x.	CLEMIN ROGERS.

9. JOHN S.[4] MCQUAIN *(THOMAS[3], ALEXANDER (WAR OF 1812)[2], ALEXANDER (REV WAR)[1])* was born 1851 in Nicholas Co., VA. He married NANCY GRIFFITH.

Notes for JOHN S. MCQUAIN – See page 109

Children of JOHN MCQUAINand NANCY GRIFFITH are:

	i.	LEWIS[5] MCQUAIN.
	ii.	ROBERT "BUB" MCQUAIN.
	iii.	THOMAS MCQUAIN.
	iv.	MARIAM "PUSS" MCQUAIN.
	v.	"BIRD" MCQUAIN.
	vi.	LULA MCQUAIN.
16.	vii.	GROVER CLEVELAND MCQUAIN.
	viii.	LAURA MCQUAIN.

10. WILLIAM PITT[4] MCQUAIN *(THOMAS[3], ALEXANDER (WAR OF 1812)[2], ALEXANDER (REV WAR)[1])* was born 1854 in VA.

Child of WILLIAM PITT MCQUAIN is:

	i.	LOUIS[5] MCQUAIN.

11. THOMAS MARSHALL⁴ MCQUAIN *(THOMAS³, ALEXANDER (WAR OF 1812)², ALEXANDER (REV WAR)¹)* was born 24 Oct 1855 in Nicholas Co., VA, and died 1928 in Kanawha Co., WV. He married MAHALA ROSE ANN DRAKE 21 Mar 1878 in Roane Co., WV, daughter of CHARLES DRAKE and SARAH BISHOP. She was born 11 May 1855.

Notes for MAHALA ROSE ANN DRAKE: Mahala Drake is related to the Grahams.

Children of THOMAS MCQUAIN and MAHALA DRAKE are:
17.   i.   LEWIS WETZEL⁵ MCQUAIN, b. 01 Feb 1879, Roane Co. Census, WV; d. 10 Oct 1957, Cotton, WV, Roane Co.
      ii. CHARLES MCQUAIN, b. Mar 1886; d. Nov 1950; m. LOLA BOWYER.

          Notes for CHARLES MCQUAIN:
          Called Sugar Bowl McQuain, hit in head by a waitress.

12. CAROLINE DIXIE⁴ MCQUAIN *(THOMAS³, ALEXANDER (WAR OF 1812)², ALEXANDER (REV WAR)¹)* was born 05 Dec 1860 in Clay Co., WV, and died 17 Mar 1921 in Newton, WV, Roane Co. She married WILLIAM GEORGE ROGERS 09 Oct 1884 in Roane Co., WV, son of ROBERT RODGERS and SARAH SMITH. He was born 03 Oct 1848 in Webster Co., Virginia, and died 06 Feb 1937 in Newton, Roane Co., West Virginia.

Notes for WILLIAM GEORGE ROGERS – See page 91

Children of CAROLINE MCQUAIN and WILLIAM ROGERS are:
18.   i.   CORA BELLE⁵ ROGERS, b. 10 Jan 1882, Virginia; d. Unknown.
19.   ii.   ALICE BLANCHE ROGERS, b. 23 Aug 1885, Roane Co., WV; d. 1964.
20.   iii. NEWTON PAUL ROGERS, b. 02 Nov 1886, Roane Co., WV; d. 19 Jan 1919.
21.   iv.   SARA ELIZABETH ROGERS, b. 19 Feb 1892, Roane Co., WV; d. 25 Jan 1962.
22.   v.   LUCY JONE ROGERS, b. 19 Sep 1894, Roane Co., WV; d. 19 Sep 1981, Springdale, WV, Fayette Co.
      vi.   WILLIAM CHARLES ROGERS, b. 22 Aug 1896, Roane Co., WV; d. 04 Sep 1933, Roane Co., WV.

          Notes for WILLIAM CHARLES ROGERS:
          Roane Co. WV Death Index, page 143. Cause of Death: He was shot.

23.   vii. JAHU CLARK ROGERS, b. 12 Aug 1899, Newton, WV, Roane Co.; d. Abt. Oct 1961, Newton, WV, Roane Co.
24.   viii. ERNEST FREAR ROGERS, b. 15 Mar 1902, Newton, Roane Co., WV; d. 25 Apr 1993, Chas., Kanawha Co., WV.

Generation No. 5

13. THOMAS BRYAN[5] MCQUAIN *(THOMAS CHARLES[4], HUGH[3], ALEXANDER (WAR OF 1812)[2], ALEXANDER (REV WAR)[1])* was born 09 Apr 1897, and died 11 Nov 1988. He married OPAL ALDAH MORRISON 30 Nov 1922.

More about THOMAS BRYAN MCQUAIN:
Christened: U.S.Marines (served in France) WWI

Children of THOMAS MCQUAIN and OPAL MORRISON are:
- i. MIRIAM[6] MCQUAIN, b. 1925, Gilmer   Co., VA (WV); m. (1) DELBERT FORD; m. (2) KENNETH LOOKER.
- ii. JESABEL MCQUAIN, b. 1927, Gilmer   Co., VA (WV); m. JOHN RICHARD LINSCOTT.
- iii. THOMAS MCQUAIN, b. 1930; m. (1) MOLLIE STOUT; m. (2) DAISY FRALEY.
- iv. DAVID MCQUAIN, m. SHARON ULDRICH.

14. RETTA[5] ROGERS *(JOANNA[4] MCQUAIN, THOMAS MCQUAIN[3], ALEXANDER (WAR OF 1812)[2], ALEXANDER (REV WAR)[1])* She married PRESTON J. TAWNEY, son of DAVID TAWNEY and CYNTHIA CARPER. He was born 02 Feb 1900, and died 12 Sep 1985.

Children of RETTA ROGERS and PRESTON TAWNEY are:
- i. JACK L.[6] TAWNEY.
- ii. JUANITA FLORENCE TAWNEY, b. Abt. 1926, Newton, Roane Co., West Virginia.
- iii. FRANKLIN D. TAWNEY.
- iv. WANDA LEE TAWNEY, m. UNKNOWN SIMMONS.

15. ESTER ELIZABETH[5] ROGERS *(JOANNA[4] MCQUAIN, THOMAS[3], ALEXANDER (WAR OF 1812)[2], ALEXANDER (REV WAR)[1])* was born 22 Jun 1880 in Roane Co, WV, and died 09 Aug 1956 in Clay Co, WV. She married EARLY BRAGG 18 May 1899 in Clay Co, WV, son of MORGAN BRAGG and SARAH FRAME. He was born 08 Dec 1871 in Clay Co, WV, and died 17 Sep 1949 in Clay Co, WV.

Children of ESTER ROGERS and EARLY BRAGG are:
- i. ORVILLE[6] BRAGG, b. 08 Mar 1900, Clay Co, WV; d. Unknown.
- ii. PEARL BRAGG, b. 13 Dec 1902, Clay Co, WV; d. Unknown; m. FRANK WHITE, 29 Apr 1924; d. Unknown.
- iii. JODA "JOANNA" BRAGG, b. 14 Jun 1905, Clay Co, WV; d. Unknown; m. LANTE SEARS, 12 Apr 1927; d. Unknown.
- iv. WARDEN EMMETT BRAGG, b. 17 Aug 1907, Clay Co, WV; m. BESSIE JONES, 24 Dec 1930.
- v. JOHN MORGAN BRAGG, b. 19 Feb 1910, Clay Co, WV; d. 18 Dec 1944, WV.
- vi. ELSIE HATTIE BRAGG, b. 19 Jan 1912, Clay Co, WV; m. DAYTON WILMOTH, 06 Oct 1933.
- vii. THOMAS WOODEROW BRAGG, b. 02 Aug 1914, Clay Co, WV; m. JUANITA WILMOTH, 07 Nov 1940.
- viii. WILLIAM IRA BRAGG, b. 31 Mar 1917, Clay Co, WV; m. HALCIE MATHENY, 31 Jul 1949.
- ix. ALICE MARION BRAGG, b. 15 Dec 1919, Clay Co, WV; m. JAMES HEFLIN, 05 Dec 1938.

     x.   DOROTHY ANNABELLE BRAGG, b. 28 Sep 1923, Clay Co, WV; m. CHARLES CARROLL, 14 Jun 1946.

    xi.   CLIFTON STERRETT BRAGG, b. 15 Dec 1925, Clay Co, WV.

16. GROVER CLEVELAND[5] MCQUAIN *(JOHN S.[4], THOMAS[3], ALEXANDER (WAR OF 1812)[2], ALEXANDER (REV WAR)[1])*

Children of GROVER CLEVELAND MCQUAIN are:

     i.   GEORGE[6] MCQUAIN.
    ii.   FRANK MCQUAIN.
   iii.   UNKNOWN MCQUAIN.
   iv.   UNKNOWN MCQUAIN.
    v.   UNKNOWN MCQUAIN.
   vi.   UNKNOWN MCQUAIN.

17. LEWIS WETZEL[5] MCQUAIN *(THOMAS MARSHALL[4], THOMAS[3], ALEXANDER (WAR OF 1812)[2], ALEXANDER (REV WAR)[1])* was born 01 Feb 1879 in Roane Co. Census, WV, and died 10 Oct 1957 in Cotton, WV, Roane Co.   He married (1) LILLY ALICE FIELDS.   She was born 1884, and died May 1925.   He married (2) DOROTHY MCKOWN 1899.

Notes for LEWIS WETZEL MCQUAIN:
Wilford Post Office not there anymore. Dedicated bridge on I-79. Lewis McQuainuseto live on old road to Charleston, at the foot of hill. Close to Clendenin exit about 4 miles. Burial: Grannies Creek Cemetery, Roane Co, WV.

Notes for LILLY ALICE FIELDS:
She died giving birth to twin sons, one of which died.   The youngest living son is George who has lived at Big Piney, Wyoming about 30 years, according to information given by John McQuain during a phone conversation between Charlotte Dilno and John on Dec 6, 1997.

More about LILLY ALICE FIELDS:
Cause of Death: Childbirth

Children of LEWIS MCQUAIN and LILLY FIELDS are:

     i.   JOHN ALBERT[6] MCQUAIN, b. 12 Jul 1921; m. RUTH ANN UNKNOWN.

        Notes for JOHN ALBERT MCQUAIN:
        Ten sons in the family were in the military service at the same time during WWII.   One brother, Earl, could not go because he was injured; was an engineer on the railroad.

        John lived near where Big Sandy runs into the Elk River.   Go down 119 to dead end, go over bridge that crosses Big Sandy and turn left, then take another left on Cobb Street.   He lives right across from the swimming pool.

    ii.   MABEL GRACE MCQUAIN, b. 01 Feb 1905; d. Unknown; m. CLARENCE HENSLEY.
   iii.   GEORGE LEWIS MCQUAIN, b. 1925.
   iv.   EARL MCQUAIN, b. 1927.
    v.   EVELYN MCQUAIN, b. 1913.
   vi.   UNKNOWN MCQUAIN.
  vii.   UNKNOWN MCQUAIN.

  viii. UNKNOWN MCQUAIN.
   ix. UNKNOWN MCQUAIN.
    x. UNKNOWN MCQUAIN.
   xi. UNKNOWN MCQUAIN.
  xii. UNKNOWN MCQUAIN.

Children of LEWIS MCQUAIN and DOROTHY MCKOWN are:
  xiii. UNKNOWN[6] MCQUAIN.
  xiv. UNKNOWN MCQUAIN.
   xv. UNKNOWN MCQUAIN.
  xvi. UNKNOWN MCQUAIN.

18. CORA BELLE[5] ROGERS *(CAROLINE DIXIE[4] MCQUAIN, THOMAS[3], ALEXANDER (WAR OF 1812)[2], ALEXANDER (REV WAR)[1])* was born 10 Jan 1882 in Virginia, and died Unknown. She married WILLIAM ROBERT SMITH. He was born Abt. 1882, and died Unknown.

Notes for WILLIAM ROBERT SMITH:
William Robert Smith had a store and Ernest Rogers worked for him.

Children of CORA ROGERS and WILLIAM SMITH are:
    i. JASON CARL[6] SMITH, d. Apr 1993; m. IRENE UNKNOWN.
   ii. KERMIT SMITH, d. Unknown.
  iii. ELIZABETH "Betty" SMITH, d. Unknown.
  iv. VIRGINIA BELLE SMITH, b. 24 Jul 1916, Fayette Co., WV; m. BASIL ESTES COOK, 17 Aug 1934, Logan Co., WV; b. Logan Co., WV; d. 23 Dec 2004.

19. ALICE BLANCHE[5] ROGERS *(CAROLINE DIXIE[4] MCQUAIN, THOMAS[3], ALEXANDER (WAR OF 1812)[2], ALEXANDER (REV WAR)[1])* was born 23 Aug 1885 in Roane Co.,   WV, and died 1964. She married ROBERT SAMUEL HENSLEY.

Children of ALICE ROGERS and ROBERT HENSLEY are:
     i. CLIFFORD[6] HENSLEY, d. Unknown; m. ANN UNKNOWN.
    ii. RAYMOND HENSLEY, b. 27 Jun 1923; m. RUTH MAE UNKNOWN.
   iii. OLIVER HENSLEY, b. 03 Oct 1926; m. LELA MAE UNKNOWN.
   iv. PIERCE HENSLEY, b. 03 Aug 1929.
    v. HENSLEY, b. Abt. 1907; m. EARL RAFFERTY.
   vi. DIXIE FAY HENSLEY-DOUGLAS, m. ERWIN DOUGLAS.
  vii. OPAL HENSLEY-DOUGLAS, m. VERNON DOUGLAS.
  viii. CHLOISE HENSLEY.
   ix. GLADYS HENSLEY, b. Abt. 03 Oct.
    x. VIRGINIA HENSLEY-WILLIAMS, m. UNKNOWN WILLIAMS.
   xi. WILLARD HENSLEY.

20. NEWTON PAUL⁵ ROGERS *(CAROLINE DIXIE⁴ MCQUAIN, THOMAS³, ALEXANDER (WAR OF 1812)², ALEXANDER (REV WAR)¹)* was born 02 Nov 1886 in Roane Co., WV, and died 19 Jan 1919. He married HESTER BOGGS 21 Nov 1913 in Roane Co., WV. She was born 1892, and died Unknown.

Children of NEWTON ROGERS and HESTER BOGGS are:
- i. SNOWDEN⁶ ROGERS, d. Unknown; m. HATTIE UNKNOWN.
- ii. LESLIE ROGERS, d. Unknown.
- iii. IMOGENE ROGERS, m. UNKNOWN GESBRECHT.

21. SARA ELIZABETH⁵ ROGERS *(CAROLINE DIXIE⁴ MCQUAIN, THOMAS³, ALEXANDER (WAR OF 1812)², ALEXANDER (REV WAR)¹)* was born 19 Feb 1892 in Roane Co., WV, and died 25 Jan 1962. She married EDWARD HUGHES. Death date unknown.

Child of SARA ROGERS and EDWARD HUGHES is:
- i. ROLAND KESTER⁶ ROGERS, b. Abt. 1911; d. Unknown.

22. LUCY JONE⁵ ROGERS *(CAROLINE DIXIE⁴ MCQUAIN, THOMAS³, ALEXANDER (WAR OF 1812)², ALEXANDER (REV WAR)¹)* was born 19 Sep 1894 in Roane Co., WV, and died 19 Sep 1981 in Springdale, WV, Fayette Co. She married WILLIAM LOWRY. He was born 22 Oct 1892, and died 26 Feb 1968 in Springdale, WV, Fayette Co.

Children of LUCY ROGERS and WILLIAM LOWRY are:
- i. IMOGENE⁶ LOWRY.
- ii. ADELEE LOWRY.
- iii. JOAN LOWRY.
- iv. ROGER LOWRY.

23. JAHU CLARK⁵ ROGERS *(CAROLINE DIXIE⁴ MCQUAIN, THOMAS³, ALEXANDER (WAR OF 1812)², ALEXANDER (REV WAR)¹)* was born 12 Aug 1899 in Newton, WV, Roane Co., and died Abt. Oct 1961 in Newton, WV, Roane Co. He married ORVA HICKS. She was born 17 Feb 1903, and died 27 Apr 1992 in Spencer, WV, Roane Co.

Children of JAHU CLARK ROGERS and ORVA HICKS are:
- i. HENRY HERSEY⁶ ROGERS, b. 24 Apr 1924, Newton, WV; d. Sep 1993, Spencer, WV, Roane Co.; m. MARY BELLE JUSTICE.
- ii. WILLIAM GAIL ROGERS, b. Abt. 1926, Newton, WV, Roane Co.
- iii. JAMES FORREST ROGERS, b. 22 Jan 1930, Newton, WV, Roane Co.; d. 06 Dec 1993, Spencer, WV, Roane Co.; m. NORA MARCEL MULLIN, 10 Apr 1962.
- iv. LAWANDA ROGERS, b. 03 Aug 1932, Newton, WV, Roane Co.; m. PAUL HICKLE; b. Abt. 1932; d. Maryland.

24. ERNEST FREAR⁵ ROGERS *(CAROLINE DIXIE⁴ MCQUAIN, THOMAS³, ALEXANDER (WAR OF 1812)², ALEXANDER (REV WAR)¹)* was born 15 Mar 1902 in Newton, Roane Co., WV, and died 25 Apr 1993 in Chas., Kanawha Co., WV. He met LULA "MABEL" TAWNEY 17 May 1926 in Akron, OH, daughter of AARON TAWNEY and FLORA GRAHAM. She was born 23 Mar 1906 in Left Hand, Roane Co., WV, and died 30 May 2003 in Newton, Roane Co., WV.

Notes for ERNEST FREAR ROGERS – See Page 24

More about ERNEST FREAR ROGERS:
Burial: Tawney Family Cemetery
Cause of Death: arteriosclerosis
Medical Information: Emphysema in later years (likely due to smoking to the age of about 62). Hernia surgery. Prostrate trouble. Ernest suffered from emphysema and osteoporosis.

Notes for MABEL TAWNEY – See Page 23

More about LULA "MABEL" TAWNEY:
Burial: 04 Jun 2003, Tawney Family Cemetery
Medical Information: Gull bladder operation. Later years had respiratory problems (including asthma). Pneumonia a few times over the years. Congestive heart disease.

Children of ERNEST ROGERS and LULA TAWNEY are:

    i.   MARDELL ADELEE[6] ROGERS, b. 06 Feb 1927, Akron, Summit Co., OH; m. (1) GILBERT MCCLELLAND, Akron, OH, Summit Co.; b. 23 Jun 1924; d. 20 May 1983; m. (2) HAROLD EDGAR JOHNSON, 23 Oct 1951, Las Vegas, NV; b. 08 Sep 1924.

    ii. ROBERT KEITH ROGERS, b. 05 Aug 1928, Akron, Summit Co. OH; d. 23 Dec 2008, Gallipolis, OH;   m. (1) MARIE PARSONS, 28 Jul 1950, Cartlettsburg, Boyd Co., KY; b. 9 Jun 1929;   m. (2) NANCY LARCH.

       Keith remembers being in the woods with Ernest and at the age of 75, Ernest was swinging on a grapevine.   Keith was a fox hunter, the same as Ernest. They hunted together from the time Keith was young, until Ernest was no longer able to go on the hills. At the age of 85, however, Ernest was still able to go on the hills. After that, Keith visited and they talked about the hunt and their fox hounds.   They both worked at Du Pont and rode together for many years.

    iii. ALMA   "DELORES" ROGERS, b. 23 Mar 1930, Akron, Summit Co., OH; m. (2) DELBERT DENNIS, 22 Jan 1958; b. 22 Dec 1928, Lake Lynn, PA.

    iv. KERMIT ADOLPH ROGERS, b. 23 Feb 1934, Newton, Roane Co., WV; m. BETTY LOU BIRD, 12 Aug 1954; b. 29 Oct 1936, Clay Co., WV.

    v. DORMA KATHERN ROGERS, b. 24 Mar 1936, Newton, Roane Co., WV; m. (1) JAMES HENRY BIRD, Sep 1955; b. 12 Jun 1933; d. May 1986; m. (2) JAMES DRAKE, 22 Jul 1997, Gatlinburg, Tennessee; b. 02 Mar 1939.

    vi. CARROLL AARON ROGERS, b. 10 May 1938, Newton, Roane Co., WV; m. MARIA FELICIA GRECO, 19 Nov 1960, Morgantown, WV; b. 25 May 1941.

    vii. CHARLOTTE ANN ROGERS, b. 16 Mar 1940, Newton, Roane Co., WV; m. (1) DAVID ALEXANDER RICHMOND, 22 Aug 1959, Inglewood, LA Co., CA; b. 02 Jun 1937, Boston, Suffolk Co., Mass; d. 03 Aug 2008; m. (2) DONALD JOHN OSTROM, 30 Oct 1972, Las Vegas, Clark Co., NV; b. 20 Mar 1939, Oconomowoc, Waukesha Co., WI; m. (3) GUY LEROY DILNO, 14 Dec 1980, Plainwell, Allegan Co., MI; b. 22 Aug 1946, Kalamazoo, MI, Kalamazoo Co.

       More about CHARLOTTE ANN ROGERS:
       Divorced: 16 Nov 1969, Santa Ana, Orange Co., CA

More about DAVID ALEXANDER RICHMOND:
Divorced: 16 Nov 1969, Santa Ana, Orange Co., CA
Medical Information: Polio at 9 years of age.

viii.   PATRICIA RONDELL ROGERS, b. 05 Feb 1943, Newton, Roane Co., WV; m. HOMER LEE CONLEY, 11 Aug 1962, Clover Ridge, Roane Co., WV; b. 14 Mar 1940, Uler, Roane Co., WV.

  ix.   BARBARA CAROLINE ROGERS, b. 07 Sep 1945, Charleston, Kanawha Co., WV; d. 05 Jun 2005, Riverside, Riverside Co., CA; m. ROGER BEISTLE, Las Vegas, NV; b. 25 Jul 1941, Riverside Co., CA.

Notes for BARBARA CAROLINE ROGERS – See Page 53

Genealogy Report of Robert Jahu Rodgers

Generation No. 1

1. ROBERT JAHU² RODGERS *(UNKNOWN¹)* was born Bet. **1805** - 1816 in Nicholas Co., Virginia, and died in Newton, WV, Roane Co.   He married SARAH ELIZABETH "SALLY" SMITH 14 May 1835 in Pocahontas Co., VA (now WV), daughter of JOHN SMITH and SARAH MOORE.   She was born Abt. 1805 in Stony Creek, Pocahontas Co., VA, and died in Nicholas Co., WV.

Notes for ROBERT JAHU RODGERS:
Ernest Rogers always told us that his Grandfather Robert (Bobby)Rogers was a Confederate Scout. William George Rogers (son of Robert Rogers) recalled to Ernest that he remembered troops arriving and Robert leaving with them on a horse and would tell them something such as "I'll be back" or "I'll see you."

Ernest always told us that Robert's full name was Robert Jahu Rodgers and he was called by "Bobby." He was a blacksmith.

Both the 1850 Census in Nicholas Co., VA   (now WV) has him listed as just Robert Rogers and his wife listed as just Sarah Rogers.

Kermit Rogers told that William George Rogers came to the Blown Timber area with his parents and they moved into the Clay Smith hollow. William Rogers was 12 at the time, 1861. They came to this area with other relatives.

Marriage Notes for ROBERT RODGERS and SARAH SMITH:
Married by Rev. E. A. Nicholson, page 84, Roane Co. Marriage Index. William George Rogers told his son, Ernest, that he came to the Roane Co. area when he was twelve years old. His parents settled in the Clay Hollow off the Blown Timber Road. William George bought the Rogers farm and a deed is recorded in the Roane Co. Records.

Children of ROBERT RODGERS and SARAH SMITH are:

       i.   JOHN HERSEY³ ROGERS, b. Abt. 1838, VA.

            Notes for JOHN HERSEY ROGERS:
            He died when ambushed serving in the Civil War in Webster County.

      ii.   ELIZABETH ROGERS, b. Abt. 1836.

            Notes for ELIZABETH ROGERS:
            Elizabeth is buried on the Russell Hensley property on Blown Timber, near Newton, at the top of a hill. William George Rogers told Mabel Rogers that Elizabeth was buried by a pine tree to mark the spot. I believe that Kermit Rogers remembers this story about where she was buried.

    iii.   SARAH ROGERS, b. Abt. 1837.

    iv.   JULIE A. ROGERS, b. Abt. 1846.

2.   v.   WILLIAM GEORGE ROGERS, b. 03 Oct 1848, Webster Co., Virginia; d. 06 Feb 1937, Newton, Roane Co., West Virginia.

     vi.   JAMES H. ROGERS, b. Abt. 1852, Kanawha Co., VA; m. ANNIE SCHOOLCRAFT, 04 Oct 1896.

Notes for JAMES H. ROGERS:
It is noted Ernest Rogers said that James Rogers moved to Oklahoma and they never heard from him again. It is thought that he died of pneumonia after going West. It is said that he had two sons.

Generation No. 2

2. WILLIAM GEORGE[3] ROGERS *(ROBERT JAHU[2] RODGERS, UNKNOWN[1])* was born 03 Oct 1848 in Webster Co., Virginia, and died 06 Feb 1937 in Newton, Roane Co., West Virginia. He married CAROLINE DIXIE MCQUAIN 09 Oct 1884 in Roane Co., WV, daughter of THOMAS MCQUAIN and CAROLINE SUMMERS. She was born 05 Dec 1860 in Clay Co., WV, and died 17 Mar 1921 in Newton, WV, Roane Co.

Notes for WILLIAM GEORGE ROGERS:
William George Rogers told his son Ernest that he came to the Roane Co. area when he was twelve years old. His parents settled in the Clay hollow off Blown Timber Road. William George Rogers bought the Rogers farm and a deed is recorded in the Roane Co. Records.

Marriage Notes for WILLIAM ROGERS and CAROLINE MCQUAIN:
Marriage License of Wm. G. Rogers and Caroline McQuain. Married in bride's residence, by E. A. Nicholson, minister of the N.P. (or M.P.) Church. Bride was 23 and born in Clay Co., WV. Groom born in Webster Co., VA. (Roane Co. Records, Marriage Index, page 84. They lived in Roane Co., Geary District in 1880 according to the Federal Census. It was reported that William George Rogers (about 30) and a (10-year old) granddaughter lived in the household in 1880. The age reported for R. Rodgers was 75 and for Sarrah was age 74.

Children of WILLIAM ROGERS and CAROLINE MCQUAIN are:
3.   i.   CORA BELLE[4] ROGERS, b. 10 Jan 1882, Virginia; d. Unknown.
4.   ii.   ALICE BLANCHE ROGERS, b. 23 Aug 1885, Roane Co., WV; d. 1964.
5.   iii.   NEWTON PAUL ROGERS, b. 02 Nov 1886, Roane Co., WV; d. 19 Jan 1919.
6.   iv.   SARA ELIZABETH ROGERS, b. 19 Feb 1892, Roane Co., WV; d. 25 Jan 1962.
7.   v.   LUCY JONE ROGERS, b. 19 Sep 1894, Roane Co., WV; d. 19 Sep 1981, Springdale, WV, Fayette Co.
     vi.   WILLIAM CHARLES ROGERS, b. 22 Aug 1896, Roane Co., WV; d. 04 Sep 1933, Roane Co., WV.

          Notes for WILLIAM CHARLES ROGERS:
          Roane Co. WV Death Index, page 143.

8.   vii.   JAHU CLARK ROGERS, b. 12 Aug 1899, Newton, WV, Roane Co.; d. Abt. Oct 1961, Newton, WV, Roane Co.
9.   viii.   ERNEST FREAR ROGERS, b. 15 Mar 1902, Newton, Roane Co., WV; d. 25 Apr 1993, Chas., Kanawha Co., WV.

Generation No. 3

3. CORA BELLE[4] ROGERS *(WILLIAM GEORGE[3], ROBERT JAHU[2] RODGERS, UNKNOWN[1])* was born 10 Jan 1882 in Virginia, and died 24 Jul 1916. She married WILLIAM ROBERT SMITH. He was born Abt. 1882; death date unknown.

Notes for WILLIAM ROBERT SMITH:
William Robert Smith had a store and Ernest Rogers worked for him.

Children of CORA ROGERS and WILLIAM SMITH are:
	i.	JASON CARL[5] SMITH, d. Apr 1993; m. IRENE.
	ii.	KERMIT SMITH; death date unknown.
10.	iii.	ELIZABETH SMITH; death date unknown.
11.	iv.	VIRGINIA BELLE SMITH, b. 24 Jul 1916, Fayette Co., WV.

4. ALICE BLANCHE[4] ROGERS *(WILLIAM GEORGE[3], ROBERT JAHU[2] RODGERS, UNKNOWN[1])* was born 23 Aug 1885 in Roane Co., WV, and died 1964. She married ROBERT SAMUEL HENSLEY.

Children of ALICE ROGERS and ROBERT HENSLEY are:
12.	i.	CLIFFORD[5] HENSLEY, d. Unknown.
13.	ii.	RAYMOND HENSLEY, b. 27 Jun 1923.
14.	iii.	OLIVER HENSLEY, b. 03 Oct 1926.
	iv.	PIERCE HENSLEY, b. 03 Aug 1929.
15.	v.	EDNA HENSLEY, b. Abt. 1907.
	vi.	DIXIE FAY HENSLEY-DOUGLAS, m. ERWIN DOUGLAS.
16.	vii.	OPAL HENSLEY-DOUGLAS.
	viii.	CHLOISE HENSLEY.
	ix.	GLADYS HENSLEY, b. Abt. 03 Oct.
	x.	VIRGINIA HENSLEY-WILLIAMS, m. UNKNOWN WILLIAMS.
	xi.	WILLARD HENSLEY.

5. NEWTON PAUL[4] ROGERS *(WILLIAM GEORGE[3], ROBERT JAHU[2] RODGERS, UNKNOWN[1])* was born 02 Nov 1886 in Roane Co., WV, and died 19 Jan 1919. He married HESTER BOGGS 21 Nov 1913 in Roane Co., WV. She was born 1892, and died Unknown.

Children of NEWTON ROGERS and HESTER BOGGS are:
17.	i.	SNOWDEN[5] ROGERS; death date unknown.
	ii.	LESLIE ROGERS; death date unknown.
	iii.	IMOGENE ROGERS, m. UNKNOWN GESBRECHT.

6.   SARA ELIZABETH[4] ROGERS *(WILLIAM GEORGE[3], ROBERT JAHU[2] RODGERS, UNKNOWN[1])* was born 19 Feb 1892 in Roane Co.,   WV, and died 25 Jan 1962.   She married EDWARD HUGHES; death date unknown.

Child of SARA ROGERS and EDWARD HUGHES is:
18.   i.   ROLAND KESTER[5] ROGERS, b. Abt. 1911; death date unknown.

7.   LUCY JONE[4] ROGERS *(WILLIAM GEORGE[3], ROBERT JAHU[2] RODGERS, UNKNOWN[1])* was born 19 Sep 1894 in Roane Co.,   WV, and died 19 Sep 1981 in Springdale, WV, Fayette Co.   She married WILLIAM LOWRY.   He was born 22 Oct 1892, and died 26 Feb 1968 in Springdale, WV, Fayette Co.

Children of LUCY ROGERS and WILLIAM LOWRY are:
        i.   IMOGENE[5] LOWRY.
       ii.   ADELEE LOWRY.
      iii.   JOAN LOWRY.
       iv.   ROGER LOWRY.

8.   JAHU CLARK[4] ROGERS *(WILLIAM GEORGE[3], ROBERT JAHU[2] RODGERS, UNKNOWN[1])* was born 12 Aug 1899 in Newton, WV, Roane Co., and died Abt. Oct 1961 in Newton, WV, Roane Co. He married ORVA HICKS.   She was born 17 Feb 1903, and died 27 Apr 1992 in Spencer, WV, Roane Co.

Children of JAHU ROGERS and ORVA HICKS are:
19.   i.   HENRY HERSEY[5] ROGERS, b. 24 Apr 1924, Newton, WV; d. Sep 1993, Spencer, WV, Roane Co.
20.   ii.   WILLIAM GAIL ROGERS, b. Abt. 1926, Newton, WV, Roane Co.
          iii.   JAMES FORREST ROGERS, b. 22 Jan 1930, Newton, WV, Roane Co.; d. 06 Dec 1993, Spencer, WV, Roane Co.; m. NORA MARCEL MULLIN, 10 Apr 1962.
21.   iv.   LAWANDA ROGERS, b. 03 Aug 1932, Newton, WV, Roane Co.

9.   ERNEST FREAR[4] ROGERS *(WILLIAM GEORGE[3], ROBERT JAHU[2] RODGERS, UNKNOWN[1])* was born 15 Mar 1902 in Newton, Roane Co., WV, and died 25 Apr 1993 in Chas., Kanawha Co., WV.   He met LULA "MABEL" TAWNEY 17 May 1926 in Akron, OH, daughter of AARON TAWNEY and FLORA GRAHAM.   She was born 23 Mar 1906 in Left Hand, Roane Co., WV, and died 30 May 2003 in Newton, Roane Co., WV.

Notes for ERNEST FREAR ROGERS – See Page 24

Notes for LULA "MABEL" TAWNEY See Page 23

More about ERNEST ROGERS and MABEL TAWNEY:
Death of Ernest: 25 Apr 1993, Charleston, Kanawha County, WV

Children of ERNEST ROGERS and MABEL TAWNEY are:
22.   i.   MARDELL ADELEE[5] ROGERS, b. 06 Feb 1927, Akron, Summit Co., OH.
23.   ii.   ROBERT KEITH ROGERS, b. 05 Aug 1928, Akron, Summit Co. OH; d. 23 Dec 2008, Gallipolis, OH.
24.   iii.   ALMA DELORES ROGERS, b. 23 Mar 1930, Akron, Summit Co., OH.
25.   iv.   KERMIT ADOLPH ROGERS, b. 23 Feb 1934, Newton, Roane Co., WV.
26.   v.   DORMA KATHERN ROGERS, b. 24 Mar 1936, Newton, Roane Co., WV.

27.   vi.   CARROLL AARON ROGERS, b. 10 May 1938, Newton, Roane Co., WV.
28.   vii.   CHARLOTTE ANN ROGERS, b. 16 Mar 1940, Newton, Roane Co., WV.
29.   viii. PATRICIA RONDELL ROGERS, b. 05 Feb 1943, Newton, Roane Co., WV.
30.   ix.   BARBARA CAROLINE ROGERS "BOBBIE," b. 07 Sep 1945, Charleston, Kanawha Co., WV; d. 05 Jun 2005, Riverside, Riverside Co., CA.

Generation No. 4

10. ELIZABETH[5] SMITH "BETTY" *(CORA BELLE[4] ROGERS, WILLIAM GEORGE[3], ROBERT JAHU[2] RODGERS, UNKNOWN[1];* death date unknown.

Child of ELIZABETH SMITH is:
31.   i.   LINDA CAMPBELL[6] SMITH.

11. VIRGINIA BELLE[5] SMITH *(CORA BELLE[4] ROGERS, WILLIAMGEORGE[3], ROBERT JAHU[2] RODGERS, UNKNOWN[1])* was born 24 Jul 1916 in Fayette Co., WV.   She married BASIL ESTES COOK 17 Aug 1934 in Logan Co., WV, son of JAMES COOK and JOSEPHINE BALLARD.   He was born in Logan Co., WV, and died 23 Dec 2004.

Children of VIRGINIA SMITH and BASIL COOK are:
32.   i.   WILLIAM ROBERT[6] COOK, b. 14 Aug 1935, Logan Co., WV.
33.   ii.   BETTY JEAN COOK, b. 02 Oct 1937.

12. CLIFFORD[5] HENSLEY *(ALICE BLANCHE[4] ROGERS, WILLIAM GEORGE[3], ROBERT JAHU[2] RODGERS, UNKNOWN[1])* died Unknown.   He married ANN UNKNOWN.

Child of CLIFFORD HENSLEY and ANN UNKNOWN is:
        i.   DANNY[6] HENSLEY.

13. RAYMOND[5] HENSLEY *(ALICE BLANCHE[4] ROGERS, WILLIAM GEORGE ROGERS [3], ROBERT JAHU[2] RODGERS, UNKNOWN[1])* was born 27 Jun 1923.   He married RUTH MAE UNKNOWN.

Children of RAYMOND HENSLEY and RUTH UNKNOWN are:
34.   i.   JUDY MAE[6] HENSLEY, Adopted child.
       ii.   JOANNE MARIE HENSLEY, m. TERRY CONLEY.

14. OLIVER[5] HENSLEY *(ALICE BLANCHE[4] ROGERS, WILLIAM GEORGE ROGERS[3], ROBERT JAHU[2] RODGERS, UNKNOWN[1])* was born 03 Oct 1926.   He married LELA MAE UNKNOWN.

Child of OLIVER HENSLEY and LELA UNKNOWN is:
        i.   SUSAN[6] HENSLEY.

15. HENSLEY[5] *(ALICE BLANCHE[4] ROGERS, WILLIAM GEORGE[3], ROBERT JAHU[2] RODGERS, UNKNOWN[1])* was born Abt. 1907.   She married EARL RAFFERTY.

Children of HENSLEY and EARL RAFFERTY are:
  i.   DALE[6] RAFFERTY.
  ii. GEORGE RAFFERTY.
  iii. ALMA RAFFERTY-MCFADDEN, m. UNKNOWN MCFADDEN.
  iv. ALICE RAFFERTY-BUSH, m. UNKNOWN BUSH.
  v.   MARY RAFFERTY-LAKE, m. UNKNOWN LAKE.

16. OPAL[5] HENSLEY-DOUGLAS *(ALICE BLANCHE[4] ROGERS, WILLIAM GEORGE[3], ROBERT JAHU[2] RODGERS, UNKNOWN[1])*   She married VERNON DOUGLAS.

Child of OPAL HENSLEY-DOUGLAS and VERNON DOUGLAS is:
  i.   HERBIE[6] DOUGLAS.

17. SNOWDEN[5] ROGERS *(NEWTON PAUL[4], WILLIAM GEORGE[3], ROBERT JAHU[2] RODGERS, UNKNOWN[1])* died Unknown.   He married HATTIE UNKNOWN.

Children of SNOWDEN ROGERS and HATTIE UNKNOWN are:
  i.   WADE[6] ROGERS, b. Unknown.
  ii. JAMES ROGERS, b. Abt. 1943.

18. ROLAND KESTER[5] ROGERS *(SARA ELIZABETH[4], WILLIAM GEORGE[3], ROBERT JAHU[2] RODGERS, UNKNOWN[1])* was born Abt. 1911; death date unknown.

Children of ROLAND KESTER ROGERS are:
  i.   MARY BETH[6] ROGERS.
  ii. LINDA ROGERS.
  iii. KAREN ROGERS.

19. HENRY HERSEY[5] ROGERS *(JAHU CLARK[4], WILLIAM GEORGE[3], ROBERT JAHU[2] RODGERS, UNKNOWN[1])* was born 24 Apr 1924 in Newton, WV, and died Sep 1993 in Spencer, WV, Roane Co.   He married MARY BELLE JUSTICE.

Children of HENRY ROGERS and MARY BELLE JUSTICE are:
  i.   MARILYN ANN[6] ROGERS, b. 22 May 1957.
  ii. INFANT ROGERS, b. 14 May 1959; d. Abt. 14 May 1959.

20. WILLIAM GAIL[5] ROGERS *(JAHU CLARK[4], WILLIAM GEORGE[3], ROBERT JAHU[2] RODGERS, UNKNOWN[1])* was born Abt. 1926 in Newton, WV, Roane Co.

Children of WILLIAM GAIL ROGERS are:
  i.   THOMAS[6] ROGERS, b. 25 Jan 1946; d. Unknown.
  ii. LARRY ROGERS, b. 31 Jan 1946; d. Unknown.

21. LAWANDA[5] ROGERS *(JAHU CLARK[4], WILLIAM GEORGE[3], ROBERT JAHU[2] RODGERS, UNKNOWN[1])* was born 03 Aug 1932 in Newton, WV, Roane Co. She married PAUL HICKLE. He was born Abt. 1932, and died in Maryland.

Children of LAWANDA ROGERS and PAUL HICKLE are:
    i. BRYAN[6] HICKLE.
    ii. BOY HICKLE.

22. MARDELL ADELEE[5] ROGERS *(ERNEST FREAR[4], WILLIAM GEORGE[3], ROBERT JAHU[2] RODGERS, UNKNOWN[1])* was born 06 Feb 1927 in Akron, Summit Co., OH. She met (1) GILBERT MCCLELLAND in Akron, OH, Summit Co., son of STANLEY MCCLELLAND and MARY DAVIS. He was born 23 Jun 1924, and died 20 May 1983. She married (2) HAROLD EDGAR JOHNSON 23 Oct 1951 in Las Vegas, NV, son of ADOLPH JOHNSON and ERNA BROOE. He was born 08 Sep 1924.

More about GILBERT MCCLELLAND and MARDELL ROGERS:
Single: Akron, OH, Summit Co.

More about HAROLD JOHNSON and ADELEE ROGERS:
Marriage: 23 Oct 1951, Las Vegas, NV

Child of ADELEE ROGERS and GILBERT MCCLELLAND is:
35.   i. MARY GILLETTE "SHELLEY"[6] MCCLELLAND, b. 04 Jan 1945, Akron, OH.

Children of ADELEE ROGERS and HAROLD JOHNSON are:
36.   ii. DALE ADOLPH[6] JOHNSON, b. 10 May 1953, Santa Monica, Los Angeles Co., CA.
37.   iii. TERESA ANN JOHNSON, b. 29 Jan 1955, Torrance, Los Angeles Co., CA.

23. ROBERT KEITH[5] ROGERS *(ERNEST FREAR[4], WILLIAM GEORGE[3], ROBERT JAHU[2] RODGERS, UNKNOWN[1])* was born 05 Aug 1928 in Akron, Summit Co. OH, and died 23 Dec 2008 in Gallipolis, OH. He married (1) MARIE PARSONS 28 Jul 1950 in Cartlettsburg, Boyd Co., KY, daughter of WILLIAM PARSONS and ICIE BISHOP. She was born 9 Jun 1929. He married (2) NANCY LARCH, daughter of WESLEY ADAMS LARCH.

Notes for ROBERT KEITH ROGERS – See page 50:

Children of ROBERT ROGERS and MARIE PARSONS are:
38.   i. INA GALE[6] ROGERS, b. 11 Mar 1949, Charleston, Kanawha Co., WV.
39.   ii. MICHAEL KEITH ROGERS, b. 03 Oct 1950, Charleston, Kanawha Co., WV.
40.   iii. RHONDA DIANE ROGERS, b. 10 May 1952, Charleston, Kanawha Co., WV.
41.   iv. DEBRA JEANNE ROGERS, b. 08 Aug 1953, Charleston, Kanawha Co., WV.
42.   v. TIMOTHY LEE ROGERS, b. 31 Jul 1954, Charleston, Kanawha Co., WV.
43.   vi. ROBERT RANDALL ROGERS, b. 10 Aug 1955, Charleston, Kanawha Co., WV.

24. ALMA "DELORES" [5] ROGERS *(ERNEST FREAR[4], WILLIAM GEORGE[3], ROBERT JAHU[2] RODGERS, UNKNOWN[1])* was born 23 Mar 1930 in Akron, Summit Co., OH. She married (2) DELBERT DENNIS 22 Jan 1958. He was born 22 Dec 1928 in Lake Lynn, PA.

Child of DELORES ROGERS is:
44.   i.   ANDREW JACKSON[6] ROGERS, b. 27 Mar 1952, Culver City, CA.

Child of DELORES ROGERS and DELBERT DENNIS is:
45.   ii. SHEILA MARLENE[6] DENNIS, b. 26 Mar 1959, Union Town, PA.

25. KERMIT ADOLPH[5] ROGERS *(ERNEST FREAR[4], WILLIAM GEORGE[3], ROBERT JAHU[2] RODGERS, UNKNOWN[1])* was born 23 Feb 1934 in Newton, Roane Co., WV.   He married BETTY LOU BIRD 12 Aug 1954, daughter of ALFRED BIRD and ORA TRUMAN.   She was born 29 Oct 1936 in Clay Co., WV.

Children of KERMIT ROGERS and BETTY BIRD are:
46.   i.   KATHLEEN ANN[6] ROGERS, b. 14 Jan 1955, Charleston, WV, Kanawha Co.
47.   ii.   CHERYL LYNN ROGERS, b. 10 Mar 1956, Charleston, WV, Kanawha Co.
48.   iii. DAWN ARLENE ROGERS, b. 15 May 1960, Charleston, WV, Kanawha Co.

26. DORMA KATHERN[5] ROGERS *(ERNEST FREAR[4], WILLIAM GEORGE[3], ROBERT JAHU[2] RODGERS, UNKNOWN[1])* was born 24 Mar 1936 in Newton, Roane Co., WV.   She married (1) JAMES HENRY BIRD Sep 1955, son of ALFRED BIRD and UNKNOWN SPOUSE.   He was born 12 Jun 1933, and died May 1986.   She married (2) JAMES DRAKE 22 Jul 1997 in Gatlinburg, Tennessee.   He was born 02 Mar 1939.

More about JAMES BIRD and DORMA ROGERS:
Death of one spouse: Indiana

More about JAMES DRAKE and DORMA ROGERS:
Marriage: 22 Jul 1997, Gatlinburg, Tennessee

Children of DORMA ROGERS and JAMES BIRD are:
         i.   JIMMY LEE[6] BIRD, b. 12 Jul 1956.
49.   ii.   NENA MARIE BIRD, b. 11 Mar 1958, Charleston, WV, Kanawha Co.
50.   iii. LISA CAROL BIRD, b. 30 Jun 1960.
51.   iv.   ERNEST SCOTT BIRD, b. 16 Aug 1962, Huntington, IN.

27. CARROLL AARON[5] ROGERS *(ERNEST FREAR[4], WILLIAM GEORGE[3], ROBERT JAHU[2] RODGERS, UNKNOWN[1])* was born 10 May 1938 in Newton, Roane Co., WV.   He married MARIA FELICIA GRECO 19 Nov 1960 in Morgantown, WV, daughter of FRANK GRECO and LOUISE NAPOLILLO.   She was born 25 May 1941.

Children of CARROLL ROGERS and MARIA GRECO are:
52.   i.   MARC ROBERT[6] ROGERS, b. 05 May 1962, Morgantown, WV, Monongalia Co.
53.   ii.   MICHELE LYNN ROGERS, b. 06 Apr 1964, Springfield, OH, Clark Co.
54.   iii. NATHAN ERIC ROGERS, b. 10 Jul 1970, Morgantown, WV, Monongalia Co.

28. CHARLOTTE ANN[5] ROGERS *(ERNEST FREAR[4], WILLIAM GEORGE[3], ROBERT JAHU[2] RODGERS, UNKNOWN[1])* was born 16 Mar 1940 in Newton, Roane Co., WV.   She married (1) DAVID ALEXANDER RICHMOND 22 Aug 1959 in Inglewood, LA Co., CA, son of JAMES ALEXANDER RICHMOND and LOIS HEMING.   He was born 02 Jun 1937 in Boston, Suffolk Co., Mass, and died 03 Aug 2008.   She married (2) DONALD JOHN OSTROM 30 Oct 1972 in Las Vegas, Clark Co., NV, son of RALPH OSTROM and ESTELLE DUDLEY.   He was born 20 Mar 1939 in Oconomowoc, Waukesha

Co., WI.   She married (3) GUY LEROY DILNO 14 Dec 1980 in Plainwell, Allegan Co., MI, son of MILFORD DILNO and WILDA PHILLIPS.   He was born 22 Aug 1946 in Kalamazoo, MI, Kalamazoo Co.

More about DAVID RICHMOND and CHARLOTTE ROGERS:
Divorce: 16 Nov 1969, Santa Ana, Orange Co., California
Marriage: 22 Aug 1959, Inglewood, LA Co., CA

More about DONALD OSTROM and CHARLOTTE ROGERS:
Divorce: 02 Nov 1979, Allegan, MI (Allegan Co.)
Marriage: 30 Oct 1972, Las Vegas, Clark Co., NV

More about GUY DILNO and CHARLOTTE ROGERS:
Marriage: 14 Dec 1980, Plainwell, Allegan Co., MI

Children of CHARLOTTE ROGERS and DAVID RICHMOND are:
55.   i.   BRAD ALEXANDER[6] RICHMOND, b. 17 Sep 1960, Inglewood, Los Angeles Co.,   CA.
56.   ii.   KIMBERLY ANNE RICHMOND, b. 11 Nov 1963, Riverside, Riverside Co., CA.

Child of CHARLOTTE ROGERS and DONALD OSTROM is:
57.   iii. LANCE JOHN[6] OSTROM, b. 29 Feb 1972, Phoenix, Maricopa Co., AZ.

29.   PATRICIA RONDELL[5] ROGERS *(ERNEST FREAR[4], WILLIAM GEORGE[3], ROBERT JAHU[2] RODGERS, UNKNOWN[1])* was born 05 Feb 1943 in Newton, Roane Co., WV.   She married HOMER LEE CONLEY 11 Aug 1962 in Clover Ridge, Roane Co., WV, son of HOWARD CONLEY and LOCIE MILLER.   He was born 14 Mar 1940 in Uler, Roane Co., WV.

Children of PATRICIA ROGERS and HOMER CONLEY are:
          i.   GREGORY LEE[6] CONLEY, b. 24 Jul 1963; m. PRISCILLA CATHERN NAYLOR, 24
                Feb 1993, Newton, Roane Co., WV; b. 11 Nov 1965.

          ii.   MICHAEL GARRETT CONLEY, b. 22 Jan 1966; m. (1) SHANNA CLAUDINE PUGH,
                Jul 1988, March AFB, Riverside Co., CA (Divorced); m. (2) JENNIFER REBECCA
                FRENCH, 30 Jun 1996 (Divorced); b. 14 Aug 1969, Grand Forks, ND; m. (3) SHIRLEY
                ANN BIRD, 19 May 2009, Newton, Roane Co., WV; b. 02 Jun 1952.
58.   iii. STEPHEN WAYNE CONLEY, b. 28 Sep 1967.
59.   iv.   STACY RONDELL CONLEY, b. 21 Sep 1972, Charleston, Kanawha Co., WV.

30.   BARBARA CAROLINE[5] ROGERS "BOBBIE" *(ERNEST FREAR[4], WILLIAM GEORGE[3], ROBERT JAHU[2] RODGERS, UNKNOWN[1])* was born 07 Sep 1945 in Charleston, Kanawha Co., WV, and died 05 Jun 2005 in Riverside, Riverside Co., CA.   She married ROGER BEISTLE in Las Vegas, NV. He was born 25 Jul 1941 in Riverside Co., CA.

Notes for BARBARA "BOBBIE" CAROLINE ROGERS – See Page 53:

Children of "BOBBIE" ROGERS and ROGER BEISTLE are:
          i.   GREGORY ALLEN[6] BEISTLE, b. 19 Jan 1966, Riverside, CA, Riverside Co.
60.   ii.   THERESE MARIE BEISTLE, b. 19 Jun 1968, Riverside, CA, Riverside Co.

Generation No. 5

31. LINDA CAMPBELL⁶ SMITH *(ELIZABETH⁵, CORA BELLE⁴ ROGERS, WILLIAM GEORGE³, ROBERT JAHU² RODGERS, UNKNOWN¹)*

Children of LINDA CAMPBELL SMITH are:
   i. JESSICA⁷ SMITH, b. 12 May 1992.
61. ii. STEPHEN ALEXANDER SMITH.

32. WILLIAM ROBERT⁶ COOK *(VIRGINIA BELLE⁵ SMITH, CORA BELLE⁴ ROGERS, WILLIAM GEORGE³ RODGERS, ROBERT JAHU² RODGERS, UNKNOWN¹)* was born 14 Aug 1935 in Logan Co., WV. He married PATTI L. STANLEY 31 Jul 1956 in Raleigh, NC.

Notes for WILLIAM ROBERT COOK:
William R. Cook

Obituary from the Charleston Gazette. William "Bobby" R. Cook, 69, a retired photoengraver with the CIA for 25 years, died from leukemia Nov. 25, 2004, at his home in Fairfax Station, Va.

He was born in Mallory, W.Va., and graduated from Sherman High School in Seth, W.Va., in 1953. Mr. Cook served an apprenticeship in photoengraving at Charleston Engraving Company. He was first employed by the Charleston Gazette in Charleston, W.Va. He came to the Washington area in 1960, and worked for Lanman Lithoplate and Rex Engraving. Mr. Cook joined the CIA in 1969, and served three separate overseas tours. He retired in 1995, receiving the Career Intelligence Medal. He was an avid golfer, and a volunteer at Twin Lakes Golf Course. He was also a member of the Bad Ems Alumni Golf Association.

Mr. Cook was a member of Fairfax Baptist Church. Survivors include his wife of 48 years, Patti Cook of Fairfax Station, Va.; four children, Cathy Vermaas of Boynton Beach, Fla., Lisa Whitney of Fairfax, Va., Greg Cook of Cheyenne, Wyoming, and Doug Cook of Leesburg, Va.; eight grandchildren; mother, Virginia Cook of Romney, W.Va.; and sister, Linda Campbell of Stephens City, Va.

Children of WILLIAM COOK and PATTI STANLEY are:
62. i. KATHY DELANE⁷ COOK, b. 10 Mar 1957.
   ii. LISA RENAE COOK, b. 29 Jun 1959; m. ROBERT WHITNEY.
   iii. ROBERT GREGORY COOK, b. 01 Sep 1960.
   iii. WILLIAM DOUGLAS COOK, b. 19 Oct 1965.
33. BETTY JEAN⁶ COOK *(VIRGINIA BELLE⁵ SMITH, CORA BELLE⁴ ROGERS, WILLIAM GEORGE³, ROBERT JAHU² RODGERS, UNKNOWN¹)* was born 02 Oct 1937. She married EARL LANCTOT. She is deceased.

Children of BETTY COOK and EARL LANCTOT are:
   i. CANDICE⁷ LANCTOT, b. 28 Nov 1969; m. JEFF DODRILL.
   ii. EDWARD EARL LANCTOT, b. 30 Jan 1970; m. TRACY NAME UNKNOWN.

34. JUDY MAE[6] HENSLEY *(RAYMOND[5], ALICE BLANCHE[4] ROGERS, WILLIAM GEORGE[3], ROBERT JAHU[2] RODGERS, UNKNOWN[1])* She married DENNIS LEROY ACHESON.

Children of JUDY HENSLEY and DENNIS ACHESON are:
    i.   ANGELA MAE[7] ACHESON, b. 27 Jun 1972.
    ii. BRIAN LEROY ACHESON, b. 17 Aug 1976.

35. MARY GILLETTE "SHELLEY"[6] MCCLELLAND *(MARDELL ADELEE[5] ROGERS, ERNEST FREAR[4], WILLIAM GEORGE[3] ROGERS, ROBERT JAHU[2] RODGERS, UNKNOWN[1])* was born 04 Jan 1945 in Akron, OH. She married (1) MARVIN JOHNSON; divorced He died Jun 2005. She married (2) BILL PANETTI; divorced.

Child of MARY MCCLELLAND and MARVIN JOHNSON is:
63.   i.   KATRINA LEIGH[7] JOHNSON, b. 08 Feb 1965.

Child of MARY MCCLELLAND and BILL PANETTI is:
    ii. MASON JEFFREY[7] PANETTI, b. 04 Jul 1968; m. NADINE F. MULLEN; b. 27 Dec 1961, Perth, Western Australia.

36. DALE ADOLPH[6] JOHNSON *(MARDELL ADELEE[5] ROGERS, ERNEST FREAR[4], WILLIAM GEORGE[3], ROBERT JAHU[2] RODGERS, UNKNOWN[1])* was born 10 May 1953 in Santa Monica, Los Angeles Co., CA. He married (1) SANDRA ANN BROWN 18 Sep 1976 in Orange Co., CA; divorced. She was born 10 Jul 1954. He married (2) DEBORAH JEAN MANUEL 17 Mar 2002 in Las Vegas, NV, daughter of UNKNOWN MANUEL and UNKNOWN WATSON. She was born 02 Jul 1950 in Tallahassee, Florida.

Children of DALE JOHNSON and SANDRA BROWN are:
    i.   MATTHEW RICHARD[7] JOHNSON, b. 01 Jul 1979; m. DENISSE CAROLINA SANCHEZ SOTO 09 Dec 2006, Los Mochis, Sinaloa, Mexico. She was born 16 Dec 1986.
    ii. RUSSELL KENNETH JOHNSON, b. 03 Feb 1981.
    iii. TIFFANY ANN JOHNSON, b. 10 Jul 1983.

37. TERESA ANN[6] JOHNSON *(MARDELL ADELEE[5] ROGERS, ERNEST FREAR[4], WILLIAM GEORGE[3] ROGERS, ROBERT JAHU[2] RODGERS, UNKNOWN[1])* was born 29 Jan 1955 in Torrance, Los Angeles Co., CA. She married KEITH CRAIG JACKSON 10 Apr 1982 in Castro Valley, Alameda Co., CA, son of WILLIAM JACKSON and MARY READING. He was born 08 May 1955.

Children of TERESA JOHNSON and KEITH JACKSON are:
    i.   LAUREN NICOLE[7] JACKSON, b. 21 May 1985, Petaluma, Sonoma Co., CA.
    ii. LEAH MICHELLE JACKSON, b. 06 Apr 1987, Petaluma, Sonoma Co., CA.
    iii. KYLE WILLIAM JACKSON, b. 16 Feb 1990, Petaluma, Sonoma Co., CA.

38. INA GALE[6] ROGERS *(ROBERT KEITH[5], ERNEST FREAR[4], WILLIAM GEORGE[3], ROBERT JAHU[2] RODGERS, UNKNOWN[1])* was born 11 Mar 1949 in Charleston, Kanawha Co., WV. She married JAMES KERMIT CARPER, son of GUY CARPER and RUBY GRAHAM. He was born 05 Jun 1941.

Children of GALE ROGERS and JAMES CARPER are:
	i.	JAMES DARIN[7] CARPER, b. 27 Nov 1967.
64.	ii.	BRIAN CHRISTOPHER CARPER, b. 23 Jun 1969.
65.	iii.	BRANDI LEE CARPER, b. 03 Feb 1975.

39. MICHAEL KEITH[6] ROGERS *(ROBERT KEITH[5], ERNEST FREAR[4], WILLIAM GEORGE[3], ROBERT JAHU[2] RODGERS, UNKNOWN[1])* was born 03 Oct 1950 in Charleston, Kanawha Co., WV. He married DEBORAH LEIGH LEGG (Divorced). She was born 16 Aug 1955.

Children of MICHAEL ROGERS and DEBORAH LEGG are:
| 66. | i. | MABEL LYNN[7] ROGERS, b. 24 Jul 1971. |
| | ii. | CHESTER KEITH ROGERS, b. 26 May 1976. |

40. RHONDA DIANE[6] ROGERS *(ROBERT KEITH[5], ERNEST FREAR[4], WILLIAM GEORGE[3], ROBERT JAHU[2] RODGERS, UNKNOWN[1])* was born 10 May 1952 in Charleston, Kanawha Co., WV. She married RANDALL KEITH CARPER 27 Mar 1971 in Roane Co., WV, son of BRADFORD CARPER and MABEL WESTFALL. He was born 21 Feb 1950.

Child of RHONDA ROGERS and RANDALL CARPER is:
| | i. | LISA DAWN[7] CARPER, b. 16 Mar 1980, Cuyahoga Falls, OH; m. BRIAN STOTT; b. 15 Feb 1976, Cuyahoga Falls, OH. |

41. DEBRA JEANNE[6] ROGERS *(ROBERT KEITH[5], ERNEST FREAR[4], WILLIAM GEORGE[3], ROBERT JAHU[2] RODGERS, UNKNOWN[1])* was born 08 Aug 1953 in Charleston, Kanawha Co., WV. She married (1) COLLEN WALDECK. She married (2) IVAN LOGSDON 19 Aug 1974 in Parsons, WV, Tucker Co; he died 1 May 2010.

More about COLLEN WALDECK and DEBRA ROGERS:
Marriage date: Divorced

More about IVAN LOGSDON and DEBRA ROGERS:
Marriage: 19 Aug 1974, Parsons, WV, Tucker Co.

Child of DEBRA ROGERS and COLLEN WALDECK is:
| 67. | i. | CHRISTINA LYNN[7] CONLEY, b. 25 Jan 1970, Parkersburg, WV, Wood Co. |

Children of DEBRA ROGERS and IVAN LOGSDON are:
| 68. | ii. | AMBER DAWN[7] LOGSDON, b. 21 Oct 1975, Parkersburg, WV, Wood Co. |
| | iii. | TRAVIS EUGENE LOGSDON, b. 30 May 1980, Parkersburg, WV, Wood Co.; m. HEATHER LYNN HEANEY, 28 Jun 2003, Vienna, WV. Divorced. |

42. TIMOTHY LEE[6] ROGERS *(ROBERT KEITH[5], ERNEST FREAR[4], WILLIAM GEORGE[3], ROBERT JAHU[2] RODGERS, UNKNOWN[1])* was born 31 Jul 1954 in Charleston, Kanawha Co., WV. He married KAREN TAWNEY; divorced. She was born 23 Oct 1954.

Children of TIMOTHY ROGERS and KAREN TAWNEY are:
69.   i.   CHADRICK LEE[7] ROGERS, b. 09 Feb 1977.
70.   ii.   KELLY JO ROGERS, b. 19 Feb 1979.

43. ROBERT RANDALL[6] ROGERS *(ROBERT KEITH[5], ERNEST FREAR[4], WILLIAM GEORGE[3], ROBERT JAHU[2] RODGERS, UNKNOWN[1])* was born 10 Aug 1955 in Charleston, Kanawha Co., WV. He married LORAINE MARIE BARONE, daughter of VITO BARONE and ANGELA UNKNOWN.

Marriage Notes for ROBERT ROGERS and LORAINE BARONE:
Divorced.

Child of ROBERT RANDALL ROGERS and LORAINE BARONE is:
     i.   JOSEPH RANDALL[7] ROGERS, b. 23 Feb 1978, Akron, OH, Summit Co.

44. ANDREW JACKSON[6] ROGERS *(ALMA DELORES [5], ERNEST FREAR[4], WILLIAM GEORGE[3], ROBERT JAHU[2] RODGERS, UNKNOWN[1])* was born 27 Mar 1952 in Culver City, CA. He married (1) CAROLINE CARTE (Divorced). She was born 23 Jun 1950 and died 03 Aug 2006 in Clay, WV. He married (2) TAMMY LYNN GRAY 05 Sep 1997 in Clifton Forge, VA, daughter of SHIRLEY GRAY and SANDRA TAWNEY. She was born 27 Jun 1973 in Jackson Co. Hospital, Ripley, WV.

Notes for ANDREW JACKSON ROGERS – See Page 57

Child of ANDREW ROGERS and CAROLINE CARTE is:
71.   i.   ANDREA JACQUELINE[7] ROGERS, b. 22 Dec 1976.

45. SHEILA MARLENE[6] DENNIS *(ALMA "DELORES" [5] ROGERS, ERNEST FREAR[4], WILLIAM GEORGE[3], ROBERT JAHU[2] RODGERS, UNKNOWN[1])* was born 26 Mar 1959 in Union Town, PA. She married ROGER ALAN BREMER 08 Mar 1980 in Fort Wayne, IN, son of KENNETH BREMER and RUTH WOLFE. He was born 10 Sep 1960.

Children of SHEILA DENNIS and ROGER BREMER are:
72.   i.   JAMI MARLENE[7] BREMER, b. 24 Aug 1980, Fort Wayne, IN.
         ii.   ASHLEY MARLENE BREMER, b. 29 Jul 1985, Fort Wayne, IN.
73.   iii.   LINDSEY MARLENE BREMER, b. 29 Jul 1985, Fort Wayne, IN.

46. KATHLEEN ANN[6] ROGERS *(KERMIT ADOLPH[5], ERNEST FREAR[4], WILLIAM GEORGE[3], ROBERT JAHU[2] RODGERS, UNKNOWN[1])* was born 14 Jan 1955 in Charleston, WV, Kanawha Co. She married (2) ROGER SMITH 01 Dec 1973; divorced. He was born 31 Jan 1947. She married (1) KARL HOLCOMB; divorced.

Children of KATHLEEN ROGERS and ROGER SMITH are:
74.   i.   KERRIE ANN[7] SMITH, b. 28 Dec 1979.
75.   ii.   KACIE JO SMITH, b. 31 Oct 1985.

47. CHERYL LYNN[6] ROGERS *(KERMIT ADOLPH[5], ERNEST FREAR[4], WILLIAM GEORGE[3], ROBERT JAHU[2] RODGERS, UNKNOWN[1])* was born 10 Mar 1956 in Charleston, WV, Kanawha Co. She met PAUL HOLCOMB 22 Sep 1973.   He was born 16 Jun 1949 in Indore, Clay Co., WV; divorced.

Children of CHERYL ROGERS and PAUL HOLCOMB are:

      i.   JENNIFER DAWN[7] HOLCOMB, b. 22 Oct 1974, Charleston, Kanawha Co., West Virginia; m. MARK TANNER, 22 Apr 2000, Monroe, NC; b. 05 Apr 1973, Charleston, Kanawha Co., West Virginia.

76.   ii.   LEAH MICHELE HOLCOMB, b. 07 Nov 1976, Charleston, Kanawha Co., West Virginia.

48. DAWN ARLENE[6] ROGERS *(KERMIT ADOLPH[5], ERNEST FREAR[4], WILLIAM GEORGE[3], ROBERT JAHU[2] RODGERS, UNKNOWN[1])* was born 15 May 1960 in Charleston, WV, Kanawha Co. She married CHARLES RICHARD WILKINSON in Arnoldsburg, WV, Calhoun Co.   He was born 26 Nov 1949.

Children of DAWN ROGERS and CHARLES WILKINSON are:

77.   i.   LUKE AARON[7] WILKINSON, b. 27 Jul 1979.

      ii.   CARRISSA DAWN WILKINSON, b. 08 Oct 1980; m. JAMES FOSTER.

     iii. JESSY KATHLYNN WILKINISON, b. 20 Oct 1984.

78.   iv. REBECCA KAY WILKINSON, b. 08 May 1986.

      v.   JULIE MARIE WILKINSON, b. 11 Oct 1988.

49. NENA MARIE[6] BIRD *(DORMA KATHERN[5] ROGERS, ERNEST FREAR[4], WILLIAM GEORGE[3], ROBERT JAHU[2] RODGERS, UNKNOWN[1])* was born 11 Mar 1958 in Charleston, WV, Kanawha Co.   She married (1) RICKY GENE COPPOCK 19 Jun 1976 in Huntington, IN, son of HARRY COPPOCK and EVELYN CAMPBELL.   He was born 11 Sep 1957, and died 10 May 2000. She married Randall Lee Hobbs on 10 April, 2010.   Randy was born on 06 Dec 1955.

Children of NENA BIRD and RICKY COPPOCK are:

79.   i.   SCOTT LEE[7] COPPOCK, b. 15 Jul 1978, Bluffton, Indiana, Wells Co.

      ii.   KATHRYN IRENE COPPOCK, b. 29 Sep 1982, Hartford City, IN, Blackford Co.; m. CHASE GARRETT HILL, 28 Dec 2002, First Baptist Church, Alexandria, IN. He was born 04 Aug 1983.

          Notes for KATHRYN IRENE COPPOCK:
          Nena said Kathryn Irene was named after grandmothers.
          Information provided by Nena Coppock.   Information from Nena Coppock 9-17-96.

50. LISA CAROL[6] BIRD *(DORMA KATHERN[5] ROGERS, ERNEST FREAR[4], WILLIAM GEORGE[3], ROBERT JAHU[2] RODGERS, UNKNOWN[1])* was born 30 Jun 1960.   She married STEVE TACKETT 03 Aug 1979.   He was born 17 Oct 1956.

Children of LISA BIRD and STEVE TACKETT are:

      i.   BOBBY WAYNE[7] TACKETT, b. 19 Aug 1980.

80.   ii.   JAMES LEE TACKETT JR., b. 19 Aug 1980.

     iii. STEVEN DANIEL TACKETT, b. 20 May 1987.

51. ERNEST SCOTT[6] BIRD *(DORMA KATHERN[5] ROGERS, ERNEST FREAR[4], WILLIAM GEORGE[3], ROBERT JAHU[2] RODGERS, UNKNOWN[1])* was born 16 Aug 1962 in Huntington, IN. He married APRIL SHOEMAKER 14 Nov 2008.

Children of ERNEST BIRD and APRIL SHOEMAKER are:
  i. KYLIE MAY[7] BIRD, b. 30 Dec 1992.
  ii. MCKENNA SHOEMAKER, b. 25 Aug 2000.
  iii. JOSEPH SCOTT BIRD, b. 05 May 2005.

52. MARC ROBERT[6] ROGERS *(CARROLL AARON[5], ERNEST FREAR[4], WILLIAM GEORGE[3], ROBERT JAHU[2] RODGERS, UNKNOWN[1])* was born 05 May 1962 in Morgantown, WV, Monongalia Co. He married MELANIE BAKER 19 Dec 1998 in Wesley Methodist Church, High St., Morgantown, WV. She was born 01 May 1964 in Honolulu, Hawaii.

Children of MARC ROGERS and MELANIE BAKER are:
  i. MATTHEW PERRY[7] ROGERS, b. 02 Feb 2001 in Russia
  ii. MIKALA POLINA ROGERS, b. 01 Sep 2003 in Russia

53. MICHELE LYNN[6] ROGERS *(CARROLL AARON[5], ERNEST FREAR[4], WILLIAM GEORGE[3], ROBERT JAHU[2] RODGERS, UNKNOWN[1])* was born 06 Apr 1964 in Springfield, OH, Clark Co. She married (1) MICHAEL TARRANTINI; divorced; he was killed in an auto accident from falling rocks. She married (2) GREGORY WES MCDONALD 20 Sep 1992 in Morgantown, WV, Monongalia Co. He was born 22 Oct 1963.

Children of MICHELE ROGERS and GREGORY MCDONALD are:
  i. HEATHER NOEL[7] MCDONALD, b. 15 Dec 1993, Morgantown, WV, Monongalia Co.
  ii. WESLEY AARON MCDONALD, b. 10 May 1997, Morgantown, WV, Monongalia Co.

54. NATHAN ERIC[6] ROGERS *(CARROLL AARON[5], ERNEST FREAR[4], WILLIAM GEORGE[3], ROBERT JAHU[2] RODGERS, UNKNOWN[1])* was born 10 Jul 1970 in Morgantown, WV, Monongalia Co. He married VICKIE SUE DECARLO 22 Jun 1996 in Morgantown, WV, Monongalia Co., daughter of DONALD DECARLO and SANDRA ASHLEY. She was born 26 Jun 1970 in Warren, OH, Trumbell Co.

Children of NATHAN ROGERS and VICKIE DECARLO are:
  i. ISIAH JACKSON[7] ROGERS, b. 24 Oct 2001.
  ii. FRANKLIN JEREMIAH ROGERS, b. 26 Jun 2003.
  iii. WINSTON NEHEMIAH ROGERS, b. 26 Jun 2003.
  iv. HUDSON ELIJAH ROGERS, b. 13 Oct 2008.

55. BRAD ALEXANDER[6] RICHMOND *(CHARLOTTE ANN[5] ROGERS, ERNEST FREAR[4], WILLIAM GEORGE[3], ROBERT JAHU[2] RODGERS, UNKNOWN[1])* was born 17 Sep 1960 in Inglewood, Los Angeles Co., CA. He married (1) DAWN MARIE GAUTHIER 30 Nov 1979 in Otsego, Allegan Co., MI, daughter of GEORGE GAUTHIER and BEATRICE BARBER. She was born 17 Jul 1961 in Plainwell, Allegan Co., MI. He married (2) VICKIE LYNNE NICKELSON 22 Aug 2008 in Rockford, MI, daughter of UNKNOWN NICKELSON. She was born 09 Jan 1962 in Henipin County, Minneapolis, MN.

Notes for BRAD ALEXANDER RICHMOND – See page 63.:

Notes for DAWN MARIE GAUTHIER:
Divorced. Graduated from Grand Canyon University in 2009.

More about BRAD RICHMOND and DAWN GAUTHIER:
Divorce: 2006, Grand Rapids, Kent Co., MI
Marriage: 30 Nov 1979, Otsego, Allegan Co., MI

Children of BRAD RICHMOND and DAWN GAUTHIER are:
     i. BROOKE ALEXANDRIA[7] RICHMOND, b. 27 Jun 1983, Plainwell, Allegan Co., MI.
    ii. BRENTON ALEXANDER RICHMOND, b. 11 Jan 1987, Plainwell, Allegan Co., MI.
   iii. BRITTANY ANASTASIA RICHMOND, b. 24 Feb 1990, Plainwell, Allegan Co., MI.

Children of BRAD RICHMOND and VICKIE NICKELSON are:
   iv. MARTIN ANDREW[7] MONZO, b. 19 Mar 1991, Ingham County, Lansing, MI.
    v. RACHEL MONZO, b. 25 Jun 1993, Kent County, Grand Rapids, MI.

56. KIMBERLY ANNE[6] RICHMOND *(CHARLOTTE ANN[5] ROGERS, ERNEST FREAR[4], WILLIAM GEORGE[3], ROBERT JAHU[2] RODGERS, UNKNOWN[1])* was born 11 Nov 1963 in Riverside, Riverside Co., CA. She married MICHAEL CHARLES HICKEY 09 Apr 1982 in Yucca Valley, CA, son of PATRICIA WEBSTER. He was born 26 May 1961 in Pittsburgh, PA.

Notes for KIMBERLY ANNE RICHMOND – see page 64.

Notes for MICHAEL CHARLES HICKEY – See Page 64.

Children of KIMBERLY RICHMOND and MICHAEL HICKEY are:
81.   i. MATTHEW MICHAEL[7] HICKEY, b. 15 Nov 1984, Nuremberg, Germany.
    ii. KRISTIN ANN HICKEY, b. 30 Oct 1988, Spanaway, Washington; m. JEFFERY LORSUNG, 10 Feb 2009, Radcliff, Kentucky; b. Coquille, Oregon.

More about JEFFERY LORSUNG and KRISTIN HICKEY:
     Marriage: 10 Feb 2009, Radcliff, Kentucky

57. LANCE JOHN[6] OSTROM *(CHARLOTTE ANN[5] ROGERS, ERNEST FREAR[4], WILLIAM GEORGE[3], ROBERT JAHU[2] RODGERS, UNKNOWN[1])* was born 29 Feb 1972 in Phoenix, Maricopa Co., AZ. He married LAUREL LEE LACOUR 09 Sep 2001 in Saline, MI, daughter of CHARLES LACOUR and JEAN. She was born 14 Apr 1975.

Notes for LANCE JOHN OSTROM – See Page 64.

Child of LANCE OSTROM and LAUREL LACOUR is:
      i.   JACOB DAVIS[7] OSTROM, b. 18 Jun 2008, Concord, MA.
      ii. CLAIRE ANN OSTROM, b. 21 Apr 2010, Concord, MA.
      iii. MAYA JEAN OSTROM, b. 21 Apr 2010, Concore, MA.

      Notes for JACOB DAVIS OSTROM -- See Page 65.

      Notes for CLAIRE ANN OSTROM. and MAYA JEAN OSTROM – See Page 65:

58. STEPHEN WAYNE[6] CONLEY *(PATRICIA RONDELL[5] ROGERS, ERNEST FREAR[4], WILLIAM GEORGE[3], ROBERT JAHU[2] RODGERS, UNKNOWN[1])* was born 28 Sep 1967.   He married (1) VERA ELLEN HIGHLANDER.

Children of STEPHEN CONLEY and VERA HIGHLANDER are:
      i.   GABRIEL WAYNE[7] CONLEY, b. 30 Dec 2001, West Virginia. Born at Thomas Memorial Hospital, Charleston, WV.

      ii. JOSHUA HIGHLANDER CONLEY, b. 25 Apr 2006, WV at Thomas Memorial Hospital..

Child of STEPHEN CONLEY and MELISSA BAILEY is:
82.   iii. ASHLEY NICOLE[7] BAILEY, b. 12 Feb 1993, So. Charleston, Kanawha Co., WV.

59. STACY RONDELL[6] CONLEY *(PATRICIA RONDELL[5] ROGERS, ERNEST FREAR[4], WILLIAM GEORGE[3], ROBERT JAHU[2] RODGERS, UNKNOWN[1])* was born 21 Sep 1972 in Charleston, Kanawha Co., WV.   She married AARON MICHAEL ROMANO 30 May 1992 in Newton, WV, Roane Co., son of JOHN ROMANO and RUTH SHEPPER.   He was born 07 Sep 1971.

Notes for STACY RONDELL CONLEY:
Information from Stacy Conley Sept. 4, 1996.
Born Charleston Memorial Hospital.

Children of STACY CONLEY and AARON ROMANO are:
      i.   BRYAN GREGORY[7] ROMANO, b. 03 May 1994, Spencer, WV, Roane Co., Roane General Hospital.

      ii. JUSTIN MATTHEW ROMANO, b. 17 Oct 1995, Great Falls, Montana; born Columbus Hospital.

      iii. SARA ELIZABETH ROMANO, b. 07 Sep 1998, Florida; born Shands Hospital at University of Florida.

60. THERESE MARIE[6] BEISTLE *(BARBARA CAROLINE[5] ROGERS, ERNEST FREAR[4], WILLIAM GEORGE[3], ROBERT JAHU[2] RODGERS, UNKNOWN[1])* was born 19 Jun 1968 in Riverside, CA, Riverside Co.   She married KEVIN PEDERSON; divorced in Riverside Co., Riverside, CA

Children of THERESE BEISTLE and KEVIN PEDERSON are:
      i.   BRITNEY TAYLOR[7] PEDERSON, b. 28 Jan 1994, Riverside, CA, Riverside Co.
      ii. CHRISTIAN KEVIN PEDERSON, b. 25 Apr 1995, Riverside, CA, Riverside Co.

Generation No. 6

61. STEPHEN ALEXANDER[7] SMITH *(LINDA CAMPBELL[6], ELIZABETH[5], CORA BELLE[4] ROGERS, WILLIAM GEORGE[3], ROBERT JAHU[2] RODGERS, UNKNOWN[1])* He married SUSAN NAME UNKNOWN.

Children of STEPHEN SMITH and SUSAN UNKNOWN are:
    i. MORGAN[8] SMITH.
   ii. WILLIAM SMITH.

62. KATHY DELANE[7] COOK *(WILLIAM ROBERT[6], VIRGINIA BELLE[5] SMITH, CORA BELLE[4] ROGERS, WILLIAM GEORGE[3], ROBERT JAHU[2] RODGERS, UNKNOWN[1])* was born 10 Mar 1957. She married ERIC PHILLIPS.

Child of KATHY COOK and ERIC PHILLIPS is:
    i. UNKNOWN[8] SON.

63. KATRINA LEIGH[7] JOHNSON *(MARY GILLETTE "SHELLEY"[6] MCCLELLAND, MARDELL ADELEE[5] ROGERS, ERNEST FREAR[4], WILLIAM GEORGE[3], ROBERT JAHU[2] RODGERS, UNKNOWN[1])* was born 08 Feb 1965. She married MATT HESSLER. Divorced.

Child of KATRINA JOHNSON and MATT HESSLER is:
    i. KAYLA ELL[8] HESSLER, b. 05 Aug 1989.

64. BRIAN CHRISTOPHER[7] CARPER *(INA GALE[6] ROGERS, ROBERT KEITH[5], ERNEST FREAR[4], WILLIAM GEORGE[3], ROBERT JAHU[2] RODGERS, UNKNOWN[1])* was born 23 Jun 1969. He married Cindy Robinson. She was born 24 Feb 1970.

Child of BRIAN CHRISTOPHER CARPER is:
   iii. KYLIE PAGE[8] CARPER, b. 22 Jun 2003.
   iv. COURTNEY BROOK CARPER b 04 Feb 2005.

65. BRANDI LEE[7] CARPER *(INA GALE[6] ROGERS, ROBERT KEITH[5], ERNEST FREAR[4], WILLIAM GEORGE[3], ROBERT JAHU[2] RODGERS, UNKNOWN[1])* was born 03 Feb 1975. She married James Ward.

Child of BRANDI LEE CARPER is:
    i. MORGAN NICHOLE[8] CARPER WALKER, b. 23 Mar 1994.

66. MABEL LYNN[7] ROGERS *(MICHAEL KEITH[6], ROBERT KEITH[5], ERNEST FREAR[4], WILLIAM GEORGE[3], ROBERT JAHU[2] RODGERS, UNKNOWN[1])* was born 24 Jul 1971.

Children of MABEL LYNN ROGERS are:
    i. JOSHUA NEIL[8] SHIREY, b. 17 Aug 1989.
   ii. LOREN MONTANA LEGG, b. 04 Jul 1991.
   iii. WHITNEY RAY SHIREY, b. 09 Jun 1993.
   iv. CHRISTINA DANIELLE PECK, b. 09 Nov 1995.

67. CHRISTINA LYNN[7] CONLEY *(DEBRA JEANNE[6] ROGERS, ROBERT KEITH[5], ERNEST FREAR[4], WILLIAM GEORGE[3], ROBERT JAHU[2] RODGERS, UNKNOWN[1])* was born 25 Jan 1970 in Parkersburg, WV, Wood Co. She married (1) GARY SCOTT DEUSENBERRY 30 Dec 1988 in Newton, WV (Divorced). He was born 30 Dec 1969. She married (2) MIKE WHITTMAN 22 Jul 2000. He was born 30 Dec 1969.

Child of CHRISTINA CONLEY and GARY DEUSENBERRY is:
     i. KAYLA COLLEEN[8] DEUSENBERRY, b. 10 Dec 1990.

68. AMBER DAWN[7] LOGSDON *(DEBRA JEANNE[6] ROGERS, ROBERT KEITH[5], ERNEST FREAR[4], WILLIAM GEORGE[3], ROBERT JAHU[2] RODGERS, UNKNOWN[1])* was born 21 Oct 1975 in Parkersburg, WV, Wood Co. She married TONY HUBER.

Children of AMBER LOGSDON and TONY HUBER are:
     i. CODY LEE[8] HUBER, b. 10 Oct 2000.
     ii. KINDRA NICOLE HUBER, b. 02 Feb 1998.

69. CHADRICK LEE[7] ROGERS *(TIMOTHY LEE[6], ROBERT KEITH[5], ERNEST FREAR[4], WILLIAM GEORGE[3], ROBERT JAHU[2] RODGERS, UNKNOWN[1])* was born 09 Feb 1977.

Child of CHADRICK LEE ROGERS is:
     i. JAYDEN[8] ROGERS, b. 2003.

70. KELLY JO[7] ROGERS *(TIMOTHY LEE[6], ROBERT KEITH[5], ERNEST FREAR[4], WILLIAM GEORGE[3], ROBERT JAHU[2] RODGERS, UNKNOWN[1])* was born 19 Feb 1979. She married DAVID STONE.

Child of KELLY ROGERS and DAVID STONE is:
     i. HAYDEN ZANE[8] STONE, b. Abt. 12 Feb 2003.

71. ANDREA JACQUELINE[7] ROGERS *(ANDREW JACKSON[6], ALMA DELORES[5], ERNEST FREAR[4], WILLIAM GEORGE[3], ROBERT JAHU[2] RODGERS, UNKNOWN[1])* was born 22 Dec 1976. She married (2) ROBERT WHITE.

Child of ANDREA JACQUELINE ROGERS is:
     i. HUNTER LEE[8] BOWMAN, b. 26 Jan 1996.

     Notes for HUNTER LEE BOWMAN:
     Hunter's biological father is Larry Bowman of Virginia. Larry is also enlisted with the U.S.M.C. as of 3-1-99.

Child of ANDREA ROGERS and ROBERT WHITE is:
     ii. JORJA KENZLEIGH[8] WHITE, b. 13 Aug 2003.

     Notes for JORJA KENZLEIGH WHITE: At birth: 7 pounds, 19 inches long.

72. JAMI MARLENE[7] BREMER *(SHEILA MARLENE[6] DENNIS, ALMA[5] DELORES ROGERS, ERNEST FREAR[4], WILLIAM GEORGE[3], ROBERT JAHU[2] RODGERS, UNKNOWN[1])* was born 24 Aug 1980 in Fort Wayne, IN. She married CASEY LEE ADAMS 16 Aug 2003 in Ft. Wayne, IN. He was born 28 Nov 1978.

Children of JAMI BREMER and CASEY ADAMS are:
>   i. SPENCER LEE[8] ADAMS, b. 01 Dec 2005, Ft. Wayne, IN.
>   ii. CHLOE RENEE ADAMS, b. 17 Oct 2008, Ft. Wayne, IN.

73. LINDSEY MARLENE[7] BREMER *(SHEILA MARLENE[6] DENNIS, ALMA DELORES[5] ROGERS, ERNEST FREAR[4], WILLIAM GEORGE[3], ROBERT JAHU[2] RODGERS, UNKNOWN[1])* was born 29 Jul 1985 in Fort Wayne, IN.

Child of LINDSEY MARLENE BREMER is:
>   i. GRACYN RYLIN[8] SPILLERS, b. 07 Nov 2009, Ft. Wayne, IN.

74. KERRIE ANN[7] SMITH *(KATHLEEN ANN[6] ROGERS, KERMIT ADOLPH[5], ERNEST FREAR[4], WILLIAM GEORGE[3], ROBERT JAHU[2] RODGERS, UNKNOWN[1])* was born 28 Dec 1979. She married (2) JAMES DRAKE 03 Jun 2000 in Newton, WV, Roane Co. She married (3) RICHARD L. YOUNG, JR. 04 Jan 2003 in United Me. Church, Clendenin, WV.

More about RICHARD YOUNG. and KERRIE SMITH:
Marriage: 04 Jan 2003, United Me. Church, Clendenin, WV

Child of KERRIE ANN SMITH is:
>   i. CLOIE PAGE[8] HART, b. 04 Sep 2007.

Child of KERRIE SMITH and RICHARD YOUNG. is:
>   ii. KAITLYNN BRIELLE[8] YOUNG, b. 27 Sep 2003.

75. KACIE JO[7] SMITH *(KATHLEEN ANN[6] ROGERS, KERMIT ADOLPH[5], ERNEST FREAR[4], WILLIAM GEORGE[3], ROBERT JAHU[2] RODGERS, UNKNOWN[1])* was born 31 Oct 1985. She married (2) ROBERT "SCOTT" HOLCOMB 22 Jun 2009. He was born 08 Jan 1982.

Child of KACIE JO SMITH is:
>   i. MAHAILEY JO[8] SMITH, b. 02 Dec 2005.
Child of KACIE JO SMITH AND SCOTT HOLCOMB is:
>   ii. MARISSA BROOKE HOLCOMB b. 25 Jan 2010.

76. LEAH MICHELE[7] HOLCOMB *(CHERYL LYNN[6] ROGERS, KERMIT ADOLPH[5], ERNEST FREAR[4], WILLIAM GEORGE[3], ROBERT JAHU[2] RODGERS, UNKNOWN[1])* was born 07 Nov 1976 in Charleston, Kanawha Co., West Virginia. She married JEREMY QUINN. He was born 30 Jun 1974 in Charleston, Kanawha Co., West Virginia.

Children of LEAH HOLCOMB and JEREMY QUINN are:
>   i. GARRETT MONTEVILLE[8] QUINN, b. 10 Mar 2001.
>   ii. JACKSON HENRY QUINN, b. 09 Jun 2006.

77. LUKE AARON[7] WILKINSON *(DAWN ARLENE[6] ROGERS, KERMIT ADOLPH[5], ERNEST FREAR[4], WILLIAM GEORGE[3], ROBERT JAHU[2] RODGERS, UNKNOWN[1])* was born 27 Jul 1979.

Child of LUKE AARON WILKINSON is:
  i. KYLIN LEVI[8] WILKINSON, b. 29 Jan 1999, Kirksville, MO.

78. REBECCA KAY[7] WILKINSON *(DAWN ARLENE[6] ROGERS, KERMIT ADOLPH[5], ERNEST FREAR[4], WILLIAM GEORGE[3], ROBERT JAHU[2] RODGERS, UNKNOWN[1])* was born 08 May 1986. She married ADAM DUANE STOCK. He was born 03 Feb 1982 in Alexandria, LA.

Children of REBECCA WILKINSON and ADAM STOCK are:
  i. BRAXTON GRAHAM[8] STOCK, b. 30 Jun 2006, Missouri.
  ii. OWEN BRADFORD STOCK, b. 24 Oct 2008.

79. SCOTT LEE[7] COPPOCK *(NENA MARIE[6] BIRD, DORMA KATHERN[5] ROGERS, ERNEST FREAR[4], WILLIAM GEORGE[3], ROBERT JAHU[2] RODGERS, UNKNOWN[1])* was born 15 Jul 1978 in Bluffton, Indiana, Wells Co. He married LILLIAN E. "FROSYNI" Douramacos" 08 Jun 2002 in Alexandria, IN. She was born 15 Oct 1978 in Anderson, IN, Madison Co.

Notes for SCOTT LEE COPPOCK:
Scott's mother said he was named after three uncles.

Notes for LILLIAN E FROSYNI" DOURAMACOS:
Married at First Christina Church, 215 West Berry, Alexandria, IN.

Child of SCOTT COPPOCK and LILLIAN DOURAMACOS is:
  i. DAVID JAMES[8] COPPOCK, b. 11 Jun 2008, Carmel, Indiana.

80. JAMES LEE TACKETT[7] JR. *(LISA CAROL[6] BIRD, DORMA KATHERN[5] ROGERS, ERNEST FREAR[4], WILLIAM GEORGE[3], ROBERT JAHU[2] RODGERS, UNKNOWN[1])* was born 19 Aug 1980. He married KRISTINE LOUISE WHITE. She was born 29 Oct 1983.

Children of JAMES JR. and KRISTINE WHITE are:
  i. HALEY KRISTINE[8] TACKETT, b. 14 Jul 2004.
  ii. JAMES LEE TACKETT II, b. 02 Nov 2001.
  iii. CHRISTIAN DAVID TACKETT, b. 04 Feb 2008.

81. MATTHEW MICHAEL[7] HICKEY *(KIMBERLY ANNE[6] RICHMOND, CHARLOTTE ANN[5] ROGERS, ERNEST FREAR[4], WILLIAM GEORGE[3], ROBERT JAHU[2] RODGERS, UNKNOWN[1])* was born 15 Nov 1984 in Nuremberg, Germany. He married ROCHELLE LYNN DOVIN in Plainwell, Allegan Co., MI. She was born 11 Mar 1985 daughter of DAMIAN DOVIN and KARINA DOVIN.

Children of MATTHEW HICKEY and ROCHELLE DOVIN are:
  i. RYLEIGH ELIZABETH[8] HICKEY, b. 06 Feb 2006, Kalamazoo, Kalamazoo Co., MI.
  ii. JACKSON MATTHEW HICKEY, b. 31 May 2009, Kalamazoo, Kalamazoo Co., MI.

82. ASHLEY NICOLE[7] BAILEY *(STEPHEN WAYNE[6] CONLEY, PATRICIA RONDELL[5] ROGERS, ERNEST FREAR[4], WILLIAM GEORGE[3], ROBERT JAHU[2] RODGERS, UNKNOWN[1])* was born 12 Feb 1993 in So. Charleston, Kanawha Co., WV.

Notes for ASHLEY NICOLE BAILEY:
Born at Thomas Memorial Hospital.

Child of ASHLEY NICOLE BAILEY is:
      i. BRAYDONN JAMES[8] BAILEY, b. 05 Jul 2009, Ohio.

Family Photographs

Figure 5 - Ernest F. Rogers and L. Mabel Tawney
May 17, 1926—Akron, Ohio

Ernest and Mabel were born in Roane County, WV near Newton. Ernest was born March 16, 1902 and Mabel was born March 23, 1906. They were married in Akron, Ohio, Summit County on May 17, 1926 and raised ten children. Ernest was a 1st Class Pipefitter at E. I. Dupont in Belle, WV and lived on a farm at Newton. In later years he became an ordained minister and, along with Mabel, was a member of the Newton Methodist Church. Mabel was a homemaker and, before she married, was an elementary school teacher. After all her children were of school age, she was a cook at the Newton Grade School and rode the school bus with her children.

Family Photographs —Tawney Family

Figure 6 - 1994.   Florence, Mamie, Mabel, Dan, Clark,
Garrison and Clement Tawney.
Brothers and Sisters. Left Hand. WV.   Memorial Day.

Figure 7 - 1996 Reunion. The Tawney Brothers and Sisters.
Front L-R Clark, Garrison, Florence, Clement, Mamie, Mabel.   Back L-R:
Dan, Anna and "Buzz."

Family Photographs—Tawney Family

Figure 8 - 1996 Family Reunion.   Tawney Brothers and Sisters

Front L-R: Frances, Mamie, Florence, Mabel and Bea.   Back L-R: Clement, Garrison, "Buzz" and Clark.   Family Reunion.   Left Hand, WV.

Figure 9 - Aaron and Almon Tawney Home.   Left Hand, WV.   Built about 1912.

Family Photographs—Tawney Family

Figure 11 - "Buzz" Jarrett Tawney.
First All-Class Reunion at
Spencer High.

Figure 10 - Mamie Tawney-Haines
and Clement Tawney.

Figure 12 - 1996.   Mabel Tawney-Rogers and Florence Tawney-Dalton.
Reunion.   Left Hand, WV.

Family Photographs—Tawney Family

Figure 16 - 1994. Opal Nester-Tawney.

Figure 15 - 1994. Clark Tawney and
Bea Summers-Tawney.

Figure 13 - 1994. Mamie
Tawney-Haines.

Figure 14 - Dan Tawney and Hazel Short-Tawney.

Family Photographs—Tawney Family
Aaron Tawney and Flora Almon Graham-Tawney

Figure 18 - About 1916. Aaron Tawney with children.

L-R: Clement, Aaron, Mabel and Mamie Tawney.

Figure 17 - About 1914. Children of Aaron and Almon Tawney:

Clement, Mamie, Garrison, Florence, Mamie, Mabel and Ernest Tawney.

Family Photographs—Tawney Family
Aaron Tawney and Flora Almon Graham-Tawney

Figure 20 - 1919. Family of Aaron and Almon Graham-Tawney.
Front: L-R: Clement, Almon holding Jarrett "Buzz," Garrison,
Clark, Aaron and Florence. Back L-R: Ernest, Mamie and Mabel.

Figure 19 - About 1926.
Almon Tawney with son
Daniel and daughter Anna.

Figure 22 - About 1915. L-R: Gracie Ann Graham
Mary Elizabeth Sergent-Graham, Mabel
Tawney (standing) and Almon
Graham-Tawney.

Figure 21 - William Isaac Graham
Born May 27, 1859
Died June 17, 1938.

Family Photographs—Tawney Family
Aaron Tawney and Flora Almon Graham-Tawney

Figure 23 - Almon Tawney.

Figure 24 - Aaron Tawney.

Figure 25 - About 1960.   Aaron Tawney. Dog Creek School in background.

Aaron Tawney was born August 27, 1876 in Roane County, West Virginia. On August 22, 1903 he married Flora Almon Graham (known as Almon). Aaron and Almon had eleven children. Aaron died October 8, 1966 at the age of 90 of congestive heart failure. Almon was born November 15, 1884 and died October 12, 1960 at the age of 75 of cancer. Aaron was a cattleman and a farmer. In the background of the above photograph sits the Dog Creek School where he was school trustee. He donated the property for the school to be built for the several children in the area to have a school to attend. There was no bus service and no other nearby schools at that time.

Figure 26 - 1950s. Almon and Aaron Tawney.

158

Family Photographs — Rogers Family
Ernest Rogers and Mabel Tawney-Rogers

Figure 29 - 2000. Mabel Tawney-Rogers.

Figure 28 - 2000. Mabel Tawney-Rogers.

Figure 27 - 1940. Mabel Rogers & Anna Group.

Front: Kermit Rogers. Back: Mrs. Cook,
Mabel holding Charlotte, and Anna Tawney.

Figure 30 - About 1948. Anna
Tawney-Desposito.

Anna holding son Michael. Front: Carroll ,
Charlotte, Barbara and Pat Rogers.
Newton, WV.

Family Photographs — Rogers Family Newton Community
Ernest Rogers and Mabel Tawney-Rogers

Figure 31 - About 1916.   Blown Timber School.

Blown Timber One-Room School
Roane County, WV

About 1916.   First through Eighth Grade. Second from left in back row is believed to be my father Ernest Rogers. Families represented are believed to be Smith, Jarvis, Rogers, and Allen. In later years, some of their own children attended this school that sat on a bank off the Blown Timber Road. The school was eventually sold to Cecil and Cleo Hensley-Taylor who converted it into a residence where they raised their two sons, Cecil and Ronnie. In 2009 it is the residence of Cleo's niece and husband who also raised their family there.

This photograph is included in this edition as several are long time Roane County residents. Martha Jarvis-Vineyard (daughter of Gary and Mary Jarvis) was very kind to furnish this from her collection. Martha lived with her family on the Blown Timber farm prior to Ernest and Mable buying it from her parents; the original owner was Danny Salyer.

Family Photographs — Rogers Family Newton Community
Ernest Rogers and Mabel Tawney-Rogers

Figure 32 - Tri-Area Senior Citizens 1996 Annual Picnic.

Tri-Area Senior Citizens 1996 Annual Picnic
Roane County, WV

Front L-R: Majel Bloom, Maxine Smith, Opal Nester-Tawney, Sylvia Vineyard and Margaret Wright. 2nd row L-R: Mabel Tawney-Rogers, Walter Combs, Arnetta Combs, Bob Wright, Marylou Wright, Vesta King, Norma Knight, Clement Tawney and Pat Rogers-Conley. Back: Jerry Knight. Newton, WV.

Family Photographs — Rogers Family Newton Community
Ernest Rogers and Mabel Tawney-Rogers

Figure 33 - Tri-Area Senior Citizens. August 24, 1988, Newton, WV
1-Ernest Rogers, 2-Harry Bloom, 3-Majel Bloom, 4-May Rowe and 5-John Rowe,
6-Loreen Jarrell, 7-Opal Nester-Tawney, 8-Retta Tawney, 9-Claudine Keen, 10-Lona Swager,
11-Sybil Hunt, 12-Daryl Elmore, 13-Norma Knight, 14-Lester Taylor, 15-Elmo Jarrell,
16-Bob King, 17-Vesta King, 18-Mabel Tawney-Rogers, 19-Maxine Smith, 20-Smith
Knight, 21-Lona Iker, and 22-Austin Boomer.

Family Photographs — Rogers Family
(Summers, McQuain and Tawney)

Figure 34 - 1920's Lucy and Sarah Rogers in Group

Front L-R: Harley Ross, unknown, unknown, Lucy Rogers-Lowry, Spurgeon Ross, unknown, unknown, unknown. Back L-R: Unknown, Sarah Rogers-Hughes, Clarence Smith, unknown, Clay Smith & Mary Westfall-Smith (husband and wife).

Figure 35 - 1920's McQuain Children

John S. McQuain and Nancy Griffith-McQuain and family.   Robert "Bub", Laura Hicks, Thomas, Mariam "Puss," "Bird," Lula and Grover McQuain.

Figure 37 - Newton Methodist Church
Newton, WV.

Figure 36 - Ernest Rogers with his Bible,
1956.

Figure 39 - Ernest Rogers holding his Mother's
coffee grinder.

Figure 38 - Sarah Rogers and Ernest
Rogers.

Pre-World War I . . .

Figure 40 - Pre WWI photo of Charley Rogers
The photo was furnished by Hersey Rogers for printing in The Times Record.
This is reproduced here with the permission of Spencer Newspapers.

Later identified as l-r: Clay Taylor, Bill (Willie) Wilmoth, **Charles (Charley) Rogers** (brother of Ernest), Patrick Rogers (killed in France during WWI), and Willis Ross (father of Howard Ross).

**Figure 41 - 1960.   Ernest Rogers, Keith Rogers and Clark Rogers.
Foxchasing Night.   Blown Timber.**

Figure 42 - Mothers' Day at Newton Methodist Church. Newton. WV.

L-R front: Kacie Smith, Mabel Rogers, Adelee and Harold Johnson; L-R back: Homer and
Pat Rogers Conley, Carroll Rogers, Charlotte Rogers-Dilno.

Figure 43 - Keith Rogers, Charlotte Rogers-Dilno,
Kermit Rogers. Blown Timber Farm.

Family Photographs — Rogers Family

Figure 45 - Orva Hicks-Rogers, Sarah Rogers-Hensley, Mabel Tawney, and
Lucy Rogers-Lowry.

Figure 44 - Charlotte Rogers-Dilno, Delores Rogers-Dennis, and
Barbara Rogers-Beistle.

Rogers Sisters in 1982. Yucca Valley, CA.

Family Photographs — Rogers Family

Figure 48 - Family of Orva Hicks-Rogers and Clark Rogers.

Gail, Lawanda, Forrest and Hersey.

Figure 49 - Gail Rogers.

Figure 47 - 1972. Brad Richmond and Grandpa Ernest Rogers and the foxhounds.

Figure 46 - About 1967-1968. Ernest Rogers and Grandson Brad Richmond at Disneyland, Anaheim, CA.

Figure 51 - About 1958 - Ernest & Mabel Home Place.
L-R: Young children are Michael, Diane, Gale and Andy Rogers.   Back L-R: Bobbie,
Charlotte, Pat, Carroll and Jim Bird standing behind the horse, Flicka.   Rogers Farm.

Figure 50 - 1996 - Rogers Girls.
Front. L-R: Bobbie Beistle and Delores Dennis.
Back L-R: Adelee Johnson, Charlotte Dilno, Dorma Drake and Pat Conley.

Family Photographs — Mardell "Adelee" Rogers Family

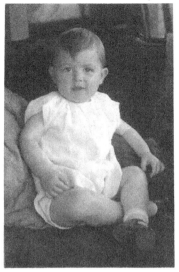

Figure 52 - Adelee Rogers. Akron, OH.

Figure 54 - L-R: Delores, Adelee and Dorma Rogers. Left Hand, WV.

Figure 55 - Adelee & Keith Rogers.

Figure 57 - Adelee Rogers. Blown Timber Farm. Early 1950s.

Figure 53 - Adelee Rogers. Blown Timber. About 1940. Rogers Farm.

Figure 56 - 1996. Mabel, Kayla, Shelley, Mason and Adelee.

L-R Sitting: Gr-Gr-Grandma Mabel. Standing: Gr-Gr-Granddaughter Kayla Hessler. Standing L-R: Grandma Mary "Shelley" McClelland-Panetti with son Mason Panetti, and Gr-Grandma Adelee Johnson.

Family Photographs — Mardell "Adelee" Rogers Family

Figure 58 - K.C. and Theresa Jackson Family.
Standing: L-R: Lauren, Leah and Kyle Jackson.

Figure 59 - 2000. Mardell Adelee
and Harold Johnson.

Figure 62 - "The Jackson Five."
L-R: K.C., Theresa, Lauren, Leah and Kyle.

Figure 61 - Dale Johnson and Children.
Dale Johnson standing with L-R: Russell,
Tiffany with puppy and Matthew.

Figure 60 - Mabel. Adelee, Matt, Dale and
Russ Johnson.

Family Photographs — Robert "Keith" Rogers Family

Figure 66 - About 1960. Gale & Mike Rogers
Molasses time with Rogers grandparents.

Figure 67 - Ernest Rogers and
son Robert "Keith" Rogers.

Figure 63 - Brothers Keith and Carroll Rogers.

Figure 65 - Keith and Marie Rogers Children.

Front L-R: Diane, Gale and Jeanne.
Back L-R: Tim, Randy and
Mike Rogers.

Figure 64 - Keith and Adelee Rogers.
Blown Timber Farm.

Family Photographs — Alma "Delores" Rogers Family

Figure 74 - Delores Rogers.

Figure 71 - Delores
Rogers and Son Andy.

Figure 70 - Delores Rogers-Dennis, Jami
Bremer, Casey Adams, and Delbert Dennis.

Figure 73 - Andy Rogers and Sister Sheila Bremer

Figure 69 - Ashley, Jami, Sheila, Roger
and Lindsey Bremer.

Figure 68 - Delores Rogers
and Son Andy.

Figure 72 - At Dennis Home with Family.

Front L-R: Delores Dennis and Dorma Drake.
Sitting L-R: Ashley Bremer, Mabel Rogers,
Charlotte Dilno, Sheila and Lindsey Bremer.

Family Photographs — Kermit A. Rogers Family

Figure 77 - Kermit Rogers with cousins Anne
Tawney-Goff and Janice Tawney-Cooper.

Figure 78 - 1951.   Delores Rogers, Kermit
Rogers and Mary McClelland.

Figure 75 - About 1946.   Kermit
Rogers and Tony the horse.

Figure 76 - About 1946. Ernest and Kermit Rogers with Tony.

Figure 80 - Leah Holcomb-Quinn and Jeremy Quinn.

Figure 81 - Jennifer Holcomb-Tanner and Mark Tanner.

Figure 79 - Betty Bird-Rogers with Granddaughters.

Julie Wilkinson, Kacie Smith, Rebecca and Jessy Wilkinson.

Figure 83 - 1940. Charlotte, Carroll, & Dorma.
At our birthplace. Front: Charlotte Rogers. Blown Timber.

Figure 84 - Jim Drake, Nena Bird-Coppock, Dorma
Rogers-Drake, Kylie May and E. Scott Bird.

Figure 82 - Jimmy Lee Bird and Mother
Dorma Rogers-Drake.

Figure 87 - Dorma Rogers-Drake and Lisa
Bird-Tackett.

Figure 86 - Dorma Rogers-Drake and Jim
Drake on their Wedding Day.

Figure 85 - Kathy Coppock, Dorma Rogers-Bird and Scott Coppock.

Family Photographs – Dorma K. Rogers Family

Figure 90 - Scott Coppock Graduation.

Nena Coppock, Dorma Drake and Kylie May Bird.

Figure 89 - 1996. Scott, Rick, Nena and Kathy Coppock.

Figure 88 - 1996 Reunion.   Coppock, Tackett, Bremer, Richmond, and Smith Children.

Back: Steve and Lisa Tackett with Nena and Rick Coppock. Front L-R: Jamie Tackett, Ashley Bremer, Brooke Richmond, Kacie Smith, Kathy and Scott Coppock.
On the bridge at grandparent's Left Hand home.

Figure 91 - 1940. Carroll and
Charlotte Rogers. Blown Timber.

Figure 93 - November 2000.   Carroll and Maria
Greco-Rogers.   40th Wedding Anniversary.

Figure 92 - Carroll Rogers Family.

Heather McDonald; Carroll and Maria Rogers; and Wesley McDonald.   Back:
L-R: Vicki and Nathan Rogers; Greg and Shelly McDonald; Marc
and Melanie Rogers.

Family Photographs — Carroll A. Rogers Family

Figure 96 - 2000.   Melanie and Marc Rogers.

Figure 95 - 2000. Wesley, Michele, Greg and Heather McDonald.

Figure 94 - November 2000.   Vicki and Nathan Rogers.

Family Photographs — Charlotte A. Rogers Family

Figure 100 - 1998.   Lance Ostrom and President Bill
Clinton.

Figure 99 - Laurel LaCour-Ostrom and
Lance Ostrom.
Plainwell. MI.

Figure 97 - 2009. Kimberly Richmond-Hickey
and Michael Hickey Family.

Front L-R: Rochelle Hickey, Kimberly and
Kristin Hickey-Lorsung. Children are
Ryleigh-Hickey and Jackson Hickey.
Back L-R: Matthey Hickey,
Michael Hickey and Jeff Lorsung.

Figure 98 - 2000. Brad Richmond Family.

Brent, Brad, Dawn, Brittany and Brooke.

Family Photographs — Charlotte A. Rogers Family

Figure 102 - 1946. Patricia and Charlotte Rogers at Marmet, WV.

Figure 101 - Charlotte and Guy Dilno. Looneyville, WV.

Figure 104 - Circa 1989, Charlotte Rogers-Dilno and children.

Kimberly Richmond, Brad Richmond and Lance Ostrom. Plainwell, MI.

Figure 103 - Lance Ostrom and Big Dog Silver.

Plainwell, MI.

Figure 107 - 2008. Brad Richmond's Family.
Front L-R: Brooke R., Brittany R., Vickie R. and Rachel
Monzo. Back L-R: Brad R., Brent R., and Martin Monzo.

Figure 105 - Brooke Richmond.

Figure 106 - Brittany Richmond.
11th Birthday.

Figure 109 - Kristin
Hickey. Playing dress-up
at grandma's in MI.

Figure 111 - Charlotte Dilno and
Brooke Richmond at South
Haven, MI.

Figure 108 - 2000. Brenton
Richmond. Wyoming, MI.

Figure 110 - 2000. Matthew
Hickey and Mom Kimberly
Richmond-Hickey in MI.

Family Photographs — Patricia R. "Pat" Rogers Family

Figure 114 - Pat and Charlotte Rogers. Marmet, WV.

Figure 115 - Pat Rogers.

Figure 118 - Pat Rogers.

Figure 112 - Christy Conley-Whittman with daughter Kayla Deusenberry.

Figure 113 - 1996. Sisters Charlotte Dilno and Pat Conley.

Figure 117 - Pat and Homer Conley Family.
Sitting: Homer Conley, Mabel Rogers and Pat Conley.
Standing L-R: Stacy, Christy, Wayne, Mike and Gregg Conley.   Newton, WV.

Figure 116 - 1958. Pat and Charlotte Rogers.

Family Photographs — Patricia R. "Pat" Rogers Family

Figure 120 - Cousins Pat, Janice, Bobbie, and Anne.

Pat Rogers-Conley, Janice Tawney-Cooper, Bobbie Rogers-Beistle and Anne Tawney-Goff.

Figure 119 - 1996.   Lance Ostrom and Wayne Conley.

Figure 122 - Easter at Grandma Rogers house.

Brooke Richmond, Ashley Bailey, Kayla Deusenberry and Corey.

Figure 121 - 2000.   Mabel Tawney-Rogers with Sara, Bryan and Justin Romano.

Figure 126 - 1997. Greg Beistle, Roger Beistle and Bobbie Rogers-Beistle. Riverside, CA.

Figure 125 - 1998. Roger and Bobbie Beistle. Left Hand, WV.

Figure 124 - Therese Beistle-Peterson, Britney and Christian Peterson and Greg Beistle.

Figure 123 - 1998. Bobbie Rogers-Beistle and Mabel Tawney-Rogers.

Family Photographs — Barbara C. " Bobbie" Rogers Family

Figure 128 - Therese Beistle-Pederson with her children Britney and Christian in Riverside, CA.

Figure 127 - Christian Pederson. Riverside, CA.   Figure 129 - Britney Pederson. Riverside, CA.

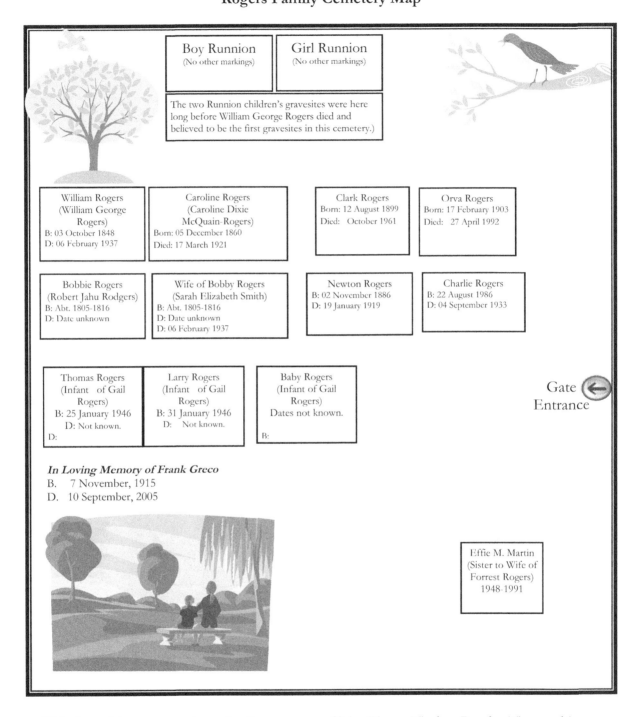

Boy Runnion
(No other markings)

Girl Runnion
(No other markings)

The two Runnion children's gravesites were here long before William George Rogers died and believed to be the first gravesites in this cemetery.)

William Rogers
(William George Rogers)
B: 03 October 1848
D: 06 February 1937

Caroline Rogers
(Caroline Dixie McQuain-Rogers)
Born: 05 December 1860
Died: 17 March 1921

Clark Rogers
Born: 12 August 1899
Died: October 1961

Orva Rogers
Born: 17 February 1903
Died: 27 April 1992

Bobbie Rogers
(Robert Jahu Rodgers)
B: Abt. 1805-1816
D: Date unknown

Wife of Bobby Rogers
(Sarah Elizabeth Smith)
B: Abt. 1805-1816
D: Date unknown
D: 06 February 1937

Newton Rogers
B: 02 November 1886
D: 19 January 1919

Charlie Rogers
B: 22 August 1986
D: 04 September 1933

Thomas Rogers
(Infant   of Gail Rogers)
B: 25 January 1946
D: Not known.
D:

Larry Rogers
(Infant   of Gail Rogers)
B: 31 January 1946
D: Not known.

Baby Rogers
(Infant of Gail Rogers)
Dates not known.
B:

Gate Entrance ←

In Loving Memory of Frank Greco
B.   7 November, 1915
D.   10 September, 2005

Effie M. Martin
(Sister to Wife of Forrest Rogers)
1948-1991

This fenced-in cemetery is on family property off the Blown Timber Road.   The road is unpaved and access is best by 4-wheel drive vehicle in 2009.   Access off the Blown Timber Road is first by private drive and continues up a wooded hill to the gate entrance.

In 2009 there are 14 gravesites and cremains of one.

Dedication to our Soldiers

The year is 2010. Unfortunately we again find ourselves in armed conflict and it is reflective to consider how many of our family members have served, or are serving, in the United States Military. I have added this section to the third edition to honor all of those who served or are currently serving. You are greatly respected and appreciated.

The young men in this newspaper clipping were later identified as: L-R: Clay Taylor, Bill "Willie" Wilmoth, William Charles "Charley" Rogers (brother of Ernest), Patrick Rogers (killed in France during WWI), Willis Ross (father of Howard Ross).

Pre-World War I . . .

Henry H. Rogers brought in this old photo of five young Roane County lads gathered for a photograph before two of them left the county to serve in World War I.

Rogers noted that he is only able to identify the three men in the middle and named them as (left to right) Willie Wilmoth, Charles Rogers and Patrick Rogers.

The two Rogers were cousins and left the area soon after the photograph was taken to serve the country in the great war.

The photo was taken near the home of Lee Ellis of Newton but the exact date and the names of the two young men on the ends have been misplaced over the years.

Figure 130 - The Times Record Pre WWI clipping of Charlie Rogers.

Figure 131 – Left - WWI Frederick Graham.

Top Left: Frederic Luther Graham. Born: 01 Jan 1893. Died around 1985 in a Charleston, WV hospital.

Top Right: Charley Goff Graham. Born 11 Aug 1889. Date of death unknown. Both are sons of William Isaac Graham and Mary Elizabeth Sergent. Their grandfather was William Edward Graham, born 09 May 1864 in Nicholas County, VA and died 09 May 1864. He served in the Civil War and was killed at Cloyds Mountain, Pulaski County. It was hat told his body was never found.

Figure 132 - WWI – Charley Graham.

Roane County, WV
World War I

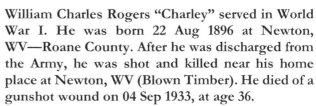

Figure 133 - Left - Charles Rogers and Edna Rafferty.

William Charles Rogers "Charley" served in World War I. He was born 22 Aug 1896 at Newton, WV—Roane County. After he was discharged from the Army, he was shot and killed near his home place at Newton, WV (Blown Timber). He died of a gunshot wound on 04 Sep 1933, at age 36.

The woman is believed to be Edna Rafferty, his 1st cousin. Charley's parents were William George Rogers and Caroline Dixie McQuain of Newton, WV.

Figure 137 - WW II. Champ "Clark" Tawney with Mother Almon Tawney at Tawney farm. Home town: Left Hand, Roane Co., WV.

Figure 134 - WW II. Jarrett "Buzz" Tawney. Born 02 Apr 1919. 1943-1946. 634th Engineers, Light Equipment Co., 9th Army, 13th Core. Home town: Left Hand, Roane Co., WV.

Figure 136 - WW II. C. Clark Tawney. Born 28 Nov 1915 at Left Hand, WV, Roane Co.

Figure 135 - WW II 1942-1945. Anna E. Tawney. First group of women to serve in U. S. Marines. Born 11 Sep 1921. Roane Co., WV. Lives in Rio Rancho, NM.

Figure 139 - WWII (WV National Guard).
Ernest F. Rogers and Mabel Tawney-Rogers.

Figure 140 - U.S. Marines. Anna
Tawney-Desposito on Mike's
bike.

Figure 138 - WWII. 1943. U.S.Marines.   Anna
Tawney - Desposito and Mike Desposito.

Figure 141 - WW II. Anna E. Tawney
and brother Jarrett "Buzz" Tawney
in California.

Figure 144 - Anna Tawney and the Mohave Pioneers.

Mohave Pioneers—First group of women to enter the U.S. Marines. Anna E. Desposito belonged to this unit and was stationed in the Mohave Desert, California. She was born Sep. 11, 1921 at Left Hand, WV, Roane Co. (See enlargement below.) Anna and Mike moved to Rio Rancho, NM after Mike retired from the New York City Police Force and became a banker in Rio Rancho. Since retirement both have given of themselves to volunteer service, including Anna at the Veteran's Hospital in Albuquerque, New Mexico. Anna is a member of the Daughters of the American Revolution—Charles Dibrell Chapter in Albuquerque.

Figure 142 - WW II U. S. Marines - 1943. Anna and Mike Desposito.

Figure 143 - Anna Tawney and the Mohave Pioneers.

Figure 146 - WW II. U.S. Army. Milford Lee
Dilno.

Figure 145 - U.S. Marines. Michael E. Desposito
and Anna E. Tawney.
Married 11 Aug 1945 in Bakersfield, CA.   Mike
served 1942-1945. Anna served 1943-45.

Figure 148 - WWII. Clark Tawney and
Sister Mamie.
Tawney farm and I believe that is Aunt
Mamie's car.

Figure 147 - WWII. 1943. Jarrett "Buzz" Tawney.

Photo background is CBS in Hollywood,
CA. Married Francis Roberts, deceased.

Figure 149 - McQuain Family.

John Albert McQuain, first left in front row. Others are sons and daughter of Lewis Wetzel McQuain.

Dedication of the McQuain Bridge in Kanawha County, WV

SENATE (sic) CONCURRENT RESOLUTION NO. 39

(By Senators Ross, McKenzie, Oliverio, Love, Kessler, Dittmar, Redd and Plymale)

———————

[Originating in the Committee on Transportation;
reported March 8, 2000.]

Requesting the Commissioner of the Division of Highways name that certain bridge which crosses over U. S. Route 119 and Lefthand Fork, on Interstate 79 near Hellford, as the "McQuain Brothers Bridge".

Whereas, First Sgt. John McQuain served twenty-seven months in the South Pacific, being attached to the anti-aircraft unit and the fifty caliber machine gun unit. He later became a member of the Regimental Combat Team, one of the elite fighting units of the Army; and
Whereas, Ten McQuain brothers, in addition to First Sgt. John McQuain, served in various fields of service:

Sgt. Ralph McQuain served in the Air Force from 1942 to 1945;

Seaman 1-C Clyde McQuain served in the Coast Guard from 1943 to 1945;

S-Sgt. Jack McQuain served in the Army as an infantryman from 1942 to 1945, attached to the Regimental Combat Team, one of the elite fighting units of the Army, and holder of the Bronze Star and the Purple Heart;

Cpl. Roy McQuain served in the Army as an infantryman in 1942 and was a German POW for twenty-six months;

Coxswain Herbert McQuain served in the Navy in 1943 and reenlisted from 1946 to 1950;

Seaman 1-C Paul McQuain served in the Navy Sea-Bees from 1939 to 1946;

Seaman 1-C Gene McQuain served in the Navy from 1946 to 1948;

PFC. Porter McQuain was a combat veteran of the Korean War and served from 1948 to 1950;

George McQuain served in the Navy for twenty years and received the Purple Heart;

T-Sgt. Donald Noe served in the 8th Air Force as a radioman;

Earl McQuain attempted to join the service with his brothers but was deferred; and

Whereas, The McQuain Brothers are believed to hold a national record for the amazing total of eleven brothers who served this country, they being decedents of a long line of West Virginians from Roane County and

Whereas, The service and dedication of the McQuain brothers is deserving of high honor and gives them a place in American history; therefore be it

Resolved by the Legislature of West Virginia

That the Legislature hereby requests the Commissioner of the Division of Highways designate that certain bridge which crosses over U. S. Route 119 and Lefthand Fork, on Interstate 79 near Hellford, as the "McQuain Brothers Bridge";

and, be it

Further Resolved, That the Commissioner of the Division of Highways is requested to have made and be placed, at either end of the bridge, signs identifying the bridge as the "McQuain Brothers Bridge"; and, be it

Further Resolved, That the Clerk of the Senate is hereby directed to forward a copy of this resolution to the Commissioner of the Division of Highways and to the capitol press corps.

Reference WV Senate Resolution No. 39, 8 March, 2000:

www.legis.state.wv.us/Bill_Text_HTML/2000_SESSIONS/rs/BILLS/scr39%20org.htm

Figure 150 - U.S. Navy. Kermit A.
Rogers—U.S.S. Orca.
Home town: Roane Co., WV.
Married Betty Bird of Belle, WV.

Figure 152 - U.S. Army–CPL Delbert
Dennis—1950s.
Home town: Smithfield, PA.
Married A. Delores Rogers.

Figure 151 - U.S. Navy. James H. Bird -   U.S.S. Hornet. 1950s.
With Delbert Drake. Home town: Belle, Kanawha Co., WV. Married Dorma Rogers.

Figure 155 - U.S. Army Reserves. Carroll
Aaron Rogers.
Training: Ft. Knox, KY and Ft. Sill, OK.
6-mo.active. 5 ½-yrs inactive. Home town:
Newton, Roane Co., WV
Married Maria Greco-Rogers.

Figure 156 - U.S. Army. Spec 5 Homer Lee
Conley 1962-1967.
Mechanics. Basic training at Fort Jackson,
SC. Stationed in Germany. Home town:
Newton, Roane Co., WV.
Married Pat Rogers.

Figure 153 - Army Reserves. Brothers L-R:
Robert Keith Rogers and Carroll Aaron
Rogers.
Home town: Newton, Roane Co., WV.

Figure 154 - U.S. Army - Guy L. Dilno. 1966 - 1968.

545th Ordnance Co. Stationed in Munster,
W. Germany. Home town: Plainwell, MI.
Married to Charlotte Rogers.

Figure 158 - U.S. Navy. Michael Edward Desposito, Jr.

7th Atlantic Fleet. Served during Vietnam.
Stationed in Italy.

Figure 157 - U.S. Air Force. Danny Desposito
with wife Jan.

Served during Vietnam.

Figure 159 - Jim Drake. Home town—Belle
(Kanawha Co.), WV.
Married to Dorma-Rogers-Bird.

Figure 160 - U.S. Marines. Andrew Jackson
Rogers.
Home town: Left Hand, WV.

Figure 162 - U.S. Air Force. Michael G. Conley.

1989. Non-Commissioned Officer Ceremony at
March AFB. Home town: Newton, WV.
Married Shirley Bird 2009.

Figure 163 - USAF.   Michael G. Conley.
1985-94.
Basic at Lackland AFB - San Antonio, TX.
March-April 1985. A.I.T. at Lackland AFB
in San Antonio, TX.   May-June 1985.

Figure 161 - U.S Marines.   Travis
Logsdon.
Home town: Vienna, WV.

Figure 164 - U.S. Marines.
Travis Eugene Logsdon
Served in Iraq during Operation Desert
Storm. Home town: Vienna, WV.

Figure 165 - 1990. U.S. Army.
Lance John Ostrom
Basic training at Ft. Benning, GA.
Stationed in Germany. Served in Kuwait
during Operation Desert Storm.
Home town: Plainwell, MI.

Figure 166 - U.S. Army. 1981.
Kimberly Anne Richmond
Hometown: Plainwell, MI.

Figure 167 - U.S. Army. 1990.
Lance John Ostrom
Home town: Plainwell, MI.

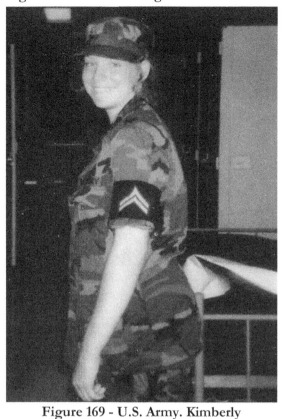

Figure 169 - U.S. Army. Kimberly
Richmond-Hickey.

Figure 170 - U.S. Army.   SGM Michael C.
Hickey. Baghdad, Iraq.

Basic Training at Ft. McClelland, Alabama,
June 1982. Army National Guard.

Figure 168 - Left - U.S. Marines.
Travis Logsdon.

Served in the USMC 1998-2003.
Graduated from Paris Island, SC.
Stationed at Camp LeJeune, NC.
Promoted to Corporal before leaving the
Corps in 2003. Served in Iraq January 1,
2003 to May 15, 2003. Served in Spain
with Dynamic Mix.   Parkersburg High
School 1998. Home town: Vienna, WV.

Figure 172 - U.S. Air Force. Michael G. Conley.

1st Duty Station 22nd Security Police Squadron, March AFB Moreno Valley, CA. 1985-1990; T.D.Y. Temporary Duty ILLinakan (Hellinikon) AB in Athens Greece.   Apr--Jun. 1986;   2nd Duty Station 8th SPS Kunsan AFB, South Korea. 1990-1991;   3rd Duty Station 847th SPS Grand Forks AFB at Grand Forks, North Dakota 1991-1994. Separated USAF Dec. 12 1994.   Home town: Newton, WV.

Left:

Figure 171 - U.S. Army. Scott L. Coppock.

Army National Guard. Enlisted: Oct 18, 2002. Supply Specialist units: C Co, 138th Signal Battalion in Elwood, IN; 259th and 258th Engineer Co's. in Phoenix; transferred to HHC, 138th Signal Battalion in Anderson, IN which became A Co, 38th STB in 2008.   Basic Training at Ft. Jackson, SC. Advanced Individual Training (AIT) at Ft. Lee, VA.
Home town: Alexandria, IN.

Figure 175 - U.S. Army. SGM Michael C. Hickey in his Bunker in Iraq.

Figure 173 - Stacie Lea Tawney-Peterson.

Home town: Left Hand, WV.

Figure 174 - U.S. Army. Lance John Ostrom.
Kuwait during Operation Desert Storm.

U.S. Army. Michael Charles Hickey in Iraq, with his M16. Hometown—Pitcairn, PA.

Figure 177 - U.S. Army. SGM Michael C. Hickey in Iraq, now retired.

Figure 176 - U.S. Army. SGM Michael Charles Hickey.
May 1979-May 31, 2009.
Served in Korea, Germany, Iraq (2 tours), and the U.S. As Sergeant Major he served
in HHT 1/4 Cav. 1st Infantry Division, Schweinfurt Germany, 1-77 Armor
Battalion, 1st Infantry Division, Schweinfurt, Germany, 194th Armor Training
Brigade, Fort Knox, Kentucky.

Figure 179 - Dec 2009. Major
Mike Peterson serving in
Afghanistan, and
Singer Billy Ray Cyrus.

Figure 180 - Feb 2009. Major Mike Peterson in Afghanistan.

Figure 178 - U.S. Army. Lance J. Ostrom. Kuwait.

Figure 182 - U.S. Army. Lance John Ostrom.
Kuwait. 125 degrees and miserable.
Home town: Plainwell, MI.
He married Laurel LaCour-Ostrom.

Figure 183 - U.S. Army. Lance John Ostrom in
Kuwait with a buddy.
Pretty hot here too. Oil fires in the
background.

Left:

Figure 181 - U.S. Army.   Lance John Ostrom.

Oil well fires (background), Kuwait.
Enlisted 1990. Basic training at Ft.
Benning, GA. Home town: Plainwell, MI.

Figure 187 - U.S. Army. Adam Duane Stock. 21 M Firefighter.

Figure 186 - U.S. Army.   Adam Stock. 21 M Firefighter.

Stationed at Fort Stewart ,GA with the 24th Ordnance. Stationed at Fort Hood TX in 507th Firefighter Detachment. Prior to that he was National Guard Firefighter stationed out of Columbia, SC. He entered the U.S. Army in October 2005 and Basic Training at Fort Leonard Wood, MO. E-4 is his rank. Married Rebecca Wilkinson.

Figure 184 - Adam Stock and son Braxton.

Figure 185 - Adam Stock in his firefighting gear.

Figure 189 - U.S. Army. Stacie Lea Tawney-Peterson in Iraq.
Stationed in Saudi Arabia During Desert Storm..

Figure 188 - Kimberly Anne Richmond-Hickey.
Germany.

U.S. Army Award for Volunteerism.

Left:

Figure 190 - 2005. U.S. Marine Corps. Sgt. Robert Scott Holcomb.

Camp Ramadi, Iraq. Served 8 years. Military Police Officer. Another tour as Squad Leader for Field Military Police Battalion. Home town: Clay, WV. Married to Kacie Smith.

No photos were provided for many others who served:

U.S. Air Force.
Aaron Romano
He left for Basic Training in Texas on May 1994, at Lackland AFB; Tech School at Keesler AFB, Biloxi, Mississippi; stationed at Malmstrom AFB in Great Falls, Montana; and separated after 3 years with an early out honorable discharge. Married Stacy Conley.

• • •

U.S. Air Force.
James Darin Carper.
4 Years

• • •

U.S. Army.
Brian Christopher Carper. Married Cindy Robinson.
2 Years, 6 Months
Called back to duty after 2 years for Desert Storm

• • •

U.S. Army.
SPC Jeffery Allen Lorsung
Born in Coquille, OR. Basic training in Fort Leonard Wood, MO. Present rank is E4 and stationed at Fort Knox, KY. Married Kristin Anne Hickey.

• • •

California National Guard.
Roger Beistle. Married Barbara Caroline Rogers

Descendants of John Jacob Tawney and Elizabeth Price

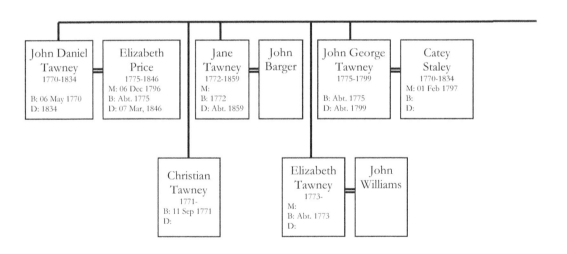

Descendants of John Jacob Tawney and Elizabeth Price

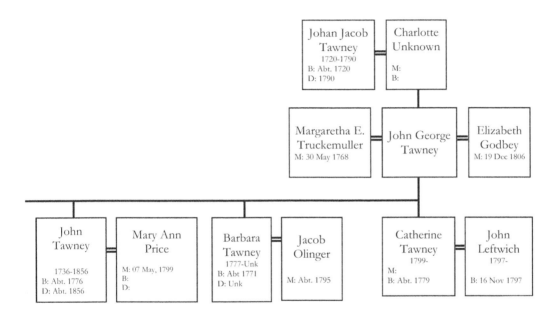

Descendants of John Daniel Tawney and Elizabeth Price

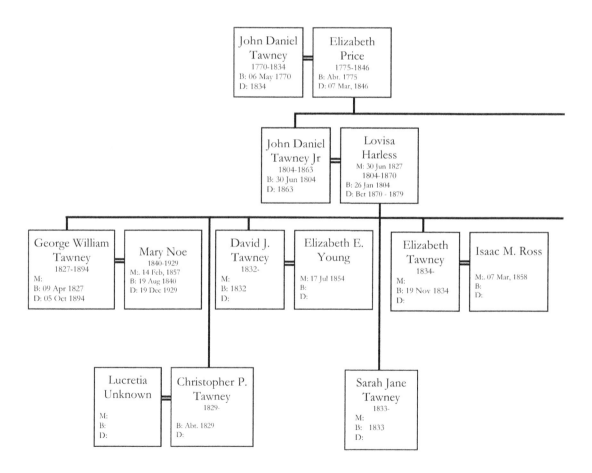

Descendants of John Daniel Tawney and Elizabeth Price

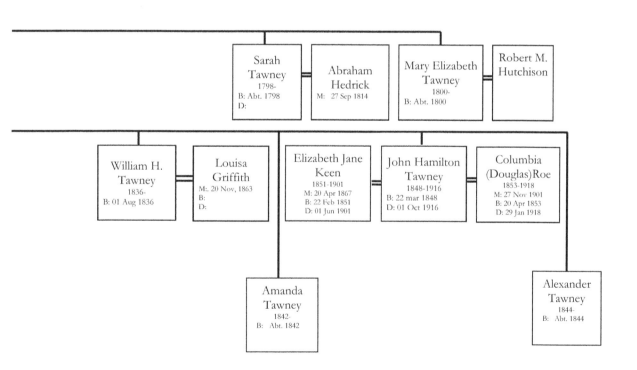

Descendants of George Tawney and Mary Noe

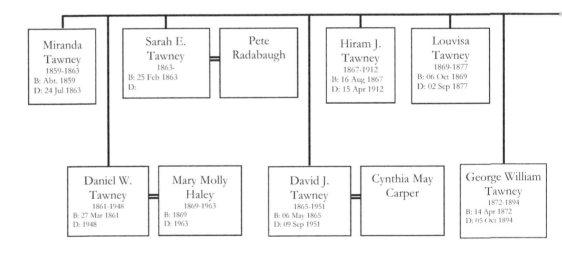

Descendants of George Tawney and Mary Noe

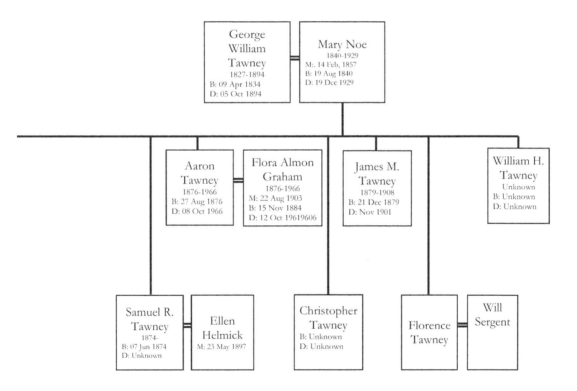

Descendants of Aaron Tawney and Flora Almon Graham

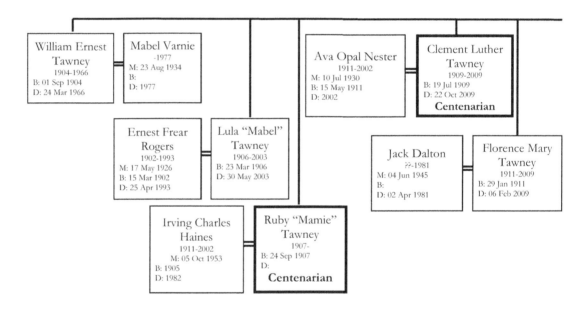

Descendants of Aaron Tawney and Flora Almon Graham

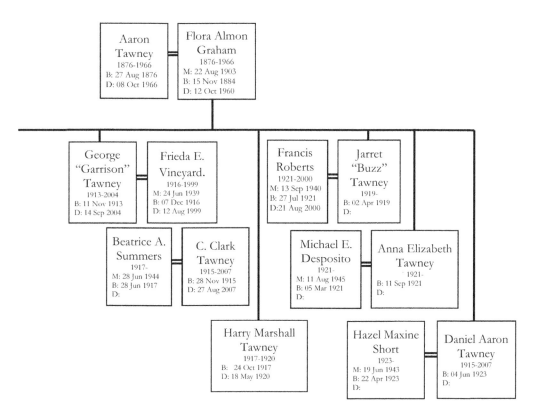

Descendants of W. Ernest Tawney and Mabel Varnie

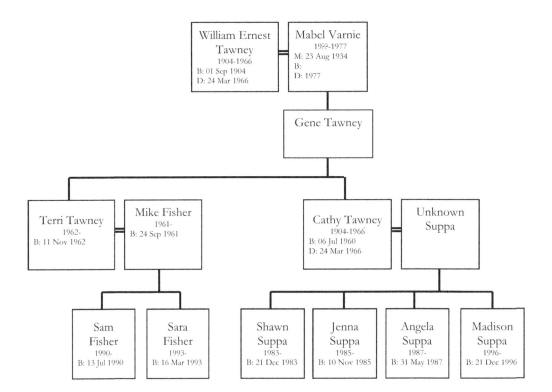

Descendants of Lula Mabel Tawney and Ernest Frear Rogers

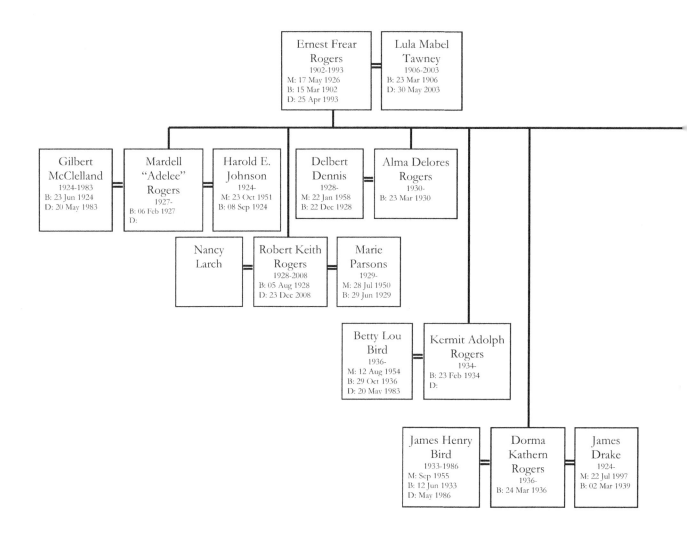

Descendants of L. Mabel Tawney and Ernest Rogers

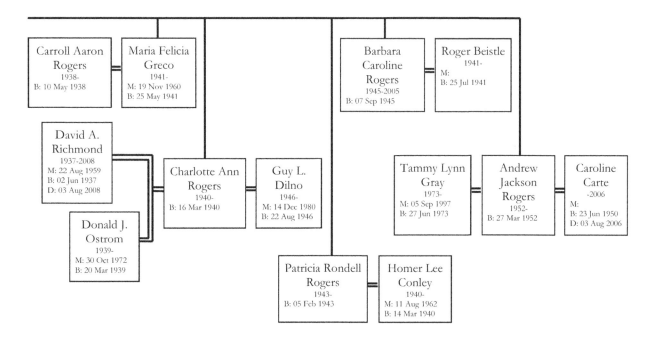

Descendants of M. Adelee Rogers, Gilbert McClelland, and Harold Johnson

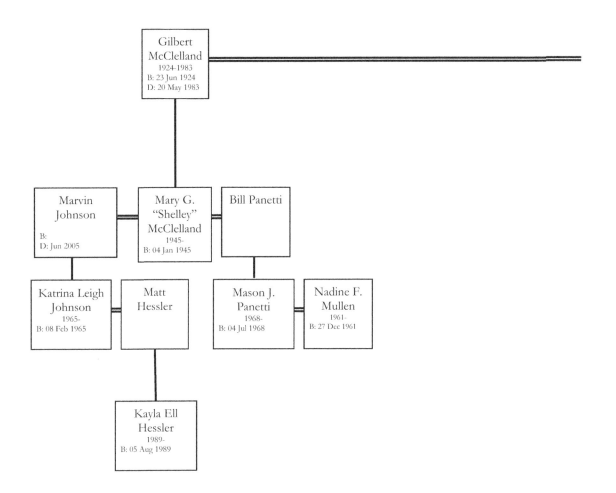

Descendants of M. Adelee Rogers, Gilbert McClelland, and Harold Johnson

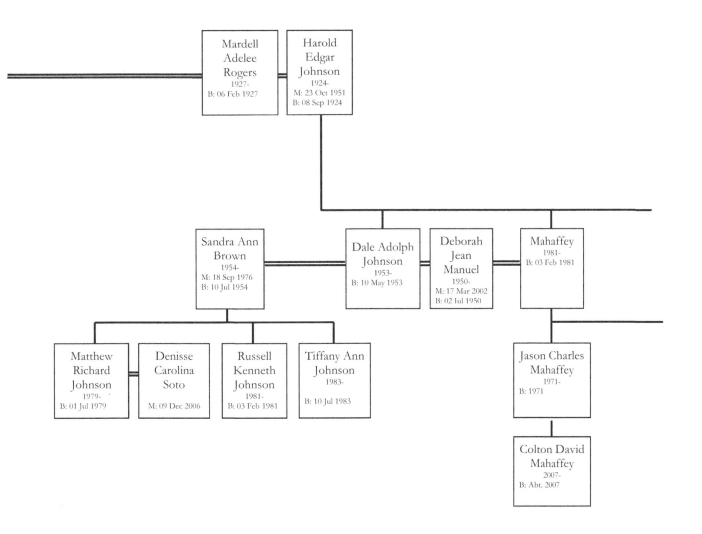

Descendants of M. Adelee Rogers, Gilbert McClelland, and Harold Johnson

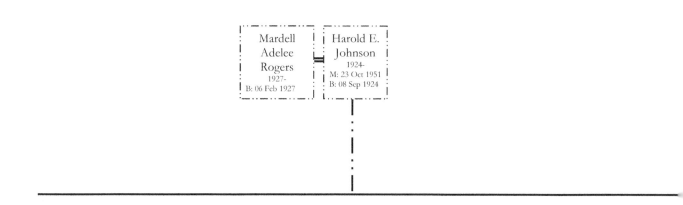

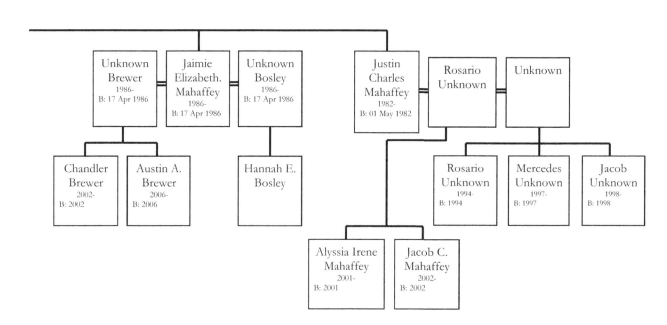

Descendants of M. Adelee Rogers, Gilbert McClelland, and Harold Johnson

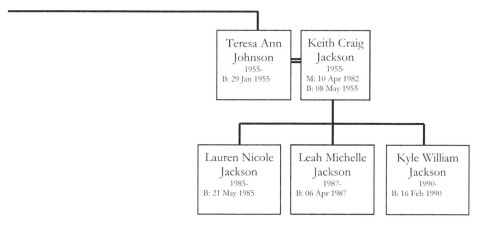

Descendants of Robert Keith Rogers and Marie Parsons

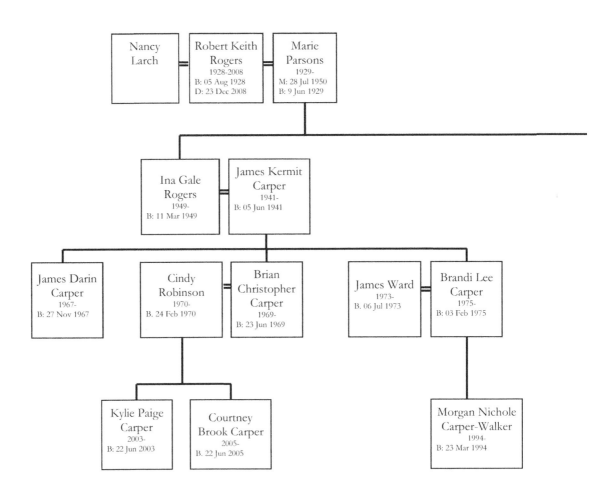

Descendants of Robert Keith Rogers and Marie Parsons

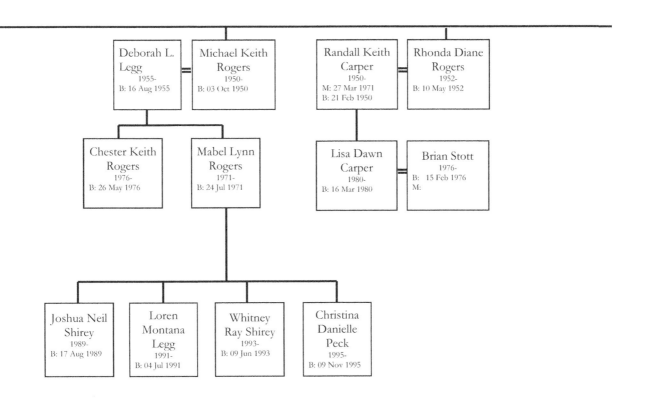

Descendants of Robert Keith Rogers and Marie Parsons

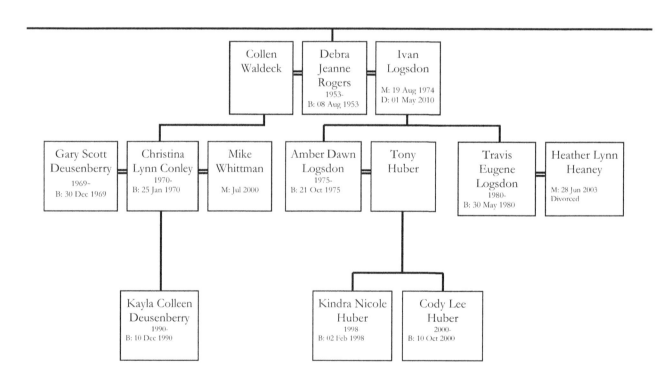

Descendants of Robert Keith Rogers and Marie Parsons

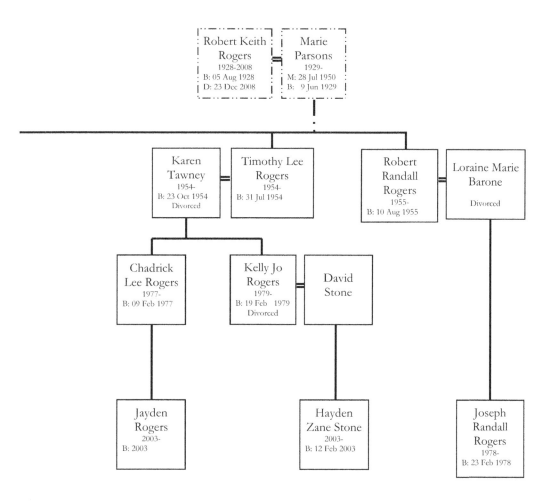

Descendants of Alma "Delores" Rogers and Delbert Dennis

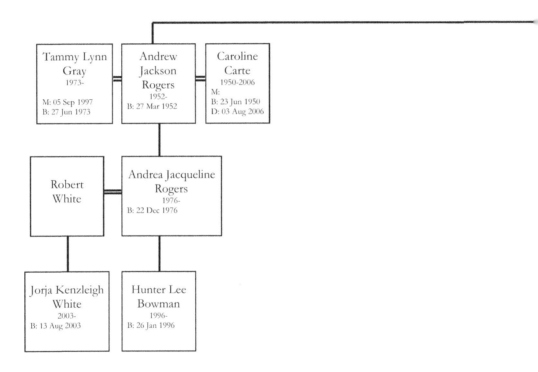

Descendants of Alma "Delores" Rogers and Delbert Dennis

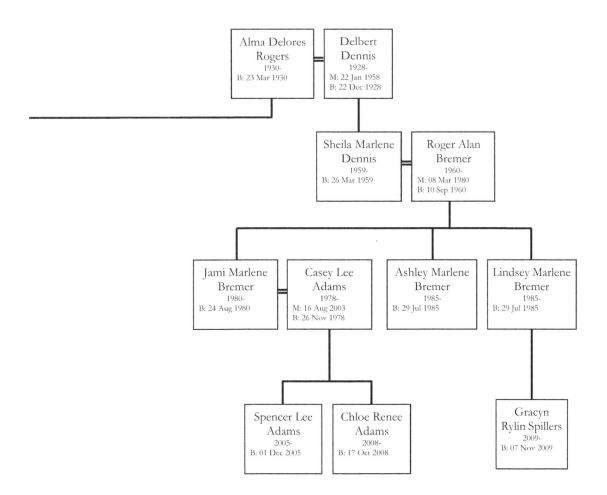

Descendants of Kermit Rogers and Betty Lou Bird

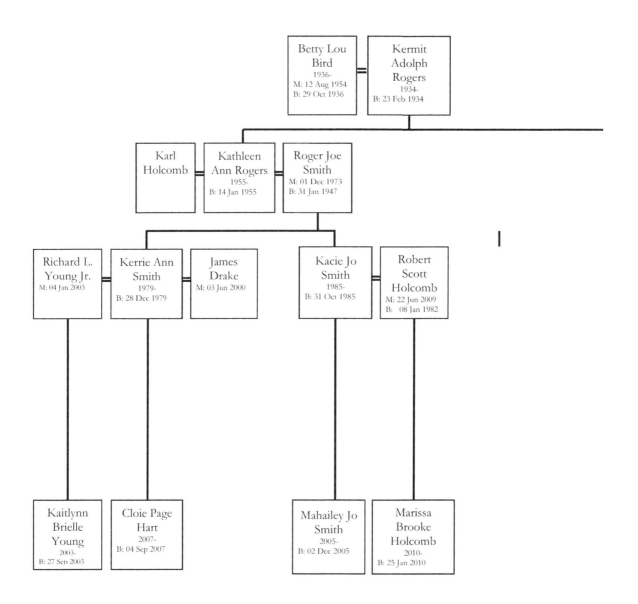

Descendants of Kermit Rogers and Betty Lou Bird

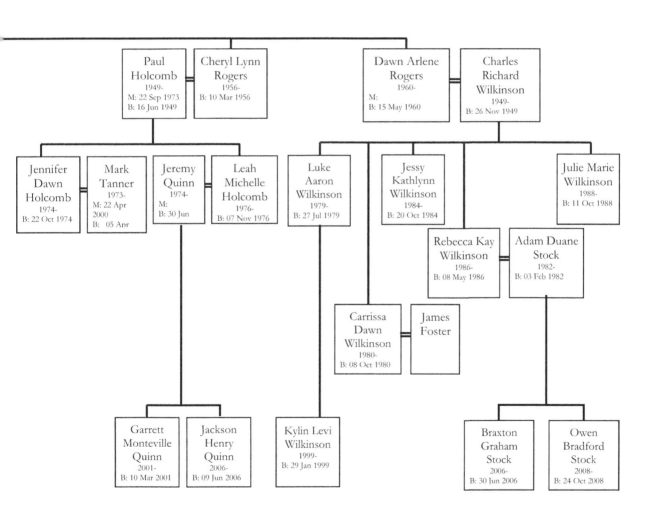

Descendants of Dorma Rogers and James Bird

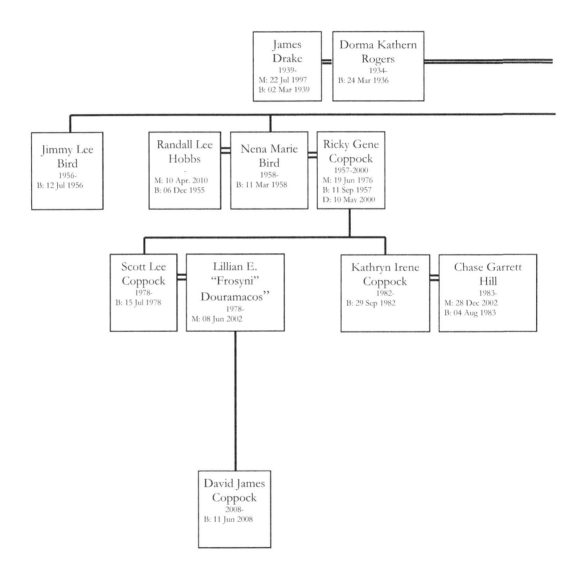

Descendants of Dorma Rogers and James Bird

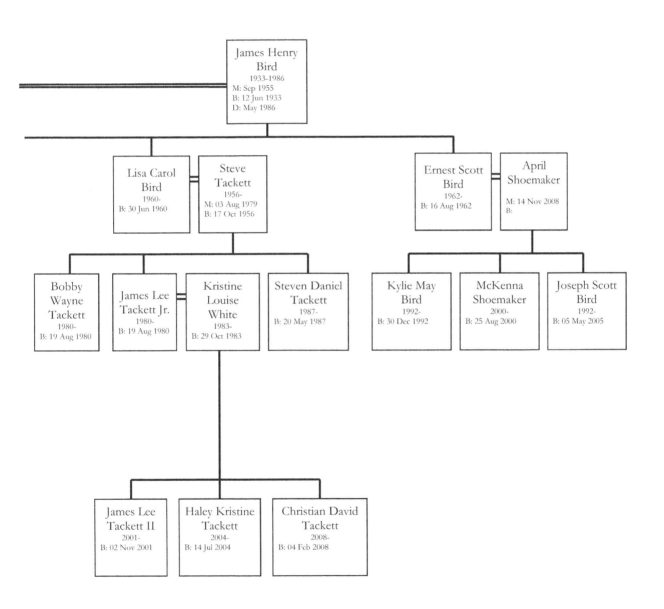

Descendants of Carroll Rogers and Maria Greco

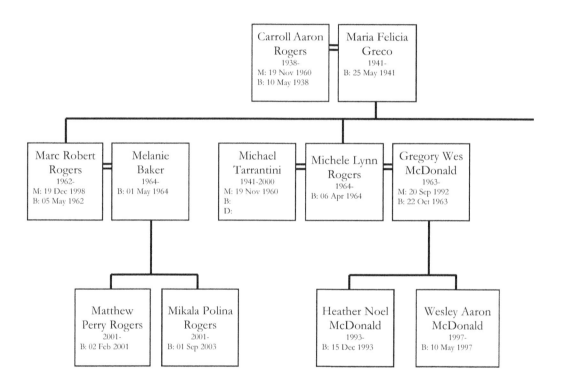

Descendants of Carroll Rogers and Maria Greco

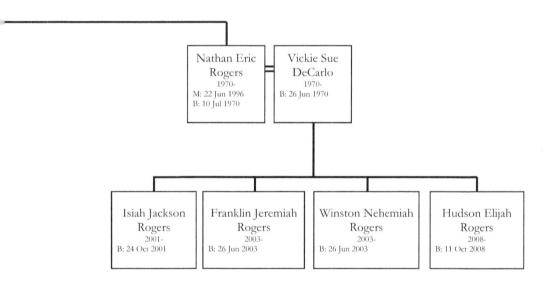

Descendants of Charlotte Rogers, David Richmond, and Don Ostrom

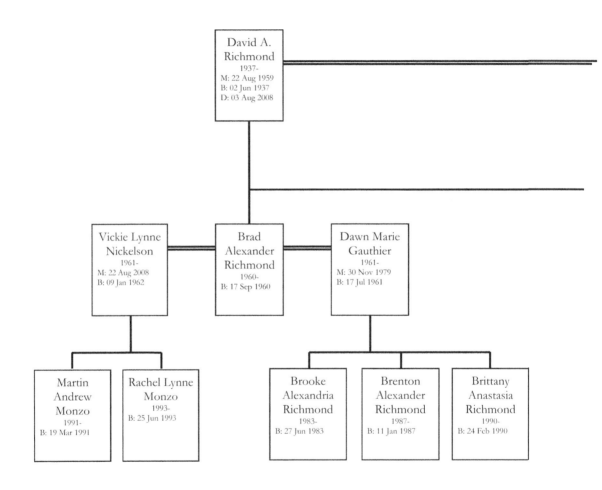

Descendants of Charlotte Rogers, David Richmond, and Don Ostrom

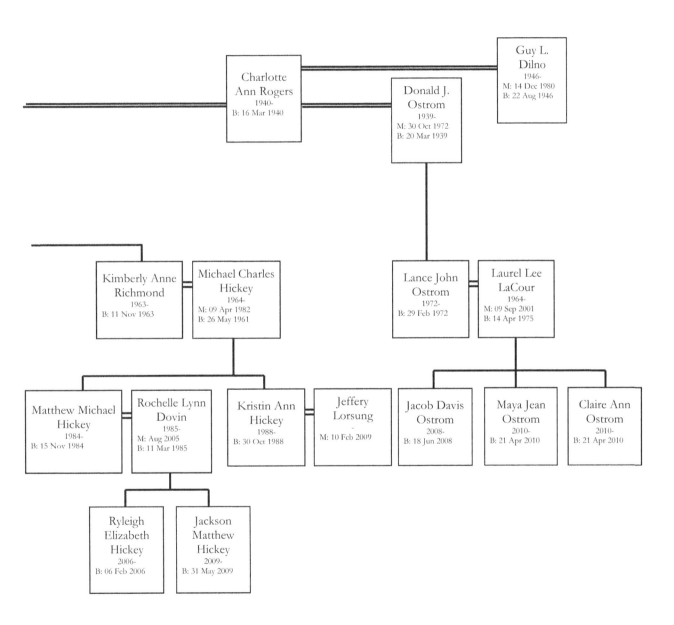

Descendants of Patricia "Pat" Rogers and Homer Conley

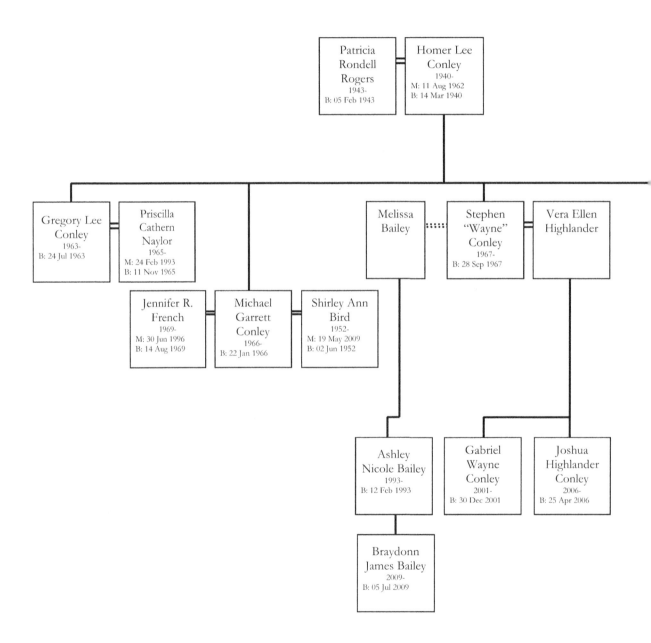

Descendants of Patricia "Pat" Rogers and Homer Conley

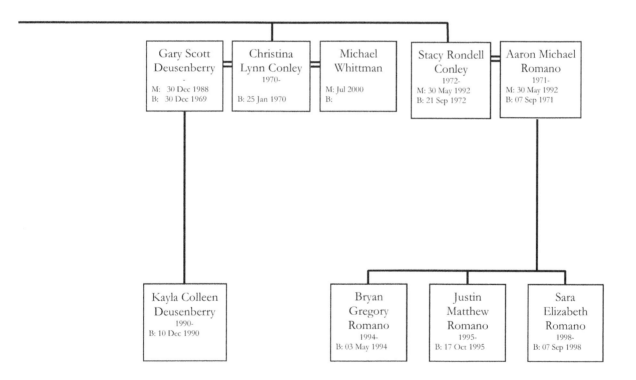

Descendants of Barbara "Bobbie" Rogers and Roger Beistle

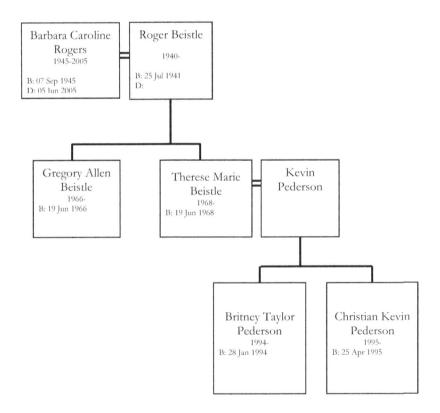

Descendants of Clement Tawney and A. Opal Nester

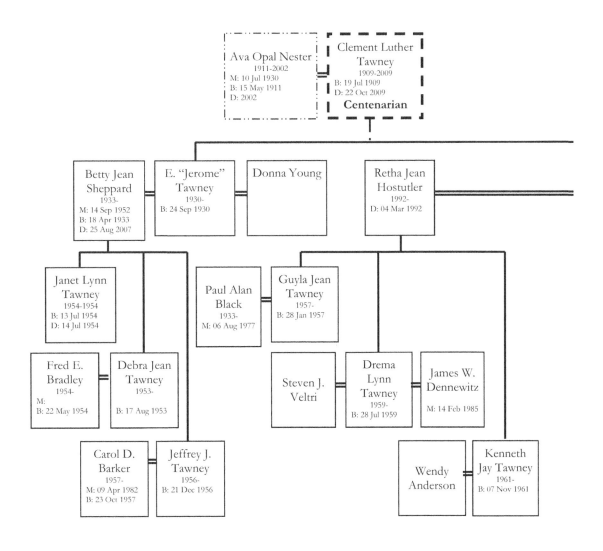

Descendants of Clement Tawney and A. Opal Nester

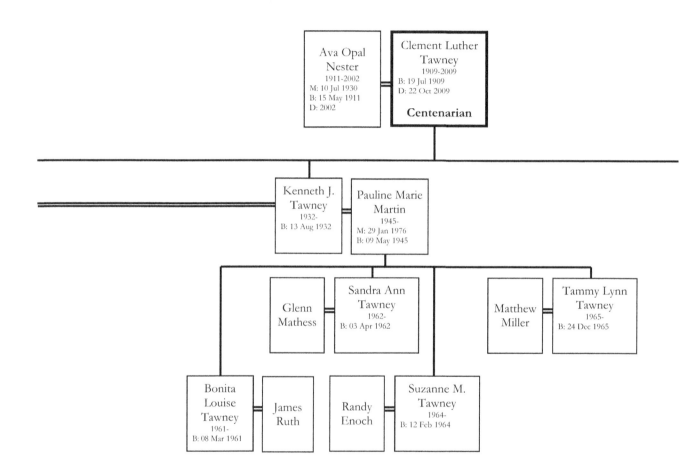

Descendants of Clement Tawney and A. Opal Nester

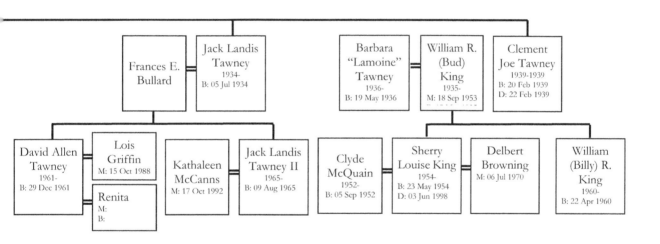

Descendants of George "Garrison" Tawney and Frieda Vineyard

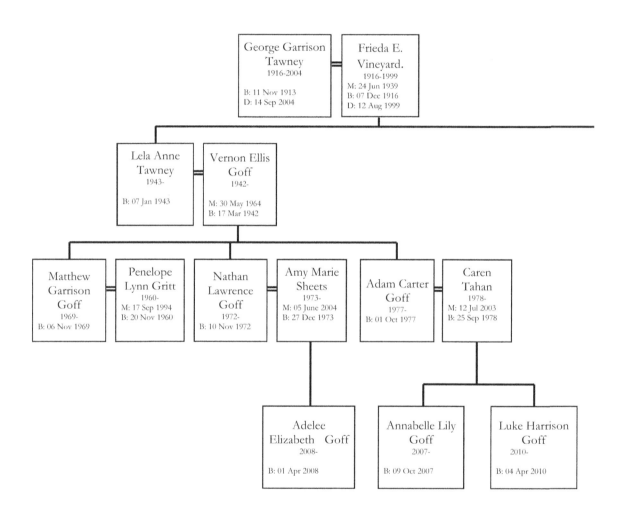

Descendants of George "Garrison" Tawney and Frieda Vineyard.

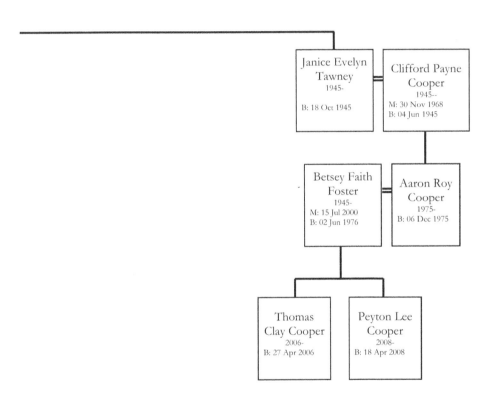

Descendants of C. "Clark" Tawney and Beatrice Summers

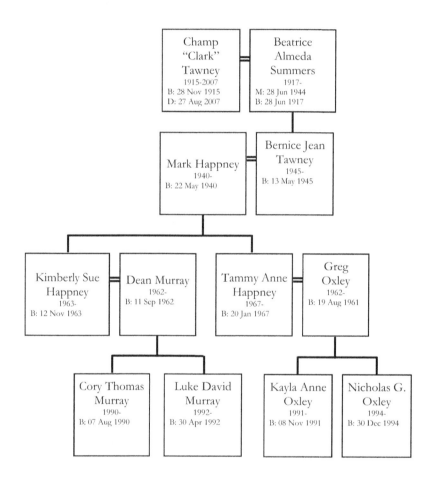

Descendants of Jarrett "Buzz" Tawney and Francis Roberts

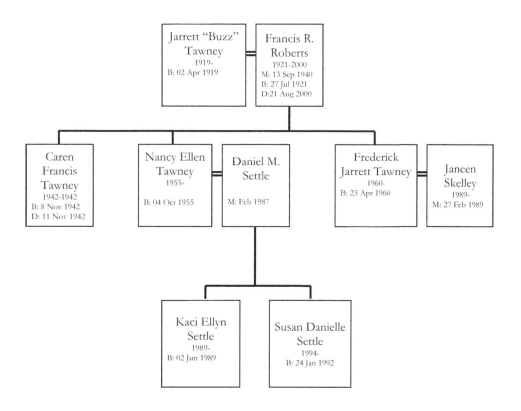

Descendants of Anna Tawney and Michael Desposito

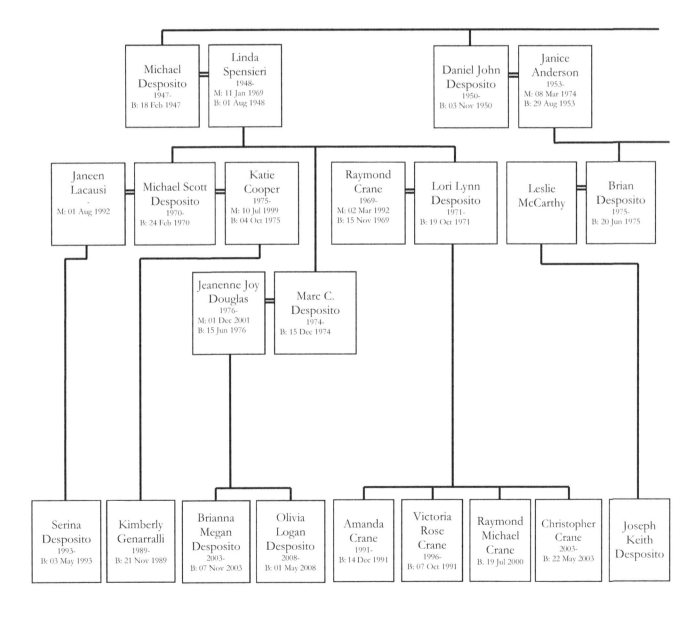

Descendants of Anna Tawney and Michael Desposito

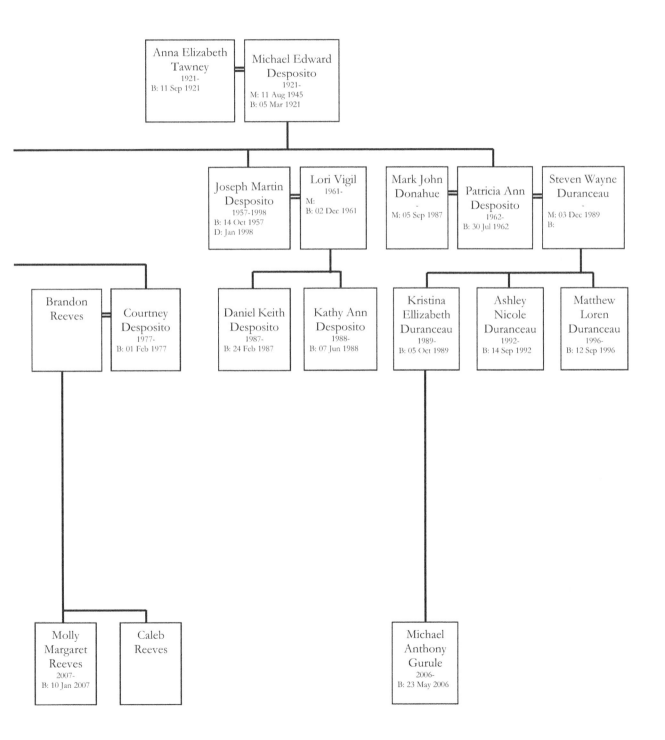

Descendants of Daniel Tawney and Hazel Short

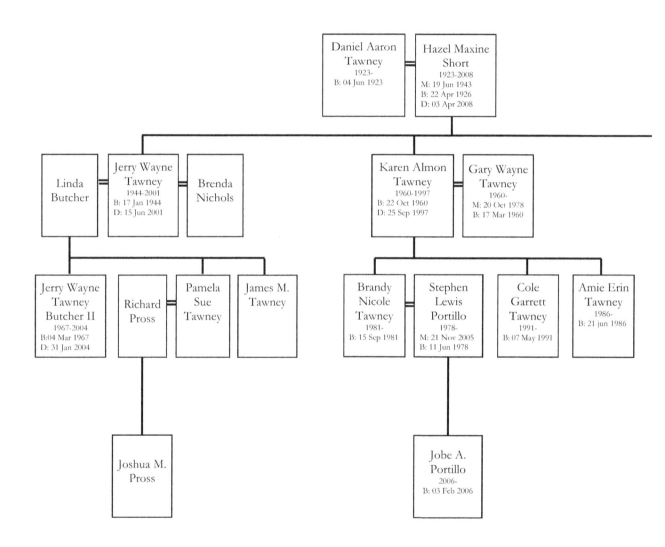

Descendants of Daniel Tawney and Hazel Short

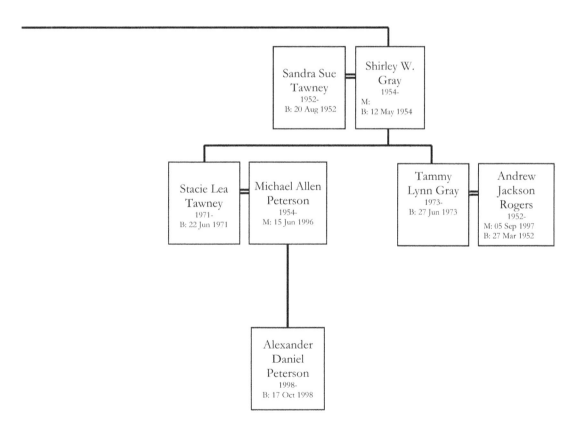

Descendants of Alexander (Rev War) McQuain and Mary Bodkin

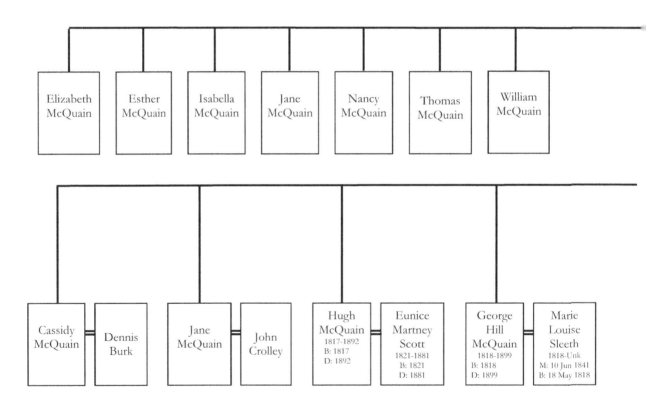

Descendants of Alexander (Rev War) McQuain and Mary Bodkin

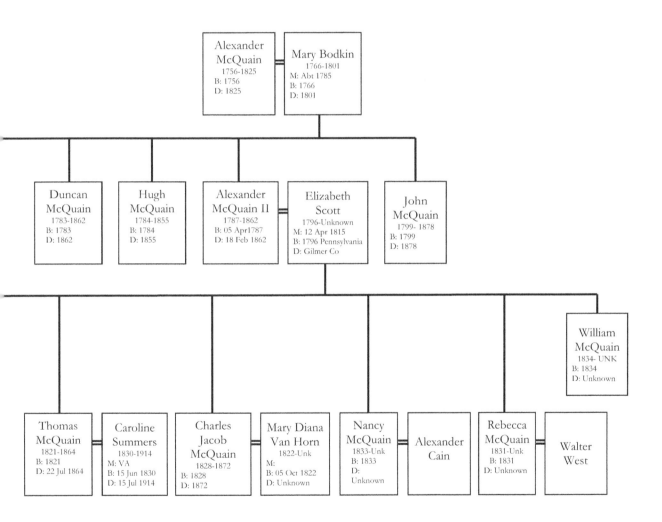

Descendants of Thomas Hughes and Nellie Foster
(Useful for Daughters of the American Revolution – Thomas Hughes is the Patriot)

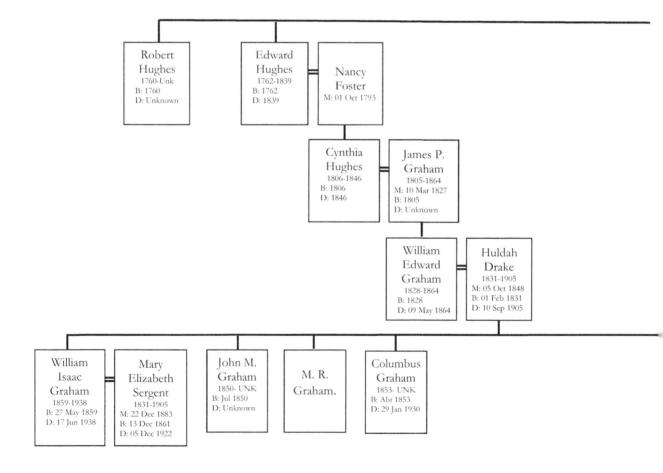

Robert
Hughes
1760-Unk
B: 1760
D: Unknown

Edward
Hughes
1762-1839
B: 1762
D: 1839

Nancy
Foster
M: 01 Oct 1793

Cynthia
Hughes
1806-1846
B: 1806
D: 1846

James P.
Graham
1805-1864
M: 10 Mar 1827
B: 1805
D: Unknown

William
Edward
Graham
1828-1864
B: 1828
D: 09 May 1864

Huldah
Drake
1831-1905
M: 05 Oct 1848
B: 01 Feb 1831
D: 10 Sep 1905

William
Isaac
Graham
1859-1938
B: 27 May 1859
D: 17 Jun 1938

Mary
Elizabeth
Sergent
1831-1905
M: 22 Dec 1883
B: 13 Dec 1861
D: 05 Dec 1922

John M.
Graham
1850- UNK
B: Jul 1850
D: Unknown

M. R.
Graham.

Columbus
Graham
1853- UNK
B: Abt 1853
D: 29 Jan 1930

Descendants of Thomas Hughes (DAR useful) and Nellie Foster

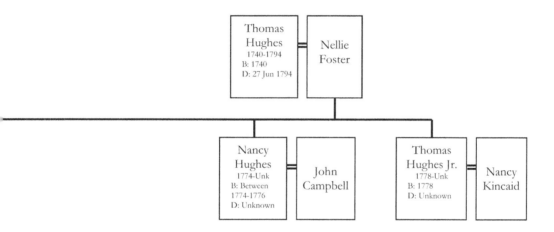

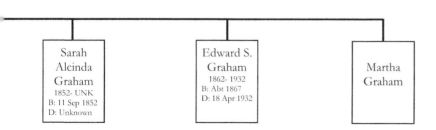

Descendants of William Isaac Graham and Mary Sergent

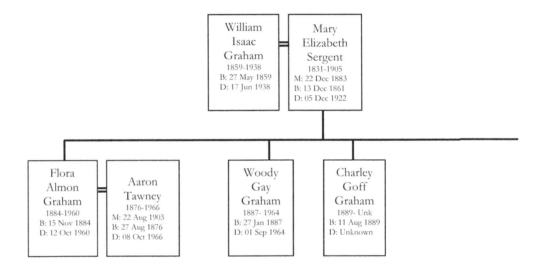

Descendants of William Isaac Graham and Mary Sergent

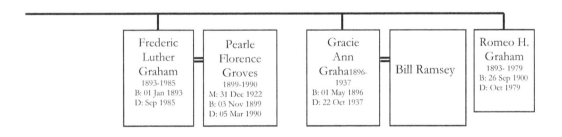

Descendants of Levi Moore and Susannah Crist
(Ancestor of Caroline Dixie McQuain)

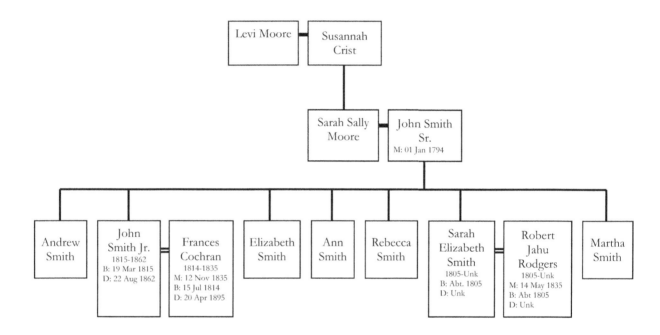

Descendants of Robert Jahu Rodgers ("Bobby" Rogers) & Sarah Smith

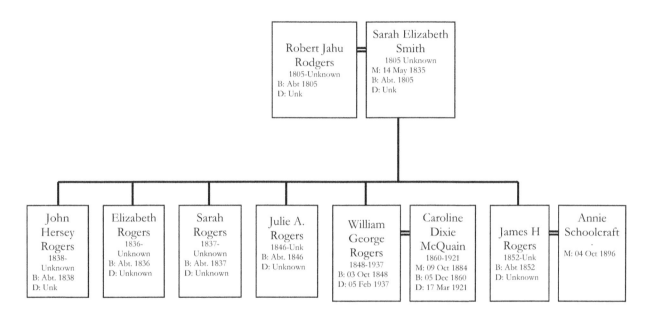

Descendants of Johann Summers and Maria Metz

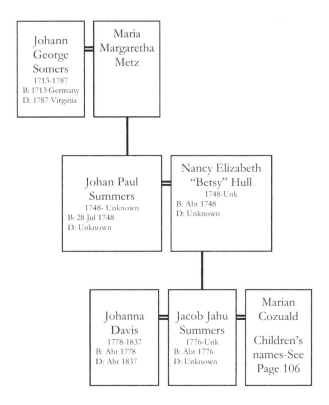

Descendants of Jacob Jahu Summers and Johanna Davis

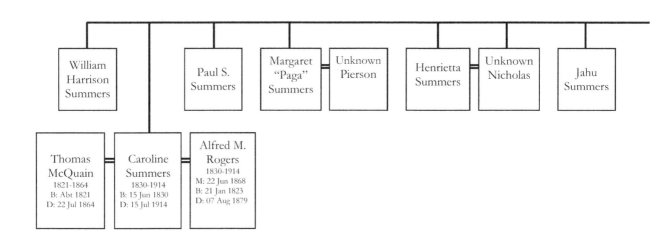

Descendants of Jacob Jahu Summers and Johanna Davis

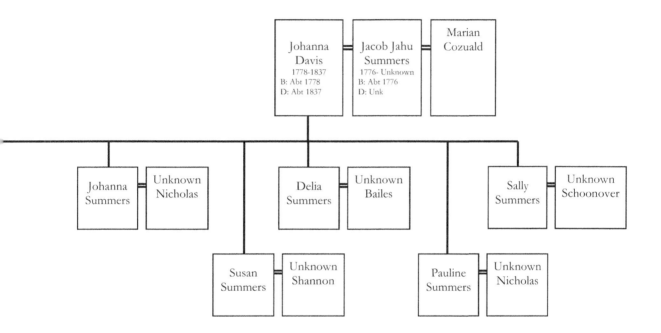

Descendants of Caroline Summers, Thomas McQuain, and Alfred Rogers

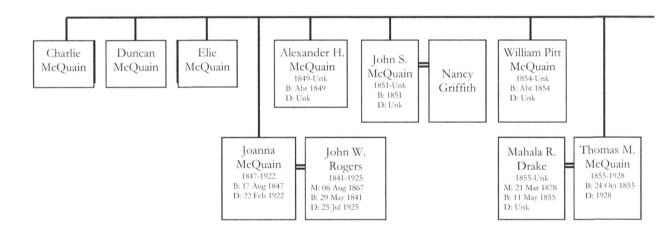

Descendants of Caroline Summers, Thomas McQuain, and Alfred Rogers

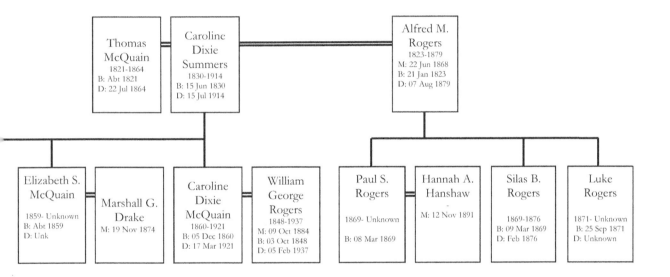

Descendants of William George Rogers and Caroline Dixie McQuain

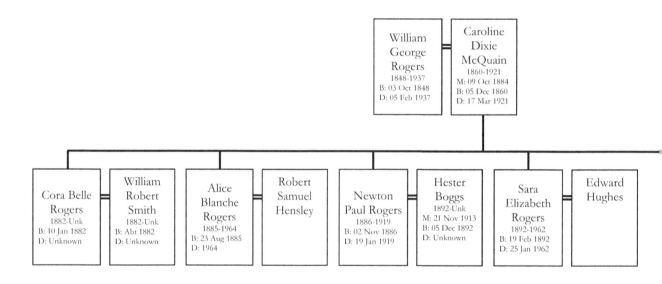

Descendants of William George Rogers and Caroline Dixie McQuain

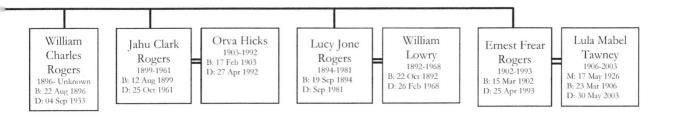

William Charles Rogers	Jahu Clark Rogers	Orva Hicks	Lucy Jone Rogers	William Lowry	Ernest Frear Rogers	Lula Mabel Tawney
1896- Unknown	1899-1961	1903-1992	1894-1981	1892-1968	1902-1993	1906-2003
B: 22 Aug 1896	B: 12 Aug 1899	B: 17 Feb 1903	B: 19 Sep 1894	B: 22 Oct 1892	B: 15 Mar 1902	M: 17 May 1926
D: 04 Sep 1933	D: 25 Oct 1961	D: 27 Apr 1992	D: Sep 1981	D: 26 Feb 1968	D: 25 Apr 1993	B: 23 Mar 1906
						D: 30 May 2003

Kinship of Lula "Mabel" Tawney

Name	Relationship with Lula Tawney	Civil	Canon
Acheson, Angela Mae	Great-grandniece of the husband		
Acheson, Brian LeRoy	Great-grandnephew of the husband		
Adams, Casey Lee	Husband of the great-granddaughter		
Adams, Chloe Renee	2nd great-granddaughter	IV	4
Adams, Spencer Lee	2nd great-grandson	IV	4
Adkins, Irene Jane	2nd great-grandmother	IV	4
Allen, Freddie D.	Husband of the 2nd cousin once removed		
Allen, Helen G.	Wife of the 2nd cousin once removed		
Anderson, Janice	Wife of the nephew		
Anderson, Wendy	Wife of the grandnephew		
Armstead, Faye	1st cousin once removed	V	3
Armstead, Freda	1st cousin once removed	V	3
Armstead, George	1st cousin once removed	V	3
Armstead, Harold	1st cousin once removed	V	3
Armstead, I. W.	Husband of the 1st cousin		
Armstead, Richard	1st cousin once removed	V	3
Armstead, unknown	1st cousin once removed	V	3
Ashley, Stella G.	Wife of the 2nd cousin		
Atkins, Albert J.	2nd cousin twice removed	VIII	5
Atkins, Clarissa "Clary"	2nd cousin twice removed	VIII	5
Atkins, George H.	2nd cousin twice removed	VIII	5
Atkins, Hiram	Husband of the 1st cousin 3 times removed		
Atkins, John	2nd cousin twice removed	VIII	5
Atkins, Lewis	2nd cousin twice removed	VIII	5
Atkins, Mary Jane	2nd cousin twice removed	VIII	5
Atkins, Moses	2nd cousin twice removed	VIII	5
Atkins, Robert	2nd cousin twice removed	VIII	5
Ayer, Charles C.	Husband of the 2nd cousin		
Bailey, Ashley Nicole	Great-granddaughter	III	3
Bailey, Braydonn James	2nd great-grandson	IV	4
Bailey, Melissa	Mother of great-granddaughter		
Baker, Melanie	Wife of the grandson		
Banckhard, Anna Ursula	4th great-grandmother	VI	6
Barger, Abram H.	1st cousin 3 times removed	VII	5
Barger, Daniel	1st cousin 3 times removed	VII	5
Barger, George Washington	1st cousin 3 times removed	VII	5
Barger, Harriet	1st cousin 3 times removed	VII	5
Barger, James Jr.	1st cousin 3 times removed	VII	5
Barger, John	Husband of the 2nd great-grandaunt		
Barger, John Jr.	1st cousin 3 times removed	VII	5
Barger, Nancy	1st cousin 3 times removed	VII	5
Barger, Phillip	1st cousin 3 times removed	VII	5
Barger, Polly	1st cousin 3 times removed	VII	5
Barger, William I.	1st cousin 3 times removed	VII	5
Barker, Carol D.	Wife of the grandnephew		
Barnes, Nancy A.	Wife of the 1st cousin once removed		

Family History of L. Mabel Tawney-Rogers and Ernest F. Rogers

Name	Relationship with Lula Tawney	Civil	Canon
Barone, Loraine Marie	Wife of the grandson		
Becker, Elizabeth	6th great-grandmother	VIII	8
Beistle, Gregory Allen	Grandson	II	2
Beistle, Roger	Son-in-law		
Beistle, Therese Marie	Granddaughter	II	2
Belknap, Conklin	Husband of the 2nd cousin		
Beller, Nannie E.	Wife of the 2nd cousin twice removed		
Beller, William H.	Husband of the 2nd cousin twice removed		
Birchard, William	Husband of the 2nd cousin		
Bird, Betty Lou	Daughter-in-law		
Bird, Ernest Scott	Grandson	II	2
Bird, James Henry	Son-in-law		
Bird, Jimmy Lee	Grandson	I	2
Bird, Joseph Scott	Great-grandson	II	3
Bird, Kylie May	Great-granddaughter	III	3
Bird, Lisa Carol	Granddaughter	II	2
Bird, Nena Marie	Granddaughter	II	2
Bird, Shirley Ann	Wife of the grandson		
Black, Paul Alan	Husband of the grandniece		
Bodkin, Mary	2nd great-grandmother of the husband		
Boggs, Ruby	Wife of the 1st cousin		
Bosley, Hannah Elizabeth	2nd great-granddaughter	IV	4
Bosley, Unknown	Husband of the great-granddaughter		
Bowman, Hunter Lee	Great-grandson	III	3
`	2nd great-grandson	IV	4
Bradley, Angela Denise	Great-grandniece	V	4
Bradley, Fred E.	Husband of the grandniece		
Bradley, Jennifer Lynn	Great-grandniece	V	4
Bragg, Alice Marion	1st cousin once removed of the husband		
Bragg, Clifton Sterrett	1st cousin once removed of the husband		
Bragg, Dorothy Annabelle	1st cousin once removed of the husband		
Bragg, Elsie Hattie	1st cousin once removed of the husband		
Bragg, Joda "Joanna"	1st cousin once removed of the husband		
Bragg, John Morgan	1st cousin once removed of the husband		
Bragg, Orville	1st cousin once removed of the husband		
Bragg, Pearl	1st cousin once removed of the husband		
Bragg, Thomas Wooderow	1st cousin once removed of the husband		
Bragg, Warden Emmett	1st cousin once removed of the husband		
Bragg, William Ira	1st cousin once removed of the husband		
Bremer, Ashley Marlene	Great-granddaughter	III	3
Bremer, Jami Marlene	Great-granddaughter	III	3
Bremer, Lindsey Marlene	Great-granddaughter	III	3
Bremer, Roger Alan	Husband of the granddaughter		
Brewer, Austin A.	2nd great-grandson	IV	4
Brewer, Chandler E.	2nd great-grandson	IV	4
Brewer, Unknown	Husband of the great-granddaughter		
Brown, Sandra Ann	Ex-wife of the grandson		

Family History of L. Mabel Tawney-Rogers and Ernest F. Rogers

Name	Relationship with Lula Tawney	Civil	Canon
Browning, Delbert	Husband of the grandniece		
Browning, Fanny	Wife of the 2nd cousin		
Buchannon, Anthony	Husband of the 1st cousin once removed		
Bullard, Frances Eloise	Wife of the nephew		
Burdette, Odessa W.	Wife of the 2nd cousin		
Butcher, Linda	Wife of the nephew		
Campbell, John	Husband of the 3rd great-grandaunt		
Carper, Brandi Lee	Great-granddaughter	III	3
Carper, Callahan Calvin	Husband of the grandaunt		
Carper, Brian Christopher	Great-grandson	III	3
Carper, Courtney Brooke	2nd great-granddaughter	IV	4
Carper, Cynthia May	Wife of the uncle		
Carper, James Darin	Great-grandson	III	3
Carper, James Kermit	Husband of the granddaughter		
Carper, Lisa Dawn	Great-granddaughter	III	3
Carper, Morgan Nichole	2nd great-granddaughter	IV	4
Carper, Kylie Paige	2nd great-granddaughter	IV	4
Carper, Randall Keith	Husband of the granddaughter		
Carte, Caroline	Ex-wife of the son		
	Ex-wife of the grandson		
Catharina, Anna	5th great-grandmother	VII	7
Conley, Christina Lynn	Granddaughter	II	2
	Great-granddaughter	III	3
Conley, Gabriel Wayne	Great-grandson	III	3
Conley, Gregory Lee	Grandson	II	2
Conley, Homer Lee	Son-in-law		
Conley, Joshua Highlander	Great-granddaughter	III	3
Conley, Michael Garrett	Grandson	II	2
Conley, Stacy Rondell	Granddaughter	II	2
Conley, Stephen Wayne	Grandson	II	2
Cook, Betty Jean	Grandniece of the husband		
Cook, C. C.	Husband of the grandaunt		
Cook, Caroline	Wife of the granduncle		
Cook, Kathy Delane	Great-grandniece of the husband		
Cook, Lisa Renae	Great-grandniece of the husband		
Cook, Robert Gregory	Great-grandnephew of the husband		
Cook, William Douglas	Great-grandnephew of the husband		
Cook, William Robert	Grandnephew of the husband		
Cooper, Aaron Roy	Grandnephew	IV	3
Cooper, Clifford Payne	Husband of the niece		
Cooper, Katie	Wife of the grandnephew		
Cooper, Peyton Lee	Great-grandnephew	V	4
Cooper, Thomas Clay	Great-grandnephew	V	4
Coppock, David James	2nd great-grandson	IV	4
Coppock, Kathryn Irene	Great-granddaughter	III	3
Coppock, Ricky Gene	Husband of the granddaughter		
Coppock, Scott Lee	Great-grandson	III	3

Family History of L. Mabel Tawney-Rogers and Ernest F. Rogers

Name	Relationship with Lula Tawney	Civil	Canon
Cox, Mary	2nd great-grandmother	IV	4
Crabtree, Mary L. (Carey)	Wife of the 2nd cousin once removed		
Crane, Amanda	Great-grandniece	V	4
Crane, Christopher	Great-grandnephew	V	4
Crane, Raymond	Husband of the grandniece		
Crane, Raymond Michael	Great-grandnephew	V	4
Crane, Victoria Rose	Great-grandniece	V	4
Crist, Susannah	2nd great-grandmother of the husband		
Cromwell, Margaret	Wife of the granduncle		
Cross, Laura M.	Wife of the 2nd cousin once removed		
Dalton, Jack	Brother-in-law		
Daugherty, Emma	Half 1st cousin twice removed	VI	4
Daugherty, Ruby	Half 2nd cousin once removed	VII	4
Davis, Johanna	Great-grandmother of the husband		
Davisson, Zelda	Wife of the 2nd cousin		
DeCarlo, Vickie Sue	Wife of the grandson		
Dennewitz, James William	Husband of the grandniece		
Dennis, Delbert	Son-in-law		
Dennis, Sheila Marlene	Granddaughter	II	2
Desposito, Brian	Grandnephew	IV	3
Desposito, Brianna Megan	Great-grandniece	V	4
Desposito, Courtney	Grandniece	IV	3
Desposito, Daniel John	Nephew	III	2
Desposito, Daniel Keith	Grandnephew	IV	3
Desposito, Joseph Keith	Great-grandnephew	V	4
Desposito, Joseph Martin	Nephew	III	2
Desposito, Kathy Ann	Grandniece	IV	3
Desposito, Lori Lynn	Grandniece	IV	3
Desposito, Marc Christopher	Grandnephew	IV	3
Desposito, Michael (Jr) Edward	Nephew	III	2
Desposito, Michael Edward	Brother-in-law		
Desposito, Michael Scott	Grandnephew	IV	3
Desposito, Olivia Logan	Great-grandniece	V	4
Desposito, Patricia Ann	Niece	III	2
Desposito, Serina	Great-grandniece	V	4
Deusenberry, Gary Scott	Ex-Husband of the granddaughter		
	Ex-Husband of the great-granddaughter		
Deusenberry, Kayla Colleen	Great-granddaughter	III	3
	2nd great-granddaughter	IV	4
Dilno, Guy LeRoy	Son-in-law		
Donahue, Mark John	Husband of the niece		
Douglas, Herbie	Grandniece of the husband		
Douglas, Jeanenne Joy	Wife of the grandnephew		
Douramacos, Lillian E. Frosyni"	Wife of the great-grandson		
Dovin, Rochelle Lynn	Wife of the great-grandson		
Drake, Carlos	2nd cousin	VI	3
Drake, Charles W.	Husband of the 1st cousin once removed		

Name	Relationship with Lula Tawney	Civil	Canon
Drake, Darrell W.	2nd cousin	VI	3
Drake, Finetta	Wife of the half great-granduncle		
Drake, Floyd	Husband of the 1st cousin		
Drake, Huldah	Great-grandmother	III	3
Drake, James	Husband of the great-granddaughter		
Drake, James	Son-in-law		
Drake, James G.	Husband of the 2nd cousin once removed		
Drake, Julia A.	Wife of the 1st cousin once removed		
Drake, Lester H.	2nd cousin	VI	3
Drake, Lula S.	Wife of the 1st cousin once removed		
Drake, Olive	2nd cousin	VI	3
Drake, Ollie	2nd cousin	VI	3
Drake, Otmer S.	2nd cousin	VI	3
Duranceau, Ashley	Grandniece	IV	3
Duranceau, Kristina Elizabeth	Grandniece	IV	3
Duranceau, Matthew	Grandnephew	IV	3
Duranceau, Steven	Husband of the niece		
Dye, Ruby Mildred	Wife of the half 2nd cousin once removed		
Eagleson, Thomas	Husband of the 1st cousin 3 times removed		
Echols, Harrison P.	Husband of the 2nd cousin twice removed		
Elizabeth, Mary	1st cousin once removed	V	3
Ellison, Joseph H.	Husband of the 2nd cousin		
Engle, Aura	2nd cousin	VI	3
Engle, Gladys	2nd cousin	VI	3
Engle, John J. "Joe"	2nd cousin	VI	3
Engle, Julia E.	2nd cousin	VI	3
Engle, Lynne	Wife of the 2nd cousin		
Engle, Mahalia	Wife of the 2nd cousin		
Engle, Orva	2nd cousin	VI	3
Engle, Shirley	Wife of the 2nd cousin		
Engle, Thurley	2nd cousin	VI	3
Engle, William Homer	Husband of the 1st cousin once removed		
Enoch, Randy	Husband of the grandniece		
Erickson, Ruby	Wife of the 2nd cousin		
Ethel Tawney, Eva	2nd cousin	VI	3
Falls, Roxie Sylvia	Wife of the 2nd cousin		
Farrer, Russell	Husband of the 1st cousin once removed		
Fisher, Mike	Husband of the grandniece		
Fisher, Sam	Great-grandnephew	V	4
Fisher, Sara	Great-grandniece	V	4
Flint, Roscoe R.	Husband of the 2nd cousin once removed		
Ford, Bruce Firlis	2nd cousin twice removed of the husband		
Ford, Gloria	2nd cousin twice removed of the husband		
Ford, Kevin	2nd cousin twice removed of the husband		
Ford, Mary Ruth	2nd cousin twice removed of the husband		
Foster, Betsey Faith	Wife of the grandnephew		
Foster, James	Husband of the great-granddaughter		

Family History of L. Mabel Tawney-Rogers and Ernest F. Rogers

Name	Relationship with Lula Tawney	Civil	Canon
Foster, Nancy	3rd great-grandmother	V	5
Foster, Nellie	4th great-grandmother	VI	6
Fox, Patrick Henry	Husband of the 2nd cousin		
French, Jennifer Rebecca	Ex-Wife of the grandson		
Gauthier, Dawn Marie	Ex-wife of the grandson		
Genarralli, Kimberly	Great-grandniece	V	4
Godbey, Elizabeth	Wife of the 3rd great-grandfather		
Goebel, John F.	Husband of the 1st cousin once removed		
Goff, "Dick" Vernon Ellis	Husband of the niece		
Goff, Adam Carter	Grandnephew	IV	3
Goff, Adelee	Great-grandniece	V	4
Goff, Annabelle Lily	Great-grandniece	V	4
Goff, Luke Harrison	Great-grandnephew	V	4
Goff, Matthew Garrison	Grandnephew	IV	3
Goff, Nathan Lawrence	Grandnephew	IV	3
Gold, Margaret	4th great-grandmother	VI	6
Goodwin, Bill	Husband of the 1st cousin once removed		
Graham, Barney	1st cousin	IV	2
Graham, Charley Goff	Uncle	III	2
Graham, Columbus	Grandaunt	IV	3
Graham, Delbert Richard	1st cousin	IV	2
Graham, Edward S.	Granduncle	IV	3
Graham, Flora Almon	Mother	I	1
Graham, Frederic Luther	Uncle	III	2
Graham, Gracie Ann	Aunt	III	2
Graham, James P.	2nd great-grandfather	IV	4
Graham, John M.	Granduncle	IV	3
Graham, Luther Edward	1st cousin	IV	2
Graham, M. R.	Grandaunt	IV	3
Graham, Martha	Grandaunt	IV	3
Graham, Nell Marie	1st cousin	IV	2
Graham, Romeo Henderson	Uncle	III	2
Graham, Sarah Alcinda	Grandaunt	IV	3
Graham, William Barney	1st cousin	IV	2
Graham, William Edward	Great-grandfather	III	3
Graham, William Isaac	Grandfather	II	2
Graham, Woody Gay	Uncle	III	2
Gray, Shirley Wyatt (Jr.)	Husband of the niece		
Gray, Tammy Lynn	Grandniece	IV	3
	Daughter-in-law		
	Wife of the grandson		
Greathouse, Evelyn M.	Wife of the 2nd cousin once removed		
Greathouse, Locie	Wife of the 1st cousin		
Greco, Maria Felicia	Daughter-in-law		
Griffin, Lois	Wife of the grandnephew		
Griffith, Louisa	Wife of the granduncle		
Gritt, Penelope Lynn	Wife of the grandnephew		

Name	Relationship with Lula Tawney	Civil	Canon
Groves, Pearle Florence	Wife of the uncle		
Gurule, Michael Anthoney	Great-grandnephew	V	4
Haines, Irving Charles	Brother-in-law		
Haley, Mary Molly	Wife of the uncle		
Hall, Harrison Dale	Husband of the 2nd cousin		
Hamric, Brian	2nd cousin 3 times removed of the husband		
Happney, Kimberly Sue	Grandniece	IV	3
Happney, Mark	Husband of the niece		
Happney, Tammy Anne	Grandniece	IV	3
Harlass, Ferdinand	5th great-grandfather	VII	7
Harless, Heinrick	6th great-grandfather	VIII	8
Harless, John Phillip, Sr.	4th great-grandfather	VI	6
Harless, Lovisa "Levicy"	Great-grandmother	III	3
Harless, Margaret	4th great-grandaunt	VIII	7
Harless, Martin	3rd great-grandfather	V	5
Harless, Michael	2nd great-grandfather	IV	4
Harold, Charles H.	Husband of the 2nd cousin		
Harold, Goldie E.	2nd cousin once removed	VII	4
Harold, Jessie	Wife of the 2nd cousin		
Harold, John	Husband of the 2nd cousin		
Harold, Maude	Wife of the 2nd cousin		
Harold, Paul H.	2nd cousin twice removed	VIII	5
Harold, Rex K.	2nd cousin once removed	VII	4
Harold, Ralph R.	2nd cousin once removed	VII	4
Hart, Cloie Page	2nd great-granddaughter	IV	4
Heaney, Heather Lynn	Wife of the great-grandson		
Hedrick, Abraham	Husband of the great-grandaunt		
Helmick, Ellen	Wife of the uncle		
Hensley	Niece of the husband		
Hensley, Chloise	Nephew of the husband		
Hensley, Clifford	Nephew of the husband		
Hensley, Danny	Grandnephew of the husband		
Hensley, Gladys	Niece of the husband		
Hensley, Joanne Marie	Grandniece of the husband		
Hensley, Judy Mae	Grandniece of the husband		
Hensley, Oliver	Nephew of the husband		
Hensley, Pierce	Nephew of the husband		
Hensley, Raymond	Nephew of the husband		
Hensley, Susan	Grandniece of the husband		
Hensley, Willard	Nephew of the husband		
Hensley-Douglas, Dixie Fay	Niece of the husband		
Hensley-Douglas, Opal	Niece of the husband		
Hensley-Williams, Virginia	Niece of the husband		
Hessler, Kayla Ell	2nd great-granddaughter	IV	4
Hessler, Matt	Husband of the great-granddaughter		
Hickey, Jackson Matthew	2nd great-grandson	IV	4
Hickey, Kristin Ann	Great-granddaughter	III	3

Family History of L. Mabel Tawney-Rogers and Ernest F. Rogers

Name	Relationship with Lula Tawney	Civil	Canon
Hickey, Matthew Michael	Great-grandson	III	3
Hickey, Michael Charles	Husband of the granddaughter		
Hickey, Ryleigh Elizabeth	2nd great-granddaughter	IV	4
Hickle, Boy	Grandnephew of the husband		
Hickle, Bryan	Grandnephew of the husband		
Highlander, Vera Ellen	Wife of the grandson		
Hill, Chase Garrett	Husband of the great-granddaughter		
Hobbs, Randall Lee	Husband of the granddaughter		
Hodge, Elizabeth	3rd great-grandmother	V	5
Hoffman, Agnes	5th great-grandmother	VII	7
Holcomb, Jennifer Dawn	Great-granddaughter	III	3
Holcomb, Karl	Ex-husband of the granddaughter		
Holcomb, Leah Michele	Great-granddaughter	III	3
Holcomb, Marissa Brooke	2nd great-granddaughter	IV	4
Holcomb, Paul	Ex-husband of the granddaughter		
Holcomb, Robert Scott	Husband of the great-granddaughter		
Hostutler, Retha Jean	Wife of the nephew		
Huber, Cody Lee	2nd great-grandson	IV	4
Huber, Kindra Nicole	2nd great-granddaughter	IV	4
Huber, Tony	Husband of the great-granddaughter		
Hughes, Cynthia	2nd great-grandmother	IV	4
Hughes, Edward	3rd great-grandfather	V	5
Hughes, Nancy	3rd great-grandaunt	VII	6
Hughes, Robert	3rd great-granduncle	VII	6
Hughes, Thomas	4th great-grandfather	VI	6
Hughes, Thomas Jr.	3rd great-granduncle	VII	6
Hull, Nancy Elizabeth "Betsy"	2nd great-grandmother of the husband		
Hull, Peter	3rd great-grandfather of the husband		
Hunt, Dona	Wife of the 1st cousin		
Hunt, Martha	Wife of the 2nd cousin		
Hunter, Elizabeth	Wife of the 1st cousin 3 times removed		
Hutchison, Robert M.	Husband of the great-grandaunt		
Hyden, Sheryl	Wife of the half 3rd cousin once removed		
Igo, Rebecca	Wife of the 2nd cousin		
Jackson, Keith Craig	Husband of the granddaughter		
Jackson, Kyle William	Great-grandson	III	3
Jackson, Lauren Nicole	Great-granddaughter	III	3
Jackson, Leah Michelle	Great-granddaughter	III	3
James, Coty Allen	2nd great-grandnephew	VI	5
James, Greg	Husband of the great-grandniece		
Jarvis, Greely	Husband of the 2nd cousin		
Jean, Barbara	2nd cousin twice removed of the husband		
Johnson, Dale Adolph	Grandson	II	2
Johnson, Harold Edgar	Son-in-law		
Johnson, Katrina Leigh	Great-granddaughter	III	3
Johnson, Marvin	Ex-husband of the granddaughter		
Johnson, Matthew Richard	Great-grandson	III	3

Family History of L. Mabel Tawney-Rogers and Ernest F. Rogers

Name	Relationship with Lula Tawney	Civil	Canon
Johnson, Russell Kenneth	Great-grandson	III	3
Johnson, Teresa Ann	Granddaughter	II	2
Johnson, Tiffany Ann	Great-granddaughter	III	3
Kanske, Charles	Husband of the 2nd cousin		
Kee, Norma	Wife of the 1st cousin once removed		
Keen, Elizabeth Jane	Wife of the granduncle		
Keen, Loise	2nd cousin once removed of the husband		
Keen, Wesley Franklin	2nd cousin of the husband		
Kincaid, Nancy	Wife of the 3rd great-granduncle		
King, Dora	Wife of the 2nd cousin		
King, Elizabeth "Betty"	Great-grandmother	III	3
King, Franklin	Great-grandaunt	V	4
King, George	Great-grandaunt	V	4
King, Jake	Husband of the 2nd cousin		
King, John	Great-grandaunt	V	4
King, Lewis	Great-grandaunt	V	4
King, Mabel	Wife of the 2nd cousin		
King, Samuel	2nd great-grandfather	IV	4
King, Samuel	Great-grandaunt	V	4
King, Sarah Jane	Great-grandaunt	V	4
King, Sherry Louise	Grandniece	IV	3
King, William R. "Bud"	Husband of the niece		
King, William Richard	Grandnephew	IV	3
Knight, William (Billy)	Husband of the grandaunt		
Knight, Smith	1st cousin once removed	V	3
Lacausi, Janeen	Wife of the grandnephew		
LaCour, Laurel Lee	Wife of the grandson		
Lanctot, Candice	Great-grandniece of the husband		
Lanctot, Edward Earl	Great-grandnephew of the husband		
Larch, Nancy	Daughter-in-law		
Lawrence, Cynthia/Syntha	Wife of the 1st cousin 3 times removed		
Lawrence, Harry W.	Husband of the 2nd cousin		
Lee, Sarah	5th great-grandmother	VII	7
Leftwich, John	Husband of the 2nd great-grandaunt		
Legg, Deborah Leigh	Ex-wife of the grandson		
Legg, Loren Montana	2nd great-grandson	IV	4
Lingel, Catharine	3rd great-grandmother	V	5
Lingel, Johan Jacob	4th great-grandfather	VI	6
Linscott, Jane	2nd cousin twice removed of the husband		
Linscott, Joe	2nd cousin twice removed of the husband		
Linscott, John	2nd cousin twice removed of the husband		
Lockhart, Rebecca	Wife of the 2nd great-grandfather		
Logsdon, Amber Dawn	Great-granddaughter	III	3
Logsdon, Ivan	Husband of the granddaughter		
Logsdon, Travis Eugene	Great-grandson	III	3
Looney, P. D.	Wife of the granduncle		
Lorsung, Jeffery	Husband of the great-granddaughter		

Family History of L. Mabel Tawney-Rogers and Ernest F. Rogers

Name	Relationship with Lula Tawney	Civil	Canon
Lowry, Adelee	Niece of the husband		
Lowry, Imogene	Niece of the husband		
Lowry, Joan	Niece of the husband		
Lowry, Polly	Niece of the husband		
Lowry, Roger	Nephew of the husband		
Mace, Holly Davis	Husband of the 2nd cousin		
Mack, Donna J.	Wife of the 2nd cousin once removed		
Mahaffey, Alyssia Irene	2nd great-granddaughter	IV	4
Mahaffey, Colton David	2nd great-grandson	IV	4
Mahaffey, Jacob Charles	2nd great-grandson	IV	4
Mahaffey, Jaimie Elizabeth	Great-granddaughter	III	3
Mahaffey, Jason Charles	Great-grandson	III	3
Mahaffey, Justin Charles	Great-grandson	III	3
Malm, Ole	Husband of the 2nd cousin		
Manuel, Deborah Jean	Wife of the grandson		
Marks, Mary	Wife of the 1st cousin		
Martin, Pauline Marie	Wife of the nephew		
Matheney, Anthony	Husband of the 2nd cousin		
Mathess, Glenn	Husband of the grandniece		
McCanns, Kathaleen	Wife of the grandnephew		
McCarthy, Leslie	Wife of the grandnephew		
McClain, Alan R.	2nd cousin once removed	VII	4
McClain, Caroll	2nd cousin once removed	VII	4
McClain, David	2nd cousin once removed	VII	4
McClain, Dianne	2nd cousin once removed	VII	4
McClain, Edward B.	2nd cousin once removed	VII	4
McClain, Ferrell	2nd cousin once removed	VII	4
McClain, Glen	2nd cousin once removed	VII	4
McClain, John Henry	Husband of the 2nd cousin		
McClain, John L.	2nd cousin once removed	VII	4
McClain, Kathy	2nd cousin once removed	VII	4
McClain, Lula Ermal	Wife of the 2nd cousin		
McClelland, Gilbert	Ex-husband of the daughter		
McClelland, Mary Gillette	Granddaughter	II	2
McDonald, Greg	Husband of the granddaughter		
McDonald, Gregory Wes	Husband of the granddaughter		
McDonald, Heather Noel	Great-granddaughter	III	3
McDonald, Wesley Aaron	Great-grandson	III	3
McGann, Virginia	Wife of the 2nd cousin		
McQuain, "Bird"	1st cousin of the husband		
McQuain, Adam Scott	1st cousin once removed of the husband		
McQuain, Alexander (Rev War)	2nd great-grandfather of the husband		
McQuain, Alexander II, War of 1812	Great-grandfather of the husband		
McQuain, Alexander Hamilton	Uncle of the husband		
McQuain, Alexander Marshall	1st cousin once removed of the husband		
McQuain, Alexander Scott	1st cousin once removed of the husband		
McQuain, Barry	2nd cousin twice removed of the husband		

Family History of L. Mabel Tawney-Rogers and Ernest F. Rogers

Name	Relationship with Lula Tawney	Civil	Canon
McQuain, Betty	Aunt of the husband		
McQuain, Caroline Dixie	Mother-in-law		
McQuain, Cassidy	Grandaunt of the husband		
McQuain, Catherine E.	1st cousin once removed of the husband		
McQuain, Catherine K.	1st cousin once removed of the husband		
McQuain, Charles	1st cousin of the husband		
McQuain, Charles Jacob	Granduncle of the husband		
McQuain, Charlie	Uncle of the husband		
McQuain, Chelsey Nicole	2nd great-grandniece	VI	5
McQuain, Clemmie Lois	2nd cousin of the husband		
McQuain, Clyde	Husband of the grandniece		
McQuain, Crystal Lynn	Great-grandniece	V	4
McQuain, David	2nd cousin once removed of the husband		
McQuain, Duncan	Uncle of the husband		
McQuain, Duncan	Great-granduncle of the husband		
McQuain, Earl	1st cousin once removed of the husband		
McQuain, Edna Columbia	2nd cousin of the husband		
McQuain, Elie	Uncle of the husband		
McQuain, Elizabeth	Great-grandaunt of the husband		
McQuain, Elizabeth Scott	Aunt of the husband		
McQuain, Ellen Luvernia	1st cousin once removed of the husband		
McQuain, Esther	Great-grandaunt of the husband		
McQuain, Eunice Elizabeth	2nd cousin of the husband		
McQuain, Evelyn	1st cousin once removed of the husband		
McQuain, Frank	1st cousin once removed of the husband		
McQuain, George	1st cousin once removed of the husband		
McQuain, George Hill	Granduncle of the husband		
McQuain, George Lewis	1st cousin once removed of the husband		
McQuain, George Newton	1st cousin once removed of the husband		
McQuain, George William	1st cousin once removed of the husband		
McQuain, George William	2nd cousin of the husband		
McQuain, Grover Cleveland	1st cousin of the husband		
McQuain, Helen Leah	2nd cousin of the husband		
McQuain, Hugh	Great-granduncle of the husband		
McQuain, Hugh	Granduncle of the husband		
McQuain, Isabella	Great-grandaunt of the husband		
McQuain, Jane	Grandaunt of the husband		
McQuain, Jane	Great-grandaunt of the husband		
McQuain, Jesabel	2nd cousin once removed of the husband		
McQuain, Joanna	Aunt of the husband		
McQuain, John	Great-granduncle of the husband		
McQuain, John Albert	1st cousin once removed of the husband		
McQuain, John Ellet Hays	1st cousin once removed of the husband		
McQuain, John S.	Uncle of the husband		
McQuain, Karen	2nd cousin twice removed of the husband		
McQuain, Kent	2nd cousin twice removed of the husband		
McQuain, Laura	1st cousin of the husband		

Family History of L. Mabel Tawney-Rogers and Ernest F. Rogers

Name	Relationship with Lula Tawney	Civil	Canon
McQuain, Lewis	1st cousin of the husband		
McQuain, Lewis Wetzel	1st cousin of the husband		
McQuain, Louis	1st cousin of the husband		
McQuain, Lula	1st cousin of the husband		
McQuain, Mabel Grace	1st cousin once removed of the husband		
McQuain, Mariam "Puss"	1st cousin of the husband		
McQuain, Marie Columbia	1st cousin once removed of the husband		
McQuain, Mark	2nd cousin twice removed of the husband		
McQuain, Mary A.	1st cousin once removed of the husband		
McQuain, Mary Diana "Molly"	1st cousin once removed of the husband		
McQuain, Mary Jane	1st cousin once removed of the husband		
McQuain, Meadow Rose	2nd great-grandniece	VI	5
McQuain, Miriam	2nd cousin once removed of the husband		
McQuain, Myra Pauline	2nd cousin of the husband		
McQuain, Nancy	Great-grandaunt of the husband		
McQuain, Nancy	Grandaunt of the husband		
McQuain, Nancy Elizabeth	1st cousin once removed of the husband		
McQuain, Oliver Cromwell	1st cousin once removed of the husband		
McQuain, Perry Hugh	2nd cousin of the husband		
McQuain, Rebecca	Grandaunt of the husband		
McQuain, Robert "Bub"	1st cousin of the husband		
McQuain, Rosetta Jane	1st cousin once removed of the husband		
McQuain, Sarah C.	1st cousin once removed of the husband		
McQuain, Thomas	1st cousin of the husband		
McQuain, Thomas	Great-granduncle of the husband		
McQuain, Thomas	2nd cousin once removed of the husband		
McQuain, Thomas Bryan	2nd cousin of the husband		
McQuain, Thomas Charles	1st cousin once removed of the husband		
McQuain, Thomas Marshall	Uncle of the husband		
McQuain, Thomas, Sr.	Grandfather of the husband		
McQuain, Travis Scott	Great-grandnephew	V	4
McQuain, Twin son	1st cousin twice removed of the husband		
McQuain, Unknown	1st cousin once removed of the husband		
McQuain, Unknown	1st cousin once removed of the husband		
McQuain, Unknown	1st cousin once removed of the husband		
McQuain, Unknown	1st cousin once removed of the husband		
McQuain, Unknown	1st cousin once removed of the husband		
McQuain, Unknown	1st cousin once removed of the husband		
McQuain, Unknown	1st cousin once removed of the husband		
McQuain, Unknown	1st cousin once removed of the husband		
McQuain, Unknown	1st cousin once removed of the husband		
McQuain, Unknown	1st cousin once removed of the husband		
McQuain, Unknown	1st cousin once removed of the husband		
McQuain, Unknown	1st cousin once removed of the husband		
McQuain, Unknown	1st cousin once removed of the husband		
McQuain, Unknown	1st cousin once removed of the husband		
McQuain, Unknown	1st cousin once removed of the husband		

Family History of L. Mabel Tawney-Rogers and Ernest F. Rogers

Name	Relationship with Lula Tawney	Civil	Canon
McQuain, Unknown	1st cousin twice removed of the husband		
McQuain, Unknown	1st cousin twice removed of the husband		
McQuain, William	Great-granduncle of the husband		
McQuain, William	Granduncle of the husband		
McQuain, William Pitt	Uncle of the husband		
McQuain, Zachary Caleb	2nd great-grandnephew	VI	5
Metz, Maria Margaretha	3rd great-grandmother of the husband		
Miller, Matthew	Husband of the grandniece		
Milster, John W.	Husband of the 1st cousin once removed		
Monzo, Martin Andrew	Great-grandson	III	3
Monzo, Rachel	Great-granddaughter	III	3
Moore, Levi	2nd great-grandfather of the husband		
Moore, Sarah Sally	Great-grandmother of the husband		
Morrison, Timothy	Husband of the 2nd cousin		
Mullen, Nadine F.	Wife of the great-grandson		
Murray, Cory Thomas	Great-grandnephew	V	4
Murray, Dean	Husband of the grandniece		
Murray, Luke David	Great-grandnephew	V	4
Murray, Mary W.	Wife of the 2nd cousin		
Music, Rhonda	Wife of the great-grandnephew		
Naylor, Priscilla Cathern	Wife of the grandson		
Nester, Ava Opal	Sister-in-law		
Nester, Charles	Husband of the 2nd cousin		
Nexter, Mattie Lucille	Wife of the 2nd cousin		
Nichols, Brenda	Wife of the nephew		
Nickelson, Vickie Lynne	Wife of the grandson		
Nida, John	Husband of the 1st cousin		
Noe, Aaron J.	Husband of the 2nd cousin		
Noe, Hiram	Granduncle	IV	3
Noe, Mary	Grandmother	II	2
Noe, Sally	Grandaunt	IV	3
Noe, William "Billy"	Great-grandfather	III	3
Ogden, Robbert Kellis	Husband of the 2nd cousin		
Olinger, Jacob	Husband of the 2nd great-grandaunt		
Ostrom, Claire Ann	Great- granddaughter	III	3
Ostrom, Maya Jean	Great- granddaughter	III	3
Ostrom, Donald John	Ex-husband of the daughter		
Ostrom, Jacob Davis	Great-grandson	III	3
Ostrom, Lance John	Grandson	II	2
Oxley, Greg	Husband of the grandniece		
Oxley, Kayla Anne	Great-grandniece	V	4
Oxley, Nicholas Gregory	Great-grandnephew	V	4
Panetti, Bill	Ex-husband of the granddaughter		
Panetti, Mason Jeffrey	Great-grandson	III	3
Parsons, Marie	Daughter-in-law		
Parsons, Mayzel	Wife of the 2nd cousin		
Pearson, Henning	Husband of the 2nd cousin		

Family History of L. Mabel Tawney-Rogers and Ernest F. Rogers

Name	Relationship with Lula Tawney	Civil	Canon
Peck, Christina Danielle	2nd great-granddaughter	IV	4
Pederson, Britney Taylor	Great-granddaughter	III	3
Pederson, Christian Kevin	Great-grandson	III	3
Pederson, Kevin	Husband of the granddaughter		
Peterson, Alexander Daniel	Great-grandnephew	V	4
Peterson, Michael Allen	Husband of the grandniece		
Portillo, Jobe Alexander	Great-grandnephew	V	4
Portillo, Stephen Lewis	Husband of the grandniece		
Preisch, David	5th great-grandfather	VII	7
Preisch, Johan Heinrich	6th great-grandfather	VIII	8
Preisch, Johannes Heinricus	7th great-grandfather	IX	9
Price, Anna Margaretta (Preiss)	4th great-grandmother	VI	6
Price, David	3rd great-grandfather	V	5
Price, David, Sr.	4th great-grandfather	VI	6
Price, Elizabeth	2nd great-grandmother	IV	4
Price, Mary Ann	Wife of the 2nd great-granduncle		
Pross, Joshua Matthew	Great-grandnephew	V	4
Pross, Richard	Husband of the grandniece		
Pugh, Shanna Claudine	Wife of the grandson		
Quinn, Garrett Monteville	2nd great-grandson	IV	4
Quinn, Jackson Henry	2nd great-grandson	IV	4
Quinn, Jeremy	Husband of the great-granddaughter		
Radabaugh, Howard	1st cousin	IV	2
Radabaugh, Kista Christenia	1st cousin	IV	2
Radabaugh, Mary	1st cousin	IV	2
Radabaugh, Omar	1st cousin	IV	2
Radabaugh, Pete	Husband of the aunt		
Rafferty, Dale	Grandnephew of the husband		
Rafferty, George	Grandnephew of the husband		
Rafferty-Bush, Alice	Grandniece of the husband		
Rafferty-Lake, Mary	Grandniece of the husband		
Rafferty-McFadden, Alma	Grandniece of the husband		
Ramsey, Bill	Husband of the aunt		
Ramsey, Granville	1st cousin	IV	2
Ramsey, Lavaughn	1st cousin	IV	2
Ramsey, Myrtle	Wife of the 2nd cousin		
Reed, Georgia Pauline	Wife of the half 3rd cousin		
Reeves, Brandon	Husband of the grandniece		
Reeves, Caleb	Great-grandnephew	V	4
Reeves, Molly Margaret	Great-grandniece	V	4
Richmond, Brad Alexander	Grandson	II	2
Richmond, Brenton Alexander	Great-grandson	III	3
Richmond, Brittany Anastasia	Great-granddaughter	III	3
Richmond, Brooke Alexandria	Great-granddaughter	III	3
Richmond, David Alexander	Ex-husband of the daughter		
Richmond, Kimberly Anne	Granddaughter	II	2
Roberts, Francis	Sister-in-law		

Family History of L. Mabel Tawney-Rogers and Ernest F. Rogers

Name	Relationship with Lula Tawney	Civil	Canon
Robinson, Cindy	Wife of Great-Grandson		
Rodgers, Robert Jahu	Grandfather of the husband		
Rogers, Alice Blanche	Sister-in-law		
Rogers, Alma "Delores"	Daughter	I	1
Rogers, Andrea Jacqueline	Granddaughter	II	2
	Great-granddaughter	III	3
Rogers, Andrew Jackson	Son	I	1
	Grandson	II	2
	Husband of the grandniece		
Rogers, Barbara Caroline	Daughter	I	1
Rogers, Carroll Aaron	Son	I	1
Rogers, Chadrick Lee	Great-grandson	III	3
Rogers, Charley	Brother-in-law		
Rogers, Charlotte Ann	Daughter	I	1
Rogers, Cheryl Lynn	Granddaughter	II	2
Rogers, Chester Keith	Great-grandson	III	3
Rogers, Clemin	1st cousin of the husband		
Rogers, Cora Belle	Sister-in-law		
Rogers, Dawn Arlene	Granddaughter	II	2
Rogers, Debra Jeanne	Granddaughter	II	2
Rogers, Dorma Kathern	Daughter	I	1
Rogers, Elizabeth	Aunt of the husband		
Rogers, Ernest Frear	Husband		
Rogers, Ester Elizabeth	1st cousin of the husband		
Rogers, Franklin Jeremiah	Great-grandson	III	3
Rogers, Frederick Alfred	1st cousin of the husband		
Rogers, Heather	Wife of the great-grandnephew		
Rogers, Henry Hersey	Nephew of the husband		
Rogers, Hudson Elijah	Great-grandson	III	3
Rogers, Imogene	Niece of the husband		
Rogers, Ina Gale	Granddaughter	II	2
Rogers, Infant	Grandniece of the husband		
Rogers, Isiah Jackson	Great-grandson	III	3
Rogers, Jahu Clark	Brother-in-law		
Rogers, James	Grandnephew of the husband		
Rogers, James Forrest	Nephew of the husband		
Rogers, James H.	Uncle of the husband		
Rogers, James John	1st cousin of the husband		
Rogers, Jayden	2nd great-granddaughter	IV	4
Rogers, John Hersey	Uncle of the husband		
Rogers, Joseph Randall	Great-grandson	III	3
Rogers, Julie A.	Aunt of the husband		
Rogers, Karen	Grandniece of the husband		
Rogers, Kathleen Ann	Granddaughter	II	2
Rogers, Kelly Jo	Great-granddaughter	III	3
Rogers, Kermit Adolph	Son	I	1
Rogers, Larry	Grandnephew of the husband		

Family History of L. Mabel Tawney-Rogers and Ernest F. Rogers

Name	Relationship with Lula Tawney	Civil	Canon
Rogers, Leslie	Nephew of the husband		
Rogers, Lawanda	Niece of the husband		
Rogers, Lillie Ellen	1st cousin of the husband		
Rogers, Linda	Grandniece of the husband		
Rogers, Lon Earl	1st cousin of the husband		
Rogers, Lucy Jone	Sister-in-law		
Rogers, Luke	Half uncle of the husband		
Rogers, Mabel Lynn	Great-granddaughter	III	3
Rogers, Mahala Caroline	1st cousin of the husband		
Rogers, Marc Robert	Grandson	II	2
Rogers, Mardell Adelee	Daughter	I	1
Rogers, Marilyn Ann	Grandniece of the husband		
Rogers, Mary Beth	Grandniece of the husband		
Rogers, Matthew Perry	Great-grandson	III	3
Rogers, Michael Keith	Grandson	II	2
Rogers, Michele Lynn	Granddaughter	II	2
Rogers, Mikala Polina	Great-granddaughter	III	3
Rogers, Nathan Eric	Grandson	II	2
Rogers, Newton Paul	Brother-in-law		
Rogers, Patricia Rondell	Daughter	I	1
Rogers, Paul S.	Half uncle of the husband		
Rogers, Retta	Wife of the 1st cousin of the husband		
Rogers, Rhonda Diane	Granddaughter	II	2
Rogers, Robert Keith	Son	I	1
Rogers, Robert Randall	Grandson	II	2
Rogers, Roland Kester	Nephew of the husband		
Rogers, Sara Elizabeth	Sister-in-law		
Rogers, Sarah	Aunt of the husband		
Rogers, Silas B.	Half uncle of the husband		
Rogers, Snowden	Nephew of the husband		
Rogers, Thomas	Grandnephew of the husband		
Rogers, Timothy Lee	Grandson	II	2
Rogers, Tyre Bennett	1st cousin of the husband		
Rogers, Wade	Grandnephew of the husband		
Rogers, William Charles	Brother-in-law		
Rogers, William Gail	Nephew of the husband		
Rogers, William George	Father-in-law		
Rogers, William Pitt	1st cousin of the husband		
Rogers, Winston Nehemiah	Great-grandson	III	3
Romano, Aaron Michael	Husband of the granddaughter		
Romano, Bryan Gregory	Great-grandson	III	3
Romano, Justin Matthew	Great-grandson	III	3
Romano, Sara Elizabeth	Great-granddaughter	III	3
Rosario	Wife of the great-grandson		
Rose, Virginia L.	Wife of the 2nd cousin		
Ross, Armetha L.	1st cousin once removed	V	3
Ross, Claude Mark	2nd cousin	VI	3

Name	Relationship with Lula Tawney	Civil	Canon
Ross, Dallas C.	2nd cousin	VI	3
Ross, Dixie Artie	2nd cousin	VI	3
Ross, Don L.	2nd cousin	VI	3
Ross, Doris Ruth	2nd cousin	VI	3
Ross, Emma E.	2nd cousin once removed	VII	4
Ross, Harley E.	2nd cousin	VI	3
Ross, Homer Daniel	2nd cousin	VI	3
Ross, Imogene	2nd cousin	VI	3
Ross, Isaac M.	Husband of the grandaunt		
Ross, John A.	1st cousin once removed	V	3
Ross, Leona	Wife of the 1st cousin once removed		
Ross, Lynn	2nd cousin	VI	3
Ross, Mary J.	1st cousin once removed	V	3
Ross, Max H.	2nd cousin once removed	VII	4
Ross, Max Hamilton	2nd cousin	VI	3
Ross, Nancy Annabelle	Wife of the 1st cousin once removed		
Ross, Paul H.	2nd cousin once removed	VII	4
Ross, Rex Philip	2nd cousin	VI	3
Ross, Richard C.	2nd cousin once removed	VII	4
Ross, Ruby Claire	2nd cousin	VI	3
Ross, Spurgeon Charles	Husband of the 1st cousin once removed		
Ross, Stanley F.	Husband of the 2nd cousin		
Ross, Ulysses Simpson	Husband of the 1st cousin once removed		
Ross, W.C./William	1st cousin once removed	V	3
Ross, Willis C.	2nd cousin	VI	3
Runnion, Mary	Wife of the great-grandfather		
Ruth, James	Husband of the grandniece		
Samms, Lester Ray	Husband of the 2nd cousin		
Scott, Elizabeth	Great-grandmother of the husband		
Scott, George	Husband of the 1st cousin once removed		
Scott, John	2nd great-grandfather of the husband		
Sergent, Annie	Grandaunt	IV	3
Sergent, Charity	Grandaunt	IV	3
Sergent, David	2nd great-grandfather	IV	4
Sergent, David	Granduncle	IV	3
Sergent, Elizabeth Kelly	Half great-grandaunt	V	4
Sergent, Ephraim	3rd great-grandfather	V	5
Sergent, Ephraim	Granduncle	IV	3
Sergent, Fannie	Half 1st cousin twice removed	VI	4
Sergent, Henderson	Half great-granduncle	V	4
Sergent, Henry Carl	Half 2nd cousin once removed	VII	4
Sergent, Henry David	Half great-granduncle	V	4
Sergent, James Madison	Half great-granduncle	V	4
Sergent, Leah Sinnett	Half great-grandaunt	V	4
Sergent, Malissa	Grandaunt	IV	3
Sergent, Mark Gerald	Half 3rd cousin once removed	IX	5
Sergent, Mary Elizabeth	Grandmother	II	2

Family History of L. Mabel Tawney-Rogers and Ernest F. Rogers

Name	Relationship with Lula Tawney	Civil	Canon
Sergent, Peter	Granduncle	IV	3
Sergent, Presley	Granduncle	IV	3
Sergent, Rachel A.	Grandaunt	IV	3
Sergent, Ralph Edward	Half 3rd cousin	VIII	4
Sergent, Robert Lawrence	Half 3rd cousin	VIII	4
Sergent, Roxie	Half 1st cousin twice removed	VI	4
Sergent, Sarah	Half 1st cousin twice removed	VI	4
Sergent, Sarah Combs	Half great-grandaunt	V	4
Sergent, Stephen	4th great-grandfather	VI	6
Sergent, Will	Husband of the aunt		
Sergent, William	5th great-grandfather	VII	7
Sergent, William Daryl	Half 2nd cousin once removed	VII	4
Sergent, Will Henderson	Great-grandfather	III	3
Sergent, William Madison	Half 1st cousin twice removed	VI	4
Settle, Daniel M.	Husband of the niece		
Settle, Kaci Ellyn	Grandniece	IV	3
Settle, Susan Danielle	Grandniece	IV	3
Shaw, Rabe Lee	Husband of the 2nd cousin		
Sheets, Amy Marie	Wife of the grandnephew		
Sheppard, Betty Jean	Wife of the nephew		
Shirey, Joshua Neil	2nd great-grandson	IV	4
Shirey, Whitney Ray	2nd great-granddaughter	IV	4
Shoemaker, April	Wife of the grandson		
Shoemaker, McKenna	Great-granddaughter	III	3
Short, Hazel Maxine	Sister-in-law		
Siers, Porter	Husband of the 2nd cousin		
Simmons, Carl W.	Husband of the 2nd cousin		
Skelly, Janeen	Wife of the nephew		
Skidmore, M.	2nd great-grandmother	IV	4
Smith, Albert L.	Husband of the 1st cousin		
	2nd cousin once removed of the husband		
Smith, Alice D.	2nd cousin of the husband		
Smith, Andrew	Granduncle of the husband		
Smith, Ann	Grandaunt of the husband		
Smith, Anna Susan	2nd cousin of the husband		
Smith, Barbara Jean	2nd cousin twice removed of the husband		
Smith, Brooks	2nd cousin once removed of the husband		
Smith, Buena A.	2nd cousin of the husband		
Smith, Carolyn Sue	1st cousin once removed	V	3
	2nd cousin twice removed of the husband		
Smith, Carrie	2nd cousin of the husband		
Smith, Cary Stephen	2nd cousin twice removed	VIII	5
Smith, Charles L.	2nd cousin of the husband		
Smith, Cora	Niece of the husband		
Smith, Coy	2nd cousin twice removed of the husband		
Smith, David	2nd cousin twice removed of the husband		
Smith, David D.	1st cousin once removed of the husband		

Family History of L. Mabel Tawney-Rogers and Ernest F. Rogers

Name	Relationship with Lula Tawney	Civil	Canon
Smith, David Hall	2nd cousin twice removed of the husband		
Smith, Debra	2nd cousin twice removed of the husband		
Smith, Diane	2nd cousin twice removed of the husband		
Smith, Elizabeth	Niece of the husband		
Smith, Elizabeth	1st cousin once removed of the husband		
Smith, Elizabeth (1)	Grandaunt of the husband		
Smith, Ella	Wife of the 2nd cousin		
Smith, Ellen Suzanne	2nd cousin twice removed of the husband		
Smith, Eloise	2nd cousin twice removed of the husband		
Smith, Emma	2nd cousin of the husband		
Smith, Eric Charles	2nd cousin twice removed of the husband		
Smith, Fannie	Wife of the 2nd cousin		
Smith, Flora Gale	2nd cousin of the husband		
Smith, Floyd	2nd cousin of the husband		
Smith, Franklin	1st cousin once removed of the husband		
Smith, Frederick	2nd cousin of the husband		
Smith, Gary	2nd cousin twice removed of the husband		
Smith, Geneva	2nd cousin once removed of the husband		
Smith, Geneva	Wife of the 2nd cousin		
Smith, George Brooks	2nd cousin of the husband		
Smith, Gladys	2nd cousin once removed of the husband		
Smith, Glen	2nd cousin once removed of the husband		
Smith, Glen	2nd cousin twice removed of the husband		
Smith, Hannah Virginia	2nd cousin of the husband		
Smith, Hunter Paul	2nd cousin once removed of the husband		
Smith, Hunter Paul	2nd cousin twice removed of the husband		
Smith, Ida	2nd cousin of the husband		
Smith, Ira D.	2nd cousin of the husband		
Smith, Jacob Blaine	2nd cousin of the husband		
Smith, James Clay	2nd cousin of the husband		
Smith, James John Jr	1st cousin once removed of the husband		
Smith, Jason Carl	Nephew of the husband		
Smith, Jessica	Great-grandniece of the husband		
Smith, Jim	2nd cousin once removed of the husband		
Smith, Jo Ann	1st cousin once removed	V	3
	2nd cousin twice removed of the husband		
Smith, John (of Blown Timber)	2nd cousin of the husband		
Smith, John (Sr.)	Great-grandfather of the husband		
Smith, John B.	1st cousin once removed	V	3
	2nd cousin twice removed of the husband		
Smith, John Calvin	2nd cousin once removed of the husband		
Smith, John Jr.	Granduncle of the husband		
Smith, Joseph Nelson	1st cousin once removed of the husband		
Smith, Julia	2nd cousin of the husband		
Smith, Kacie Jo	Great-granddaughter	III	3
Smith, Kenneth	2nd cousin once removed of the husband		
Smith, Kermit	Nephew of the husband		

Family History of L. Mabel Tawney-Rogers and Ernest F. Rogers

Name	Relationship with Lula Tawney	Civil	Canon
Smith, Kerrie Ann	Great-granddaughter	III	3
Smith, Laura	2nd cousin once removed of the husband		
Smith, Lecta	1st cousin once removed of the husband		
Smith, Lillie	Wife of the 2nd cousin		
Smith, Linda Campbell	Grandniece of the husband		
Smith, Lionel	2nd cousin once removed of the husband		
Smith, Lona	2nd cousin once removed of the husband		
Smith, Loretta	2nd cousin twice removed of the husband		
Smith, Lucy	2nd cousin once removed of the husband		
Smith, Lydia	1st cousin once removed of the husband		
Smith, Mahailey Jo	2nd great-granddaughter	IV	4
Smith, Margaret	1st cousin once removed of the husband		
Smith, Margarette	2nd cousin once removed of the husband		
Smith, Martha	Grandaunt of the husband		
Smith, Martha	1st cousin once removed of the husband		
Smith, Mary	Half 1st cousin twice removed	VI	4
Smith, Mary	1st cousin once removed of the husband		
Smith, Mary F.	Wife of the 1st cousin once removed		
Smith, Mary Lou	1st cousin once removed	V	3
	2nd cousin twice removed of the husband		
Smith, Merle Louise	2nd cousin twice removed of the husband		
Smith, Mildred	2nd cousin once removed of the husband		
Smith, Morgan	2nd great-grandniece of the husband		
Smith, Newton	1st cousin once removed of the husband		
Smith, Newton Jasper	2nd cousin of the husband		
Smith, Raymond	Husband of the 2nd cousin		
Smith, Raymond	2nd cousin once removed of the husband		
Smith, Rebecca	Grandaunt of the husband		
Smith, Rebecca	2nd cousin twice removed of the husband		
Smith, Robert L.	1st cousin once removed	V	3
	2nd cousin twice removed of the husband		
Smith, Roger	Husband of the granddaughter		
Smith, Rosa	2nd cousin once removed of the husband		
Smith, Rose Mary	2nd cousin once removed of the husband		
Smith, Sarah Elizabeth "Sally"	Grandmother of the husband		
Smith, Scott Andrew	2nd cousin twice removed of the husband		
Smith, Stephen Alexander	Great-grandnephew of the husband		
Smith, Stephen Blake	Husband of the 2nd cousin once removed		
Smith, Theresa	2nd cousin twice removed of the husband		
Smith, Thomas Frederick	2nd cousin of the husband		
Smith, Tom	2nd cousin twice removed of the husband		
Smith, Virginia	Wife of the 2nd cousin		
Smith, Virginia Belle	Niece of the husband		
Smith, Virginia Gay	2nd cousin twice removed of the husband		
Smith, Walter B.	Husband of the 2nd cousin		
Smith, Wanda	2nd cousin twice removed of the husband		
Smith, William	2nd cousin twice removed of the husband		

Name	Relationship with Lula Tawney	Civil	Canon
Smith, William Clyde	Husband of the 2nd cousin		
Smith, William Hunter	2nd cousin of the husband		
Smith, William Young	1st cousin once removed of the husband		
Somers, Johann George	3rd great-grandfather of the husband		
	2nd great-grandniece of the husband		
Soto, Denisse Carolina Sanchez	Wife of the great-grandson		
Southworth, Doris E.	Wife of the 2nd cousin		
Spencer, Clifford Duane	2nd cousin twice removed of the husband		
Spensieri, Linda	Wife of the nephew		
Sperling, John	Husband of the 2nd cousin		
Spillers, Gracyn Rylin	2nd great-grandson	IV	4
Sproul, Mary Eunice	2nd great-grandmother of the husband		
Staley, Catey	Wife of the 2nd great-granduncle		
Starcher, Marilyn	Wife of the 2nd cousin		
Stevens, Minnie D.	Wife of the 2nd cousin		
Stock, Adam Duane	Husband of the great-granddaughter		
Stock, Braxton Graham	2nd great-grandson	IV	4
Stock, Owen Bradford	2nd great-grandson	IV	4
Stone, David	Husband of the great-granddaughter		
Stone, Hayden Zane	2nd great-grandson	IV	4
Stott, Brian	Husband of the great-granddaughter		
Summers, Almira	Half grandaunt of the husband		
Summers, America	Half grandaunt of the husband		
Summers, Andrew Jackson	Half granduncle of the husband		
Summers, Beatrice Almeda	Sister-in-law		
Summers, Caroline Dixie	Grandmother of the husband		
Summers, Crockett	Great-grandfather of the husband		
Summers, David Crockett	Half granduncle of the husband		
Summers, Deba	Grandaunt of the husband		
Summers, Delia	Grandaunt of the husband		
Summers, George Clarke	Half granduncle of the husband		
Summers, Henrietta	Grandaunt of the husband		
Summers, Jacob Jahu	Great-grandfather of the husband		
Summers, Jahu (twin to Paul)	Granduncle of the husband		
Summers, Johan Paul	2nd great-grandfather of the husband		
Summers, Johanna	Grandaunt of the husband		
Summers, Lois	Half grandaunt of the husband		
Summers, Margaret "Paga"	Grandaunt of the husband		
Summers, Pauline	Grandaunt of the husband		
Summers, Sally	Grandaunt of the husband		
Summers, Susan	Grandaunt of the husband		
Summers, Thomas Benton	Half granduncle of the husband		
Summers, William Harrison	Granduncle of the husband		
Suppa, Angela	Great-grandniece	V	4
Suppa, Jenna	Great-grandniece	V	4
Suppa, Madison	Great-grandniece	V	4
Suppa, Shawn	Great-grandniece	V	4

Family History of L. Mabel Tawney-Rogers and Ernest F. Rogers

Name	Relationship with Lula Tawney	Civil	Canon
Sutphin, Hazel M.	2nd cousin	VI	3
Sutphin, Peter T.	Husband of the 1st cousin once removed		
Swain, Lowell	Husband of the 2nd cousin		
Tackett, Bobby Wayne	Great-grandson	III	3
Tackett, Christian David	2nd great-grandson	IV	4
Tackett, Haley Kristine	2nd great-granddaughter	IV	4
Tackett, James Lee II	Great-grandson	III	3
Tackett, Steve	Husband of the granddaughter		
Tackett, Steven Daniel	Great-grandson	III	3
Tahan, Caren	Wife of the grandnephew		
Tanner, Mark	Husband of the great-granddaughter		
Tany, Johan Jacob	4th great-grandfather	VI	6
Tarrantini, Michael	Ex-Husband of the granddaughter		
Tawney, Aaron	Father	I	1
Tawney, Adam Christopher	Great-grandnephew	V	4
Tawney, Add S.	1st cousin	IV	2
Tawney, Agnes	1st cousin 3 times removed	VII	5
Tawney, Albert/Herbert	1st cousin once removed	V	3
Tawney, Alexander	Granduncle	IV	3
Tawney, Amanda	Grandaunt	IV	3
Tawney, Amie Erin	Grandniece	IV	3
Tawney, Anna Elizabeth	Sister	II	1
Tawney, Anne	Niece	III	2
Tawney, Arlie M.	2nd cousin	VI	3
Tawney, Armentha M.	1st cousin once removed	V	3
Tawney, Armetha A.	1st cousin once removed	V	3
Tawney, Armitta E.	1st cousin once removed	V	3
Tawney, Barbara	2nd great-grandaunt	VI	5
Tawney, Barbara Lamoine	Niece	III	2
Tawney, Bernice G.	2nd cousin	VI	3
Tawney, Bernice Jean	Niece	III	2
Tawney, Bett	Aunt	III	2
Tawney, Betty Gladys	2nd cousin	VI	3
Tawney, Bonita Louise	Grandniece	IV	3
Tawney, Brandy Nicole	Grandniece	IV	3
Tawney, Buck	Great-grandfather	III	3
Tawney, Buzz	Brother	II	1
Tawney, Carl Hamilton	2nd cousin	VI	3
Tawney, Carrie Neva	2nd cousin	VI	3
Tawney, Catherine	2nd great-grandaunt	VI	5
Tawney, Cathy	Grandniece	IV	3
Tawney, Champ "Clark"	Brother	II		1
Tawney, Charles	2nd cousin once removed	VII	4
Tawney, Christian	2nd great-granduncle	VI	5
Tawney, Christopher	Uncle	III	2
Tawney, Christopher P.	Granduncle	IV	3
Tawney, Clara	1st cousin	IV	2

Family History of L. Mabel Tawney-Rogers and Ernest F. Rogers

Name	Relationship with Lula Tawney	Civil	Canon
Tawney, Clara	1st cousin once removed	V	3
Tawney, Clara Fay	2nd cousin	VI	3
Tawney, Clark	1st cousin	IV	2
Tawney, Clement Joe	Nephew	III	2
Tawney, Clement Luther	Brother	II	1
Tawney, Cole Garrett	Grandnephew	IV	3
Tawney, Cora	1st cousin	IV	2
Tawney, Daniel Aaron	Brother	II	1
Tawney, Dan Carey	1st cousin once removed	V	3
Tawney, Dan W. "Link"	Uncle	III	2
Tawney, DavidAllen	Grandnephew	IV	3
Tawney, David J.	Granduncle	IV	3
Tawney, David Jackson	Uncle	III	2
Tawney, David James	1st cousin 3 times removed	VII	5
Tawney, Debra Jean	Grandniece	IV	3
Tawney, Donald Clyde	2nd cousin	VI	3
Tawney, Dora Ellen	1st cousin once removed	V	3
Tawney, Drema Lynn	Grandniece	IV	3
Tawney, Edwin A.	1st cousin once removed	V	3
Tawney, Elbert L.	2nd cousin	VI	3
Tawney, Elizabeth	2nd great-grandaunt	VI	5
Tawney, Elizabeth	Grandaunt	IV	3
Tawney, Emma	1st cousin	IV	2
Tawney, Emma	1st cousin once removed	V	3
Tawney, Ernest R.	1st cousin once removed	V	3
Tawney, Eupha Iona	2nd cousin	VI	3
Tawney, Eva Ethyl	2nd cousin	VI	3
Tawney, Ewuell Jerome	Nephew	III	2
Tawney, Florence	Aunt	III	2
Tawney, Florence	1st cousin	IV	2
Tawney, Florence Mary	Sister	II	1
Tawney, Floyd M.	1st cousin once removed	V	3
Tawney, Franklin D.	1st cousin once removed	V	3
	1st cousin once removed of the husband		
Tawney, Freda Mae	2nd cousin once removed	VII	4
Tawney, Freddie	Nephew	III	2
Tawney, Freddie D.	2nd cousin	VI	3
Tawney, Frederick Jarrett	Nephew	III	2
Tawney, Gary Wayne	Husband of the niece		
Tawney, Gene	Nephew	III	2
Tawney, George	1st cousin	IV	2
Tawney, George	1st cousin 3 times removed	VII	5
Tawney, George "Garrison"	Brother	II	1
Tawney, George W.	2nd cousin	VI	3
Tawney, George William	Grandfather	II	2
Tawney, Grover	1st cousin	IV	2
Tawney, Guyla Jean	Grandniece	IV	3

Family History of L. Mabel Tawney-Rogers and Ernest F. Rogers

Name	Relationship with Lula Tawney	Civil	Canon
Tawney, Gypsy	1st cousin	IV	2
Tawney, Harry Marshall	Brother	II	1
Tawney, Hester	1st cousin	IV	2
Tawney, Hiram J. "High"	Uncle	III	2
Tawney, Hugh H.	1st cousin once removed	V	3
Tawney, Ina	2nd cousin	VI	3
Tawney, Infant	1st cousin once removed	V	3
Tawney, Iris Ethel	2nd cousin	VI	3
Tawney, Jack L.	1st cousin once removed	V	3
	1st cousin once removed of the husband		
Tawney, Jack Landis	Nephew	III	2
Tawney, Jack Landis II	Grandnephew	IV	3
Tawney, Jacob	1st cousin 3 times removed	VII	5
Tawney, James Delmar	2nd cousin	VI	3
Tawney, James Henry	1st cousin	IV	2
Tawney, James M.	1st cousin once removed	V	3
Tawney, James M.	Uncle	III	2
Tawney, James Matthew	Grandnephew	IV	3
Tawney, James Wellington	1st cousin once removed	V	3
Tawney, Jane	2nd great-grandaunt	VI	5
Tawney, Janet Lynn	Grandniece	IV	3
Tawney, Janice Evelyn	Niece	III	2
Tawney, Jarrett "Buzz"	Brother	II	1
Tawney, Jeffrey Jerome	Grandnephew	IV	3
Tawney, Jennings	1st cousin	IV	2
Tawney, Jerry W II.	Grandnephew	IV	3
Tawney, Jerry Wayne	Nephew	III	2
Tawney, Johan Jacob	4th great-grandfather	VI	6
Tawney, John	1st cousin	IV	2
Tawney, John	2nd cousin	VI	3
Tawney, John	1st cousin 3 times removed	VII	5
Tawney, John	2nd great-granduncle	VI	5
Tawney, John D.	1st cousin once removed	V	3
Tawney, John Daniel	2nd great-grandfather	IV	4
Tawney, John Daniel, Jr.	Great-grandfather	III	3
Tawney, John George	3rd great-grandfather	V	5
Tawney, John George Jr,	2nd great-granduncle	VI	5
Tawney, John Hamilton	Granduncle	IV	3
Tawney, John Spencer	1st cousin once removed	V	3
Tawney, Juanita Florence	1st cousin once removed	V	3
	1st cousin once removed of the husband		
Tawney, Karen	Ex-wife of the grandson		
Tawney, Karen Almon	Niece	III	2
Tawney, Katherine	1st cousin 3 times removed	VII	5
Tawney, Kenneth Jay	Grandnephew	IV	3
Tawney, Kenneth Jenoal	Nephew	III	2
Tawney, Kenneth Joseph	Great-grandnephew	V	4

Name	Relationship with Lula Tawney	Civil	Canon
Tawney, LaMoine	Niece	III	2
Tawney, Lela Anne	Niece	III	2
Tawney, Leona Helen	2nd cousin	VI	3
Tawney, Lettice	1st cousin 3 times removed	VII	5
Tawney, Lewis C.	1st cousin once removed	V	3
Tawney, Locie D.	2nd cousin	VI	3
Tawney, Louvisa	Aunt	III	2
Tawney, Lovica M.	1st cousin once removed	V	3
Tawney, Lucy Alaphair	1st cousin once removed	V	3
Tawney, Lula "Mabel"	Self		0
Tawney, Mae Belle	1st cousin once removed	V	3
Tawney, Maggie	1st cousin	IV	2
Tawney, Martha A.	1st cousin once removed	V	3
Tawney, Mary	1st cousin	IV	2
Tawney, Mary A.	1st cousin once removed	V	3
Tawney, Mary Elizabeth	Great-grandaunt	V	4
Tawney, Mary F.	1st cousin once removed	V	3
Tawney, Mary "Polly"	1st cousin 3 times removed	VII	5
Tawney, Mattie L.	1st cousin once removed	V	3
Tawney, Miranda	Aunt	III	2
Tawney, Nancy Audra	Wife of the 2nd cousin		
Tawney, Nancy Audra	2nd cousin	VI	3
	Wife of the 2nd cousin		
Tawney, Nancy Ellen	Niece	III	2
Tawney, Nancy Emma	1st cousin once removed	V	3
Tawney, Nora Hester	2nd cousin	VI	3
Tawney, Omar Willard	2nd cousin	VI	3
Tawney, Pamela Sue	Grandniece	IV	3
Tawney, Phillip G.	1st cousin once removed	V	3
Tawney, Preston J.	1st cousin	IV	2
Tawney, Rebecca J. `	1st cousin once removed	V	3
Tawney, Regina Fay	2nd cousin once removed	VII	4
Tawney, Rhuami Florence	1st cousin	IV	2
Tawney, Robert L.	1st cousin once removed	V	3
Tawney, Rosa Forrest	1st cousin once removed	V	3
Tawney, Roxie Fay	1st cousin once removed	V	3
Tawney, Ruamie	Wife of the great-grandfather		
Tawney, Ruby "Mamie"	Sister	II	1
Tawney, Russell D.	2nd cousin	VI	3
Tawney, Samuel Richard	Uncle	III	2
Tawney, Sandra	2nd cousin once removed	VII	4
Tawney, Sandra Ann	Grandniece	IV	3
Tawney, Sandra Sue	Niece	III	2
Tawney, Sara Elizabeth "Bett"	Aunt	III	2
Tawney, Sara "Sally"	Great-grandaunt	V	4
Tawney, Sara Jane	Grandaunt	IV	3
Tawney, Stacie Lea	Grandniece	IV	3

Family History of L. Mabel Tawney-Rogers and Ernest F. Rogers

Name	Relationship with Lula Tawney	Civil	Canon
Tawney, Stella	1st cousin	IV	2
Tawney, Stillborn	1st cousin once removed	V	3
Tawney, Stillborn	1st cousin once removed	V	3
Tawney, Suzanne Marie	Grandniece	IV	3
Tawney, Tammy Lynn	Grandniece	IV	3
Tawney, Terri	Grandniece	IV	3
Tawney, Vesta G.	2nd cousin	VI	3
Tawney, Vivian Joyce	2nd cousin once removed	VII	4
Tawney, W Cecil	2nd cousin	VI	3
Tawney, W Clay	1st cousin	IV	2
Tawney, Wanda Lee	2nd cousin once removed	VII	4
Tawney, Wanda Lee	1st cousin once removed	V	3
	1st cousin once removed of the husband		
Tawney, William	1st cousin 3 times removed	VII	5
Tawney, William	1st cousin once removed	V	3
Tawney, William "Ernest"	Brother	II	1
William George	Uncle	III	2
Tawney, William H.	Granduncle	IV	3
Tawney, William	Uncle	III	2
Tawney, William M.	1st cousin once removed	V	3
Tawney, William P.	1st cousin once removed	V	3
Tawney, Wilson	1st cousin	IV	2
Thany, John George	3rd great-grandfather	V	5
Tinsley, Cleopatric	Wife of the 2nd cousin twice removed		
Titus, Carol J.	Wife of the 2nd cousin once removed		
Truckemuller, Margaretha Elisabeth	3rd great-grandmother	V	5
Tucker, Whit	Husband of the 2nd cousin		
Unknown, Catharina	6th great-grandmother	VIII	8
Unknown, Charlotte	4th great-grandmother	VI	6
Unknown, Jacob	2nd great-grandson	IV	4
Unknown, Katherine	3rd great-grandmother	V	5
Unknown, Lucretia	Wife of the granduncle		
Unknown, Matoka	Wife of the 2nd cousin		
Unknown, Mercedes	2nd great-granddaughter	IV	4
Unknown, Name	Husband of the grandniece		
Unknown, Rosario	2nd great-granddaughter	IV	4
Varnie, Mabel	Sister-in-law		
Veltri, Christopher Joseph	Great-grandnephew	V	4
Veltri, Stephanie Marie	Great-grandniece	V	4
Veltri, Steven Joseph	Husband of the grandniece		
Vigil, Lori	Wife of the nephew		
Vineyard, Cynthia	Great-grandmother	III	3
Vineyard, Frieda E.	Sister-in-law		
Vineyard, Maude	Wife of the half 1st cousin twice removed		
Waldeck, Collen	Husband of the granddaughter		
Ward, James	Husband of great-granddaughter		
White, Bruce H.	2nd cousin	VI	3

Family History of L. Mabel Tawney-Rogers and Ernest F. Rogers

Name	Relationship with Lula Tawney	Civil	Canon
White, Dixie A.	2nd cousin	VI	3
White, Ernest	Husband of the 2nd cousin		
White, Grace	Wife of the 2nd cousin		
White, Homer	Husband of the 1st cousin		
White, John W.	2nd cousin	VI	3
White, Jorja Kenzleigh	Great-granddaughter	III	3
	2nd great-granddaughter	IV	4
White, Kristine Louise	Wife of the great-grandson		
White, Okey E.	Husband of the 1st cousin once removed		
White, Olive C.	2nd cousin	VI	3
White, Robert	Husband of the granddaughter		
White, Zoe	Wife of the 2nd cousin		
Whittman, Mike	Husband of the granddaughter		
Wilkinison, Jessy Kathlynn	Great-granddaughter	III	3
Wilkinson, Carrissa Dawn	Great-granddaughter	III	3
Wilkinson, Charles Richard	Husband of the granddaughter		
Wilkinson, Julie Marie	Great-granddaughter	III	3
Wilkinson, Kylin Levi	2nd great-grandson	IV	4
Wilkinson, Luke Aaron	Great-grandson	III	3
Wilkinson, Rebecca Kay	Great-granddaughter	III	3
Williams, John	Husband of the 2nd great-grandaunt		
Wilson, Buena	2nd cousin	VI	3
Wilson, Clara	2nd cousin	VI	3
Wilson, Clark	2nd cousin	VI	3
Wilson, Clida	2nd cousin	VI	3
Wilson, Cora	2nd cousin	VI	3
Wilson, Everett	2nd cousin	VI	3
Wilson, Fannie	2nd cousin	VI	3
Wilson, Goff	2nd cousin	VI	3
	Husband of the 2nd cousin		
Wilson, Harry	2nd cousin	VI	3
Wilson, Hunter	2nd cousin	VI	3
Wilson, John W.	2nd cousin	VI	3
Wilson, Julia	2nd cousin	VI	3
Wilson, Robert	2nd cousin	VI	3
Wilson, Robert Filmore	Husband of the 1st cousin once removed		
Wilson, Thelma	2nd cousin	VI	3
Witte, Samuel	Husband of the 2nd cousin		
Young, Cassidy Ava	2nd great-grandniece	VI	5
Young, Elizabeth E.	Wife of the granduncle		
Young, Kaitlynn Brielle	2nd great-granddaughter	IV	4
Young, Richard L., Jr.	Husband of the great-granddaughter		
Young, Roy	Husband of the great-grandniece		

References

1. Barnes, Pat Smith and Ted; Ancestor Charts of the members of the Roane Co.Historical Society, Inc.; Volume 2; Published by Roane Co. Historical Society, Spencer WV; Printed by Closson Press, Apollo, PA; 1997.

2. Roane Co. Family History Committee; Roane Co. West Virginia Family History 1989; Walsworth Publishing Company; 1990; LC# 90-71348.

3. Ross, Clara Mae (Alt); John H. Tawney, 1848-1916; His ancestors from Giles Co., Virginia to Pennsylvania and His Descendants of Roane Co., West Virginia; Dogwood Printing; Ozark, MO; 1996.

4. Lockhart, Flora J. Taylor; PedigreeChart; Prepared 4 March, 1998. Florida.

5. Yates, Garnette C.; Family Group Records; 1997 & 1998; Norfolk, Virginia.

6. Yates, Garnette C.; Personal Letter; Undated; Norfolk, Virginia.

7. West Virginia Senate Concurrent Resolution No. 39, March 8, 2000

www.legis.state.wv.us/Bill_Text_HTML/2000_SESSIONS/rs/BILLS/scr39%20org.htm

H

I

J

K

U

Uldrich, Sharon, 122
Updike, Patty Louise, 67

V

Van Horn, Mary Diana, 119, 257
Van Horn, Thomas, 119
Varnie, Mabel, 45, 80, 84, 88, 220, 297
Veltri, Christopher Joseph, 297
Veltri, Stephanie Marie, 66, 297
Veltri, Steven Joseph, 66, 245, 297
Vigil, Lori, 56, 297
Vigil, Steven, 56
Vineyard, Cynthia, 77, 79, 83, 297
Vineyard, Frederick Kirby, 46
Vineyard, Frieda E., 1, 34, 46, 80, 84, 88, 219, 248, 249, 297
Vineyard, Janet Celest, 69
Vineyard, Maude, 83, 297

W

Waldeck, Collen, 60, 101, 139, 230, 297
Ward, James, 228
Watson, Unknown, 58, 138
Webster, Patricia, 64, 143
West, Hazel Mae, 57
West, Walter, 117, 257
Westfall, Mabel, 59, 139
White, Bruce H., 43, 297
White, Dixie A., 43, 298
White, Ernest, 42, 298
White, Frank, 111, 122
White, Grace, 43, 298
White, Homer, 39, 87, 298
White, James D., 43
White, John W., 43, 298
White, Jorja Kenzleigh, 72, 147, 298
White, Joseph Kenzleigh, 232
White, Kristine Louise, 74, 149, 237, 298
White, Okey E., 43, 298
White, Olive C., 43, 298
White, Robert, 72, 147, 232, 298
White, Zoe, 42, 298
Whitney, Robert, 137
Whittman, Mike, 71, 147, 230, 243, 298
Wilkinison, Jessy Kathlynn, 141, 298

Wilkinson, Carrissa Dawn, 61, 141, 235, 298
Wilkinson, Charles Richard, 61, 102, 141, 235, 298
Wilkinson, Jessy Kathlynn, 61, 235
Wilkinson, Julie Marie, 61, 141, 235, 298
Wilkinson, Kylin Levi, 73, 149, 235, 298
Wilkinson, Luke Aaron, 61, 73, 141, 149, 235, 298
Wilkinson, Marc Robert, 62
Wilkinson, Rebecca Kay, 61, 73, 76, 141, 149, 235, 298
Williams, John, 34, 212, 298
Williams, Unknown, 113, 124, 130
Wilmoth, Dayton, 111, 122
Wilmoth, Juanita, 111, 122
Wilson, Buena, 41, 298
Wilson, Clara, 41, 298
Wilson, Clark, 41, 298
Wilson, Clida, 41, 298
Wilson, Cora, 41, 298
Wilson, Everett, 41, 298
Wilson, Fannie, 41, 298
Wilson, Goff, 41, 44, 298
Wilson, Harry, 41, 298
Wilson, Hunter, 41, 298
Wilson, John W., 41, 298
Wilson, Julia, 41
Wilson, Julia Ann, 93, 298
Wilson, Malinda, 106
Wilson, Robert, 41, 298
Wilson, Robert Filmore, 41, 298
Wilson, Thelma, 41, 298
Wilson, Walter, 41
Wise, Cornelius I.D., 119
Witte, Samuel, 41, 298
Wolfe, Kathern, 118
Wolfe, Ruth, 140

Y

Yarra, Minnie, 108, 120
Young, Brielle Young, 148
Young, Casidy Ava, 75
Young, Cassidy Ava, 298
Young, Dola Vae, 54
Young, Elizabeth E., 38, 214, 298
Young, Kaitlynn Brielle, 72, 298
Young, Richard L. Jr., 72, 148, 234
Young, Roy, 75, 298

Made in the USA
Coppell, TX
08 June 2023

17842858R00184